THE VOICE OF THE FOREIGN SERVICE

**Related Titles**

*Career Diplomacy: Life and Work in the US Foreign Service, Fourth Edition*
Harry W. Kopp and John Naland

*Inside a U.S. Embassy: Diplomacy at Work, Third Edition*
Shawn Dorman, Editor

# THE VOICE OF THE FOREIGN SERVICE

A History of the
American Foreign Service
Association at 100

SECOND EDITION

Harry W. Kopp

FOREIGN SERVICE BOOKS | WASHINGTON, D.C.

Library of Congress Control Number: 2023947707

ISBN-13: 979-8-9882530-0-6 (paperback)
ISBN-13: 979-8-9882530-1-3 (e-book)

26   25   24        1   2   3   4   5   6   7   8   9   10

Composition: BookComp, Inc.
Cover design: Erin Kirk

Printed in the United States of America

# CONTENTS

# BOXES

# ILLUSTRATIONS

*Following page 146*

# FOREWORD

We owe a debt of gratitude to Harry Kopp for this newest edition of *The Voice of the Foreign Service* as we look back in 2024 on 100 years of the modern Foreign Service and the creation of the American Foreign Service Association (AFSA) as its professional association. There is much to celebrate. With the passage of the Rogers Act of 1924, the basic foundations of a diplomatic career were laid, many of which still exist to this day. This includes the establishment of a highly competitive entry process, promotion by merit, provision of benefits and allowances, and a rudimentary retirement system. Thus began the building of an organization with an esprit de corps that has marked Foreign Service members as a distinct cadre within the federal government.

But there is also much to reflect and build on. The Foreign Service in the wake of the Rogers Act was almost entirely male and white. The lone black diplomat on staff, Clifton R. Wharton, was nearly denied entry and had to suffer innumerable slights and inequities from the beginning of his career in 1925. As for women, they would only have the right to be full members of the Foreign Service with the landmark *Palmer* decisions in 1972 and 1976 that overturned the State Department requirement that women FSOs resign if they marry and provided for other measures to bring about equity.

At its birth, AFSA deferred greatly to the State Department and defended the department on all matters as vital to the survival of the profession. As Kopp notes, "Nothing in the records of the early work of the association indicates that its leadership or membership ever considered challenging or bargaining with the Department of State." AFSA would only start to defend its members in earnest decades later, with, among things, its advocacy during the Vietnam War for the Dissent Channel, an official, internal means to express opposition to matters of U.S. foreign policy.

Most importantly, with the groundbreaking work of the "Young Turks"—especially Lannon Walker and Charles Bray, whose election to AFSA's leadership in 1967 ended the association's deference to the Department of State, and Tom Boyatt, Bill Harrop, and Tex Harris, who led AFSA's drive to become the sole collective bargaining agent of the Foreign Service. By 1973, AFSA was a dues-paying labor union that supported its members on an individual and collective basis, negotiating with the department and often at odds with the way in which personnel policy was implemented.

With this second edition, Kopp brings the story from the end of the Obama administration through the tumultuous Trump administration to the Biden administration and with that the return to climate of respect and support for the Foreign Service with the advent of the Biden administration. While there were serious challenges for AFSA throughout this period, it was the Trump years that really put AFSA in the spotlight and represented an almost existential threat to the Foreign Service. This period also showed what AFSA's leadership was made of. The Trump administration practically bristled with hostility toward the career Foreign Service (and basically all federal workers), proposed a 33 percent cut to the Fiscal Year 2018 foreign affairs budget, and instituted an 18-month-long hiring freeze for the State Department.

Kopp documents how then–AFSA President Barbara Stephenson made the case that nonpartisan professionalism, sacrifice, and call to duty were (and are) the hallmarks of the Foreign Service—and that these men and women deserve our support and respect. This case found resonance on Capitol Hill: the final FY 2018 foreign affairs budget was more than $14 billion above the administration's request.

The passages in this book that deal with the response to the first Trump impeachment trial in the fall of 2019 illustrate AFSA standing up for the Foreign Service. The Governing Board, ably led by Ambassador Eric Rubin, confronted the summary recall of our ambassador in Kyiv, Masha Yovanovitch, and the unprecedented spectacle of our members having to answer a congressional subpoena with the administration pressuring them not to. As Kopp explains it, "Ambassador Yovanovitch—along with members of the Foreign Service, the Civil Service, and the armed services, and others whose testimony was sought—was trapped between the rock of a legislative branch with subpoena power and the hard place of an executive branch that demanded silence."

AFSA sprang into action to defend its members who had to testify. We successfully got pro bono legal assistance changed from a "gift," the value of which would be disallowed under ethics rules, to a benefit of AFSA membership—which meant unfettered access to the AFSA Legal Defense Fund. As State Department AFSA vice president during this time, I attended a fundraising event with Ambassador Rubin to help raise money for the fund. The responses from this event and the general call for donations were overwhelming and humbling. AFSA was even able to get the State Department to pay a share of these legal costs, as supporting employees who had to testify in the course of their official duties was a clear agency responsibility. As Kopp points out, not one of our members who had to testify was out one penny for legal costs, and after this period, our legal defense fund still had a $300,000 balance.

The new Biden administration brought relief, such as the immediate repeal of the so-called Schedule F initiative from the previous administration. This would have lifted the labor protections of some 50,000 civil servants in policymaking positions, making it easier to fire them if they were not seen to be supportive enough of the president's political agenda. New issues rose to the forefront. This included greater attention to the issue of Anomalous Health Incidents (AHIs) or "Havana syndrome" that had afflicted our members in Cuba, China, and elsewhere—and now had the personal involvement of the Secretary of State—and a new assignment restrictions policy, as there was some evidence that the previous policy had been used in a discriminating fashion against Asian American employees and others.

While AFSA's relationship with management improved under the Biden administration, Kopp is right to emphasize that the great bipartisan legislative breakthroughs he details were largely the result of AFSA's efforts on Capitol Hill, not the administration's. Also, while the percentage of career officials in ambassadorial and other high-level positions was better than in the Trump administration, this percentage was still too small and took away opportunities from professional career diplomats. Coupled with this, the slow rate of nominations making their way out of the White House had been extremely disappointing.

The issue of reform of the Foreign Service has also not gotten the attention it deserves from the administration. Although Secretary Antony Blinken did announce a modernization program for the whole of the State Department in the fall of 2021, there was no specific large-scale initiative for the Foreign Service. AFSA largely supports the reform ideas, for example, detailed in the 2020 and 2022 American Diplomacy Project (Phase I and Phase II) reports from the

Belfer Center and Arizona State University, but has not been able to effectively engage with the department on these ideas.

A journalist recently asked me whether AFSA has concerns about a future administration having animosity toward federal employees. I responded that AFSA weathered the storm in the past because it did not allow itself to stray from being a nonpartisan, professional cadre of individuals motivated to serve our nation, sometimes in the hardest and most dangerous places, and to provide our elected leaders with the best information so that they can make the best decisions for the American people. Come what may, I see no reason to deviate from this path.

As I write this in the fall of 2023, in office only a few months as AFSA president and anticipating our centennial year ahead, I look to the future with optimism. The 2024 election year likely means partisan rancor will be at an even greater fever pitch. But, as Harry Kopp has shown in this new edition, AFSA has shown itself capable of forging bipartisan consensus, even in the most difficult times, to support the needs of its members and the health of the Foreign Service.

*Tom Yazdgerdi*
*AFSA President*
*Washington, D.C.*
*September 2023*

# PREFACE

This edition of *The Voice of the Foreign Service: A History of the American Foreign Service Association* marks 100 years since AFSA's founding in August 1924. It expands on an earlier edition published in 2015 and brings the story forward as close as possible to the date of publication.

The book was commissioned by the American Foreign Service Association (AFSA) itself and approved for publication by members of AFSA's Governing Board. The author's research relied heavily on the recollections of AFSA members, officers, and staff; the records kept by the association's Governing Boards; and the archives of AFSA's own *Foreign Service Journal*. The result is a book that is unashamedly pro-AFSA: Readers will find here no snarky critiques or juicy exposés. Failures and scandals are not ignored, but neither are they highlighted.

Writing is said to be lonely work, but in writing this book I was not at all alone. I had help from scores of people connected to AFSA, many of whom sat for hours of interviews to share their knowledge and experiences. Thanks to them all.

I am especially grateful to the redoubtable Shawn Dorman, editor of the *Foreign Service Journal* and director of Foreign Service Books, and to Kathryn Owens, who wrangled a bunch of untidy files through the production process.

Susan Maitra, John Naland, Sharon Papp, Eric Rubin, and Ásgeir Sigfússon read portions of the draft and flagged many errors of commission and omission. Copy editor Vicki Chamlee cleared many more. The mistakes that remain are all on me.

*Harry W. Kopp*
*Baltimore, February 2023*

# ABBREVIATIONS

| | |
|---|---|
| AAFSW | Association of American Foreign Service Women |
| ACDA | Arms Control and Disarmament Agency |
| ADST | Association for Diplomatic Studies and Training |
| ADST OHP | Association for Diplomatic Studies and Training's Oral History Program |
| AFGE | American Federation of Government Employees |
| AFL-CIO | American Federation of Labor and Congress of Industrial Organizations |
| AFSA | American Foreign Service Association |
| AFSA-PAC | American Foreign Service Association's Political Action Committee |
| *AFSJ* | *American Foreign Service Journal* |
| AFSPA | American Foreign Service Protective Association |
| APHIS | Animal and Plant Health Inspection Service |
| CSRA | Civil Service Reform Act |
| DACOR | Diplomatic and Consular Officers, Retired |
| DCM | deputy chief of mission |
| DOS | Department of State |
| DRI | Diplomatic Readiness Initiative |
| DS | Diplomatic Security |
| ECA | Economic Cooperation Administration |
| EEO | equal employment opportunity |
| EEOC | Equal Employment Opportunity Commission |
| EFM | eligible family member |
| EMRC | Employee-Management Relations Commission |

| | |
|---|---|
| FAC | Foreign Affairs Council |
| FAS | Foreign Agricultural Service |
| FCS | Foreign Commercial Service |
| FERS | Federal Employees' Retirement System |
| FLO | Family Liaison Office (now GCLO, Global Community Liaison Office) |
| FLRA | Federal Labor Relations Authority |
| FLRC | Federal Labor Relations Council |
| FSGB | Foreign Service Grievance Board |
| FSIDP | Foreign Service Impasse Disputes Panel |
| *FSJ* | *Foreign Service Journal* |
| FSL | Foreign Service Limited |
| FSLRB | Foreign Service Labor Relations Board |
| FSO | Foreign Service officer |
| FSOA | Foreign Service Oral Assessment |
| FSOT | Foreign Service Officer Test |
| FSRU | Foreign Service Reserve Unlimited |
| FSS | Foreign Service staff and Foreign Service specialist |
| GAO | Government Accountability Office |
| GLIFAA | Gays and Lesbians in Foreign Affairs Agencies (now glifaa) |
| GS | General Schedule (Civil Service pay grades) |
| IBB | International Broadcasting Bureau (now USAGM) |
| IDCA | International Development Cooperation Agency |
| IG | interdepartmental group |
| IRG | interdepartmental regional groups |
| JFSOC | Junior Foreign Service Officers Club |
| LEAP | law enforcement availability pay |
| LM | Labor Management Office |
| LNC | limited non-career |
| MSI | meritorious service increase |
| NFFE | National Federation of Federal Employees |
| NSAM | National Security Action Memorandum |
| NSC | National Security Council |
| OBC | Overseas Briefing Center |
| OC | counselor, Foreign Service grade |
| OCP | overseas comparability pay |
| OIG | Office of the Inspector General |
| OLMS | Office of Labor-Management Standards |

| | |
|---|---|
| OMB | Office of Management and Budget |
| PAC | Political Action Committee |
| PATCO | Professional Air Traffic Controllers Organization |
| PIT | part-time, intermittent, temporary (employment) |
| PRO | Professional Renewal Organization |
| PRP | President's Reorganization Project |
| PRT | Provincial Reconstruction Team |
| QDDR | Quadrennial Diplomacy and Development Review |
| REA | Reemployed Annuitant (formerly WAE) |
| RIF | reduction in force |
| SES | Senior Executive Service |
| SFS | Senior Foreign Service |
| SIG | senior interdepartmental group |
| SY | Office of Security |
| TIC | time in class |
| USAGM | U.S. Agency for Global Media (formerly IBB) |
| USAID | U.S. Agency for International Development |
| USIA | U.S. Information Agency |
| USICA | U.S. International Communications Agency |
| WAE | When Actually Employed (now REA) |
| WAO | Women's Action Organization |

# 1

## Diplomats and Consuls, 1789–1924

The U.S. Foreign Service and the American Foreign Service Association were born together in 1924, the direct and indirect progeny of an act of Congress. It had been a long gestation.

Public dissatisfaction with America's representation abroad had been building as the country began to emerge as a global commercial, financial, and military power in the late nineteenth century. Rep. John Jacob Rogers (R-Mass.) had spent five years working with Wilbur J. Carr, a State Department official, to craft a bill that would merge the country's amateurish and patronage-ridden consular and diplomatic services into a single, professional Foreign Service of the United States.

The Foreign Service Act that President Calvin Coolidge signed on May 24, 1924, gave the Service the attributes of a profession and a career: entrance at the bottom by examination, association of rank with the individual, advancement based on peer review, a school for practitioners, and a schedule of pay, allowances, and benefits.[1] The act passed Congress with few dissenting votes, despite opposition from a handful of diplomats who protested that they had not signed up for consular work.[2] Most diplomats and consuls, however, embraced the new order.[3]

To mark the moment, a number of diplomats in Washington at the time joined the six-year-old American Consular Association, which changed its name to the American Foreign Service Association. The new organization, said its founders, was "formed for the purpose of fostering *esprit de corps* among the members of the Foreign Service, to strengthen Service spirit and to establish a center around which might be grouped the united efforts of its members for the improvement of the Service."[4]

Rogers and Carr did not write on a blank page. One hundred and fifty years of history had been shaping the Foreign Service since the earliest years of the republic, even before the Declaration of Independence. Diplomatic service shone with the brilliance and prestige of its practitioners. The names of many diplomats—Benjamin Franklin, Thomas Jefferson, John Adams, John Quincy Adams, and John Jay—still resonate.

Benjamin Franklin, rightly called the "father" of the Foreign Service, had in the 1750s and 1760s been a colonial agent—specifically, a diplomat in the service of the Pennsylvania Colony—in England and France. After war with England broke out but before the colonies announced their independence, Franklin, then based in Philadelphia, organized a network of agents in European centers. The agents were to provide intelligence to the new Continental Congress (which promised to pay them) and explore possibilities for "assistance or alliance" for the colonies in their struggle with Britain.

After the Declaration of Independence, when Congress claimed full authority in foreign affairs, Franklin returned to France with Silas Deane and Thomas Jefferson as representatives of the United States. Their diplomatic success in securing French financial and military support for the Revolutionary War made possible the military success that followed. When Franklin presented his credentials to Louis XVI on March 23, 1779, he became the first American to hold the title of minister plenipotentiary.[5] John Adams and John Jay—on missions to the Netherlands and Spain, respectively—soon followed in that rank, as did Thomas Jefferson when he replaced Franklin in Paris.

Foreign affairs in the nation's early years attracted such men of great standing. Of the first 10 to serve as Secretary of State, five—Jefferson, James Madison, James Monroe, John Quincy Adams, and Martin Van Buren—went on to become president. But the eminence of America's early diplomats did not secure respect for their profession.

On the contrary, the new republic regarded diplomacy with suspicion. The rigid forms and elegant niceties of European courts made diplomacy seem a tool for kings and princes, not for a country where the people were sovereign. Americans wanted more direct action and faster results. Even John Adams, hardly a backwoodsman, advocated what he called "militia diplomacy." Just as irregular forces could use unconventional tactics to defeat trained British soldiers, he said, so militia diplomatists, by flouting custom and the rules of protocol, would be able to secure recognition and financial aid for the self-proclaimed republic.[6]

Following this approach, Congress in 1776 dispatched envoys to Spain, Prussia, Austria, Russia, and Tuscany. Unlike the famous Franklin, who was well known in France and had prepared the ground for his mission in talks in Philadelphia with agents of the French foreign minister, the militia diplomatists were unknown in the capitals to which they sailed unprepared. All were rudely treated, and all failed.[7]

During and after the revolution, American diplomacy suffered as well from the lack of an executive authority. Franklin had proposed in 1775 that "the power and duty of Congress shall extend to the determining on war and peace," and other matters of relations with foreign powers. Congress created a Committee of Secret Correspondence, later named the Committee for Foreign Affairs, to oversee foreign relations. Membership in the committee changed constantly, and the committee's instructions and advice to American agents abroad changed with the membership. Congress often added confusion by creating special committees to handle matters, such as negotiation of a peace treaty with Great Britain, that logically should have been within the purview of the Committee for Foreign Affairs.[8] Only the skill and perseverance of its envoys, and their willingness to act without instructions, allowed the new republic to overcome its self-imposed hindrances.

Ratification of the Constitution in 1788 created an executive authority, but it fell to Congress to organize and fund that authority for the conduct of foreign affairs. When Congress convened in New York in the spring of 1789, James Madison, a member of the House and a principal author of the Constitution, introduced a bill to establish a department of foreign affairs. The bill passed in July and President George Washington signed it into law, but the department—the first created under the Constitution—did not last two months. By September, Congress had decided that the department was underemployed and added to its responsibilities a number of state functions that had belonged to the secretary of Congress under the Articles of Confederation.

With the change of function came a change of name. Very quickly, the new Department of State became a department of everything else, vested with responsibility for taking the census, dealing with patents and copyrights, printing laws and keeping the archives, handling federal pardons and commissions, maintaining weights and measures, and, as Jefferson said, managing "the whole domestic administration (war and finance excepted)." Diplomatic and consular duties were not an afterthought, but neither were they the secretary's sole preoccupation. Washington appointed Jefferson the first Secretary of State. Congress authorized the hiring of two clerks, three assistant clerks, a part-time French translator, and two messengers.[9]

The Constitution assigned certain functions in foreign affairs. It gave Congress the power to declare war, the Senate to ratify treaties, and the president to appoint "Ambassadors, other public Ministers, and Consuls," with senatorial advice and consent. With respect to other functions, however, it was largely silent. The primacy of the executive was established largely through practice and experience. Presidents Washington and John Adams, without asking the consent of the Senate, named special envoys to carry out particular missions.[10] President Jefferson, who came to the office after years of diplomatic practice abroad and at home, made international affairs an exception to his general antagonism to a strong executive. He ordered naval attacks on the Barbary pirates without asking Congress for a declaration of war, and he and his minister in France, Robert Livingston, negotiated the purchase of the Louisiana Territory without prior legislative approval or consultations.[11] Subsequent presidents built on this precedent.

The exercise of executive power did not require an army of diplomats, and in fact the new country's strategic approach to international relations suggested a small diplomatic establishment. President Washington warned against American involvement in European disputes, most famously in his farewell address: "The great rule of conduct for us in regard to foreign nations is, in extending our commercial relations, to have with them as little political connection as possible."[12] It was a doctrine that would endure for more than a hundred years.

## DIPLOMATS AND CONSULS

The development of the country's overseas presence followed logically from this premise. Secretary Jefferson established separate diplomatic and consular services—the former to deal with political affairs and state-to-state relations, the latter with the country's maritime and commercial interests and the protection of its citizens. To conserve funds, Jefferson told Congress he would maintain representation at "the lowest grades admissible."[13] In keeping with the primacy of commerce over politics, the consuls outnumbered the diplomats:

- In 1800 the United States had just six diplomatic missions but 52 consular posts.
- In 1860 the numbers had risen to 33 diplomatic missions and 282 consular posts.
- By 1900 the count was 41 diplomatic missions, 323 consular posts, and 430 consular agencies.[14]

The great number of consular establishments was largely a function of law and practice in maritime trade, which, beginning in 1818, required a consular

seal or certification on invoices and manifests of all shipments of goods des-
tined to a U.S. consignee. The practice lasted well into the twentieth century—
consular officers and agents certified more than half a million invoices in 1921
alone—before finally fading away in the 1930s.[15]

Consuls and diplomats had no formal training in their duties. In 1790
Secretary Jefferson defined consular duties to include reporting on American
merchant vessels and sending useful commercial and political information,
particularly relating to military preparations, about the ports in which they
served. Congress in a 1792 act tasked consuls with the protection of American
citizens, particularly merchant seamen.[16] In the 1830s, consular duties expanded
to include detailed reporting on local commercial laws and practices, and the
promotion of American commercial interests. Trade promotion became a principal consular function after the U.S. Civil War.[17]

The consular service and diplomatic service had little to do with each other,
and neither had much to do with the home or departmental service, the name
given to the body of employees who worked for the Department of State in
Washington. Throughout the nineteenth century, the departmental service was
by far the smallest of the three. In 1860 the department had only 42 employees in
the United States. As late as 1909, when the United States was an emerging world
power with a colony in the Philippines, a two-ocean navy, and a global financial
center in New York, the department had a total of just 209 employees, including
35 officers and 135 clerks.[18]

The department had shed many of its domestic duties by 1900.[19] Its 91 domestic employees were essentially devoted to foreign affairs. The spoils system functioned only weakly in the department. Civil Service reforms had largely removed
the clerks from political control, and the bureau chiefs—there were only seven—
were paid salaries of around $2,100, not enough to attract many office seekers.[20]

It is clear from the numbers, as well as from the archives, that the small staff in
Washington gave little supervision to the country's 41 diplomatic and nearly 800
consular establishments abroad. A fictional consul in a 1904 story by O. Henry
(who had been a fugitive in Honduras and knew the consular service well) complained that he had twice cabled the department, first "for a couple of gunboats
to protect American citizens. The department sent me a pair of gum boots. The
second time was when a man named Pease was going to be executed here. They
referred that appeal to the Secretary of Agriculture."[21]

Throughout the nineteenth century, neither the diplomatic service nor the
consular service was in any sense professional. Diplomats and consuls were all
presidential appointees. With very few exceptions, they were not paid until 1856,

when Congress authorized the first salaries or stipends. Salaries for diplomats varied according to post; the highest salaries went to principal officers in Great Britain and France and then to those in Mexico and China. The 1856 law set a salary cap of $17,500, an amount that remained unchanged for 90 years.[22]

Consuls, who had been able to keep most of the money they collected in fees as compensation for their services, were also put on salary and were required to remit their fees, for which they now had to issue receipts, to the U.S. Treasury. They were also prohibited from engaging in trade. But these provisions applied only to senior consuls who were American citizens. Junior consular officers and foreign citizens who held American consular commissions continued to serve without pay, retain fees as compensation, and engage in private business.

Until the twentieth century, the Department of State had no authority to acquire real property abroad. The department gave principal officers a small allowance for rental of office space but not for quarters. Parsimonious diplomats and consuls often lived in their offices. Nor were official funds available for entertaining.

The budget was relatively small. As late as 1900, expenditures for the Department of State, including the diplomatic, consular, and departmental services, totaled less than $3.5 million, about 0.7 percent of federal outlays. The ratio of outlays for the Department of State to all federal outlays has stayed in the range of 0.4 to 0.8 percent ever since.[23]

Nineteenth-century diplomats, facing low pay and high expenses, were nearly all men of wealth. A few had lengthy terms of service, but most were gone after one appointment. Consuls, however, were often American businessmen who lived abroad, and many held their posts for years.[24] Despite the 1856 statute, even senior consuls did not always abandon their private businesses when they received their commissions. Many used their official positions to advance their personal fortunes, conduct that was scandalous, if not criminal, by the standards of the day. An inspector from the U.S. Treasury who visited consular posts in 1870 found widespread fraud and mismanagement. "If all could be told of the consular Service," he wrote, "the excess of bad over good would be so great that the most cold and indifferent citizen would blush for the name of his country."[25]

In the early decades of the nineteenth century, presidential appointees below cabinet rank were not customarily asked to resign at the end of an administration, and presidents rarely replaced ministers or consuls who were performing well and had no wish to leave their posts. President Andrew Jackson, however, did not see much value in keeping appointees in office. "The duties of all public officers," he told Congress in 1829, "are so plain and simple that men of intelligence may readily qualify themselves for their performance. . . . More is lost by the continuance of men in office than is generally to be gained by their experience."[26]

Jackson's view of public service justified a spoils system, in which the party in power used federal patronage to reward political friends. The satirist Ambrose Bierce in his *Devil's Dictionary* defines a consul as "a person who, having failed to secure an office from the people, is given one by the administration on condition that he leave the country."[27] Secretary of State John Hay worried that his policies would suffer in Congress if he could not satisfy demands from members of the Senate for consular appointments for their favored supporters. He told his friend and neighbor Henry Adams that President William McKinley "will have promised all the consulates in the service; the senators will come to me and refuse to believe me disconsulate; I shall see all my treaties slaughtered, one by one."[28]

Presidents also used diplomatic and consular appointments to reward qualities other than political loyalty. Abraham Lincoln told Secretary of State William Seward to use consular positions to "facilitate artists a little [in] their profession."[29] Lincoln was not the first or the last president to find overseas employment for distinguished writers, musicians, and other artists. Among the artists who held diplomatic or consular appointments were Washington Irving, Nathaniel Hawthorne, James Fenimore Cooper, James Russell Lowell, James Weldon Johnson, William Dean Howells, Gen. Lew Wallace, and Bret Harte.[30]

Most officers serving between 1890 and 1900 were lawyers, businessmen, journalists, or government officials at the time of their appointment. About one in six—17 percent—had held high elective office, either in the U.S. Senate or House of Representatives, or as governor of a state. Eight percent were immigrants who had been naturalized as citizens. A large number were fluent in foreign languages. They came from all parts of the country (however, not many from the South, a Democratic stronghold during a time of Republican administrations) and varied in age from 27 to 72 years old, with the median age being about 50.[31]

These officers may have been talented in their fields, but the conduct of American diplomacy was haphazard. Every change of administration brought a wholesale change in diplomatic and consular personnel, with aptitude for the work often a minor consideration in appointment. Appointees received no training, and their instructions were often vague. Even at the end of the nineteenth century, posts did not have their own telegraphic facilities; most communications went by sea or train. Reports, if diplomats bothered to send them, were generally ignored and often lost. The department's recordkeeping was sketchy and bizarre, "pitifully inadequate for the conduct of foreign relations."[32] If American foreign policy was successful, it was because little was happening in the world that tested American diplomacy. The expansion of American commercial and naval power did not rely on the skill of the country's diplomats.

By the turn of the nineteenth century, there were calls to close down the diplomatic service entirely. A senator from New York in 1885 complained that the "Diplomatic Service is working our ruin by creating a desire for foreign customs and foreign follies." The *New York Sun* editorialized in 1889 that the service was "a costly humbug and sham" that should be abolished. The *Washington Post* in 1890 said much the same: "There is no longer any need for men of affairs in our Foreign Service, and it had better be abolished." John Hay's biographer Tyler Dennett described the Department of State in 1898 as "an antiquated feeble organization, enslaved by precedents and routine inherited from an earlier century, remote from the public gaze and indifferent to it."[33]

## REFORM AND THE ROGERS ACT

The spoils system that produced an amateur foreign service and an amateur State Department put amateurs all over the government. The deterioration of public service and the high levels of corruption led to a reform movement that began to take hold in the 1880s with the support of Presidents James Garfield, Chester Arthur, and Grover Cleveland.

But reform aimed at the domestic service, not the foreign service. When the Pendleton Civil Service Act, which introduced a merit system for appointment to federal jobs, became law in 1883, it did not apply to the consular or diplomatic services. (The Pendleton reforms made things worse. As the number of patronage jobs in the Civil Service diminished, pressure to place political appointees in the still-available overseas positions increased.) Merit system reforms came to the diplomatic and consular services only later, chiefly through administrative actions and executive orders.

In 1895 President Cleveland placed many consular positions on the merit system, requiring positions to be filled by transfer or promotion, or by new hires under competitive examination. President Theodore Roosevelt in 1905, and Congress in 1906, extended the merit system to consular positions with salaries over $1,000 and to diplomatic secretaries. Despite these reforms, Roosevelt's second Secretary of State, Elihu Root (1905–1909), could still describe the consular service as a place "to shelve broken-down politicians and to take care of failures in American life."[34]

President William Howard Taft (1909–1913), in a series of executive orders issued in 1909, extended the merit system to all diplomatic positions below the rank of minister, created a board of examiners, and required "efficiency records" to be prepared on every diplomatic officer for use in consideration of promotion, transfers, and retention. The order also prohibited consideration of the political affiliation of candidates and required his Secretary of State (Philander Knox, who took a strong interest in management of the department) to identify to the president those career officers capable of serving as chief of mission. Taft's orders were the first to use the term "Foreign Service" as a legal expression referring to the consular and diplomatic services together.[35]

An act of Congress in 1911 authorized the Department of State to purchase buildings overseas for official use. Another in 1915 provided that diplomatic and consular officers be commissioned to their rank, not to their post, and allowed officers to serve up to three years in the Department of State in Washington without loss of pay.[36]

The growing international reach of U.S. commerce, naval and military strength, and cultural influence demanded a more capable overseas presence. Between 1898 and 1918, the number of diplomatic secretaries (diplomats below the rank of counselor) grew from 24 to 122. The diplomatic service, which, more than the consular service, had been a small club of individuals, became more of an organization with a sense of hierarchy and esprit de corps.[37] These developments set the stage for the 1924 Rogers Act, the sweeping reform that created the Foreign Service of the United States.

The Rogers Act was largely the work of three men: John Rogers, Charles Evans Hughes, and Wilbur Carr. Congressman Rogers first introduced his bill on the Foreign Service in 1919 with the encouragement of Secretary of State Robert Lansing. By 1924, during a period of Republican ascendancy, Rogers had risen to the chairmanship of the House Committee on Foreign Affairs, where he was well positioned to gain his bill's passage. Secretary of State Hughes—a former governor of New York, associate justice of the Supreme Court, and Republican candidate for president—lent his great prestige to the bill when he testified in its favor in 1922 (it passed the House but was not taken up by the Senate) and again in 1924. Carr, a civil servant who had joined the Department of State as a stenographer in 1892, had directed the consular service since 1909.

Of the three, Carr was the least conspicuous but the most important. A meticulous, energetic, and apolitical officer who had long been frustrated by the uneven quality of the consular service, he was the source of most of the ideas and much of the language embodied in the act.[38]

During hearings on the bill, a succession of business leaders compared American diplomats and consular officials unfavorably with their more professional, polished, and sophisticated European counterparts. But the testimony that received the most attention was that of Hugh Gibson, then American minister to Poland but already a veteran of diplomatic assignments in Tegucigalpa, London, and, most notably, Brussels in the early years of World War I.

The structure of the diplomatic service, Gibson said, is "rickety," in large part because "a man without private means cannot remain in the public service without failing in his family duties." The country needs "the most efficient diplomatic and consular service . . . as a matter of absolute national security." He argued for allowances, not better pay, for chiefs of mission, saying that his salary of $10,000 would be fair payment for his services—that is, if he did not have to "spend all this money in order to . . . maintain the sort of an establishment which is required if the representative of the United States government is to afford proper support to American interests."[39]

Most famously, Gibson complained about the quality of "a very small minority" of the diplomatic service: "You hear very frequently about the boys with the white spats, the tea drinkers, the cookie pushers. . . . Our problem now is to attract enough men so that we will have a real choice of material and crowd out these incompetents and defectives."

Gibson's testimony was well received.[40] The bill passed the House on May 1 by a vote of 134 to 27, and the Senate adopted it two weeks later by unanimous consent. President Coolidge signed it into law on May 24, 1924. It took effect on July 1 of that year.[41]

The Rogers Act placed in statute the reforms contained in recent executive orders, and it added many new elements to ensure a professional and efficient Service. It unified the consular and diplomatic corps, creating a single Foreign Service of the United States with nine classified grades and one unclassified grade. Consular and diplomatic personnel were placed in the unified Service at the grade that most closely matched their current status; new entrants, however, were required to pass an examination and start at the bottom. To forestall grade creep and a top-heavy Service, percentage limits were placed on the number of officers in each of the top six grades. Salaries and benefits, including retirement benefits, were designed to parallel those of the Civil Service, with additional allowances, including a housing allowance and a representation allowance, to compensate for the added costs of overseas service. As in the military services, rank and pay grade were associated with the individual, not with the job or assignment.

To reduce opportunities for political interference, the Foreign Service was to be self-administered. The Service would control its own recruitment, hiring, assignments, and promotions, but ultimate authority would rest with the Secretary of State.[42] Wilbur Carr was named assistant secretary for administration and thus was able to oversee the act's implementation.

## THE AMERICAN CONSULAR ASSOCIATION FADES OUT

Consuls and diplomats celebrated the union of the two branches into a single Foreign Service of about 600 professionals. The Executive Committee of the American Consular Association, launched six years earlier by consular officers at the Department of State, began meeting with an informal committee of diplomats. On August 4, 1924, the consular association, by a resolution of its members present in Washington, authorized its Executive Committee to "take such steps as may seem to it appropriate" to create a single American Foreign Service Association.

# 2

## The Birth of AFSA, 1924–1946

On August 7, members of the diplomatic branch present in Washington met, agreed to the proposals of the consular association, and elected an Executive Committee to take charge of the new American Foreign Service Association (AFSA). The five-person Executive Committee had three members of the consular branch, including Chairman Evan Young. One of the two diplomats was 32-year-old Allen Dulles, chief of the department's Near East division, the future director of the Central Intelligence Agency, and brother of future Secretary of State John Foster Dulles. The consular association was dissolved, and its assets and liabilities were transferred to AFSA. The *American Consular Bulletin*, which had begun publication in March 1919, became the *American Foreign Service Journal*.[1]

AFSA's Resolution Number 1, adopted by the Executive Committee on August 7, 1924, contained a broad statement of purpose: "The organization of a Foreign Service Association and the publication by the Association of a Foreign Service journal, for the purpose of fostering and promoting an *esprit de corps* throughout the Service and for the purpose of advancing the interests of the Service in legitimate and appropriate ways, is deemed both opportune and appropriate."[2]

The *Journal's* statement of purpose, published in its inaugural issue in October 1924, was more impressive: "to add to the understanding of the tasks and surroundings of the Foreign Service, to maintain and enlarge the acquaintance with one another of widely scattered colleagues, and to preserve the increase the zeal of the officers in the Foreign Service for the protection and promotion of American interests."[3] (This issue, like all issues of the *Journal* and the *American Consular Bulletin*, is freely available to the public at https://afsa.org/fsj-archive.)

As one of its first tasks, AFSA's Executive Committee drafted Articles of Association, which were circulated to the membership. At the first annual meeting, held in June 1925, the articles were approved by a majority of the 36 active members in attendance. The articles provided for active, associate, and honorary members: Foreign Service officers (FSOs), ambassadors, and ministers were invited to the first category; departmental (i.e., Civil Service) and non-career officers to the second. Clerks, secretaries, and other staff employees were not eligible for membership.[4] Secretary of State Charles Evans Hughes was named honorary president, and the other senior officials—the under secretary and three assistant secretaries—were named honorary vice presidents.[5] By the end of June 1925, the new AFSA had 510 members, of whom 414 came from the American Consular Association, paying dues of $5 per year.[6]

A special meeting of the membership in December 1926 amended the articles to provide for the annual election of a president and vice president by an electoral college of 18 association members on assignment to the department. The procedure for choosing the electors was complex: At some point between the opening of the electoral season in January and its closing on May 15, each member of the association could submit a ballot with up to 18 names selected, of whom not more than 12 were to have served primarily in the consular branch and not more than six in the diplomatic branch.

The 12 consuls and the six diplomats receiving the most votes formed an electoral college and chose a president and vice president—one a consul and the other a diplomat—from among the active membership assigned to the department. The electoral college also chose an Executive Committee of three consuls and two diplomats from among active members of the association assigned to the department and retired members living within a 25-mile radius of Washington, D.C. The president, vice president, and members of the Executive Committee all served one-year terms.[7]

The American Consular Association had held most of its meetings in an upstairs room at Cushman's Restaurant at 14th and F Streets Northwest. AFSA in its early years often met in similar venues and was primarily a social and benevolent organization.[8] Some 60 or 70 officers—nearly all of the roughly 10 percent of the Service posted in Washington, D.C.—attended the association's monthly luncheons, where a speaker, sometimes from outside the government, addressed matters of foreign policy, diplomatic practice, or department administration.[9]

In its monthly magazine, the *American Foreign Service Journal* (renamed the *Foreign Service Journal* in August 1951), the association provided a record of assignments, transfers, promotions, retirements, births, marriages, and deaths.

Articles by association members—and occasionally by prominent figures in government, business, journalism, or academia—dealt with exotic posts, curiosities of diplomatic life and history, and current events in the United States, especially the World Series, from which its readers were cut off. The *Journal* published articles on consular problems, trade promotion, and post management, but—except for the texts of speeches by department officials—generally avoided matters of foreign policy.[10] The *Journal*'s formal statement of purpose made its direction quite clear:

> The main purpose of the *Journal* will be inspirational and not educational. . . . Photographs, the light touch in the narration of experience, and personal items will be constantly desired.
>
> Propaganda and articles of a tendentious nature, especially such as might be aimed to influence legislative, executive, or administrative action with respect to the Foreign Service, or the Department of State, are rigidly excluded from its columns.[11]

Nothing in the records of the early work of the association indicates that its leadership or membership ever considered challenging or bargaining with the Department of State. On the contrary, the association and its members saw the department as the guardian of their professionalism, the promoter of their welfare, and their defender against politics and parsimony in the White House and the Congress. Secretary Hughes spoke to the association at a luncheon in his honor in 1925, in what quickly became an annual tradition. The promotion of Wilbur J. Carr to assistant secretary following passage of the Rogers Act gave the professional Service a strong and able supporter at the top of the department.

Implementation of the Rogers Act kept Assistant Secretary Carr and the department's administrative staff fully engaged in the second half of the decade. Over that time, the distinctions between the consular and diplomatic branches were gradually erased. New members of the Service received dual commissions. In most capitals around the world, consular and diplomatic missions were brought into the same building. AFSA amended its Articles of Association to eliminate references to consular and diplomatic branches.[12]

In one central area, implementation of the act fell utterly short. The act had envisioned and provided for a single Foreign Service of the United States that would serve all agencies of the government with international responsibilities. But in 1927, at the urging of American business interests, Congress established a Foreign Commerce Service in the Department of Commerce to supplement the work of FSOs in trade promotion and to provide a personnel structure for Commerce Department employees already serving as commercial attachés in a number of posts abroad. In similar fashion and for similar reasons, Congress three years later created a (much smaller) Foreign Agricultural Service in the Department of Agriculture and in 1935 provided for overseas postings for employees of the Interior Department's Bureau of Mines. Members of these new services were in the Civil Service system and were not members of the U.S. Foreign Service.

Neither the records of the association nor the pages of the *Journal* suggest that AFSA's Executive Committee ever discussed these developments or that the membership registered any concern. When the Departments of State and Commerce negotiated an agreement "to avoid duplication of activity" in commercial work, AFSA played no role.[13] In 1939, largely as an economy measure, the Foreign Commerce and Agricultural Services were closed down, and their officers transferred into the Department of State and the Foreign Service. AFSA's Executive Committee welcomed the new officers and invited them to join the association.[14]

AFSA began to take a more aggressive tone in support of the Service and its professional interests in 1929. When the consul general in Dresden asked the association to support his appeal of an adverse ruling in a salary dispute with the department, the Executive Committee agreed because "the principle involved . . . affects the interests of every officer in the association."[15] Adopting "a policy of greater frankness," the committee instructed the editors of the *Journal* to initiate a series of articles and editorials by members of the Foreign Service on "problems or difficulties . . . worthy of the attention of the Service as a whole." In October 1929, the *Journal* dropped its statement of purpose from its masthead, including the reference to the rigorous exclusion of advocacy ("articles of a tendentious nature"). In December the *Journal* published an unsigned editorial supporting President Herbert Hoover's request to Congress for a substantial increase in the budget for the Service.[16]

These early initiatives did not last. Perhaps because the membership of the Executive Committee changed each year, the association found it hard to pursue long-term goals with sustained effort, a problem that would persist at least into the 1960s.

## THE FOREIGN SERVICE UNION

One class of employees had been almost wholly excluded from the benefits that the Rogers Act conferred on Foreign Service officers. Non-career employees, as they were called, included commissioned vice consuls who had not passed the Foreign Service examination and non-commissioned Americans working overseas in clerical and other staff positions. The non-career employees, who outnumbered the officers roughly 2,000 to 700, were (except for the vice consuls) excluded from membership in the association. They did not share AFSA's hesitation about how, and how vigorously, to seek improvement in their working conditions.

In 1929 non-career employees at the American embassy in Paris organized a union, Local 349 of the Washington-based National Federation of Federal Employees (NFFE), part of the American Federation of Labor. The Foreign Service Local, as it came to be called, published a forthright statement of purpose in the first edition of the *Foreign Service Employee*, a monthly publication launched in June 1929:

> Safeguarding the good name of the United States abroad, fostering a new *esprit de corps* among the non-career personnel of the American Foreign Service, and serving as a club for that body.
>
> Betterment of the economic and social conditions in the Foreign Service. . . . Obtain provisions for pay, for promotion, and for optional retirement, in keeping with the services rendered.
>
> Pursue a policy of helpful cooperation with the several departments of the government, and furnish information pertaining to the true conditions of affairs to Congress and other bodies.[17]

Within a year, the Foreign Service Local claimed 79 members "in practically every diplomatic mission and in a number of consular missions in Europe" and in "China, [the] Dutch East Indies, Egypt, French Northern Africa, [and] South America."[18]

The local and the association were often on the same side, but nothing indicates that they officially collaborated. AFSA used the pages of the *Journal* to support legislation to improve the administration of the Foreign Service and increase its salaries and benefits, but it took no other action. In the debate over what became the Moses-Linthicum Act of 1931, FSOs dealt with Congress via the Department of State, primarily through Assistant Secretary Carr, not through AFSA. Non-career employees were active, however, both through NFFE and in letters and private meetings with members. Members of the local and other clerical staff lobbied on key issues: access to allowances (especially a rent allowance) and benefits provided to officers, voluntary retirement, paid home leave, and a general level of compensation that would afford its members "American standards of living."

Signed into law on February 23, 1931, the Moses-Linthicum Act—and a series of implementing orders signed by President Hoover in June of that year—ushered in several additional changes. These provided annual step increases between minimum and maximum salaries for each FSO rank, allowed voluntary retirement after 30 years of service regardless of age, increased annuities (which had been badly eroded by inflation in the late 1920s), created a personnel division to rate FSOs and a board to recommend promotions for FSOs, and took a number of other measures that the Department of State said would place "our Foreign Service legislation on a thoroughly satisfactory basis."[19] Wilbur Carr called the act "the biggest thing that has ever happened to the Foreign Service."[20]

The Moses-Linthicum Act also recognized the contributions of the non-career employees to the extent of providing classifications of clerical jobs and promotions based on merit for staff, including non-American staff, in diplomatic and consular offices. Nevertheless, the Foreign Service Local failed to realize most of its goals, and staff remained outside the career Service until the creation of the staff corps in the Foreign Service Act of 1946. In 1933, short of funds, a struggling Local 349 opened its membership to all Foreign Service personnel, including officers.

As the country sank into economic depression, federal tax receipts withered, and the Hoover administration tried to keep the budget in balance with spending cuts. Neither AFSA nor the Local 349 nor the department itself—despite impassioned testimony by Assistant Secretary Carr—was able to do much to alleviate the effects on the Foreign Service of the budgetary contraction enacted in 1932. Appropriations were reduced, officers and other employees placed on unpaid furlough, salaries cut by 15 percent, and various allowances reduced or eliminated. Promotions were frozen within class and between classes.[21]

After the change of administration in 1933, President Franklin Delano Roosevelt stretched his authority to allow employees at posts overseas where the dollar had weakened to draw their pay and allowances in local currency at an above-market exchange rate.[22] However, this mitigation was not enough to keep the Service from falling, like the rest of the country, into hard times. The Service lost 10 percent of its members between 1932 and 1934.[23]

## AFSA'S GOOD WORKS

Even while avoiding, or not even contemplating, confrontation with the management of the department, AFSA undertook a number of projects to advance members' interests, as a group and individually, in its early years.

## The Foreign Service Honor Roll

One of the most enduring efforts began in 1929, when the Executive Committee received, from a source whose name has been lost, a list of "those in the American Foreign Service who, since the earliest days of our national existence, have died under tragic or heroic circumstances." With this list came the suggestion for creating a roll of honor and a memorial tablet or plaque as "a source of pride" for the Service and a reminder to the public that the Service "is not a life merely of pleasant toil, but one often entailing sacrifice even unto death."[24] The committee eagerly took up the idea.[25]

By 1932, contributions to AFSA to fund a memorial tablet had topped $1,100; and in 1933, following approval of the design by the Fine Arts Commission, the work was undertaken. Secretary of State Henry Stimson unveiled the plaque, then with 65 names, in the north end of the entrance area in the State, War, and Navy Building next to the White House.[26] The plaque later moved with the department to what is now Main State, first to what is now the 21st Street entrance (the Marshall wing) and in January 1961 to the C Street lobby.[27]

AFSA from the beginning has kept control of the honor roll and the memorial plaques on which the names are inscribed. Debates about the general criteria for inclusion in the roll, and about whether individual cases meet the criteria, have often roiled the AFSA Governing Board and the membership. Should the roll be restricted to career members of the Service, excluding all non-career appointees and contractors? What about Foreign Service national employees (now called locally employed staff)? What kinds of death merit recognition—all Service-related deaths or only those that are "tragic" or "heroic," however those words may be defined? These questions are grim and difficult.

John Naland, whose name appears often in these pages, has been since the early 2000s the central figure in maintaining and improving the honor roll and recording its history.[28] In June 2021, as Naland wrote, "AFSA unveiled a once-in-a-generation expansion of the memorial plaques" in the State Department's C Street lobby, reinscribing four existing panels and adding six new ones, with a total of 321 names inscribed. The expansion captured names previously overlooked or omitted under changing criteria. Separate plaques in the C Street lobby, not controlled by AFSA, memorialize deaths overseas in service to America that do not fall under AFSA's criteria. The U.S. Agency for International Development maintains its own memorial wall at its headquarters in the Reagan Building.

The honor roll is never closed. The world and duty being as they are, the plaques have room for the scores of names that surely will need to be added in the future.

## Insurance

The association's involvement with group insurance for its members began in 1926 with a cold-call solicitation from J. Alan Maphis, a broker with the Equitable Life Insurance Company of New York. That solicitation led to the incorporation in 1929 of the American Foreign Service Protective Association, an entity legally separate from AFSA but sharing AFSA's directors, to contract with underwriters for group health, life, and accident insurance for AFSA members. Alan Maphis was later hired as the protective association's insurance counselor, a position he held for more than 30 years.[29]

The AFSA Governing Board attended to smaller matters as well. Section IV of the Articles of Association empowered the Executive Committee to "make loans or in especially meritorious cases donations to members of the association or their heirs or dependents," up to 10 percent of the association's cash assets. The committee spent a good deal of time weighing requests for assistance. An officer seeking help to pay off "a note of $500 outstanding with a local institution under circumstances that make the situation embarrassing" was turned down, but the committee paid the expenses of a medical specialist to treat a gravely ill consul in Tehran (the costs were recovered from the estate), and it loaned money to cover the repatriation of the widow of a consul who died in Manchester. When a Consul Randolph sent a dispatch stating that Consul Brissel's grave in Baghdad was marked only by a wooden cross, the committee undertook to raise money for a "proper tombstone." And the association opened a line of credit for the benefit of certain personnel of the American legation in Managua following a devastating earthquake in that city.[30]

## The Scholarship Fund

The AFSA Scholarship Fund, an association jewel, is almost as old as the organization itself. It began with the death in 1926 of Oliver Bishop Harriman, who had entered the U.S. diplomatic service by examination in 1915. He was a distant cousin of railroad magnate E. H. Harriman's son Averell, who would become ambassador to Russia, ambassador to Great Britain, under secretary of State, and governor of New York. Oliver Harriman died of a heart attack at age 39 while serving as first secretary and chargé d'affaires at Embassy Copenhagen. His mother, Elizabeth Templeton Bishop Harriman, gave $25,000 to the new American Foreign Service Association to create a fund in his memory to award scholarships to children of Foreign Service members. AFSA set up a trust to receive the funds and a committee to make the awards, the first of which was granted in 1927. "I make no restrictions," wrote Mrs. Harriman, "wishing merely that something for the good of the Service should be established."[31]

The Scholarship Fund was set up as a restricted account, not to be drawn on except for its stated purpose. An AFSA Scholarship Committee began awarding scholarships on need and merit in 1927. AFSA added to Mrs. Harriman's gift with a transfer of $5,000 from its operating account, following a unanimous endorsement of the idea at the general meeting in June 1932. The funds were invested in U.S. savings bonds. Tax-free contributions from wealthy political appointees as well as from the association and its members allowed the fund to grow despite the Great Depression.[32] Scholarships for undergraduate study were awarded annually, but the association for many years fretted at the relative paucity of applications.[33]

When assets in the fund reached $8 million in 2016, AFSA stopped soliciting contributions—or, as the association's annual report put it, "[pivoted] from a fundraising posture to a focus on effectively and efficiently administering the funds."[34] At the end of 2020, the fund held more than $11 million and was considered self-sustaining.[35] In 2022 AFSA awarded $263,000 in need-based financial aid to 74 students and $143,500 in merit awards to 38 students.[36]

## Overseas Schools

The association worked in other ways to improve educational opportunities for the children of members of the Service posted overseas. An AFSA committee created in 1938 documented the problem: There were 367 children between the ages of 6 and 18 of FSOs serving at "more than 200 places" in the world, in most of which "no schools were available which were adapted to the needs of American children." Of 152 teenage children, 59 were at posts with no schools at all.[37] The committee praised a bill in Congress, supported by the department, that would set a policy of providing "opportunity for primary and secondary education" to children of U.S. citizens on duty abroad. But the bill did not pass and would not have guaranteed funding if it had; nor is there anything in the record to indicate that the committee or the association lobbied Congress for its passage. In any case, soon afterward World War II swept this issue, like so many others, away.

# THE FOREIGN SERVICE IN WARTIME

The association was no more prescient about the war than other foreign affairs institutions. In August 1940, two months after the fall of France, a stodgy editorial in the *Journal* merely urged "close study of current trends" and "realistic interpretations of the lessons of history" to prepare for "manifold tasks" that will require "the highest professional qualifications."[38]

## Foreign Service Culture

In fact, the Service was poorly equipped for war. President Franklin Roosevelt "distrusted the career diplomats" and considered them "entirely out of touch with American affairs . . . anti-immigrant, anti-Semitic, anti-black, and anti-New Deal."[39] State Department historian Donald Trask wrote that the department knew little about warfare and lacked "the expertise and institutions [needed] to exert dominant influence on the shaping of grand strategy."[40]

The department and the Service were kept on the sidelines. Secretary of State Cordell Hull was deliberately kept absent from all the major wartime conferences. The Navy, not the State Department, handled the president's communications with foreign leaders, and special emissaries, notably White House aide Harry Hopkins, handled the most sensitive diplomatic missions.[41]

Anti-Semitism in the department was only thinly veiled. Jews, women, and people of color were generally excluded from the Foreign Service.[42] At the beginning of the war, the department placed Breckinridge Long—a former ambassador to, and admirer of, Benito Mussolini's Italy—in charge of refugee affairs. Long (a political appointee, not a career member of the Foreign Service) had called Adolf Hitler's *Mein Kampf* "eloquent in opposition to Jewry and to Jews as exponents of Communism and chaos," and he administered refugee policy in accordance with that way of thinking, with support from career staff.[43] Other American diplomats said to be "known to disparage Jews" included Ambassadors William Phillips (Long's successor in Italy) and Hugh Gibson.[44]

The Service also produced its heroes. The Raoul Wallenberg Foundation, named for the Swedish diplomat who rescued hundreds of Jews in Hungary, recognized Hiram "Harry" Bingham IV (vice consul in Marseilles); J. Rives Childs (consul general in Tangier); Howard Elting Jr. (vice consul in Geneva); Myles Standish (vice consul in Marseilles); Raymond Herman Geist (consul general in Berlin); and Stephen B. Vaughan (vice consul in Breslau) as having issued many thousands of visas to Jews fleeing the Nazis, in contravention of

U.S. policy.[45] In 2002 AFSA recognized Bingham with a posthumous award for constructive dissent.[46]

## Structural Change

The war transformed the Foreign Service, just as it transformed every institution and agency in the executive branch. Demands on the Service called for its expansion, but politics and an inflexible personnel structure brought contraction instead. Recruitment was suspended to avoid interference with the military draft, so members who left (many to volunteer for military service) could not be replaced. With the total number of officers in the Service in slow decline, the percentage limits on the number of officers in each of the upper grades effectively froze promotions. To retain as many career officers as possible, the department sought draft deferments for eligible officers, costing the Service some of the support it had enjoyed on Capitol Hill and reviving the reputation for snobbery, elitism, and lack of manliness that the Service had tried so hard to overcome.[47]

The Foreign Service became less foreign as well. Before 1941, FSOs rarely served in Washington; about 90 percent of Service members were abroad at any given time.[48] But the war and the closure of posts in Europe and Asia brought officers in large numbers back home, where they worked in the Department of State and on loan to the Departments of War and the Navy, the Board of Economic Warfare, the Office of Strategic Services, the Office of War Information, and other agencies.[49] For many officers, service in Washington was a new experience, teaching lessons in bureaucracy, interagency rivalry and cooperation, and the importance of domestic politics that they had never before had occasion to learn. At the same time, the number of agencies sending personnel overseas rose to more than 50.

The department and AFSA struggled to keep up with the pace of change. Congress in 1941 authorized a Foreign Service auxiliary, allowing the department to hire officers outside the examination process to serve "for the duration of the war." Many members of the auxiliary were hired to do work that required skills or knowledge—especially in economics and finance—not readily available among regular FSOs, who called (or disparaged) them as "specialized" or "technical."[50] Disparities of pay increased the friction: Pay grades for newly hired auxiliary officers were based on their civilian experience, so auxiliary officers sometimes earned more than regular FSOs doing similar work or operating at similar levels of responsibility. And the regular officers often saw the auxiliary members as lacking the diplomatic skills the former had acquired through years of service.

## POSTWAR PLANNING

By 1943, planning for postwar demands was already underway. Congress and the department recognized that the occupation of defeated enemies, the revival of war-torn allies, and the reshaping of international relations would create an explosion of demands worldwide for civilian personnel with a variety of skills. The department's top administrative official, career FSO G. Howland Shaw, said in a speech that the Foreign Service would need to collaborate with other agencies to deal with unfamiliar problems, such as rehabilitating industries, reconstructing bombed-out areas, restoring trade and economic activity, and the like. "We shall have an immediate need for specialized personnel," he said. "Such officers may well be integrated into the Foreign Service for stated periods." In addition to the temporary officers, he saw a need for the Service to hire technical personnel and administrators.[51]

Many FSOs read Shaw's speech as a confirmation of their fears that members of the Foreign Service auxiliary would become career officers, inhibiting advancement for the regular officers and changing the character of the Service. An unsigned editorial in the *Journal*, possibly by *Journal* Editor Henry S. Villard, responded to Shaw and laid out a case for what would come to be called "generalists," setting the terms of a debate that continued through the drafting of the Foreign Service Acts of 1946 and 1980, and remains active today:

> The editors of the *Journal* believe that the trained Foreign Service officer has amply demonstrated his ability to handle most of the tasks assigned to specialists and technicians in the auxiliary branch. . . . Versatility and adaptability are the prime characteristics of the officer produced by the Rogers Act. He is either able to play successfully any role asked of him or he fails to measure up to required standards. . . . The average individual Foreign Service officer is better fitted to handle the coming postwar duties abroad than any group of specialists or technicians recruited from civil life in the United States.[52]

The editorial expressed an attitude that was widely shared but irrelevant to events. By January 1946, the 976 officers in the auxiliary outnumbered the 820 officers in the regular career Service.[53]

To improve planning and administration, the department in January 1944 merged three divisions into a single Office of Foreign Service, placing personnel, administration, and foreign buildings under one chief (initially John Erhardt) reporting to Assistant Secretary Shaw.[54] Shaw's concept of the needs of the Service differed sharply from that of the *Journal*'s editors. In Shaw's view, "The doctrine that the average Foreign Service officer can do anything and everything . . . has hampered the development of the Foreign Service in the past." Shaw's intention, he said in a speech, was to bring more specialists into the career Service so that "eventually . . . we should have a diminishing need to recruit specialists from the outside."[55] Foreign Service Officer Bill Blue, who would become chairman of the AFSA Governing Board in 1961, complained that "any significant increase of personnel along the lines [Shaw] indicated . . . will undoubtedly have an adverse effect on the morale of the career Service and will merely be an amplification of the system followed before 1939, at which time the representatives of the Departments of Agriculture and Commerce were incorporated into the Service."[56]

In the 1920s and 1930s, members of the career Service had placed full trust in the department's management, and in Wilbur Carr personally, because they saw the interests of the Foreign Service and the State Department as essentially identical. The *Journal*'s 1943 editorial and Blue's 1944 letter made clear that for many members of the Service, that identity of interest could no longer be assumed. The trust they had placed in the department's management had begun to erode.

AFSA was well supported and financially strong—in June 1942, it had 945 active members, including all but 79 of the 840 active-duty Foreign Service officers[57]—but its Executive Committee struggled to work out its views and make them known. The committee had informal exchanges with Assistant Secretary Shaw and decided in October 1943 to formalize its views in a letter. Four months later, it still had not agreed on a text.[58] Shaw discussed immediate needs and postwar planning at an AFSA luncheon in February 1944, and in March the department sent proposed legislation to Congress to allow recruitment into the Foreign Service "after suitable examination" of a permanent corps of "specialists in finance, economics, research, public relations, and other technical fields."

Career officers reacted defensively. Headed by Merle Cochran, the AFSA Executive Committee that took office on October 1, 1944, saw itself as "the only duly constituted representative of the entire Foreign Service" with a mandate to follow the bill and protect the interests "of all Foreign Service officers." The committee discussed the bill "at length and in detail" during four or five meetings in October and November 1944, and tried again to formalize its position in a letter to Assistant Secretary Shaw.[59]

As before, the committee struggled to agree. A first draft called on the department to "convince the Service beyond doubt" that it "recognizes ability and loyalty in its present career officers and intends to maintain them in positions of leadership." A second draft called the bill "wholly inadequate," urged "generous and rapid promotions" as soon as possible, and asked for assurances of rigorous entry exams for newcomers.[60]

By the time of the third draft, prepared in March 1945, a year had passed since the department's proposal had gone to Capitol Hill, Gen. Julius Holmes (a former Foreign Service officer and retired from the Army) had replaced Howland Shaw, and the Executive Committee struck a more moderate tone. The values of the career Service, AFSA said, "although intangible, are well known to you. They include discipline and devotion to duty; esprit de corps and pride in the traditions of the Service; subordination of personal interest to furthering the foreign relations of the United States; entrance at the bottom on the basis of rigorous examination; and promotion by merit without regard to political affiliation or influence."[61]

The letter went on to urge General Holmes to involve FSOs in the department's planning process, to arrange "rapid advancement throughout the Service on the basis of merit," and to pledge that newcomers would be taken into the middle and upper grades "only after strict examination and only as a temporary and emergency expedient."[62] Holmes responded warmly, promising to keep the Service engaged and to protect its principles. He asked "the Executive Committee of the association and the members of the association" to "work with us in telling the field about developments and in soliciting suggestions and comments from the field." He also promised to resume promotions "as soon as the . . . legislation goes through and the percentage limitation on the number of men in the classified ranks is lifted."[63] Congress lifted the limitation in May in a bill that also improved the status, pay, and allowances of administrative and clerical personnel.[64]

The exchange of letters marked a new relationship between AFSA and the management of the department. The department's Office of Foreign Service was tasked with developing new basic legislation to replace "the crazy-quilt pattern" of a century of law and regulation.[65] Formal and informal exchanges between the Executive Committee and the planning staff in the Office of Foreign Service became routine, especially after Loy Henderson became Executive Committee chairman in October 1945. When State set up an interdepartmental group to draft what became the Manpower Act of 1946 and the Foreign Service Act of 1946, a representative of the Executive Committee was invited to join (the committee elected FSO Edward T. Wailes). AFSA and the department's managers had frequent and sometimes strong disagreements, but each side maintained a respect for the other and trusted in its good intentions, if not its wisdom.

The fight over the Manpower Act showed the direction and extent of AFSA's influence. The act was intended to give the department emergency authority to hire additional FSOs, not necessarily into the bottom grades, after appropriate examination. AFSA argued in letters to the Office of Foreign Service and in a joint resolution of the outgoing and incoming Executive Committees that the authority should exclude the two senior-most grades and that no new hire should enter at a grade in which he would be among the youngest 10 percent of officers in that grade.[66] The department eventually accepted AFSA's position and proposed legislation to bring in an additional 120 officers. The Bureau of the Budget pushed for more new blood than the career officers were prepared to accept and insisted that hiring authority should extend to 250 officers without limitation as to grade. The department and AFSA capitulated.[67]

When the Executive Committee turned over in October 1945, the outgoing and incoming committees issued a joint resolution.[68] They accepted the need for lateral entry "in view of the apparent necessity" but urged the Department of State "not to undermine the career principle" that candidates start at the bottom and rise through promotion based on merit. They called on the department to speed the promotion of officers already in the service and to provide in-service training "so that innate ability ... may be matured ... and not wasted or deadened by prolonged concentration in routine fields." And they asked the department to accelerate the hiring of 400 new junior officers, giving preference to members and veterans of the armed forces, and to raise clerical pay.

State followed AFSA's advice on hiring, offering a special examination to military service members and veterans in the fall of 1945 and hiring 360 new officers as a result.[69] (The advice on in-service training, however, went unheeded.) Congress passed the Manpower Act in line with the request of Harry S. Truman's administration. It became law on July 3, 1946.[70]

## THE FOREIGN SERVICE ACT OF 1946

Even while the Manpower Act was no more than a rough draft, the State Department, the Bureau of the Budget, interested agencies, members of Congress, and AFSA's Executive Committee were already at work on new basic legislation for the Foreign Service. The Rogers Act, they all agreed, had been too rigid. The department and the Service had been unable to respond in a timely way to the rapid changes that the world situation had demanded. A fresh approach was overdue.

Secretary of State James F. Byrnes, nominated in July 1945 and confirmed the day after his nomination, faced immediate pressure to reorganize the department "based upon the democratization of the Foreign Service."[71] He was, however, determined to act deliberately, and he asked the Bureau of the Budget (now the Office of Management and Budget) to make recommendations to him on the organization and management of the department. He brought in his protégé, Donald Stuart Russell (later governor of South Carolina and a U.S. senator), as assistant secretary for administration.

The Bureau of the Budget urged the Secretary to consider strengthening the department by placing its Foreign Service and Civil Service employees in a single system or at least under a central personnel or planning officer. The bureau said that Foreign Service employees needed more frequent tours in the department, lest they see themselves only as reporting officers and analysts who would fail to develop the operational skills needed "to carry out the positive policies which our government in the future may adopt."[72] Civil servants would also benefit from occasional tours abroad. In its view, the closed, elite structure of the Service needed opening through legislation authorizing recruitment and entry (after examination) into the middle and upper grades. The bureau also urged more attention to building leadership, supervisory, and administrative skills, and systematic training for departmental and Foreign Service personnel, using instruction by supervisors as well as formal courses.[73]

The career Service was also looking at reform but reached different conclusions. The *Journal*, with support from AFSA's Executive Committee and funding from its own resources, supplemented by donations from active and retired officers, had in March 1944 launched a prize essay contest. Its theme was "Suggestions for improving the Foreign Service and its administration to meet its war and postwar responsibilities." Under Secretary Joseph Grew (the country's senior career diplomat) and several members of Congress were among the judges, and the best four of the 60 entries were published in the *Journal*.[74]

More formally, the director of the Office of Foreign Service, Seldin Chapin, put together a study group that prepared its own report. The AFSA Executive Committee worked closely with Chapin, a career Foreign Service officer and U.S. Naval Academy graduate, on this project. Andrew B. Foster, a member of Chapin's study group and the coauthor of what came to be called the "Chapin-Foster Report," was also a member of AFSA's 1944–1945 Executive Committee.

The Chapin-Foster Report, like the report from the Bureau of the Budget, paid close attention to "amalgamation"—building a more integrated departmental workforce by changing the relationship and roles of Foreign Service and Civil Service employees. The AFSA Executive Committee and career officers generally were opposed to, or at least quite wary of, any integration with the Civil Service that would dilute "career principles," including entry at the bottom by competitive examination, promotion by merit, rank in person, and worldwide availability. The Chapin-Foster Report proposed adding a Navy principle of "promotion up or selection-out"—mandatory retirement for officers repeatedly passed over for promotion or repeatedly ranked at the bottom of their class.

It also proposed measured amalgamation, a decade-long transition to a consolidated Service in which all members would serve at home and abroad, with "executive officers" being subject to selection-out and "staff officers" being exempt. But as Arthur Jones, a department personnel expert, wrote, "Acceptance of a plan for amalgamating the Department [of State] and the Foreign Service would undoubtedly have generated internal controversy," and Assistant Secretary Russell "clearly wished to avoid a clash between the Secretary and the Foreign Service officers." He told Chapin and Foster to go to work on draft legislation that would preserve a separate Foreign Service.[75]

Many of the Chapin-Foster concepts were adopted in the final legislation, worked out over six successive drafts circulated through the interdepartmental group on which an AFSA representative sat. Each draft went to the Bureau of the Budget (which gathered additional views from other interested agencies) and then to a special subcommittee of the House Foreign Affairs Committee.[76] Despite objections from the Bureau of the Budget, which argued that the bill empowered the Director General of the Foreign Service at the expense of the Secretary of State, President Truman signed the bill on August 13, 1946.[77]

The act created a Foreign Service that included an officer corps, a staff corps of officers and employees, and a reserve. Reserve officers received temporary commissions, up to five years, with the expectation that the reserve would fill the need for officers with specialized skills and knowledge. There was no provision for amalgamation with the departmental service, although lateral entry into any but the highest level of the Foreign Service, following examination by the Board of Examiners, was opened to members of the departmental service, the Foreign Service staff corps, and the Foreign Service Reserve corps who had at least four years of experience (three years for persons over age 31). Reserve officers were to receive pay and benefits identical to those of career officers.[78]

The staff corps, as the Chapin-Foster Report had proposed, would provide clerical, administrative, and functional specialists. Its members were not subject

Box 2.1. Employees as of December 31, 1946

| | |
|---|---|
| Foreign Service officers | 975 |
| Foreign Service Reserve officers | 166 |
| Foreign Service staff personnel | 3,120 |
| Local employees (aliens employed abroad) | 6,899 |
| Total Foreign Service | 11,193 |
| Department of State | 8,754 |

Source: Jones, *Personnel Systems*, 50.

to selection-out. It was expected that many members of the wartime auxiliary would join the staff corps.[79]

In June 1949, AFSA amended its Articles of Association to take the changes made by the 1946 Act into account and open its membership rolls to reserve and staff personnel on active duty.[80] The change greatly expanded the pool of personnel eligible for membership in AFSA.

## OTHER AFSA ACTIVITY

The debate over how to restructure the Foreign Service in wartime and for the postwar period preoccupied AFSA's Executive Committee from about 1943 to the passage of the 1946 legislation, but it was not the sole concern. Minutes of committee meetings contain references to several initiatives for which a recorded resolution is unfortunately lacking. For instance, in 1944 the Education Committee looked into obtaining a quota for entry into the U.S. military and naval academies at West Point and Annapolis for children of members of the Foreign Service "who have no basic legal residence." The results of their investigation were not recorded or have been lost.[81]

The Executive Committee also proposed an appeal to the president and Secretary of State to create a hiring preference for disabled veterans seeking to join the regular or auxiliary Foreign Service.[82] Again, there is no record of the results of this effort. In 1945 the Executive Committee endorsed a proposal by Seldin Chapin to set up a small exhibit in or near the main hall of the department with items bearing on the history of the Foreign Service.[83] No further information on the issue is available.

The Executive Committee put considerable effort into maintaining the roll of honor on the memorial plaque. In 1943 it rejected one name on the grounds that "the Honor Roll includes officers only." In 1945, after much discussion, it decided against adding the name of John J. Meily, a consul general killed in an air crash in Brazil in September 1944.[84] When a similar debate took up most of a meeting in January 1946, the committee asked its secretary, J. Graham Parsons, to compile a record of previous decisions and set up a special committee under Julian Harrington to recommend whether the standard of death under "tragic or heroic circumstances" should be retained.

Harrington's committee concluded that since all deaths are tragic, emphasis should be placed on "peculiarly heroic circumstances," adding that there should be no review of names already on the plaque. Harrington's committee also urged that names should be drawn "from the entire personnel of the Foreign Service and not limited only to diplomatic and consular officers." The *Journal* in August 1946 asked for comments on the special committee's recommendations; none was received. The committee's recommendations were finally put before an AFSA general meeting on April 21, 1948, and approved.[85]

## THE ACT OF 1946, SEEN FROM 1968

The 1946 Act is especially important in the history of AFSA and not just because it was the basic governing statute for the Foreign Service for 34 years. The act was an inspiration and lodestar for the members of the reform movement, known as the Young Turks, who took control of AFSA in 1968 and led the association on the path that brought it, five years later, recognition as a labor union.

In their study, *Toward a Modern Diplomacy*, which AFSA published in 1968, the reformers wrote, "The Foreign Service of the United States created by the Act [of 1946] provided an almost ideal instrument for the implementation abroad of U.S. policies after the war. . . . The system created by the act was a marvelously flexible instrument."[86] The study lavished praise on the Foreign Service Reserve and the provisions for lateral entry, which together "permitted an expansion or contraction as the needs of the nation might dictate." But the authors of the study concluded that "the Foreign Service Act of 1946, except for a very brief initial period, had never been implemented as intended by the Congress."[87] They believed that AFSA could become the platform on which a reform that looked backward for structure and forward for content might be constructed.

# 3

# Growth and Turmoil, 1946–1967

Passage of the Foreign Service Act of 1946 turned out to be the beginning of a long period of organizational turmoil—the growing pains of a new superpower. During the presidencies of Harry S. Truman and Dwight D. Eisenhower, the Department of State and the Foreign Service were enmeshed in bureaucratic struggles for turf, jobs, money, prestige, and power. At the same time, both institutions became targets for ferocious, reckless attacks on their loyalty and competence. The American Foreign Service Association took part in the organizational debates, but its role was minor and in no case decisive. In the face of the political attacks, the association was largely though not wholly silent. In this hesitancy it was far from alone: Neither the American Federation of Government Employees (AFGE) nor the National Federation of Federal Employees nor any other government employee organization confronted Sen. Joseph McCarthy (R-Wis.) or his allies.

## ORGANIZATION: 1940s

The State Department shed responsibilities it had acquired during the war and the demobilization that followed. Responsibility for intelligence, which State had picked up with the closure of the Office of Strategic Services in 1945, went at President Truman's request to the new Central Intelligence Agency, established by law in 1947.[1] In 1948 Congress created the Economic Cooperation Administration (ECA), a predecessor of the U.S. Agency for International Development (USAID, sometimes referred to simply as AID), to operate assistance programs under the Marshall Plan. The ECA had its own special representative in Paris, Averell Harriman, whose staff vastly outnumbered the rest of the American embassy.[2]

Information and public affairs, which had come into State with the closure of the Office of War Information, went to the U.S. Information Agency (USIA), a new agency established in 1953.[3] The Foreign Agricultural Service, which had been folded into State in 1939, was reestablished in the Department of Agriculture in 1954.[4] (The work of the Foreign Commerce Service, also merged into State in 1939, remained in State until pursuant to an act of Congress a Foreign Commercial Service was reestablished in the Commerce Department in 1980.[5]) Trade negotiations, a core function of the department, began to migrate to the White House after the creation of the Office of the Special Trade Representative in the Executive Office of the President in 1962.[6]

A series of blue-ribbon panels—the Hoover Commission (1947–1949), the Rowe-Ramspeck-DeCourcy Committee (1950), a Brookings Institution group (1951), a White House Personnel Task Force (1953–1954), and the Wriston Committee (1954)[7]—all urged the State Department to restructure. The deficiencies were well understood: The Civil Service had scant experience of conditions abroad, and the Foreign Service had only cursory exposure to the tug and tussle of policymaking in Washington. The Hoover Commission cited "a cancerous cleavage" between the Foreign Service and the civil servants who staffed the department, and later panels echoed the theme. Every report recommended a similar solution: a whole or partial amalgamation of the Foreign Service and the Civil Service. The department's management and the Service's rank and file fretted over the issue for close to a decade. The rancor that accompanied its resolution lasted a decade more.

The Hoover Commission Report recommended, "The personnel in the permanent State Department establishment in Washington and the personnel of the Foreign Service above certain levels should be amalgamated over a short period of years into a *single* foreign affairs service *obligated* to serve at home or overseas and constituting a safeguarded career group administered separately from the general Civil Service."[8] Dean Acheson, then out of the department and a member of the commission, "heartily concurred."[9] But when Acheson took office as Secretary of State in January 1949, his concern for the morale of the Service caused him to hesitate. He named a three-man committee—headed by James Rowe (a New Deal lawyer who had served on the Hoover Commission), with Civil Service Commission Chairman Robert Ramspeck and Foreign Service Officer William DeCourcy—to give the issue further study. The Rowe Commission went even further than its predecessor and called for "a single personnel system applicable to *all* people under the direct administrative control of the Secretary of State," a system "initially outside of the regular Civil

Service" and with the flexibility to exempt some members from overseas service. Employees would be divided into officers and staff support, with temporary appointments allowed in both categories.[10]

The Rowe Commission surveyed department employees and found that 81 percent of civil servants and 59 percent of Foreign Service officers supported the idea of a single, integrated Service, with both groups heavily conditioning their support on the details of implementation. Civil servants wanted assurances that they would not be penalized if they chose not to go abroad; Foreign Service officers worried about a decline in standards and feared a loss of pension and retirement benefits.[11]

AFSA, whether by intention or inertia, had little to do with the commission's report. The chairman of the Executive Committee, Hervé L'Heureux, sought and received assurances from the department's top administrative officer, John Peurifoy, that the committee would have an opportunity to comment on the completed report before any action was taken. Presumably this promise was kept, but there is no record of any committee action. At the 1950 general meeting, AFSA President George F. Kennan tried to push the issue aside. The future of the Foreign Service, he said, depended not on amalgamation but on how the Service was viewed by official Washington as a whole. "For this reason," he said, there was "not much to be gained by frantically plucking people's sleeves with a view to getting isolated decisions taken in favor of the Service against the better judgment of those who had taken them."[12]

Others shared Kennan's reluctance to lobby the department's managers, believing perhaps that it would reflect poorly on them. In his memoir, Dean Rusk relates this anecdote (from his time as director of the Office of Special Political Affairs, which later became the Office of United Nations Affairs):

> [Secretary of State George C.] Marshall ... taught us how we should conduct ourselves in public life, both by personal example and by dropping little homilies. . . . For example, soon after his appointment, Marshall was in a staff meeting with about 15 of us, and someone complained about poor departmental morale. The general straightened himself up, looked around the table, and declared, "Gentlemen, enlisted men may be entitled to morale problems, but officers are not. I expect all officers in this department to take care of their own morale." When word went around the department that there was no shoulder to cry on, morale at State went to the highest point that I had ever seen it, before or since.[13]

Members of AFSA's Executive Committee may have thought that commenting on amalgamation would be tantamount to whining about morale. Or perhaps they missed Loy Henderson's leadership. In any case, in contrast to its active role in drafting the Foreign Service Act of 1946, the association remained largely an observer on amalgamation in the early 1950s.

Despite the Hoover and Rowe Reports, the department took only modest action. A 1951 directive from the under secretary (there was then only one) liberalized the rules to allow more departmental Civil Service officers, and members of the Foreign Service Reserve and staff corps, to apply for entry into the Foreign Service officer corps. The directive opened some foreign postings to civil servants who volunteered to go abroad, and it increased the number of Washington jobs to be filled by FSOs.[14] Minutes of meetings of AFSA's Executive Committee contain no record of any discussion of the program, but the *Foreign Service Journal* praised it as "courageous and realistic."[15] Arthur Jones in a 1965 study called it "ill-fated." Its implementation "lacked a sense of urgency," and it accomplished little.[16]

## MCCARTHY

For the failure of the 1951 reform, as for so much else, a good measure of blame may fall on Sen. Joseph McCarthy. Political attacks on the Department of State and the Foreign Service began in the late 1940s and increased in intensity into the 1950s, draining the department's energy and interfering with structural reforms. Dean Acheson, under secretary from 1945 to 1947 and Secretary of State from 1949 to 1953, wrote (referring to himself in the third person) that in 1951 the department

> was already facing troubles enough at home to induce moderation in reorganizing its harassed staff. Since the first of the year, Senator Joseph McCarthy, with help from various other internal-security investigations and loyalty boards, was keeping administrative officers busy and both Foreign Service officers and departmental staff thoroughly upset. It would seem understandable that the Secretary regarded a far-reaching and basic reorganization of the status of every person in the department as General Grant might have regarded a similar proposal for the Army of the Potomac between the Wilderness and Appomattox.[17]

In the years after World War II, as after World War I, anti-communist fervor seized much of the country, as if the moral exaltation of wartime could not be demobilized but had to assert itself in a new mission. President Truman, under political pressure following the Democratic Party's loss of both houses of Congress in 1946, instituted loyalty reviews of federal employees in 1947. The House Un-American Activities Committee began its famous investigation into communist influence in the motion picture industry in the same year.

In the State Department, security concerns had arisen even before the end of the war. Maj. Gen. Patrick Hurley, a former secretary of war named special envoy and then ambassador to China in 1944, complained to President Truman in 1945 that his mission had been frustrated because "the professional Foreign Service men sided with the Chinese Communist Party."[18] One of those men, "China hand" John Stewart Service, was arrested later that year with other State Department employees and charged with passing classified documents to *Amerasia*, a small, monthly foreign affairs journal.[19] The arrests prompted the department to establish an Office of Security, the predecessor of today's Bureau of Diplomatic Security. That office set up a Security Committee (later the Loyalty Security Board), which in its first 10 months disapproved for employment or terminated 341 individuals.[20] In 1946 a rider to the State appropriations bill gave the Secretary of State "absolute discretion" to fire any employee considered a "security risk," a term the department defined to include people with "sexual peculiarities, alcoholism, or . . . an indiscreet and chronically wagging tongue; [regardless of] the individual's loyalty to this country." The rider was attached to appropriations bills for the next seven years.[21]

The Soviet testing of an atomic bomb in August 1949, the victory of the communists in China a few weeks later, and the North Korean attack on South Korea in June 1950 spurred a furious hunt for spies, communist sympathizers, and others who might be unreliable. Some Soviet agents were indeed exposed: State Department official Alger Hiss was publicly accused of spying for the Soviet Union in 1948 and convicted of perjury in February 1950; nuclear spy Klaus Fuchs was convicted (in Britain) a month later.

On February 9, 1950, at a speech before a Republican women's group in Wheeling, West Virginia, Senator McCarthy announced that he had a list of "205 individuals that were known to the Secretary of State as being members of the Communist Party and who, nevertheless, are still working and shaping policy in the State Department."[22] On the Senate floor McCarthy's ally, Sen. William E. Jenner (R-Ind.), called Secretary Acheson a "communist-appeasing, communist-protecting betrayer of America."[23] Department officials were called repeatedly to testify before various Senate committees.

As a sign of determination and zeal, between 1947 and 1950 the department fired 202 employees deemed security risks.[24] Between 1950 and 1952, the number

**Box 3.1.** Security Risk Dismissals

The China hands got the headlines, but it was alleged homosexuals, not suspected communist sympathizers, who bore the brunt of the firings. Under pressure from Senator McCarthy, and with the rationalization that gay men and women could be easily blackmailed, the security office at State in 1950 established the "M Unit" to investigate charges of homosexuality. The official history of the Bureau of Diplomatic Security writes that State's "Office of Personnel believed that 'latent tendencies can remain dormant for long periods of time—and then break through the surface without prior warning.'" The purge of suspected individuals, carried out across the federal government but with special ferocity at the Department of State, came to be known as the Lavender Scare and went on for years.

**State Department Employee Dismissals as Security Risks**

|      | Alleged homosexuals | All others | Total |
|------|---------------------|------------|-------|
| 1950 | 54                  | 12         | 63    |
| 1951 | 119                 | 35         | 154   |
| 1952 | 134                 | 70         | 204   |

Source: Adapted from U.S. Department of State, *History of the Bureau of Diplomatic Security*, 128–29.

State's security office dismissed another 306 employees in the first nine months of the Eisenhower administration and tried to block the nomination of Foreign Service Officer Charles Bohlen as ambassador to Moscow on the grounds that he had "close associations with three State Department employees suspected of homosexuality."[a]

a. U.S. Department of State, *Diplomatic Security*, 141.

rose to 421. A grand jury had unanimously refused to indict John Stewart Service after his arrest in 1945, and loyalty investigations cleared him in 1946, 1947, and 1949. But in 1951 he was fired as a security risk, as was Foreign Service Officer John Paton Davies in 1953.[25]

McCarthy's power faded rapidly after a failed investigation of the U.S. Army led to his censure by the Senate in 1954. The effect of his attacks, however, and the failure of the department's leadership to defend its employees remained "like a flash bulb witnessed up close, seen much later when one's eyes were closed."[26] John Foster Dulles, Secretary of State from 1953 to 1959, reinforced the fear among Foreign Service officers that expressing unpopular views could destroy a career. On taking office, he told department employees that he expected "competence, discipline, and *positive loyalty* to the policies that our president and the

Congress may prescribe. . . . Less than that is not tolerable at this time."[27] Such was the atmosphere of the Dulles years.

Throughout this period, AFSA was largely silent, at least for the record. Its Executive Committees and Boards of Directors issued no statements, and the presidents made no speeches. Minutes of meetings in the late 1940s and into the 1950s record no discussions of the shocks and humiliations inflicted on the Service. The strongest note of concern—under the circumstances, a courageous one—was a 1951 editorial in the *Journal*, "Career vs. Conscience." The Foreign Service officer, wrote the editors,

> is searching his conscience and examining his job in a way previously unknown to his experience. . . . He finds that a calling which has claimed his abiding loyalty, and his unexpressed but deep sense of devotion to his country, is being assailed and degraded by irresponsible demagogues. He discovers that what he may report [may] be distorted and publicly held against him. He learns that his associations can be suspect and that, instead of performing his duty by acquiring the widest possible acquaintance in the country of his assignment—as he was ever taught by his superiors and by formal instruction of the department—he is condemned for his initiative in attempting to meet individuals of unorthodox beliefs. . . .
>
> The choice is before him. Shall he remain in the Service, resolved to report only what will harmonize with the temper of the times? Shall he report honestly and fearlessly . . . knowing the dangers of honesty and the risk to his career and his reputation? Or shall he resign?
>
> Courage is needed, on the part of the department and the government. If there are disloyal members among us, no one will resist their removal forthwith. But if the rest of us are loyal, let the department have the courage to defend our loyalty and to reaffirm a creed of the Foreign Service—to serve to the best of ability, to observe keenly, to report what is seen and heard and felt, without inhibition, fear, or mental reservation—to know our enemies as well as to cultivate our friends, and to pursue as best we can the honorable profession we have chosen, in the constant and undeterred conviction that ours is the first line of defense of our country.[28]

## HERVÉ L'HEUREUX

A key figure in AFSA during this period was Hervé L'Heureux, a consular officer who had risen rapidly to become chief of the visa division and was extended for a fifth year in that position by act of Congress. L'Heureux was a World War I veteran who, as a Foreign Service officer, had entered North Africa with the invading Allied force in 1942 and served as U.S. consul in Algiers and Marseilles. After the war, when the American Legion joined those who questioned the loyalty and patriotism of the Department of State, L'Heureux established a legion post in the department and was its commander. He was vice chairman of AFSA's Executive Committee from 1947 to 1948, and when the association's first paid director, retired FSO Frank Lockhart, died in 1949, L'Heureux filled in without pay. In 1950 he was elected to the first of three consecutive terms as the committee's chairman.[29]

Under L'Heureux's leadership, the association attended to internal affairs and bread-and-butter issues. New bylaws adopted in 1951 replaced the Executive Committee with a five-person Board of Directors, chosen along with the president and vice president by an electoral college of 18, elected annually by the active membership. The bylaws gave the board the power to set dues, up to a ceiling of $12 per year (dues were set at $10).[30] The association incorporated in the District of Columbia in 1952, and its sister organization, the American Foreign Service Protective Association, purchased for $45,000 a "Georgetown-type" house at 1809 G Street Northwest where AFSA leased space. A Foreign Service Club, long debated within AFSA, opened in the G Street building in the fall.[31]

AFSA created a new legal entity, the Foreign Service Cooperative Association, to build and maintain a revolving fund on which U.S. despatch agents or the Department of State could draw in connection with nonofficial purchases and shipments of goods to individuals or commissaries at Foreign Service posts abroad. (The fund was liquidated in 1956, when the agents determined that they could not handle personal shipments.) And for the first time, the AFSA Governing Board established a standing committee to address the concerns of retirees.[32]

Despite these efforts, the association struggled. In 1952 it had 1,992 active and 546 associate members out of a pool of about 12,000 eligible for active or associate membership.[33] About a tenth of the membership was in arrears on dues. Association revenues were about $42,000, more than half of which came from advertising in the *Journal*.[34] The revenues covered expenses, including rent and a paid staff of eight (including the *Journal* staff), but just barely. Sixty volunteers handled the work of the association's six standing committees: education, entertainment, club, retirement, revolving fund, and welfare.[35]

One member, James May, suggested in a 1953 letter that the association's poor membership support was related to its failure to "campaign to improve the lot" of Foreign Service employees. May urged AFSA to fight for better pay and benefits and to take on other bread-and-butter issues. Chairman of the Board Tyler

Box 3.2. The Foreign Service League

In 1954 Joseph Grew incorporated, on the model of the Navy League, a Foreign Service League as a nonprofit organization to promote the Foreign Service. One objective was to support a television series about a Foreign Service family abroad that would be similar to the then-popular show *Navy Log*. According to minutes of meetings of the AFSA Board, David Waters of the State Department's Office of Public Affairs and Outerbridge Horsey of the AFSA Board believed at one point in 1956 that they had two proposals: one from Four Star Films for a year of weekly half-hour shows at a cost of $4.5 million, with DuPont as a sponsor, and a competing proposal from CBS. By 1957, however, Four Star and CBS had lost interest in the television project, and the Foreign Service League never became active.[a]

Promoting the Service in popular media was by no means a fanciful idea. In 1946 the State Department worked with NBC to produce a radio show, *Tales of the Foreign Service*, presenting fictionalized "true tales" of American diplomats in wartime. (Surviving episodes are available for download at RadioEchoes [https://www.radioechoes.com] and other sites.) In the 1949 Hollywood film *Assignment in China* (also known as *State Department File 649*), a Foreign Service officer outwits a Chinese warlord.[b] Diplomatic couriers appeared in heroic, or at least glamorous, roles in movies (for example, *Diplomatic Courier*, 1952) and television shows (*Passport to Danger*, 1954–1958).[c] More recent examples are cited in box 8.1, "Foreign Service Showbiz," on page 126.

a. Minutes, AFSA Board meetings, June 9, 1955, and November 9, 1955.
b. *State Department: File 649*, Film Classics, Inc., Sigmund Neufeld Pictures, 1949, https://archive.org/details/state_department.
c. *Diplomatic Courier*, directed by Henry Hathaway, Twentieth Century Fox, 1952, IMDb.com, https://www.imdb.com/title/tt0044552/?ref_=fn_al_tt_1; and *Passport to Danger*, created by Robert C. Dennis for Hal Roach Studios, 1954–1958, IMDb, https://www.imdb.com/title/tt0046634/.

Thompson rejected the idea and rebuked the writer. The association should not act "as a militant trade union type of organization," he said. Why not? Because "the loyalty of the Foreign Service to the Secretary as its chief precludes any action on the part of the association which would run counter to his decisions."[36] This view of the association as part of the apparatus of the Secretary and the Department of State prevailed until the end of the decade.

## THE WRISTON COMMITTEE AND WRISTONIZATION

Secretary of State John Foster Dulles convened a "public committee on personnel" early in 1954. He named the president of Brown University, Henry

Wriston, as chairman and appointed two career officers, Norman Armour and Robert D. Murphy, among the eight members. The chairman of AFSA's Board of Directors, Andrew B. Foster, coauthor of the 1945 Chapin-Foster Report (see chapter 2), served full time as the committee's associate staff director and sought to bring the viewpoint of the career Service "constantly to the committee's attention."[37] What precisely that viewpoint was, however, was hardly clear. The Service was divided.

Secretary Dulles wanted the committee to look to the Hoover and Rowe Reports and recommend swift, decisive action. He got his wish. The committee met for the first time in February, reported in May, and had the Secretary's approval of its recommendations in hand in June.[38] To make sure the recommendations were carried out, Dulles named one of the committee's members, former Assistant Secretary of State Charles Saltzman, under secretary for administration.

The committee's most important recommendation called for integration of the Foreign Service and the Civil Service "where their functions and responsibilities converge." The integration would involve making some 1,450 Civil Service positions in the department available to Foreign Service personnel and admitting a like number of Civil Service officers to the Foreign Service. The Foreign Service officer corps was to rise in number from around 1,300 to nearly 4,000.[39] Legislation was sought and quickly approved to allow the program to move forward.[40]

Wriston himself had expected some "emotional resistance" in the Foreign Service to "watering down" an elite corps through lateral entry.[41] Sen. Alexander Wiley (R-Wis.), at the request of Secretary Dulles, surveyed some 200 FSOs, reserve officers, and staff, mainly at European posts. He found that 83 percent of FSOs favored integration of the Foreign Service and Civil Service as a matter of principle but raised many objections to Wristonization in practice.[42] Perhaps concerned about their prospects for promotion and likely convinced that diplomatic skills are best acquired on the job, officers favored bringing new personnel in at the lower grades, not in the middle and upper grades as the Wriston program would allow.[43]

Moreover, many Foreign Service officers considered civil servants in general to be unworthy. George Kennan, although he had refused to argue against integration when he was president of AFSA, certainly held that view. Writing in high patrician style in *Foreign Affairs*, he referred to himself as an "antiquated spirit" who would prefer "25 really superior officers to 2,500 mediocre ones," and he deprecated the Wriston Report as a "pamphlet."[44]

## Speak No Evil

The AFSA Board offered Charles Saltzman, the new under secretary for administration, its "fullest cooperation and support," and he was quick to take up the offer. On August 3, 1954, Saltzman summoned AFSA Board Chairman Andrew Foster to his office. "Certain congressmen and senators" had told Saltzman that "various Foreign Service personnel" had "voiced misgivings of one kind or another" about the Wriston program. It was "deplorable and outrageous" that anyone in the Service should lobby against a program that the Secretary had approved and directed be carried out. Foster agreed that "this situation was intolerable" and that "there was no excuse for it." With the full approval of the board, Foster presented a plan to pass on to Saltzman letters to the association or the *Journal* that expressed "anxieties" about the program. Salzman accepted Foster's proposal. The *Journal* published few such letters and later stopped running them entirely.[45] Foster also conferred with the president of Diplomatic and Consular Officers, Retired (DACOR, the association for Foreign Service retirees), John Campbell White, who agreed that DACOR members should not and would not approach Congress about Wristonization.[46]

In the late 1950s, while the State Department tightened its control over the AFSA Board, the board tightened its control over the editorial policy of the *Journal*, going so far as vetting book reviews. *The Ugly American*, a best-selling 1958 novel, had painted American diplomats in a fictional East Asian country as comfortably isolated in their compound, speaking only English, obsessed with communism, and easily manipulated by corrupt local leaders. A *Journal* editorial found some positive things to say about the book and warned that the spread of government housing, commissaries, and other services tended "to divorce Foreign Service personnel from the mainstream of life in their country of assignment."[47]

The *Journal* and its staff were promptly rebuked. The chairman of the AFSA Board, J. Graham Parsons, reminded Editor W. T. M. Beale and the *Journal's* Editorial Board that they serve at the pleasure of the AFSA Board. Although the editors must have "the greatest possible freedom," said Parsons, they must also check with the AFSA Board of Directors before publishing "material of major importance."[48] A few weeks later, the *Journal's* Editorial Board decided not to opine on a bill to establish a Foreign Service Academy until the department had taken a position.[49] And in April 1959, Under Secretary (and former AFSA Board Chairman) Loy Henderson told AFSA Board members to make sure the *Journal* took no position on the issue until congressional hearings had concluded.[50]

By the end of the decade, AFSA had become reticent, even mute. In late 1959, when the Senate took up a bill to raise Foreign Service salaries and benefits, Sen. Mike Mansfield (D-Mont.) of the Committee on Foreign Relations had to write to AFSA President Joseph Satterthwaite to solicit the association's comments.[51]

## THE UNION IDEA IN THE FEDERAL GOVERNMENT

The idea that a federal employee might be a tradesman or a worker, like a carpenter in the American Federation of Labor or a steelworker in the Congress of Industrial Organizations, did not easily take hold. In the late nineteenth and early twentieth centuries, as unions in mining, steel, railroads, garments, and other industries entered a period of fierce and sometimes bloody struggle with employers, government workers formed social organizations and mutual benefit societies. They did not unionize or engage with management in labor-management discussions.[52]

The Lloyd–La Follette Amendment to the Post Office Appropriation Act of 1912 guaranteed federal workers the right to lobby Congress but not to bargain with their executive branch employers.[53] The National Labor Relations Act of 1935—named the Wagner Act after its chief sponsor, Sen. Robert Wagner (D-N.Y.)—stated that "employees shall have the right to organize and bargain collectively," but the act did not apply to the public sector. President Franklin Roosevelt told the president of the National Federation of Federal Employees that "all government employees should realize that the process of collective bargaining, as usually understood, cannot be transplanted into the public service" because "the employer is the whole people" whom administrative officials cannot fully represent or bind. And a strike against the government "by those who have sworn to support it, is unthinkable and intolerable."[54]

In the late 1940s and early 1950s, however, despite the inability of unions to bargain collectively with federal agencies, the AFGE and the NFFE expanded their presence across the federal government.

In 1958 Senator Wagner's son, New York City Mayor Robert F. Wagner Jr., issued an executive order granting collective bargaining rights to city employees. The act had national repercussions. Just three years later, after a commission reported that labor-management relations in the federal government were "chaotic," President John F. Kennedy also used an executive order to give federal employees the right to "form, join, and assist any employee organization or to refrain from any such activity." The order set a government-wide policy on collective bargaining that avoided the word "negotiate" but allowed parties to "meet and confer" on a specific list of issues.[55]

## THE UNION IDEA IN THE FOREIGN SERVICE

The order led to an expansion of union membership within the federal workforce. By 1970, nearly 50 percent of civilian federal employees were union members.[56] Soon after the order was issued, Neil M. Ruge, chief of the Employee Relations Branch in the State Department's Office of Personnel, urged AFSA to "grasp the opportunity" to organize the Foreign Service. In a 1962 letter to the *Foreign Service Journal*, Ruge compared AFSA unfavorably with medical and bar associations in advancing members' interests and warned that "other employee organizations"—meaning AFGE—"are currently engaged in recruiting members within the department and the Foreign Service."[57] Indeed, both AFGE and NFFE had local unions with Civil Service members in the Department of State and the U.S. Information Agency even before the Kennedy order.[58]

But Ruge, like James May in 1953, was ahead of his time. The Foreign Service in 1962 was a tired institution, unready for change and unreceptive to new ideas. A Kennedy administration transition task force report said the Service was just beginning to emerge from "professional deformations" due to the institutional "trauma of the Dulles-McCarthy years" and its "vast increase in size" following Wristonization. The entire Department of State, said the report, exerted a "tremendous institutional inertial force" so that "even such a distinguished career group as the Foreign Service has failed to keep pace with the novel and expanding demands of a changing world." The senior men in the Service, according to George Kennan (by this time ambassador to Yugoslavia), were "empty bundles of good manners."[59]

The American Foreign Service Association reflected this exhaustion. AFSA in the late 1950s and early 1960s was a quiet place that operated out of a couple of rented rooms. Its assets in 1960 totaled less than $200,000, including $95,000 in a dedicated Scholarship Fund. AFSA was, in the judgment of one of its members, "an effete club of elderly gentlemen whose headquarters could not be located and who took care never to fight for any cause."[60]

But pressure for change was beginning to build among what the transition report called "the young, imaginative, all too often circumscribed" officers.[61] While the organization as a whole remained passive, some in AFSA saw the association as a potential center of efforts for reform. Robert McClintock, chairman of the Editorial Board of the *Foreign Service Journal*, argued in a 1958 memorandum to the AFSA Board that AFSA should provide leadership to its members and assert itself more vigorously on their behalf in relations with the department, Congress, and the public.

When the chairman of the 1957–1958 AFSA Board, E. Allan Lightner Jr., left office in October 1958, he reported that the board had "only partially come to grips" with the questions raised in McClintock's memo. Lightner had come into office, he said, "raising soul-searching questions having to do with the fundamental nature of the association and its potentialities for better serving its membership," and he left office unsatisfied. Board Chairman Hugh Appling, in his 1962 valedictory report, noted that the board had set up a Committee on Public Relations and an ad hoc committee to examine "the propriety and desirability of . . . taking an interest in pending legislation affecting the Foreign Service."[62]

The lack of leadership did not pass unnoticed. FSO Jack Armitage wrote to the *Journal*: "It is a fact known to all that there is little, if any, deeply felt association with the AFSA on the part of the membership. Large numbers [of Foreign Service members] do not even belong. . . . I would submit that AFSA has no meaningful concept of what the Foreign Service should be and of what it—the association—should do to develop, sustain, and maintain it."[63]

Armitage was right about AFSA's reticence. As the *Journal* reported, Board Chairman Lucius Battle said in September 1963 that "AFSA 'must speak up' on issues affecting the welfare of the Foreign Service, though it should be careful to . . . avoid public difference with those in authority."[64]

Even after passage of the 1946 Act, AFSA limited "active membership" to chiefs of mission and active-duty Foreign Service personnel employed by the Department of State. State's Foreign Service retirees were eligible for "associate membership," as were American citizen career employees at USIA, the International Cooperation Agency (later USAID), and other agencies if they were "on foreign service"—that is, serving abroad.[65] In 1961 AFSA had only about 3,600 active members out of a potential pool more than twice that size.[66] It took until 1963, 17 years after passage of the act, for AFSA to extend eligibility for active membership to Foreign Service personnel of USIA, USAID, and other agencies.[67]

## PRESSURE FOR CHANGE

Elsewhere in the country, public differences with those in authority were the stuff of daily headlines. During the "Freedom Summer" of 1964, northern students headed to the Deep South to join local Black organizers in a drive to register Black people to vote; the ensuing violence brought a wave of national media attention to civil rights and civil disobedience that did not subside. That fall at the Berkeley campus of the University of California, efforts to enforce rules limiting political advocacy provoked student resistance; the following mass arrests inspired protest movements on campuses around the country. After Congress passed the Gulf of Tonkin Resolution in August 1964, the government's prosecution of the war in Vietnam intensified, as did opposition to it, especially among those eligible for the military draft. The term "generation gap" came into popular use, and, four years later, the fifties became the sixties.[68]

This spirit of dissent and dissatisfaction affected the Foreign Service in several ways. Senior officers, and the State Department itself, became concerned that domestic resistance to the government's foreign policies would weaken American diplomacy. They sought ways to improve communications between Foreign Service professionals and the academicians and journalists who were thought to have influence over public opinion. Junior officers became more willing to challenge the department, not necessarily on matters of policy but on matters of administration and personnel. Both groups often used the word "openness," which encompassed outreach, transparency, and candor.

In Congress, Sen. Henry M. Jackson (D-Wash.), chairman of the Subcommittee on National Security (part of the Committee on Government Oversight), poked and prodded the Department of State and the Foreign Service from 1959 to 1965. On the House side in 1964 and 1965, the Foreign Affairs Committee held hearings and put forward legislation proposing sweeping changes to the Foreign Service Act of 1946.

AFSA felt the push for change and responded in three areas: public relations, which today would be called "outreach"; personal well-being, or bread-and-butter issues; and professional enhancement. Upon establishing the Committee on Public Relations, the board opened its minutes to the public in 1962, and the *Journal* began publishing the minutes, or at least summaries of them, in January 1963. In 1964 the association set up two committees that would be central to its future: a Committee on Career Principles to examine "the relation of current policy and administration to the *strengthening of the Foreign Service as an instrument of foreign policy*" and a Planning Committee to map a course for AFSA itself.[69] The association also established a formal relationship with the Junior Foreign Service Officers Club (JFSOC), which had begun in 1956 as a purely social organization but by 1964 had become a locus for dissatisfied young officers eager for change.[70]

AFSA's president in 1964, and again from 1966 to 1967, was U. Alexis Johnson, the deputy under secretary for political affairs and the highest-ranking career officer in the department. Johnson and the boards he worked with—notable members included Elbert "Bert" Mathews, Martin Herz, Marshall Green, and Samuel "Sandy" Berger—saw the Service as neglected and disparaged. They looked for ways to use the association to improve public recognition of the Foreign Service as the home of professionalism, expertise, and experience in foreign affairs. To familiarize the foreign policy establishment with the Service and vice versa, AFSA amended its bylaws in 1964 to create two new classes of membership: fellows in diplomacy and corresponding members, open by invitation to distinguished academicians, journalists, and others outside the government.[71]

AFSA, DACOR, and the State Department organized the first Foreign Service Day—held as a conference of pundits and practitioners, with panels, roundtables, keynote speakers, and the like—on November 12, 1965. AFSA hoped to hold annual "assemblies to bring career diplomats and opinion-makers together, to mutual benefit." The Planning Committee, in a report prepared in 1966 and 1967, recommended turning the *Foreign Service Journal* into a professional quarterly for an audience of "those in American society with a serious interest in foreign affairs" while covering parochial matters in a non-subscription monthly for active-duty members.[72] The board also tried, with no success, to revive the failed effort from the 1950s to "bring the story of the Foreign Service to the American public" through movies and television.[73]

The same report also looked at bread-and-butter issues, which it called matters of "personal well-being." Its conclusions were timid. The association, it said, should solicit contributions from donors, but it "would never have the resources or membership requisite to effective professional lobbying with the Congress." The committee said the association should be a "sympathetic ombudsman" for aggrieved members, and it urged AFSA to build a deeper affiliation with two established organizations: AFGE, a union in the American Federation of Labor and Congress of Industrial Organizations representing more than 100,000 federal employees, and the National Federation of Professional Organizations, a trade association.[74]

Whatever the feelings of its membership, AFSA in the early 1960s was reluctant to engage with Congress or challenge the department's management. Change came slowly. The board set up an ad hoc committee in 1962 to examine the propriety, desirability, and legal ramifications of the association's taking an interest in pending legislation affecting the Service. In a replay of legislative efforts in the 1950s, Board Chairman Lucius Battle, acting this time without prior approval from State, wrote to the committees of jurisdiction in support of legislation to establish a National Academy of Foreign Affairs, comparable to the military academies.[75] In another 1950s replay, AFSA left it to retiree association DACOR to marshal support for a bill adding a cost-of-living adjustment to Service pensions. The bill, enacted in 1965, came to be called the "DACOR legislation."[76] Not until 1967, when AFSA Board Chairman Outerbridge Horsey appeared before a House subcommittee to support an administration proposal to raise all federal salaries by 4.5 percent, would AFSA testify on legislation.[77]

U. Alexis Johnson was unable to give sustained attention to association affairs and not only because his position in the department was a good deal more than full time. Elected to a one-year term that began in October 1963, he left the presidency early when he was named deputy ambassador to Vietnam. Board Chairman Taylor Belcher, elected at the same time as Johnson, served only six months before leaving to serve as chief of mission in Cyprus. Johnson returned to Washington, and to the presidency of AFSA, in 1965. Stability improved after AFSA's general meeting that year amended the bylaws to establish two-year terms for officers and directors, adding at the same time a second vice president and an 11th board member.[78] Even so, the sudden departure of officers and directors to take up critical assignments would remain a challenge for AFSA's management and leadership.

Despite the changes in leadership, the association was busy and productive in 1966 and 1967. U. Alexis Johnson published the first letter from an AFSA president in the March 1966 *Journal*.[79] A membership drive fell short of its goal but still netted 1,300 new members, raising the total membership by about 20 percent to around 7,600 (about 55 percent of those eligible).[80] And in May 1967, for $315,000 (about $2.8 million in 2022 dollars), the association bought the building at 2101 E Street Northwest, across the street from the State Department, finally giving the lie to the old canard that its headquarters could not be located.[81]

## REORGANIZATION AND REFORM

In the mid-1960s, the executive and legislative branches sought to reorganize the foreign policy machinery of the U.S. government. It had changed little since the Foreign Service Act of 1946 and the National Security Act of 1947, which created the Central Intelligence Agency and the National Security Council.

In the State Department, the deputy under secretary for administration, Bill Crockett, had big plans for restructuring the Foreign Service. Crockett, who had been an administrative officer with the Technical Cooperation Administration (a predecessor of USAID) in Beirut in the early 1950s, had transferred into the Foreign Service in 1953 and had risen quickly through the ranks. As a manager, he strengthened medical and family services and played a major role in the creation of three enduring programs: American overseas schools, art in embassies, and diplomats in residence. But he struggled with organizational reform. "I was the Foreign Service's Don Quixote," he said. "I saw wind-mills to combat and I never contemplated failure. I was naive or inordinately optimistic about what we could accomplish."[82]

Crockett's main objective was the creation of a single personnel system to cover all civilian U.S. government employees abroad, as the Rogers Act of 1924 had envisioned and as the Hoover Commission in 1948 and the Herter Committee in 1962 had recommended. Crockett enlisted the support of Rep. Wayne Hays (D-Ohio), the short-tempered, erratic chairman of the House Foreign Affairs Committee. A bill Hays introduced in the spring of 1965 would have categorized nearly all the employees of State, USIA, and USAID in the Foreign Service as regular, reserve, or staff officers, adding as well a new personnel category, foreign affairs officers, for professionals who would serve primarily but not exclusively in the United States.

Crockett saw the Hays bill as an extension of the Foreign Service Act of 1946, which, like the Rogers Act of 1924, had envisioned a single Foreign Service that would represent all agencies with international responsibilities. In a speech in 1964, Crockett praised the act effusively: "The framers of the Foreign Service Act of 1946 had a vision of greatness for the Foreign Service. They, like the framers of our Constitution, enunciated fundamental principles for achieving greatness. . . . We are not just the Foreign Service of *the State Department*! We are the Foreign Service of the United States!"[83]

AFSA, which had been passive during Wristonization, began to assert a role for itself as a place where the interests of the Service could be defined and its structure debated. The association favored the Hays bill. An editorial in the *Journal* said the bill should provide "greater administrative flexibility" that would help the department make "effective use of the Foreign Service and Civil Service employees."[84]

The Hays bill passed the House, but the Senate Foreign Relations Committee let it die without a hearing. Bill Crockett believed the bill was a casualty of the intense dislike that the Senate committee chairman, J. William Fulbright (D-Ark.), had for Wayne Hays. Hays himself blamed Sen. Claiborne Pell (D-R.I.), a member of the committee and a former Foreign Service officer, who (Hays reportedly said) "didn't like the selecting-out thing."[85]

In the White House, however, plans for reforming the foreign policy structure moved rapidly forward, and the association remained engaged. As the situation in Vietnam deteriorated, President Lyndon B. Johnson, dissatisfied with the performance and personalities of the National Security Council he inherited from President Kennedy, tried to strengthen the position of the Department of State and Secretary Dean Rusk. National Security Action Memorandum (NSAM) 341, which Johnson signed on March 2, 1966, sought to replicate in Washington the "country team" approach to managing foreign policy that ambassadors used to run their embassies overseas. NSAM 341 was largely the work of two men who had recently returned from Embassy Saigon: military adviser Gen. Maxwell Taylor, former chief of mission, and U. Alexis Johnson, former deputy ambassador and now under secretary of State for political affairs. The directive made the Secretary of State responsible for the "overall direction, coordination, and supervision" of interagency work overseas. It established a pyramid of interagency committees that was topped by a senior interdepartmental group (SIG) and chaired by State's under secretary, and supported by interdepartmental regional groups (IRGs) and ad hoc interdepartmental groups (IGs), which were chaired by State's assistant and deputy assistant secretaries, to carry out the work.[86]

The effort by the Johnson White House to put State more firmly in charge inspired and encouraged a number of FSOs who (as the Kennedy transition memo had recognized) felt undervalued and underemployed. Lannon Walker, then a junior officer newly returned from tours in North Africa, was startled to discover that others in his orientation class at the Foreign Service Institute shared concerns about the Service that he thought were unique to his experience.[87] Soon, a group of like-minded officers began to meet, sometimes at the home of Charles W. "Charlie" Bray III, then in charge of personnel in the Bureau of African Affairs.[88] The Service, they wrote in an internal memo later published in the *Journal* with minor changes, had seen a "steady erosion of [its] influence in the conduct of foreign affairs," leaving, in the absence of reform, "considerable doubt as to the validity of the concept of a career Foreign Service."[89]

The officers—Bray, Walker, Peter Constable, Morris Draper, Robert Hennemeyer, Frank Wile, David Zweifel, and others—were forward looking; the *Journal* called them "positivists."[90] But they were also looking back to a golden age that never was. As they began to develop proposals for reform, the unrealized model in the Foreign Service Act of 1946, which provided for a single career Service working for all foreign affairs agencies and administered by a Director General independent of the Department of State, seemed nearly ideal. "The principal tasks of the Foreign Service officer corps," they wrote, "must be: (1) *the elaboration of policy*; (2) *the effective coordination and direction* of the skills and resources residing elsewhere in the foreign affairs community; and . . .

(3) *assuring that policy decisions are understood and implemented* by each agency affected. These, rather than the conduct of foreign affairs at the technical level," are the essential work of the Foreign Service officer corps.[91]

The reformers drew heavily on earlier studies, not only the work by official commissions such as those of Hoover, Rowe, and Herter, but also the efforts of AFSA's Committee on Career Principles. That committee, chaired by Samuel Berger (1965–1966) and William Leonhart (1966–1967), had attracted more than 70 volunteers. They were talented officers: 13 of the 28 who signed the 1967 interim report went on to become chiefs of mission, and a 14th, Peter Tarnoff, was confirmed as an under secretary of State.[92]

What most distinguished the reformers from their predecessors was the way they pressed their case. The reformers, who came to be known as the Young Turks, believed their ideas had broad support across the career Service, and they saw the odd election system of the American Foreign Service Association as a way to demonstrate that support and gain a pulpit and platform.

By this time, Lannon Walker, then an officer in Class 5 (equivalent to today's FS-3 rank), had been assigned to the department's executive secretariat, a position that allowed him to establish connections throughout State. He organized a group of 18 officers at junior, middle, and senior grades from State, USIA, and USAID to run as a slate for AFSA's electoral college, and they pledged to choose AFSA's board from among themselves. The Group of 18 was at least as talented as the Committee on Career Principles: 10 of its members (including Walker and Bray) became chiefs of mission, and one, Philip Habib, became under secretary of State.[93]

Although 10 members of the group were on the official ballot, which included some 200 names, eight would have to compete as write-in candidates. "I got the AFSA bylaws," Walker said, "and saw there was provision for a write-in ballot." Among the group, "we knew at least one person in nearly every mission we had," enhancing the prospects for a successful write-in campaign.

Charles Bray had become staff assistant to the deputy under secretary of State for political affairs, Foy Kohler, then serving as AFSA's president. Kohler was sympathetic to the reformers. They had, he wrote later, "a predisposition to lead . . . an attitude that has not been much with us since the end of World War II, when the Foreign Service officer corps last participated actively and positively in shaping its own future."[94] Bray helped secure Kohler's support for the Reform slate and a pledge to stay on as president if the reformers were successful.

As the reformers moved from internal debate to political action, their stated objectives shifted from overhauling the country's foreign policy apparatus toward attaining goals more sharply focused on the interests of AFSA members. Their campaign platform made no reference to the Foreign Service Act of 1946 or the desirability of an independent Foreign Service. It called instead for defending the professional interests of AFSA's members and advancing their personal well-being. AFSA, the group's platform declared, "can and should expect to be heard" on personnel and administrative policies. Members "should be able to bring their professional grievances and problems to the association" and receive "prompt and energetic assistance." Employees of USAID and USIA "can and should expect equal privileges and representation" with employees of State.[95]

When the balloting ended on September 10, 1967, the entire Group of 18 had won election, including the write-ins; even the least supported among them had been named on 507 of the 1,782 ballots cast. The group met as the electoral college on September 18, named Lannon Walker chairman of the board, and reelected Foy Kohler as its president.[96] On October 1, 1967, control of AFSA passed to the reformers.

# 4

## Transformation, 1968–1973

The reformers saw the American Foreign Service Association as a platform for a campaign for institutional change to recognize the professionalism of the career Foreign Service and raise the level of responsibility entrusted to it. For Lannon Walker, Charlie Bray, and the rest of the Group of 18, this was the cause that drove their efforts.

The new board infused AFSA with energy and youth: Lannon Walker was 32; Charlie Bray, 34. They moved with a speed and audacity that the association had not seen before.

Immediately after taking office, the new board received the interim report of the Committee on Career Principles, which AFSA had created in 1965 to work on the Hays bill. In one of its first acts, the board approved the interim report and called for further work. Walker persuaded Graham Martin, then newly returned from his post as ambassador to Thailand and a new recipient of the State Department's Distinguished Honor Award, to lead the group.[1] The committee, now with many new volunteers, organized itself into eight subcommittees, whose chairs formed a steering committee that met weekly for six months.[2] The final document, published in October 1968 under the title *Toward a Modern Diplomacy*, included a 60-page chairman's report, 100 pages of reports from the subcommittees, and 20 pages of background material.[3]

## MODERN DIPLOMACY: A MANIFESTO

*Toward a Modern Diplomacy* was more conservative than radical. The authors' pride in the Foreign Service and their desire to preserve its special character are evident on almost every page. The manifesto, as the report was often called, stressed the importance of maintaining a separate Foreign Service—that is, separate from the Civil Service—with three key features: personnel who are prepared to serve anywhere in the world, rank in the individual (or rank in person) to protect flexibility and mobility, and competition for promotion that includes separation for those who fail to advance ("up or out") or who are ranked at the bottom of their class ("selection-out"). The authors praised the Foreign Service Act of 1946 as "an almost ideal instrument" that created "a basic corps of commissioned Foreign Service officers" to "furnish the hard core of our nation's representation abroad, supported by a staff corps at both officer and clerical levels," and protected from political patronage.[4]

The 1946 Act, they wrote, was "extraordinarily flexible and adaptable." Its flexibility lay in provisions for a Foreign Service Reserve that could supply extra manpower or special expertise for limited periods and in provisions for sending Foreign Service officers on detail to other agencies when overseas needs contracted. But lamentably, they wrote, the Foreign Service had its hidebound old guard—its "Horse Cavalry Colonels"—who had blocked effective implementation of the act, to the detriment of the career Service.

The authors blamed the same unnamed officers, and Secretary of State John Foster Dulles, for the department's loss of the operational functions and capabilities it had acquired after World War II and nurtured under Secretary of State George Marshall. The authors held that the Foreign Service of the United States of the 1946 Act was "a fiction. . . . [T]he Foreign Service of the Department of State is what it has become." They believed the 1946 vision remained viable, though, and recommended specific steps to lead to a unified Foreign Service for the State Department, the U.S. Agency for International Development, the U.S. Information Agency, and the Commerce and Labor Departments with a single director general, an interdepartmental advisory board of the Foreign Service, a single set of personnel policies and standards, and an easy movement of personnel among the agencies.[5]

The report presented data and careful reasoning to support recommendations that echoed past and prefigured future studies. The recommendations called for workforce planning, systematic training linked to promotions and career development, attention to interagency planning and coordination, engagement with Congress and the public, adaptation of advanced technology, and remuneration and benefits no less than accorded to other government employees in similar situations at home or abroad.[6]

To promote these ideas and raise the prestige of the Foreign Service, the new AFSA Board expanded its public relations work. Fortuitously, Secretary of State

Dean Rusk had assigned Peter Krogh, a White House fellow from his office, to work with AFSA.[7] As Lannon Walker tells it, "Peter said, 'What do you do for money? You need to get into fund-raising. Come with me to New York; we'll go tomorrow. I'll take you to see John D. Rockefeller.' He led me, and then others, by the hand. Peter Krogh was the master; he was from another world."[8] With Krogh's help, AFSA received funds from John D. Rockefeller III, the William H. Donner Foundation, Mrs. Christian Herter, and others.[9]

The money was needed. Revenue from dues and advertising in the *Journal* barely covered costs, which now included AFSA's mortgage on the building and the conversion of its lower level to a Foreign Service Club with full dining facilities. The donated funds were used "to finance programs which are clearly beyond the association's capacity to carry out from normal revenue," such as the publication of *Toward a Modern Diplomacy*.[10] Donations in 1968 and 1969 from the Harriman, Rivkin, and Herter families launched the association's program of awards recognizing members of the Foreign Service for "extraordinary accomplishment involving initiative, integrity, intellectual courage, and constructive dissent."[11] AFSA's constructive dissent awards are unique in the federal government and continue to be awarded over a half century since their creation.

The money also helped support Charlie Bray, who in 1968 took leave without pay from the Office of the Deputy Under Secretary for Political Affairs (where Charles "Chip" Bohlen had replaced the retired Foy Kohler) to work at AFSA full time for a year.[12] According to Lannon Walker, Bray "got us organized." Walker himself stayed in his job in the executive secretariat. "My wife would come down to pick me up at midnight," he said.[13]

When President Lyndon Johnson announced in March that he would not stand for reelection, the reformers knew they would have a chance to make their case to a new administration. In the summer of 1968, board members Charlie Bray and John Reinhardt went to Miami to lobby the Republican National Convention. They secured inclusion of this statement in the party's platform: "In the development and execution of the nation's foreign policy, our career Foreign Service officers play a critical role. We strongly support the Foreign Service and will strengthen it by improving its efficiency and administration and providing adequate allowances for its personnel."[14] Charlie Bray later remarked, "It's been a long time since anybody's platform has said anything like that about the Foreign Service."[15]

The press took note. When *Toward a Modern Diplomacy* was released in October, the *Washington Post* headline was "'Young Turks' of Foreign Service Seek to Modernize U.S. Diplomacy."[16] The *New York Times* called it "a 185-page

blueprint for reform" that "makes 17 recommendations for improving the conduct of United States foreign policy." Although a subsequent *Times* article said
"there is little that is novel" in the reform program, an editorial urged President-
elect Richard Nixon to "take heart from this evidence of vitality in the Service. . . . A bureaucracy that produces young men willing to stick their necks out
for self-improvement can't be all bad."[17]

The *New York Times* may have had warm thoughts about the new AFSA
Governing Board, but the department's top manager did not share them. Idar
Rimestad, who had replaced Bill Crockett as deputy under secretary for management early in 1967, was an old-line administrator. A North Dakotan, he had
started in personnel as a civilian in the Quartermaster's Office of the National
Youth Administration in 1942 and had joined the Foreign Service in 1954 after
working for the U.S. High Commissioner in Germany. Under the Wriston program, he converted from the staff corps to the officer corps in 1957.[18]

He had clear ideas and a rough tongue. Not long after the new board took
office, he asked Lannon Walker to come see him. As Walker recalled the meeting
in a 2013 interview, Rimestad "had every executive officer in the building there.
And he looked at me and said, 'Just who the f— do you think you are? You don't
represent anybody, and you're not going to get anything.'"[19]

Rimestad, interviewed in 1990, gave a similar account.

> I took Lannon Walker aside and said, "You see that certificate on the wall,
> signed by the president? I think you will see my name on the top. Where
> does it say that I am to abdicate my responsibilities to the Foreign Service
> Association? It doesn't, and I don't intend to do it." I didn't really have much
> sympathy at the time for the cry-babies—the departmental people who
> would be complaining about this or that. From the time they graduated
> from the Foreign Service Institute and were given their first assignments,
> they had a mind set to distrust administration and the people in it. They
> had already learned to resent the administrative people for having so much
> authority. . . . There wasn't a single member of the American Foreign Ser-
> vice Association Board that had any sympathy [for the] administration or
> its problems. Not one.[20]

Walker took Rimestad's assertion that AFSA represented no one as a challenge.
The AFSA Board responded with an open meeting in September 1968 that
packed State's auditorium with a noisy crowd. There was little doubt that members were angry with management and eager for a champion.

A passion for the Foreign Service and its institutional reform drove the leaders of the Group of 18, but it did not get them elected. They won election because members of the Foreign Service felt aggrieved and powerless in the face of departmental decisions on personnel, allowances, leave, transfers, health benefits, and the like.[21] The electoral program of the Group of 18 recognized this discontent and pledged to address it: "The Association can and should advance the well-being of its membership: it can and should expect to be heard before decisions of major importance in the areas of administration and personnel are made by the agencies of the foreign affairs community; its members should be able to bring their professional grievances and problems to the Association in the expectation of prompt and energetic assistance."[22]

The board tried to make good on these promises. Walker and Junior Foreign Service Officers Club President Edward "Ned" Walker testified before the Subcommittee on Compensation of the House Committee on Post Office and Civil Service to support comparability of pay between private- and public-sector employees. Lannon Walker, though, digressed from the pay issue to express general dissatisfaction with "the organization of foreign affairs." The "gross proliferation of agencies and quasi-career Foreign Services" led to a great waste of resources, he said. He complained as well of abuse of the Foreign Service Reserve with "increasing numbers of political appointments."[23]

In early 1969, Walker wrote to Idar Rimestad with a list of proposed "improvements" in allowances and benefits. Some might require legislation, Walker said, but the department could undertake most on its own. Among the issues raised were a displacement allowance, which was provided to the military and the Civil Service but not to the Foreign Service; provision for outpatient treatment in the United States for an illness contracted by a dependent while overseas; full (rather than 80 percent) advance of travel allowances; access to the federal savings program available to members of the armed forces, the U.S. Public Health Service, and the U.S. Coast and Geodetic Survey serving overseas; parity with other agencies with regard to home leave, which the department then provided only between two foreign assignments; parity between single and married employees in temporary lodging allowance; parity with members of the military in treatment of capital gains on the sale of a primary residence in the United States; and a number of other issues. The letter, which asked for discussions, got no reply.[24]

## MACOMBER TAKES OVER

As so often happens in the Foreign Service, time and transfers resolved the hostility between Walker and Rimestad. The new administration wanted its own manager at State; Rimestad moved on to become U.S. ambassador to international organizations in Geneva.

His successor was William B. Macomber Jr., nominally a Republican but a Johnson administration holdover who had been assistant secretary for legislative affairs since 1967. He had served earlier in the decade as President Kennedy's ambassador to Jordan. Macomber was a lawyer, but his real profession was public service. He was a war hero, a Marine who had twice parachuted into occupied France to work with the Resistance. He first came to the State Department in 1953 after serving in the Central Intelligence Agency. Macomber had an explosive temper but did not act in haste or out of emotion. He managed to be both thoughtful and energetic. He was persistent, and he got things done.

Unlike Rimestad, Macomber had no direct experience in management before taking the reins at State. And unlike Rimestad, he was broadly sympathetic to reform.[25] Several AFSA initiatives that had stalled moved forward even before Macomber had been confirmed: full advance of travel allowances, improvement in the overseas temporary lodging allowance, and the appointment of an ombudsman, an idea first proposed by AFSA Board member Morris Draper.[26]

Macomber quickly took on two big issues, one that he asked for and one that took him by surprise. The one he sought was a thorough examination and overhaul of management in the Department of State and the Foreign Service. The surprise was a sweeping change in labor-management relations.

## Nixon's First Order

Macomber took over as State's top manager just as the White House was preparing new rules for labor-management relations across the federal workforce, rules intended to allow unions to organize without creating an adversarial relationship with management.[27] Executive Order (E.O.) 11491—issued October 29, 1969—established a union election system with a secret ballot, a Federal Labor Relations Council (FLRC) and a Federal Services Impasses Panel to set policy and resolve negotiation stalemates, and an arbitration process to rule on complaints of unfair labor practices and other grievances. The order also clarified the key issue of who in the federal service was a supervisor. Supervisors, by definition, lived on the management side of the labor-management divide; they were excluded from the bargaining unit and, with rare exceptions, could not belong to a union or vote in a union election.[28] Under the order, a supervisor was "an employee having authority, in the interest of an agency, to hire, transfer, suspend, lay off, recall, promote, discharge, assign, reward, or discipline other employees, or responsibly to direct them."[29]

That definition led Macomber and Secretary of State William P. Rogers to oppose the application of the executive order to the Foreign Service. Macomber argued before the FLRC that the unique characteristics of the Service required a different approach. Foreign Service officers, he said, are commissioned by the president, deeply involved with national security, and thoroughly intermingled with management.[30] As State and the FLRC debated the applicability of the order to the Foreign Service, AFSA debated whether it could seek recognition under the order as a labor union and still retain its status as a professional organization.

## Diplomacy for the Seventies

On January 14, 1970, in a speech to foreign affairs personnel, Macomber announced his intention to shake up State's management. The department, he said, had not been sufficiently "systematic, competent, and aggressive" in coordinating U.S. government activities abroad and making sure they are consistent with policy. He proposed to move rapidly on reform, and he acknowledged the work of AFSA.[31]

The department set up 13 task forces, echoing the eight subcommittees that labored on *Toward a Modern Diplomacy*. Each task force had about 20 members, drawn from the Civil Service and Foreign Service and including employees of USIA and USAID. By November, the final task force reports, which included more than 500 recommendations, had been put together in a 610-page document, *Diplomacy for the 70s*.[32]

Perhaps the most important reform to come out of the exercise was the Foreign Affairs Specialist program, a Macomber initiative that tried to accomplish administratively what the Hays bill had failed to do legislatively. The program, launched in February 1971 in a management bulletin titled "Toward a Unified Personnel System," used dubious authority to allow certain Civil Service employees and Foreign Service staff officers to convert to the Foreign Service Reserve with unlimited tenure (FSRU).[33]

AFSA supported the program, but the American Federation of Government Employees, the American Federation of Labor and Congress of Industrial Organizations (AFL-CIO) affiliate union to which many members of the Civil Service belonged, opposed it. The conversion of Civil Service employees to FSRU status put them at risk of selection-out and subjected them to other Foreign Service disciplines that, to AFGE, were unacceptable conditions of employment. An AFGE lawsuit challenging the department's authority to act won a federal injunction that effectively ended the program, though many individuals who

had converted chose to retain their Foreign Service status. The death of the Foreign Affairs Specialist program ended the 30-year effort to merge the two personnel systems operating in the Department of State.

## AFSA'S UNIONISTS

AFSA had begun to talk about unionization even before the October 1969 executive order. When a *Journal* interviewer had asked Charles Bray about that pos-
sibility in April of that year, he replied, "I don't know who speaks for the Foreign
Service if AFSA does not. And I think this means that an organization such
as ours inevitably must play a more active role in advancing the welfare of its
membership. It's a long step from that to trade unionism as such, but I think one
thing the membership in the next couple of years will have to decide is whether
it wishes AFSA to take a more militant stance."[34]

In April 1969 the AFSA Board duly set up a committee to study Executive
Order 10988, the 1962 policy that still governed the role of unions in the federal
workforce, to see whether it would allow the association to operate simultaneously as a union and a professional society, "with all that the phrase implies for
style and substance."[35]

The board and the committee had heard the rumors that a new executive
order was in the works. Seeking recognition under the 1962 order, said the committee report, would put AFSA in a good position when a new order came out.
"Recognition . . . does not mean the Association will become a trade union, [but
it] will facilitate AFSA's attempts to improve both the professionalism and conditions of the Foreign Service." The report also recommended that the bargaining
unit include Civil Service and Foreign Service (officer, information officer, staff,
and reserve) employees who work on substantive foreign policy issues or serve
in U.S. missions abroad in direct support to substantive officers and that AFSA
should "move urgently" to increase its membership among civil servants. The
association, the committee said, should put recognition to a membership vote.[36]

Lannon Walker broached the subject of recognition with Director General
John Burns and Under Secretary Elliot Richardson in August, but the board did
not poll the membership and decided not to push the issue.[37]

AFSA held an election in the fall of 1969, just as the new executive order was
published. The election was the first to take place under rules, adopted that February, that replaced the electoral college with direct elections and changed the
date for the start of the new board's two-year term from October 1 to January 15.
Three slates of candidates competed. Charles Bray's winning Continuity slate

included one staff officer (Barbara Good, who became the only woman on the board), an African American (John Reinhardt), two USAID officers (Princeton Lyman and C. William Kontos), and four USIA officers (John Reinhardt, Robert Nevitt, George Lambrakis, and Alan Carter). Most subsequent slates and boards strove for similar balance.

About 30 percent of the membership cast ballots, with Bray's slate winning about half the votes for a clear plurality. A "Message from the Board" in the *Journal* described the board's immediate agenda: expand the membership, listen to the membership, stand up for the staff corps, and attend to the bread-and-butter issues that were "the bedrock of AFSA's concerns." But representing Foreign Service employees in labor-management relations—becoming a union—was not on the list.[38] After the tumult and excitement of the Walker board, the new board seemed inclined to move cautiously.

The Bray board and William Macomber shared several goals. Both wanted to exclude the Foreign Service from the executive order, though for different reasons. Macomber's main interest was to protect the authority of the Secretary of State against erosion by outside arbitrators, mediators, or appeal or grievance commissions. The AFSA Board saw that without exclusion of the Service from the order, it might face an uncomfortable either-or choice: remain a professional association with no role in employee-management negotiations or become a labor union from which supervisory personnel—the heart of the profession— were excluded. The board and Macomber both wanted to retain unique Service concepts such as rank in person, worldwide availability, and selection-out from erosion through collective bargaining. Both also had an interest in management reform, which would affect working conditions and professional development for all Foreign Service employees.

The board was less aggressive than Macomber and content to respond to the task force reports rather than try to shape them. When the reports were published in July in preliminary form, the board offered tepid comments that had little impact. The final reports were released on October 1, 1969, as *Diplomacy for the 70s*. In the end, AFSA said the task forces had produced only a "sketchy agenda" with no big picture, no broad, clear vision for the department and the Foreign Service.[39] The criticism was valid, if not constructive.

Discussions about an alternative to Executive Order 11491 began with mistrust. The department had not consulted AFSA (or AFGE) before seeking to exclude the Foreign Service, and the AFSA Board had not consulted its membership. The board and (more strongly) the junior officer organization were suspicious of the department's motives. The board felt pressure from JFSOC, which considered AFSA a "company union" that was too quick to cede to management's point of view.

The board knew that AFGE had filed organizing petitions for Foreign Service employees initially in the Bureau of African Affairs and the Africa office of the Bureau of Intelligence and Research at State, and in the international training division at USAID.[40] After AFGE invited JFSOC to appoint a member to its Executive Council (an advisory body), there seemed to be some danger that JFSOC might support AFGE in a recognition battle.[41] Growing dissent within the Service about the war in Vietnam, stirred by the U.S. incursion into Cambodia in April, further soured the atmosphere.

But as the AFSA Governing Board developed a better understanding of E.O. 11491, the risks of failing to seek exclusive recognition became more evident.[42] The definitions of "bargaining unit" (the group of employees who could vote to choose the union and would then be represented by it) and of "supervisory personnel" (considered part of management and excluded from the bargaining unit) were at best unclear. If Civil Service and Foreign Service personnel were part of one bargaining unit, AFGE, with its strength in the Civil Service, might win exclusive recognition. AFSA then could be frozen out and unable to conduct even the consultations, essential to its role as a professional association, in which it had long been engaged.

The Federal Labor Relations Council told AFSA to present its views in October; the board could temporize no longer. Bray called for a rare formal vote, and by eight to one (with two members absent), the board agreed that "the exclusive recognition option is the course of action with the greatest chance of preserving and enhancing AFSA's present role in representing the interests of all Foreign Service employees."[43] The board resolved to poll the membership but procrastinated.

The dissenting vote belonged to FSO William Bradford, who did not believe commissioned officers should unionize. He resigned from the board with an emotional open letter. He had won more votes in the 1969 AFSA election than all but one candidate, and a sizable minority shared his views.[44]

## Harrop Takes Over

Even before the membership had spoken on seeking recognition under E.O. 11491—indeed, even before the referendum package had been mailed—members of the AFSA leadership were in discussions with Macomber about an alternative to the order. The board itself was in transition. The pressure of work forced first Vice Chairman Dick Davies and then Chairman Charlie Bray to step down; Davies went on to become deputy assistant secretary for European affairs and Bray to become the department's spokesman. Board member Bill Harrop, who had replaced Davies as vice chairman, took over as chairman on January 10, 1971. The following month, F. Allen Harris, a graduate of the law school of the University of Texas who was universally known as "Tex," moved into the vacant vice chairmanship.[45] The change in leadership involved no change in policy and little change in style.

When Bill Harrop became AFSA's chairman, he had been in the Service for 17 years. Like Charlie Bray and Lannon Walker, he had served in Africa (in Congo) and in the Bureau of African Affairs. Like them also, he was calm in manner and dignified in speech, a contrast with the volatile and profane Macomber. But Harrop and Macomber were both Marines, tough, loyal, and determined. They dealt with each other with mutual respect.

Harrop faced multiple challenges. As soon as the association told the Federal Labor Relations Council that it intended to seek recognition under E.O. 11491, AFGE filed an unfair labor practices complaint, the first shot in a long skirmish, alleging that AFSA was not a labor organization and did not qualify for recognition. The association had no in-house legal staff; it turned to its outside counsel at Covington & Burling to refute the charge. Tex Harris, a lawyer and the new vice chairman, shadowed the Covington lawyer and learned labor law. Harris, who would twice be elected president of AFSA, came to handle much of the association's legal work in the years ahead.[46]

The outside counsel was expensive, and the association's finances were shaky. Expenses were rising faster than revenue. The operating deficit for Fiscal Year 1971 rose to $97,000. Assets, including the Scholarship Fund, fell over the same period by $142,000 to $1.25 million. Tax legislation in 1969 had forced the association to take care to segregate the money flowing into its five funds—general, *Journal*, club, scholarship, and awards and programs—to ensure that money received for one purpose was not diverted to another. The general fund had been borrowing from the Scholarship Fund at below-market rates, a practice that the association's outside counsel said must stop. The board raised dues, cut staff (including the executive director), shifted some legal work to Tex Harris and other volunteers, and hired a new contractor to run the money-losing club. Membership rose by 5 percent to 7,800, but the increase was below the board's target and not enough to close the gaps in the budget.

## AFSA Votes to Unionize

On January 14, 1971, Harrop, Bray, and AFSA President Ted Eliot met with Secretary of State William Rogers to present AFSA's ideas for a new labor-management program.[47] Three weeks later, in the first days of February, Macomber and the AFSA Board reached an agreement on some of the elements of a hypothetical employee-management system for the Foreign Service outside E.O. 11491. The agreement had seven points:

- Formal agency-organization consultation on personnel policies and procedures, including grievances
- Consultations to result in written agreements
- Management decisions in the absence of agreement to be conveyed in writing and made subject to appeal to the board of the Foreign Service
- Informal consultations on other management issues, not to extend to foreign policy
- Agencies to seek authority for deduction of dues from paychecks of consenting employees
- Organizations to be "bona fide representatives of significant number of Foreign Service employees" to qualify
- Agencies and organizations to review their relationships annually[48]

At an open meeting in the State Department's West (now Dean Acheson) Auditorium on February 8, 1971, Harrop defended the exclusion of the Foreign Service from the executive order. Under the order, he said, as much as half of the Service would be considered supervisors and denied representation. The seven-point agreement, he said, would give the Foreign Service the same rights as the Civil Service but allow many more employees to participate. JFSOC President Bob Maxim and members of an "ad hoc committee for the executive order" disputed Harrop's claims and demanded an immediate vote to disavow the agreement with Macomber. To avoid a likely loss, AFSA President Ted Eliot said the vote would be by referendum. He abruptly closed the meeting. "This was," the *Journal* reported, "marked by boos, cries of 'shame,' the invoking of democracy and other adverse comment." A shoving match broke out on the podium.[49]

The long-delayed referendum, now including the seven-point agreement and opposing views from JFSOC and the ad hoc committee, went out to members the next day.[50] Voters were asked for their preferred course of action under two cases: if the FLRC allowed the executive order to stand and if it did not.

When the ballots were counted on March 31, 1971, 88 percent of the 2,200 voters favored unionization under E.O. 11491. The FLRC, however, had decided to exempt the Foreign Service from the order on March 15, two weeks before the vote count, so that part of the ballot was moot.[51] Fortunately for the AFSA Board, which had already begun negotiations with State, USIA, and USAID, 60 percent of the voters still wanted to proceed toward exclusive recognition—unionization—under the seven-point agreement.[52]

The AFSA Board set up a "Committee of 40" to backstop the negotiation with State over the terms of the new program, which would take the form of a new executive order. Though as many as 40 people attended the organizational meeting, the committee relied heavily on Tex Harris (its chairman) and board members Rick Melton and Jack Binns. They developed the positions and language that AFSA would take into meetings with Bill Macomber and his staff at State. Macomber, for his part, conducted discussions simultaneously with AFGE.

Harrop and Harris met with Vernon Gill, the executive director of the FLRC, and came away with the understanding that the FLRC was unlikely to accept a program that AFSA opposed.[53] Macomber apparently operated under a similar assumption, because AFSA negotiators were able to use their presumed veto power as leverage to gain key their objectives.[54] Negotiations blew past the June 1 deadline and continued into the fall of 1971. Two State Department lawyers, Tom Byrne and Jim Michel, put the resulting concepts into legal language.[55]

## Hard Hat or Homburg?

The deal with Macomber set the framework for AFSA's eventual transformation into a union with real bargaining power. ("Union" is the right word, although the association, always fastidious, preferred "employee organization" or some other euphemism.) The crucial element was the definition of "management"—the definition that determines, in a labor-management negotiation, who sits on which side of the table. AFGE argued that a manager is a supervisor, and a supervisor is anyone with a subordinate, anyone who writes or reviews a performance rating. That definition would have excluded a large percentage, perhaps a majority, of AFSA's active-duty members from the bargaining unit. AFSA argued—to a generally sympathetic State Department—that Foreign Service employees are intermingled with management but remain and are treated as employees at least until they reach the highest levels.

The final agreement, promulgated as E.O. 11636 of December 17, 1971, drew the management-labor line just below deputy assistant secretaries and deputy

Box 4.1. Shakespeare and the Career Principle

Frank Shakespeare, the director of the U.S. Information Agency, had ordered his agency's 1971 selection boards to send him the list of candidates recommended for promotion from Class 2 to Class 1 (today's counselor to minister counselor) in unranked alphabetical order so that he could choose among them. AFSA President Bill Harrop wrote to Shakespeare: "As director, you can assign your officers, regardless of rank, to the positions best meeting your assessment of their capacity. You can delegate such responsibility as you wish, regardless of grade. You can place citations or criticisms as you wish in the personnel files, and your views are bound to have great influence upon selection boards. But as a political leader, a transient in high office, you cannot personally make the promotions without breaking the career system."[a]

When Shakespeare rejected that argument, AFSA took the dispute to the Board of the Foreign Service, which issued a decision in its favor in 1974.[b] The issue "seemed trivial to an outsider," said Tex Harris, "but it went to the heart of the system."[c]

a. The *Journal* published the letter, dated November 15, 1971, with Shakespeare's reply. See *FSJ*, January 1972, 7–8.
b. Minutes, AFSA Board meeting, November 20, 1973; and *FSJ*, January 1975, 44.
c. Tex Harris, interview, January 23, 2013.

chiefs of mission, adding also to management confidential employees and persons setting personnel policy or charged with administering labor-management relations. The definition was a great achievement for AFSA and crucial to its future. First, it allowed Foreign Service officers in middle and senior grades to join the bargaining unit and participate in the election that would choose the employee representative. These voters were solidly for AFSA over AFGE; had they been disenfranchised, the outcome might have been different. Second, and more important, the broad definition of "employee" relieved the association of having to choose whether to become a union or to remain a professional society only. Hard hat or homburg? AFSA could wear both.

AFSA won two other major points in the executive order. First, the order provided for rolling negotiations between the employee organization and management, the results of which would from time to time be written down and formalized as agreements emerged. AFGE had favored the traditional labor approach, in which an entire contract is negotiated at regular intervals, and no part is agreed until the whole package is settled. Second, the executive order required the agencies to establish grievance procedures and to consult on the issue beforehand with the employee organization. However, it also straddled the AFSA and management positions (and AFGE's) by requiring, inconsistently, that a grievance board be at once "independent of agency management" and subordinate to the Secretary of State.[56]

The order provided for elections in each agency to determine which organization would be recognized as the exclusive representative of the agency's Foreign Service employees and placed the elections under the supervision of a new Employee-Management Relations Commission (EMRC), established (with confusing nomenclature) as a committee of the Board of the Foreign Service.[57] Once recognized, an employee organization could consult with agency management on personnel policies, benefits, allowances, and working conditions; but the agency's mission, budget, and structure, as well as the number, salaries, and grades of its employees, were all off-limits.

## UNION RECOGNITION: THREE ELECTIONS, THREE VICTORIES

The 1971 AFSA Governing Board elections took place while negotiations on the rules that would guide employee-management relations were underway. Voters could choose between two slates or split their ballots among individuals. Members of the outgoing board, including Bill Harrop and Tex Harris, ran on the Participation slate against a Members' Interests slate led by former board Chairman Dave McKillop and Lars Hydle.

The challengers ran a spirited campaign. They attacked the incumbents as timid and passive, but there were no serious differences of principle. The Participation slate won with 60 percent of the vote.[58] When the new board convened in January 1972, it chose Bill Harrop as chairman and Tom Boyatt as vice chairman, and in February it unanimously elected Dave McKillop to replace Ted Eliot as president.[59] The new board turned at once to the fundamental, transformative issue: the campaign for union recognition.

In each of the agencies named in the executive order—State, USIA, and USAID—AFSA faced the same formidable opponent: AFGE. An AFL-CIO affiliate, AFGE was the largest union in the federal workforce. It was well funded, well lawyered, and well practiced in contesting union elections. AFSA was, in comparison, an amateur outfit whose unpaid volunteer leadership had full-time jobs and no experience in union organization.

Differences between the two contestants were stark. AFGE President John Griner testified that "Foreign Service personnel should be treated at home as domestic civil servants." He opposed the rank-in-person system "because it deviates from the principle of equal pay for equal work."[60] AFSA supported provisions in the 1965 Hays bill and in Macomber's Foreign Affairs Specialist program to facilitate the conversion of members of the Civil Service to Foreign Service status, but AFGE opposed the provisions because converts would lose grievance protections and become subject to selection-out.

An AFGE member wrote, "AFGE viewed the Department of State's argument of Foreign Service uniqueness as an effort to evade 'enforceable accountability' for its violations of the rights of employees and as justification of a system which—however much lip service was paid to employee participation—was paternalistic, capricious, and discriminatory."[61] AFGE was a union only, focused solely on members' benefits. Unlike AFSA, AFGE showed no interest in American diplomacy as a profession or in the need for excellence in the Foreign Service as its practitioner. With its hard-line, trade union attitude, AFGE had its base of support among staff and junior officers and among foreign affairs specialists recently converted from Civil Service status under Macomber's Foreign Affairs Specialist program.

AFSA faced two challenges: making the elections happen and winning them. AFSA Board Chairman Bill Harrop put Vice President Tom Boyatt in charge of both battles.

AFSA had beaten AFGE before, in the debate surrounding the drafting of E.O. 11636 about the definition of "supervisor" and the placement of the line separating management and labor. But the State Department had the lead in that struggle, with AFSA in a supporting role. In the union election, the department, wherever Macomber's sympathies may have lain, was scrupulously neutral.

Elections were not automatic. In each agency, a would-be union had to demonstrate a show of interest by submitting to the EMRC signed cards from at least 5 percent of the bargaining unit. All qualifying organizations would then compete for the votes of members of the bargaining unit in a secret ballot overseen by the EMRC.

AFGE sought delay by invoking hearings wherever possible and by filing formal legal challenges on basic issues. For example, despite the clear language of the executive order, AFGE asked the EMRC to disqualify AFSA's election petition on the grounds that Harrop, Boyatt, and Hank Cohen, who had signed the petition, were supervisors and therefore management officials. AFGE used the same argument to try to bar broad classes of Foreign Service members from voting. It also alleged that an AFSA member at an overseas post, who had signed an appeal to his colleagues with the words "political officer" under his signature, had thereby engaged in coercive tactics. AFGE lost on each of these claims, but its tactics kept Boyatt, other board members, and some of AFSA's election volunteers tied up in hearings before administrative law judges at the Department of Labor for days on end.[62] In the end, the EMRC rejected AFGE's claims, and the elections went forward.[63]

In all three agencies, a large part of the bargaining unit was overseas, and AFSA was better positioned than AFGE to reach overseas voters.[64] Just as Lannon Walker, Charlie Bray, and the Group of 18 had friends to turn to in every regional bureau and around the world, so did the AFSA Board under Harrop, Boyatt, Tex Harris, and Cohen. Boyatt enlisted the help of well-placed volunteers around the department, including Rick Melton, Jack Binns, David Ransom, and others, to form an election team with global reach.[65] At many posts, an AFSA member volunteered to serve as a front man, drumming up support.

By June 1972, AFSA had collected more than 2,700 cards from Foreign Service employees at State, about 500 from USIA, and about 950 at USAID. AFGE, by contrast, had 411 at State and 84 at USIA, barely meeting the threshold in those agencies. AFGE did not reach the threshold at USAID in July.[66] The show-of-interest exercise strengthened AFSA's network of overseas chapters and key men. It taught the board the importance of staying in touch with its overseas constituency.

The disparity in show-of-interest cards was one sign that AFGE was running well behind. A bellwether election at JFSOC was another. Junior officers, along with staff officers, had been AFGE's areas of greatest strength, but AFSA's resolve in the negotiation of the executive order won many over. An election in the spring of 1972 to choose JFSOC's leadership—the first contested election in JFSOC's short history—returned a pro-AFSA slate headed by Robert Boettcher and Lars Hydle, taking 70 percent of the vote, over a slate that AFGE had endorsed.[67]

AFSA won at all three agencies. After rejecting a final AFGE appeal, the EMRC certified AFSA as the winner at the Department of State with 70 percent of the vote on January 24, 1973. At USIA, where a number of labor-information officers had come out of the labor movement and had strong sympathies for traditional unions, the first count left AFSA short of a majority. Only after challenged ballots were opened and counted did the EMRC declare a winner, certifying AFSA on April 18, 1973. At USAID, management had insisted that office directors, inspectors, and auditors should be struck from the voting rolls. The EMRC decided otherwise (as it had with respect to State), but the adjudication delayed the voting until January 1973. In the end, AFSA carried almost 80 percent of the vote and was certified on March 28, 1973.[68]

Box 4.2.  A Thrice-Told Tale

A good story invites repetition. The *Foreign Service Journal* editions of June 2003, April 2013, and January–February 2023 marked the thirtieth, fortieth, and fiftieth anniversaries of the 1973 votes with celebratory first- and third-person accounts of the transformation of AFSA from a professional society to a labor union. John Harter provided a contrary view of these events in a letter to the *Journal*'s editor published in the October 2003 edition, pages 9–11.

These issues of the *Journal*, and the oral history interviews that the Association for Diplomatic Studies and Training (ADST) conducted with participants and published at https://adst.org/oral-history/, are basic sources for a history of this period.

The union elections completed a transformation that had been a decade in the making. From the 1920s into the 1960s, the association had been a professional organization dominated by Foreign Service officers and closely tied to the leadership of the Department of State. AFSA now represented all employees in the Foreign Service system—officers, staff, and reserve—in State, USIA, and USAID, and not just in terms of their professional interests and development, but also in negotiations and consultations with agency management. AFSA gained in stature and occupied a larger space. Soon able to serve full time, its leaders became familiar figures on Capitol Hill and among the press and were able to speak for a group of professionals whose voice had hitherto been muffled.

The association would struggle to adapt to its new prominence and its new role. The years after the union elections saw periods of poor governance, weak finances, and a loss of representation at USIA. But there was no turning back. By trial and error, members of the Foreign Service learned what the new AFSA could do and could be. They voted their approval with their participation and their dues. Had AFSA failed to seize the chance to unionize, it would have remained a professional society with a muted voice and a tiny treasury, and it would have been far less able to defend the Service and its people against the smears and attacks that in time would come.

# 5

## The New AFSA, 1973–1979

The American Foreign Service Association grew rapidly into its new role as the voice and defender of the Foreign Service and its members as professionals and employees. Through the association, the Service began to express a collective, institutional position on such critical issues as grievances, discrimination, and dissent. The policy choices that AFSA took on these issues in the late 1960s and early 1970s shaped its approach for decades to come.

The contest between the association and the American Federation of Government Employees overshadowed two other important AFSA elections held in 1973. In March of that year, the membership voted to approve new bylaws that replaced the Board of Directors and the title of chairman with the Governing Board headed by a president. The bylaws tied the size of the board to the size of the membership, awarding one representative for every 1,000 members in each constituency: initially, four from State, one each from the U.S. Information Agency and the U.S. Agency for International Development, and two retirees. To reduce board turnover, elections would take place in the spring, and the new board would take office in July, in line with the school year and the transfer cycle.

Bill Harrop resigned as AFSA chairman in April 1973 to take up his assignment as deputy chief of mission in Canberra. The board named Tom Boyatt as his successor and moved Tex Harris into the vice chairmanship that Boyatt had vacated. Boyatt and Harris served out their unexpired terms and then ran under the new bylaws for president and vice president, respectively, of a transitional board that would hold office until July 15, 1975. There was no rival slate. By margins of about three to one and two and a half to one, Boyatt and Harris defeated independent candidates John Hemenway for president and John Harter for vice president. The challengers, who will figure later in this history, filed unsuccessful complaints about the election with the Department of Labor. The new Governing Board and old Board of Directors held a joint meeting to mark the transition on January 15, 1974.[1]

These elections took place against a backdrop of intense activity. The new AFSA Board established 25 standing committees to deal with various aspects of professional activities, employee representation, and internal management, as well as a number of ad hoc committees. There was little precedent for much of this work; the board had to be innovative and flexible, discarding what did not work and institutionalizing what did.

## GRIEVANCES: PROCESS AND PRINCIPLE

The matter of grievances exemplified the board's efforts and struggles. The Walker-Bray Reform slate in 1967 had argued that members should be able to bring professional grievances and problems to the association and receive "prompt and energetic assistance."[2] But in 1971, Foreign Service grievants remained at the mercy of management. Civil Service rules required an independent grievance board, but employees covered by the regulations of the Foreign Affairs Manual had no such protection: Their grievances were decided by their own management officials. Decisions on promotions, assignments, and selection-out were not reviewable.[3] Three hard cases—those of Charles Thomas, John Harter, and Alison Palmer—exposed the inequities of the system. In controversial and difficult decisions, the association stayed aloof from the litigation but tried to shape the outcomes.

### Charles Thomas Case

In 1969 Charles Thomas had been a Foreign Service officer for 18 years. That year marked his eighth in Class 4, and when he was again passed over for promotion, time-in-class (TIC) rules forced his dismissal from the Service without a pension. Two years and many hundreds of job-rejection letters later, the 48-year-old Thomas took his own life in an attempt to provide an insurance settlement for his family.

Thomas believed that on the basis of his record he should have been promoted, but he could not prove it. He was not allowed to review his performance file until a year before his final consideration for promotion. The file, as he belatedly discovered, contained a negative evaluation report written three years earlier that he had never had a chance to rebut. And a 1969 inspector's report recommending him for promotion was for some time misfiled in the folder of another officer with the same name, although the department stated in a later investigation that the memo was correctly refiled before the 1967 selection boards had convened.[4]

Thomas's widow, Cynthia, a State Department employee, found support in AFGE for a lawsuit against the department. Union locals in the various foreign affairs agencies set up the Charles W. Thomas Memorial Legal Defense Fund to challenge selection-out and the absence of due process.[5] "The steelworkers, the bricklayers, the stonemasons gave money for Foreign Service due process," said Bruce Gregory, an AFGE activist in USIA. "AFSA wasn't thrilled with that."[6]

AFSA, which supported selection-out, did not contribute to the Thomas Fund and did not join the suit, but the association did enter an amicus brief calling for procedural safeguards. Judge Gerhard Gesell of the U.S. Federal District Court ruled in 1973 that an officer facing dismissal must have access to all materials in his or her case and is entitled to present evidence, interview witnesses, and be represented by counsel at a hearing before a review panel. The ruling tracked many elements of the AFSA brief, and AFSA claimed victory.[7] The suit cost the Thomas Fund over $50,000 and sharpened differences between AFSA and AFGE.[8]

The Thomas case inspired action on Capitol Hill as well as in the courts. A private bill granting financial relief to the Thomas family passed Congress and became law in January 1975.[9]

In June 1971, Sen. Birch Bayh Jr., a Democrat from Thomas's home state of Indiana, was on the board of the Thomas Fund and introduced grievance legislation based largely on work done by Tex Harris and Marian Nash, who drafted a grievance system over brown-bag lunches in the department's law library.[10] Sen. John Sherman Cooper (R-Ky.), a former ambassador to India who had great respect for the Foreign Service, was a cosponsor of the legislation, as were Sen. Hubert Humphrey (D-Minn.) and Sen. Hugh Scott (R-Pa.).[11]

The State Department reacted reflexively to any threatened curb on the Secretary's freedom of action. Management hoped to head off the bill with hastily announced "interim grievance procedures," which failed to satisfy AFSA, AFGE, or the Senate sponsors.[12] AFSA lobbied hard. The Bayh bill passed the Senate three times, but in the House, Rep. Wayne Hays (D-Ohio), chairman of the subcommittee of jurisdiction, kept the bill bottled up until 1975, when a version (not entirely satisfactory to Bayh or AFGE) passed as part of an authorization measure.[13] Once the legislation was in place, AFSA and the department quickly reached agreement on conforming grievance regulations, which took effect in 1976.[14]

## John Harter Case

John Harter, a member of the 1961 AFSA Board, had faced dismissal for time in class in 1971 because his personnel file was faulty. It included no evaluation reports covering the two years he had spent in training, and his supervisor in 1970 had filed only a memorandum, not a full evaluation report as required. Harter sought assistance from AFSA, and the board tasked Tex Harris to see what could be done. Harter later said that the AFSA Board "was ambiguous at best" about his grievance, and indeed the board did not do much to support his case.[15] But Harter received a hearing under the interim grievance procedures the department had set up in October 1971, the first officer to do so. His persistence was rewarded, and his grievance rendered moot, when he was promoted in 1972.[16]

Harter disagreed with many of the premises of *Toward a Modern Diplomacy*. He "was appalled" by AFSA's support for selection-out and by the seven-point agreement between the association and Macomber. He ran for the chairmanship of the AFSA Board in 1971 and for the vice presidency in 1973 and 1975, in the hopes of leading the association away from unionization. Those losses, he said, taught him "the immense advantage of incumbents in politics."[17]

## Alison Palmer Case

In 1970 the Foreign Service officer corps was 95 percent male (and 1 percent African American). All female officers were single and required (not by law or regulation but by unwritten rule and administrative practice) to resign if they wed.[18] Wives of officers were unpaid adjuncts and evaluated in their husbands' ratings on their performance of social and other duties.[19]

Alison Palmer joined the Service in 1958 and began to complain about discrimination in assignments and promotions in 1965. Receiving no satisfaction, she filed a lawsuit in 1971, but the department largely ignored her until 1972, when senators sympathetic to her cause blocked the confirmation of Howard Mace, the department's director of personnel, to be ambassador to Sierra Leone. She then received a promotion.[20]

In 1976 Palmer and others filed a class action suit alleging discrimination against women in hiring, promotion, and assignments.[21] AFGE, the Thomas

Fund, and the department's Women's Action Organization (founded by Barbara Good, the first woman to serve on the AFSA Board) all supported her suit and helped pay its costs, but AFSA did not.[22] So tenacious was the department's resistance to a settlement that the presiding judge, Stanley Sporkin, told State's lawyers, "The arrogance of your office is beyond belief."[23] In one form or another, the case lingered in the courts for more than 30 years, but it produced judgments in 1989, 1990, and 2002 that forced the department to give new assignments and revised performance ratings to about 600 female officers, to revise entry-test scores for another 400, and to change testing procedures to comply with court orders.[24]

## THE MERIT PRINCIPLE

The Thomas, Harter, and Palmer cases were exceptional. As Tom Boyatt pointed out in his president's report to the 1974 AFSA general meeting, the board's Grievance Committee had "helped hundreds of individuals with grievances," most of which were amicably resolved.[25]

In the Alison Palmer case and other less prominent ones, the association defended its decision to withhold full support from the grievants as an expression of its commitment to promotion according to merit. In AFSA's view, reaffirmed by successive Governing Boards, grievance boards and federal courts had no business ordering promotions as a remedy for past discrimination. The association argued that in the Foreign Service Act of 1946, Congress had limited the president's authority to promote members of the Foreign Service by prescribing the manner in which recommendations for promotion are prepared and transmitted: The Secretary of State can recommend for promotion only those individuals found deserving by a selection board.

Association leaders who had defended the selection board's lists against manipulation by the director of USIA (see page 65) made a similar argument against interference by court order or administrative decision. An editorial in the April 1972 *Foreign Service Journal* warned, "If the Director General, the Board of the Foreign Service and the Secretary can recommend these [compensatory] promotions, the door is opened for them or their successors to recommend other 'worthy' promotions, and thus open the merit promotion system to serious abuses."[26]

AFSA would struggle for many years with the tension between the merit principle and what came to be known as affirmative action. Rick Melton, a member of the Boyatt board who worked closely with Tex Harris, expressed this view of the Palmer case: "The settlement of a grievance can have unintended consequences. When you mandate set-asides, you're affecting everyone in the system. Who is right and wrong in the grievance is one thing, but the settlement is something else. In this case, the department was too willing to give away other people's equities. At AFSA, we're supposed to be custodians of the interests of the whole Service. The Service didn't commit the injustice. Settlements have to be equitable for everybody."[27]

## DISSENT

When Tom Boyatt reported to the general meeting of the membership in June 1974 on the work of the association since certification, he had plenty to say. Membership had grown with rapid increases in USAID, USIA, and the staff corps. The association's role as employee representative had only enhanced its traditional work as a professional organization. The attention and respect AFSA had gained through bargaining carried over to its vigorous defense of the integrity, courage, and ability of the Foreign Service itself.

Dissent was an important theme of Boyatt's report. Dissent in the Service could mean many things: a conflict of conscience, a dispute about strategy or tactics, a resistance to secrecy or privilege, or simply candor, the honest expression of an opinion or merely of unwelcome news.

In the 1950s, the association held as a bedrock principle that members of the Foreign Service "cannot enter the political arena."[28] When the Service was attacked, AFSA waited silently and in vain for members of Congress, the administration, or non-career ambassadors to come to its defense. In the late 1960s, Charlie Bray, Bill Harrop, and Ted Eliot could use the association's growing clout to protect individuals yet keep the organization out of policy debates.

In 1969 a group of Foreign Service employees in Hong Kong wanted to use the association as a megaphone for their views on Vietnam. Ted Eliot responded, "AFSA does not take positions on substantive foreign policy issues." Later that year, the *Journal* received instructions from the AFSA Governing Board not to publish letters or articles from members of the Service attacking administration policy.[29]

The following year, some 250 foreign affairs professionals, members of the Foreign and Civil Service, wrote to Secretary of State William Rogers to protest the incursion of U.S. armed forces into Cambodia. U. Alexis Johnson, then under secretary for political affairs, wrote in his memoir that when the letter inevitably leaked to the press, he received a phone call at two o'clock in the morning: "This is the president. I want you to make sure all of those sons of bitches are fired first thing in the morning!" Johnson and Secretary Rogers went to see the president, who was "consumed with anger."

Nixon relented on the firings but demanded the names of the signatories. Johnson ducked that demand but promised the president he would not promote the signatories or post them to Southeast Asia.[30] Separately, AFSA sought and obtained assurances from Deputy Under Secretary William Macomber that no disciplinary action would be taken against the signatories.[31] Both sides to that agreement were likely unaware of Johnson's promise. Later, when a White House investigator asked for their names, Macomber and Rogers refused to provide them.[32]

As AFSA chairman, Bill Harrop made a point of honoring dissent with a splashy luncheon in honor of John S. Service, John Emmerson, Robert Barnett, O. Edmund Clubb, and other China hands who had been vilified in the 1950s. Hundreds attended. The *New York Times* covered the event under the headline "Honor Came a Bit Late."[33]

Charlie Bray praised dissent and practiced it in its purest form. In 1973 National Security Adviser Henry Kissinger acknowledged authorizing wiretaps on several of his White House aides. When Kissinger was nominated to be Secretary of State, Bray, the department's spokesman, resigned from the Service. Bray said he would find it "distasteful" to work for someone who did not appreciate that "loyalty has to run in both directions."[34] Kissinger later defended his actions in unyielding terms. "That wiretapping is distasteful is unquestionable," he wrote in his memoirs, "but so is the willful and unauthorized disclosure of military and diplomatic secrets in the middle of a war."[35]

Boyatt's report to the June 1974 general meeting took place not many months after the coup in Chile that toppled the government of Salvador Allende. Press accounts accused the embassy in Santiago of failing to provide protection to American citizens during and immediately after the coup. Sam Hart, president of the embassy's AFSA chapter, refuted these attacks in a detailed open letter that AFSA circulated to members of the House and Senate Foreign Affairs Committees and to the press.

Boyatt, who had served in Chile early in his career and would later head to Santiago as deputy chief of mission, spoke out frequently in defense of the embassy and its staff. The media attacks did not stop, but many in Congress backed the embassy and praised its work in chaotic, dangerous conditions. Boyatt in his report made this promise to AFSA's membership: "We will never again permit McCarthyism or any other threat to impinge upon our integrity or to silence our dedication to the national interest."[36]

Box 5.1.  Tom Boyatt's Cyprus Dissent

During this period, Boyatt was moonlighting at AFSA; his day job was as country director for Cyprus. He had repeatedly warned his superiors that a Greek-
sponsored coup against Archbishop Makarios, the Cypriot leader, would lead to
a Turkish invasion and the collapse of U.S. policy. Boyatt spent many months
in a fruitless effort to win approval of a message to Greek strongman Dimi-
trios Ioannidis, "in words of one syllable that even he will understand," that the
United States would strongly oppose any Greek mischief in Cyprus. The feared
coup occurred, followed by a Turkish attack and the assassination of Rodger
Davies, the American ambassador in Nicosia. Boyatt used the Dissent Channel
to send a memorandum to the Secretary of State recommending the next steps
on Cyprus (and including a bit of "I told you so").[a]

In 1975 a House investigative committee chaired by Rep. Otis Pike (D-N.Y.)
later sought that memo and the rest of the department's Cyprus file. The department eventually turned over the material but in a form that protected the source
of the information "to insulate junior officers [officers who are not presidential
appointees] from partisan pressures."[b] Some 200 Foreign Service officers supported the department's position in a letter to Representative Pike; the AFSA
Board, then enmeshed in conflict with AFSA President John Hemenway, was
split on the issue.[c]

a. The department created the Dissent Channel in 1971 to allow employees to send their
views on important foreign policy issues directly and confidentially to the department's
most senior officials. Quote from Ambassador Boyatt's presentation at the Foreign
Service Institute, September 30, 1992, https://tile.loc.gov/storage-services/service/mss
/mfdip/2004/2004boy02/2004boy02.pdf. Henry Kissinger presents a different but
consistent picture of the Cyprus crisis; see his "Cyprus, a Case Study in Ethnic Conflict,"
Years of Renewal, chap. 7 (192–239).
b. Kissinger, Years of Renewal, 334, 330–37.
c. Minutes, AFSA Board meeting, October 6, 1975; Murrey Marder, "Kissinger Rebuffs
Pike Unit," Washington Post, October 16, 1975; and Kissinger, Years of Renewal, 334.
Kissinger's memoir states that the AFSA Board "endorsed my position in a vote of
7–0," but that vote was taken only after AFSA President John Hemenway, who opposed
Kissinger's position, had closed the meeting and left the room. A letter from the AFSA
Board to Representative Pike supporting the department was apparently never sent.

## AFSA'S STRENGTHS AND WEAKNESSES

Certification as a union changed AFSA's view of itself and what it could do. The
association and its leadership grew more confident, more assertive. The defense
of the embassy in Santiago was one facet of AFSA's readiness to take on a new
role and new responsibilities. Its claim to a role in evaluating ambassadorial
nominees was another.

Before 1973, AFSA had never taken a formal stand in opposition to a president's nominee. When Bill Harrop testified in 1972 on the controversial nomination of Howard Mace as ambassador to Sierra Leone, he expressed no opinion on Mace's fitness for the position. But that reticence would change. Tom Boyatt told this story: "On September 6, 1973, Tex Harris, Hank Cohen, and I trooped into Kissinger's White House office. For 45 minutes, we outlined our objectives and discussed matters of mutual interest. At one point, after I informed Dr. Kissinger that I would testify against an unqualified political ambassador, he responded (jokingly, I hoped): 'I realize that you have the right to testify against the president's nomination, but you must remember that I have the right to send you to Chad.'"[37]

Soon after that conversation, Boyatt and Bill Harrop appeared before the Senate Foreign Relations Committee to testify against the nomination of Leonard Firestone, a Republican contributor and fundraiser, as ambassador to Belgium. Far from provoking retribution, AFSA's principled stand, and Boyatt's early warning, may have raised the Secretary's estimate of AFSA's strength and value. After the murder of Ambassador Cleo Noel and Deputy Chief of Mission Curtis Moore in Sudan, Kissinger on his own initiative asked for a "joint [State] Department-AFSA working group to review our policies and actions" in responding to terrorist threats against diplomats and embassies.[38] Nothing in the employee-management agreement required the department to deal with AFSA on this issue, but Kissinger wanted AFSA's views.

AFSA's growing strength could be seen as well in the benefits it won as a union. Thanks to several years of work by Hank Cohen, chairman of the Members' Interests Committee, the department extended the education allowance to cover kindergarten, matching benefits provided to members of the Civil Service employed abroad. The department also agreed to pay air freight for layettes when employees with infants traveled on change of station and increased the allowance for required immunizations. Long battles about overtime pay for secretaries, communicators, and other staff were resolved in the employees' favor.[39]

AFSA used the new tools at its disposal to file unfair labor practice complaints against USAID for its handling of a reduction in force and a freeze of promotions.[40] It negotiated an agreement with State to block management interference with promotions after selection boards have done their work, and it asserted a role in the implementation of the Global Outlook Program, the department's term for a policy aimed at increasing the assignment of personnel to regions of the world with which they were unfamiliar. AFSA became engaged in more and more areas of Foreign Service life and work, demanding that its members receive both respect as professionals and fairness as employees.

AFSA's growing strength had limits, however, and they were quickly reached. Despite AFSA's testimony, Leonard Firestone was confirmed as ambassador to Belgium, where he served without incident from April 1974 to January 1977. And despite AFSA's efforts, attacks on the performance of the embassy in Santiago continued, notably in the best-selling book *The Execution of Charles Horman: An American Sacrifice* by Thomas Hauser published in 1978. (The book was credited as the basis for the movie *Missing* [1982], which won an Academy Award for its screenplay in 1983. Ambassador Nathaniel Davis, Consul Fred Purdy, and others filed libel suits that temporarily forced the book and movie off the U.S. market, but the suit was eventually unsuccessful.[41])

Two years after the union victory, signs of trouble inside the association began to multiply. Finances were weak. Costs were rising faster than revenues, and the club, after seven years, was still losing money. Relations between AFSA and USAID's management were poor, with "every issue of substance . . . the subject of an unfair practice charge, a dispute, or a consultability appeal."[42]

Unremarked and almost unnoticed, two institutional goals that AFSA had endorsed since 1946 lost much of their relevance and appeal: a single, unified, centrally administered Service for all foreign affairs agencies and the integration of Civil Service and Foreign Service employees in foreign affairs agencies through conversion of Civil Service professionals to Foreign Service status. Despite the association's many achievements, large numbers of its members remained dissatisfied, eager for confrontation with management.

## The Hemenway Episode

The board elections of 1975, with no incumbents running for the top positions, were contentious. The Department of Labor supervised the process, a result of the protest of the 1973 election by defeated candidates John Hemenway and John Harter. As in 1973, Hemenway ran for president as an independent. He faced AFSA Executive Director and Counselor Richard "Rick" Williamson, standing for president at the head of the Progress slate, and 1963 AFSA Chairman Bert Mathews, a retired FSO heading a Coalition slate. Hemenway came in third in ballots cast in the Department of State, but he won at USAID and USIA, where he had a clear majority. More than half the retired voters cast their ballots for Mathews. Of the total vote, Hemenway took more than 35 percent against 33 percent for Mathews and 31 percent for Williamson. The vice presidency went to

Dan Newberry of the Coalition slate, with Progress candidate Lars Hydle second and independent candidate John Harter third. Turnout was just over 40 percent.

Tom Boyatt took backhanded responsibility for Hemenway's success. "It was my fault," he said. "Bert Mathews was a founder of the State Department Credit Union, and sometime before the 1975 election he asked if AFSA planned to absorb it. I made a noncommittal response. I was careless, I didn't think it was important. Bert ran in the 1975 election, I think because he was motivated to save the credit union."[43]

The three-way race clearly helped Hemenway win, but Rick Williamson also credits Hemenway's campaign: "The problem was Hemenway putting out in the last couple of days different campaign ads to USAID and the retirees. To USAID, he said, the trouble is we're not enough like a real union, not tough enough on management. To the retirees, he said something like, we've got to stop all this union business. The two ads were absolutely incompatible. But there wasn't time for me to get anything out that would counter that."[44]

Hemenway's presidency quickly deteriorated into a power struggle between the president and the board. A majority of the board insisted that no one could speak in the name of the association without the board's prior approval. Nevertheless, Hemenway testified or wrote letters in opposition to the confirmation of a USIA career Foreign Service officer, Hans Tuch, as career minister and against the confirmation of Foreign Service Officer Helmut Sonnenfeldt, a close associate of Secretary Kissinger's, to the same rank. He testified against promotions for past and present AFSA Board members, including Tom Boyatt, Lars Hydle, Ed Stumpf, and LaRue Velott. He was quoted in the *Washington Post* referring to the Secretary of State as "an unmitigated disaster for our foreign policy."[45] At Hemenway's insistence, all board meetings were recorded, though there were no funds to transcribe the tapes.

The divisions in the leadership aggravated a number of issues. The vice president, secretary, and treasurer resigned in the first three months after Hemenway's election. Under the bylaws, the board chose replacements to fill out their terms. For the vice presidency, it chose Lars Hydle, the Progress slate candidate who had come in second in the race for that office. The position of counselor, last held by Rick Williamson, fell vacant. Resignations continued; by the spring of 1976, a majority of the board was unelected. Finances, never robust, grew shakier. The association resumed drawing from the Scholarship Fund to cover operating expenses, and repayment to the fund was problematic. The board considered closing the club and selling the building but could not come to consensus on any course of action.

---

**Box 5.2.** John Hemenway

John Hemenway had brilliant credentials. When he entered the Foreign Service in 1954, he was 28 years old and had completed a military trifecta: He had served in the Army, Navy, and Air Force. He held degrees from the U.S. Naval Academy and from Oxford University, where he was a Rhodes Scholar.

Hemenway entered in Class 6 (today's Class 4) and was promoted twice in his first seven years. His career then stalled. In 1969 he had reached the maximum allowable eight years in Class 4, and when he was again passed over, he was dismissed from the Service. He ran for president of AFSA in 1975 as a retiree, serving as a civilian employee at the Pentagon.[a]

Hemenway carried a grudge the way Maria Callas carried a tune. He saw conspiracies and base motives in any opposition or in any line of policy with which he disagreed. Bill Harrop, a target of one of his lawsuits, described Hemenway as "bitter . . . controversial and destructive."[b] Rep. Wayne Hays (D-Ohio) of the House Foreign Affairs Committee was less diplomatic: "I have had the man before the committee and I will say he appears to be nuttier than a Christmas fruitcake."[c]

Hemenway later earned a law degree and practiced law in the District of Columbia. He acquired some notoriety as a lawyer when, at age 83, he filed a suit challenging the eligibility of Barack Obama to be president of the United States. He told an interviewer in 2010, "I am convinced 99 percent that it's a fact that Obama was born in Mombasa, Kenya."[d]

a. Department of State, *Biographic Register*; and *FSJ*, May 1975, 30.
b. Harrop, ADST OHP interview, August 24, 1993, 43, 84.
c. Representative Hays to James Keogh, director, USIA, during hearings in 1976. Partial transcript attached to minutes of AFSA Board meeting, May 26, 1976.
d. John Hemenway, ADST OHP interview, August 10, 2010.

---

## Hemenway Is Ousted

A version of the Bayh bill to establish a grievance process for the Foreign Service reached a Senate-House conference in November 1975. Tom Boyatt and Tex Harris, acting now as individuals, endorsed the bill, which had the support of the department and a majority of the AFSA Board. But Hemenway, with the support of Cynthia Thomas (a member of AFSA but not of the board), attacked the bill in a message on AFSA letterhead to members of the conference. The bill would "kill any real system of justice," he wrote, and any suggestion that the association endorsed it was "untrue, immoral, and illegal." Hemenway had ignored the board's insistence that he not speak for the association without explicit board approval. The board voted to censure Hemenway and soon thereafter began an effort to force a recall election aimed at his ouster.[46]

The board believed it had authority under the association's bylaws to remove the president, but it chose instead to take the question to the full membership. Vice President Hydle, a political officer, had served in Saigon, Bien Hoa, and Belfast; he was no stranger to conflict. He led the board's opposition to Hemenway in long, contentious meetings at which no issue, substantive or procedural, weighty or routine, could be resolved without fierce dispute. Hydle struggled over many months to keep the association engaged in negotiations with the foreign affairs agencies on grievance procedures and other issues, and to make the board's views known on Capitol Hill despite the president's conflicting testimony.

Hydle led the recall movement but also offered to resign if Hemenway would do the same.[47] Hemenway did not take him up on that offer, and in May 1976 the recall effort, under rules adopted by the board with advice from renowned labor lawyer Joseph L. Rauh Jr., was formally launched.[48] The Washington membership and 47 overseas chapters endorsed a six-count recall indictment, which in October was sent to all members with a yes-or-no ballot. Hemenway's appeal to the federal district court to block a vote count failed. On November 17, Hemenway was removed from office by a vote of 2,751 to 175. The turnout was 57 percent, the highest in the association's history.[49]

Hemenway, John Harter, and three other AFSA members sued the association, initially asking for a halt to the recall ballot and, when that failed, seeking Hemenway's reinstatement and award of damages.[50] The suit against AFSA was dismissed at the end of 1977.[51]

## USIA Pulls Out

The distraction and paralysis in the AFSA Board during Hemenway's presidency helped AFGE replace AFSA as the exclusive representative of Foreign Service employees at the U.S. Information Agency. A month after Hemenway took office, AFGE opened a petition for a new representation election at USIA.[52]

The Foreign Service was relatively new to USIA. Although the agency had been around since 1953, its officers held limited appointments until 1968, when Congress established the Foreign Service Information Officer Corps.[53] That bill provided authority to convert Foreign Service Reserve officers with limited appointments into Foreign Service Reserve officers with unlimited tenure. In 1971 Deputy Under Secretary for Management Bill Macomber had seized on that authority to allow Civil Service employees and Foreign Service staff officers to convert to a new personnel category, foreign affairs specialist (see page 58). When the department set up the program without new legislation, AFGE sued, claiming the program lacked a basis in law. The federal district court agreed.

Court orders halted conversions in 1973 and eventually killed the program, which had been popular in USIA.[54] The AFGE unit in USIA, Local 1812, urged employees to convert to foreign affairs specialist when it was to their financial advantage and to return to the General Schedule (GS) of the Civil Service system when job reclassifications opened opportunities for promotion. Hundreds of Civil Service employees, many of whom were members of AFGE, took that advice. AFGE petitioned the Employee-Management Relations Commission to allow foreign affairs specialist employees to be part of the Foreign Service bargaining unit and to vote in representation elections. AFSA objected, arguing that foreign affairs specialist employees and other Foreign Service employees had different interests, but the EMRC sided with AFGE.[55]

In 1976, foreign affairs specialist employees in USIA may have outnumbered regular Foreign Service members.[56] Their votes, added to those of regular Foreign Service employees disgusted with AFSA, may have made the difference. When the ballots were counted in March, AFGE easily defeated AFSA, 853 to 504; 75 voted for no union. On April 16, 1975, the commission certified AFGE as the bargaining representative of Foreign Service employees in USIA.[57] AFSA's membership in USIA declined by more than 60 percent, from 636 as of June 15, 1976, to just 249 two years later.[58]

## AFSA REVIVED

Lars Hydle served as acting president until December 7, 1976, when the board chose Patricia Woodring, a State representative and one of the few remaining elected board members, to serve out Hemenway's term.[59] Woodring, the first woman to head the association, faced a difficult situation. The Hemenway episode had brought discredit on the organization and on the membership that had elected him. By the end of his presidency, AFSA was running a deficit of over $35,000 a year, drawing down its capital, and taking short-term loans to cover operating expenses.[60] Membership had fallen by 15 percent.[61]

Past and present board members, as well as the association itself, had been named in a Hemenway lawsuit. The congressionally mandated Commission on the Organization of the Government for the Conduct of Foreign Policy, named the Murphy Commission after its chairman, Career Ambassador Robert Murphy, had recommended repealing Executive Order 11636 and returning AFSA to its former status as a professional society only.[62]

In the spring of 1977, AFSA held a new round of elections, again under close Labor Department supervision. Lars Hydle put together an Alliance slate that faced opposition from a Fresh Start slate led by Mike Michaud. "That slate," Hydle said, "thought the whole Hemenway business was distasteful; we should put it behind us. I remember sending out a flyer that said, 'Where were you people when we needed you?' People agreed with that, and we won." Hydle carried 1,468 votes, 44 percent of the total and enough for a seven-point victory. John Hemenway and John Harter were on the ballot, but Hemenway received less than 4 percent of the votes and Harter even fewer.[63] The new board took office in July.

AFSA's recovery would require showing members of the Foreign Service that AFSA still served their interests as employees and professionals. The change of administration from President Gerald Ford to President Jimmy Carter meant a new round of ambassadorial appointments and a new focus on women and minorities. More broadly, the incoming administration had bold ideas for reorganizing the federal bureaucracy, including the foreign affairs agencies and the Foreign Service. If on such issues the association could show itself an effective voice for the interests of the service, recovery in membership and stabilization of finances were likely to follow.

## AMBASSADORSHIPS

Jockeying for appointments began long before the new chief executive put his hand on the Bible and looked Chief Justice Warren Burger in the eye. As early as August 1976, Lars Hydle asked the board to set up a committee on presidential appointments that "over time would develop an understanding with the Senate Foreign Relations Committee . . . [to] develop a regular procedure for rating nominees, either privately . . . or publicly."[64] A rating committee was not a new idea; at the suggestion of former Ambassador John Kenneth Galbraith, AFSA had set one up under Martin Herz in 1969, modeled on the American Bar Association's committee on the qualifications of judicial nominees.[65] A similar proposal came up in 1974, when President Nixon's lawyer, Herbert Kalmbach, gave sworn testimony during the Watergate scandal that exposed the selling of embassies for campaign contributions.[66] But the idea had no appeal to the White House or (with a few exceptions) to members of Congress. A 1973 AFSA proposal—"a major new professional initiative"—to limit non-career appointees to 15 percent of ambassadorial posts had been dead on arrival.[67]

Would the Carter administration share AFSA's views? There was reason to think so. President-elect Jimmy Carter's 1976 campaign manifesto, a short book called *Why Not the Best?*, included this observation: "For many years in the State Department we have chosen from among almost 16,000 applicants about 110 of our nation's finest young leaders to represent us in the international world. But we top this off with the disgraceful and counterproductive policy of appointing unqualified persons to major diplomatic posts as political payoffs. This must be stopped immediately."[68]

In December 1976, AFSA sent the president-elect a proposal for reforming ambassadorial appointments that included a nonpartisan review panel, a 10 percent cap on non-career appointments, and a 15 percent limit in any one geographic region. After the inauguration, when the president announced the Presidential Advisory Board on Ambassadorial Appointments, AFSA criticized its lack of career personnel. Most of the 20 panel members had been Carter delegates to the Democratic National Convention or campaign supporters, although Dean Rusk and former non-career Ambassadors Averell Harriman and William Scranton (a former Republican governor of Pennsylvania and presidential candidate) were also members.[69] When rumors surfaced that the White House planned to put some 60 campaign workers into Schedule C positions at State, Lars Hydle, then chairman of AFSA's State Standing Committee, wrote to the department's director of employee-management relations, FSO Jack Scanlan: "What in the department's view is the moral distinction between appointing 'fat cat' campaign contributors to ambassadorships, and appointing lean and hungry Carter campaign workers to the department?"[70] AFSA President Pat Woodring raised the subject of appointments in more moderate tones in a letter to Secretary of State Cyrus Vance.[71] AFSA supported efforts by Senators Abraham Ribicoff (D-Conn.), Charles Percy (R-Ill.), and Jacob Javits (R-N.Y.) to establish standards for confirming nominees to high office, including ambassadorial appointments.[72] During President Carter's first year in office, AFSA opposed five ambassadorial nominees as unqualified, one of whom withdrew.[73]

Hydle was especially hard on the administration at an AFSA awards ceremony on December 9, 1977. With National Security Adviser Zbigniew Brzezinski in attendance, Hydle pointed out the gap between campaign statements and actual performance: It "suggests that the administration does not want to use career people in senior policy-level positions." He also accused the White House of stifling dissent on human rights policy: "It is difficult to have a serious discussion with someone who thinks you're immoral; and we hoped we had seen the last of demands . . . for 'positive loyalty.'" Brzezinski replied that the

Foreign Service had a "dominant role" in the conduct of foreign relations; what he was thinking as he spoke can only be guessed at.[74]

The Foreign Service Act of 1980 picked up some of AFSA's ideas and included, for the first time in law, an exhortation on the qualities desired in a chief of mission, including knowledge of the language, history, culture, politics, and economics of the country. Chiefs of mission, the act stipulated, should "normally" be career members of the Foreign Service, although non-career appointments may be warranted "from time to time."[75] The president and the Senate never paid much attention to this legislative language. AFSA never acquired a role in the selection of ambassadors, and neither the executive nor the Senate ever acknowledged a cap on non-career appointees.

AFSA's strenuous efforts failed to change the rules or move the numbers, but the association drew attention to the issue and gained respect for its stand among professionals across the foreign affairs agencies.

The Carter administration put career people in about 73 percent of ambassadorships. The comparable figures in the Johnson, Nixon, and Ford administrations were 60, 69, and 61 percent.[76] But President Carter named fewer career people to top positions in the Department of State than his predecessors did; only six of 22 were career members of the Foreign Service, the smallest share at least since 1949.[77]

## REORGANIZING THE GOVERNMENT

The proclaimed interest of the Carter administration in appointing career officers as chiefs of mission was part of a larger fascination with the machinery of government. At the very beginning of his administration, the president set up a President's Reorganization Project (PRP), based in the Office of Management and Budget. By April 1977, he had won authority from Congress to submit reorganization plans that would take effect in 60 days unless disapproved by either chamber.[78] He used that authority boldly:

- The State Department's Bureau of Cultural Affairs was folded into the U.S. Information Agency, which became the U.S. International Communications Agency.
- The U.S. Agency for International Development absorbed the Overseas Private Investment Corporation and became the International Development Cooperation Agency (IDCA), outside the Department of State.

- Export promotion shifted from State to Commerce, where a Foreign Commercial Service, similar to the one that existed from 1927 to 1939, was established with 129 overseas State Department positions.[79]
- The Special Trade Representative, a position Congress had created in the Executive Office of the President in 1962, took on new responsibilities for policy and negotiations and became the U.S. Trade Representative with a greatly expanded staff.

The largest changes, including the creation of two new cabinet departments, Education and Energy, came about through acts of Congress. Most important for the Department of State and for AFSA were two bills that reformed the federal workforce: the Civil Service Reform Act of 1978 and the Foreign Service Act of 1980.

Reform of the Civil Service was the central project of the PRP. The president named more than a hundred individuals to a Federal Personnel Management Project and sent them off to an isolated building, where they took to calling themselves the "Buzzard Point Expeditionary Force." In less than a year, the group produced draft legislation that was introduced in Congress in March 1978 as the Civil Service Reform Act (CSRA).[80] Just seven months later, President Carter signed the bill into law.[81]

Passage of the CSRA cleared the way for debate on a new Foreign Service act to replace the Act of 1946. But even if personnel reform and reorganization had not been passions of the Carter administration, a number of deep-seated problems would likely have pushed the department's management, and AFSA, to agree on the need for change. These included persistent friction between the Civil Service and an underpaid Foreign Service, underrepresentation in the Foreign Service of women and members of racial and ethnic minorities, a personnel structure that produced more senior officers than senior positions, and treatment of the staff corps in law and practice that undervalued its expertise and professionalism.

The association was slow to appreciate the opportunity that drafting a new Foreign Service act would present. The AFSA Board under Lars Hydle believed that new legislation was "unnecessary, and perhaps dangerous."[82] In May 1979, at a meeting with Secretary of State Vance and Ben Read, his under secretary for management, AFSA representatives recognized the problems facing the Foreign Service but spoke in favor of addressing them with existing authorities and amending the 1946 Act if necessary. The Secretary, however, in a "decision made on the spot," said the State Department would go forward with a new comprehensive bill.[83]

# 6

## The Foreign Service Act of 1980

The prospect of a new basic statute was the central issue in AFSA's 1979 elections. Ken Bleakley, a mid-level officer from a union family (his father was a leader of the New York Newspaper Guild), headed a Professional Renewal Organization (PRO) slate that backed the Secretary of State in his desire for new legislation. The PRO secured support and even campaign contributions from some of the most distinguished members of the Foreign Service, including Lawrence "Larry" Eagleburger, then ambassador to Yugoslavia, and former Under Secretary for Political Affairs Philip Habib, who had retired in the spring of 1978. "We were concerned about professionalism," Bleakley said, "about the dilution of the Foreign Service. We saw a real role for the union, but we didn't want the union to replace the profession."[1] The defense of professionalism, and active campaigning by Phil Habib, helped the slate to run especially well among retired officers.

Bleakley's slate faced two others: the Representative slate led by incumbent board member Kenneth Rogers and the Unity slate led by incumbent Bob Pfeiffer. The members of the Representative slate were wary of new legislation, and the Unity slate was hostile. Bleakley and the PROs won by about 14 percentage points.[2] The PRO candidate for vice president, however, lost to Anthea "Thea" de Rouville, a staff officer who had been asked to join all three slates and chose Unity.[3] "Thea," said Bleakley, "turned out to be in many ways our most valuable resource."[4] The top vote-getter as State representative was an incumbent board member who joined the PROs, Joseph "Joe" McBride. A mid-level Foreign Service officer, McBride had been president of the Junior Foreign Service Officers Club a decade earlier and retained some of that organization's traditional impatience and suspicion of management.

Bleakley, de Rouville, and McBride were the core of AFSA's negotiating team. State's negotiators were Ben Read, the top management official; Harry Barnes, successor to Carol Laise as Director General of the Foreign Service; Bill Bacchus, director for policy in the Bureau of Personnel; and Jim Michel, deputy legal adviser.

Like Bill Macomber, Ben Read was a U.S. Marine, a World War II veteran, and a lawyer whose career was spent largely in nonpartisan public service. His first experience at the Department of State came in a brief stint as an attorney in the Office of the Legal Adviser during the Eisenhower administration. He spent time on the Hill in the office of Sen. Joe Clark (D-Pa.) but returned to State in 1963 as executive secretary under Dean Rusk. In 1969 he was named director of the Woodrow Wilson International Center for Scholars and then, in 1972, was the first president of the German Marshall Fund. He became deputy under secretary for management in August 1977 and, when the position was reestablished by Congress in 1978, the under secretary for management.[5]

Harry Barnes came to his job with a classic Foreign Service background. He had joined the Service in 1951 at age 25 with degrees from Amherst and Columbia, and two years' service in the U.S. Army. When he became Director General in 1977, he had spent 26 years in the Foreign Service, with consular, political, and administrative assignments on two continents (Europe and Asia), including a tour as chief of mission (Romania).

Bacchus and Michel were members of the Civil Service. Bacchus had an academic background. He held a doctorate in political science from Yale and had written on management at State while a professor at the University of Virginia. Carol Laise brought Bacchus into the department to respond to the Murphy Commission's report, which Bacchus had helped write. He would spend the next 26 years at State and USAID.[6] Jim Michel, a careful, brilliant lawyer, started as an attorney at State in 1965 and was put to work on the Hays bill. After passage of the 1980 Foreign Service Act, he would go on to serve as principal deputy assistant secretary in the Bureau of American Republic Affairs, ambassador to Guatemala, and acting administrator of USAID.[7]

Bleakley, de Rouville, and McBride had a generally cordial, collaborative relationship with the department's management. "We played good cop, bad cop," said Bleakley. "I was usually the good cop. The bad cop was Joe McBride." At one point in the negotiations, in a meeting with AFSA, State Department management backed away from positions it had already taken, and McBride, in a "memorable outburst," threw his papers across the table and walked out.[8] The display of temper worked to good effect. The department promised "to review

---

**Box 6.1. The Night Watch**

In 1979 the AFSA presidency was still an extracurricular activity. "I worked with the Secretary to get assigned as deputy director of the operations center," Ken Bleakley said, "where I could do a lot of my work at night and handle the AFSA job during the day." On November 4 of that year, the U.S. embassy in Tehran was overrun and more than 50 hostages taken, most of them members of the Foreign Service or the armed forces. A few months later, guerrillas in Colombia seized the Dominican embassy during a reception and took more than 60 hostages, including U.S. Ambassador Diego Asencio.

"My two jobs crossed," said Bleakley. "I was the principal contact with Penne Laingen, and with Diego's family. On the Hill we used the crises rather blatantly. We said, '[T]his is your Foreign Service, the true professionals.' It won us tremendous sympathy. We used it to get benefits for people. And I was in contact with [Chargé d'Affaires] Bruce Laingen. He had time on his hands, sitting there at the foreign ministry. I would run ideas for the [Foreign Service Act] by Bruce."[a]

---

a. Bleakley interview, August 9, 2013. Penne Laingen was the wife of Bruce Laingen, then chargé d'affaires in Tehran. He was not in the embassy when it was captured but was held, essentially under arrest, in the foreign ministry building, where he was occasionally allowed access to a telephone. He and two colleagues were eventually transferred to join the rest of the hostages. Bruce Laingen died in 2019; Penne Laingen, in 2021.

---

several . . . issues of great interest to the union, such as standby pay for those staff corps employees required to be available for duty . . . outside normal office hours, and . . . full hardship allowances to employees, notwithstanding an existing administrative ceiling."[9] As Lannon Walker and Charlie Bray understood, a little zeal can be useful.

## CRITICAL ISSUES

Only 16 months passed between the formal introduction of the Foreign Service Act in June 1979 and its final passage in October 1980. The AFSA Board held frequent meetings in Washington with constituent groups and polled its membership to set negotiating objectives and priorities.[10] The account that follows looks at AFSA's role on critical issues as the act came together.

### The Foreign Service and the Civil Service

The Foreign Service Acts of 1924 and 1946 kept the Civil Service and the Foreign Service separate, but the Hoover (1947–1949) and Rowe (1950) Commissions (among others) favored a single-service model. After the report of the Wriston Committee (1954), the State Department began to integrate the two services by bringing civil servants into the Foreign Service and rotating Foreign Service personnel through domestic assignments. AFSA backed the single-service model from Wriston through the Herter Report (1962) and the Hays bill (1965), but it changed direction with the publication of its own study, *Toward a Modern Diplomacy* (1968), which strongly favored a distinct, independent Foreign Service. In 1971 the department tried to push further toward integrating the two services with the creation of a corps of "foreign affairs specialists," essentially civil servants in the Foreign Service system who would serve only occasional tours overseas. A lawsuit filed by the American Federation of Government Employees and a subsequent court order stalled the project (see pages 57–59).[11]

The 10-year effort to build a single-system model around a hybrid foreign affairs specialist corps, which both AFGE and AFSA came to oppose, ended in May 1975, when Ambassador Carol Laise, then the new Director General of the Foreign Service, told Secretary Kissinger that the single-system model had failed.[12] The following month, yet another blue-ribbon commission, this one convoked by Congress and headed by former Ambassador Robert Murphy, came down in favor of a dual-service system.[13] The question of a dual-service or a single-service system seemed settled. When AFSA President Tom Boyatt testified before the Murphy Commission, he did not even address the issue.[14]

Ben Read embraced the emerging consensus that favored separation over integration of the Foreign and Civil Services. During the 1978 debate on the Civil Service Reform Act, Sen. Claiborne Pell (D-R.I.), a former Foreign Service officer, had sought to include the Senior Foreign Service in the proposed Senior Executive Service (SES) and to allow civil servants and Foreign Service officers to compete against each other for top jobs across government and for performance pay, a new feature of the act.[15] Read and AFSA enlisted the support of another former Foreign Service officer, Rep. Jim Leach (R-Iowa) of the Post Office and Civil Service Committee, to keep the Foreign Service and its top positions separate from the SES. When the House and Senate bills reached conference, Pell yielded the point to Leach on the basis of a promise by department officials that State's personnel system would undergo reform.[16] Civil Service managers welcomed the move. Alan (Scotty) Campbell, director of the Office of Personnel Management, testified that "the attempt to adapt [the Foreign Service system to Civil Service jobs] produced a great deal of difficulty and inequities. . . . We warmly endorse the department's proposal to establish a [separate] Senior Foreign Service."[17]

The strong consensus in favor of separate services made this question, so often analyzed and so long contested, almost incidental to the drafting of the Foreign Service Act of 1980. The act resolved what Ben Read called "a foolish, debilitating, 30-year dispute" in its "acceptance of clear distinctions" between the Foreign Service and the Civil Service "based on availability for worldwide service."[18] At State and USAID, employees who had converted to foreign affairs specialists returned to the Civil Service or the Foreign Service by the mid-1980s.[19]

## A Unified Foreign Service

When AFSA abandoned its support for increased integration of the Foreign and Civil Services, it nevertheless maintained its support for a unified Foreign Service, meaning a single Service across all foreign affairs agencies. The association argued, as it had more than a decade earlier in *Toward a Modern Diplomacy*, that a single Director General should govern the Foreign Service in all agencies, independent of the Secretary of State and other agency heads. The corollary to this position was that the Director General should have nothing to do with the Civil Service in the State Department or anywhere else.[20]

Wisely, AFSA did not push the idea, which by 1979 (if not long before) had become fanciful. Carol Laise, Director General from 1975 to 1977, said that "the director general is nothing more than the assistant secretary of State for personnel administration. The political clout and influence are in the job of under secretary for management." In her view, AFSA itself had undercut the notion that the Director General had any special role in representing the Foreign Service. "Tom Boyatt made it very clear to me that [AFSA] represented the Foreign Service on policy issues with management. They expected me to weigh in . . . but I didn't have a constituency behind me."[21] The new act, which stated that the Director General "shall perform such duties as the Secretary of State may prescribe," did nothing to contradict Ambassador Laise's view of the position.

AFSA's support for a single Foreign Service across multiple agencies found expression in provisions of the act that made the Foreign Service system available to the Department of Commerce for its new Foreign Commercial Service (FCS) and to the Department of Agriculture for its Foreign Agricultural Service (FAS). (Before passage of the act, the FAS had been operating under Civil Service rules, and Commerce had intended to use the Civil Service for the FCS.)[22] Both agencies took advantage of the greater flexibility that the rank-in-person and worldwide-availability features of the Foreign Service system provided. AFSA and State management strongly favored these decisions, which they expected would facilitate exchanges of Foreign Service personnel among the Foreign Service agencies. Those exchanges never occurred on a significant scale.

## Foreign Service Pay

Foreign Service employees had complained throughout the late 1960s that their counterparts in the private sector—in business, law, and especially international banking—were far better rewarded. By the 1970s, they said, the Foreign Service had fallen behind the Civil Service and the military as well.

AFSA's lobbying, unopposed by the department, secured a provision in the Foreign Relations Authorization Act of 1979 requiring the department to conduct an independent study of the issue. Hay Associates, a consulting firm then generally considered the best in this field, did the study and found that relative to the Civil Service, the Foreign Service was underpaid at the upper-middle ranks but not necessarily at the top (which had received a pay raise on January 1, 1977) or at the bottom.[23]

---

**Box 6.2.** Jim Leach and AFSA

Rep. Jim Leach of Iowa seemed to know more about government pay schedules than more senior members of the Post Office and Civil Service Committee and often more than government witnesses and union lobbyists. He was unusually well prepared.

In 1971 Leach, then a junior Foreign Service officer, had conducted a pay comparability study for AFSA that found the FSOs were underpaid. The study recommended a crosswalk from the Foreign Service pay schedule to the General Schedule at new and higher levels.[a]

Leach resigned from the Service in 1973 and entered Congress as a Republican member from Iowa in 1977. Throughout the debate on the Foreign Service Act, he was open to advice from AFSA and the department, and he had a Foreign Service officer, John Forbes, on his staff. Although a junior member of the minority, Leach had the substantive knowledge and political skill to bring about the pay increase he had argued for in 1971. FSO Bill Veale, who had shared an office with Leach in 1971 and who led AFSA's task force on Foreign Service pay, wrote that "Jim Leach . . . was 100-percent behind us all the way, and gave wise counsel at the end of the road."[b] Jim Leach served in Congress until 2003, always a friend to the Foreign Service.

a. Bacchus, *Inside the Legislative Process*, 38.
b. *FSJ*, June 1981, 14; and Veale, ADST OHP interview, June 27, 2000.

Against opposition from the Office of Management and Budget, and the threat of a White House veto, AFSA and State worked together to persuade Congress to translate the results of the Hay study into a new and more generous pay schedule and to reject a plan that would have matched Foreign Service and Civil Service (General Schedule) grades precisely. The latter outcome, favored by the Office of Personnel Management, would have put the Foreign Service into a 10-level system and allowed Foreign Service jobs to be reclassified according to Civil Service standards.[24] Throughout the debates on Foreign Service pay, Representative Leach provided able and essential leadership.

State's position on pay fell well short of what AFSA wanted, however, and a final deal was not reached until September 25, 1979, when the House and Senate versions of the bill were reconciled in conference. In the end, the legislation—and the administration's pledges on implementation—amounted to a $27.4 million pay increase for the Foreign Service (about $112 million in 2022 dollars). Foreign Service personnel received on average a 9.6 percent pay hike on top of a 9.1 percent government-wide pay increase that took effect at the same time—a compound increase of 19.6 percent.[25]

## Gender, Race, and Affirmative Action

In 1970 of a total of 3,084 Foreign Service officers in the Department of State, 139 were women and 34 were African Americans. Despite the requirement of the Foreign Service Act of 1946 that the Service be "broadly representative" of the American people, the department, the Foreign Service, and the American Foreign Service Association seemed unaware in the early 1970s that these numbers indicated a problem.[26] A 1972 amendment to the Civil Rights Act of 1964 required affirmative action and equal employment opportunity (EEO) programs in every federal agency and established the Equal Employment Opportunity Commission to deal with compliance, but employment policies in the department did not change.

The issue was forced at last by the Alison Palmer lawsuit, by pressure groups like the Women's Action Organization (WAO) and the Thursday Luncheon Group (formed in 1973 by a group of Black officers in foreign affairs agencies), and by the Carter administration itself.

Secretary Cyrus Vance convened an affirmative action task force under Dick Moose, the new deputy under secretary for management.[27] Why, the task force asked itself, did so few women and members of minority groups seek Foreign Service careers? Perhaps, they wrote, because the service is seen as "elitist, self-satisfied, a walled-in barony populated by smug white males, an old-boy system in which women and minorities cannot possibly hope to be treated with equity in such matters as promotions and senior-level responsibilities."[28] The Secretary and the administration were determined to change the image and the reality behind it.

The task force wanted to expand a small, mid-level hiring program begun in 1975. In assignments, an implementation working group, set up to ensure that task force recommendations took hold, urged "special consideration" for qualified women and minorities in filling "high-visibility positions" and positions "in career fields under-represented by minorities or women."[29]

AFSA was having none of it. The board sent a message to all members and published the same message as a 1978 *Journal* editorial: "We strongly oppose measures that would bestow special advantages not equally available to all members of the Foreign Service" on members of "an EEO category"—that is, on women and racial or ethnic minorities.[30]

The *Journal* reported that the reaction to the editorial was "largely favorable," which may have been true—if one ignores the reactions of the WAO, the Thursday Luncheon Group, the Hispanic Officers Group, and the Asian and Pacific American Federal Employees Council. These groups signed a joint letter charging AFSA with a "serious misunderstanding" of equal opportunity and affirmative action. State and the Foreign Service, they asserted, are "monuments to past and continuing discrimination."[31]

Others agreed. The head of JFSOC said that management's "first obligation" is to make "a statement of principle in favor of an immediate remedy" to past discrimination, to "make this Foreign Service truly representative of the American people."[32] One FSO wrote that AFSA had taken a "members' interest, trade union approach," when the "very best American trade unions recognize a national interest in furthering the interest of minorities."[33] A USIA officer, however, agreed with the AFSA Board and called the inclusion of a commitment to affirmative action in his agency's promotion precepts "ideological blackmail of the most despicable kind."[34]

As the department moved to implement the task force recommendations, the AFSA Board continued to fight against "proposals to give preferential treatment [to people] . . . simply because they are women or members of certain ethnic minority groups." The implementation working group devised proposals that AFSA warned were subject to legal challenge as discriminatory, since they were based on "an implicit assumption that there are too few women and minorities in the FSO Corps." (The assumption was, in fact, explicit.) The board objected also to special consideration in assignments except as a remedy for individuals with a "past assignment pattern" that showed discrimination.[35] It complained about "the proliferation of special interest groups and their efforts to bypass AFSA and deal directly with management," despite AFSA's right to exclusive representation of Foreign Service employees under the executive order.[36] When management dismissed or ignored AFSA's complaints, the association took the dispute to the Employee-Management Relations Commission, which brokered a compromise in the language used in the working group's final report.

Issues associated with discrimination, or more precisely with remedies for discrimination, remained divisive. AFSA's stand against what it called "the preferential reverse-discriminating aspects" of affirmative action aroused hostility in parts of its constituency. AFSA complained about "management's sweeping proposals for preferential treatment," but the Women's Action Organization thought those same proposals were inadequate and irrelevant to the problem. The State vice president of the WAO wrote that "so long as minorities and women are limited by the subjective judgments" of untrained, often prejudiced supervisors and personnel officers, discrimination will continue.[37]

Coming into the talks on the new Foreign Service act, AFSA President Ken Bleakley softened the association's position. "We were supportive," he said in a 2013 interview, "not of affirmative action necessarily, but of making the Foreign Service more representative of the American people. We were fully in agreement with that objective. We didn't think you could make it work by giving bonus points to people because they were black or female. But you should recognize that some people have a much tougher time than others, and give them credit for overcoming adversity."[38]

The 1946 Act had said that "the members of the Foreign Service should be broadly representative of the American people." The 1980 Act deleted the word "broadly."[39] After the president of the Thursday Luncheon Group pointed out in testimony that the bill did not mention affirmative action or "provide teeth for existing [EEO] laws and regulations," Congress changed the bill to address these deficiencies.[40]

Neither the department's affirmative action program nor the Foreign Service Act of 1980 had much effect on the numbers. Federal courts, however, came to accept the argument of WAO and others that data on the composition of the Foreign Service by gender, race, and ethnic background, and on the variation in rates of promotion or the patterns of assignment affecting such groups, may be evidence of discrimination sufficient to require judicial intervention. Court orders changed the department's entry testing and assignment procedures, and forced hundreds of retroactive promotions. The department over time lost much of its discretion in wide areas of personnel policy to the courts. Management's loss of control meant a loss of influence for AFSA as well: The union could not bargain with a federal judge.

## The Staff Corps

In the late 1970s, the staff corps (predecessor of today's Foreign Service specialists) was perhaps the most dissatisfied element of the Foreign Service. Disaffected members of this group, mostly secretaries and communicators, formed an affinity and advocacy group called September 17; Anthea de Rouville was one of its founders. The name referred to the date of a meeting during which the under secretary for management told her and other secretaries that they should be seen and not heard.

The staff corps's complaints were both professional and social. "We are talking about a caste system," said Pauline Slavik, a secretary with 19 years in the Service at the time. "This includes walking down a corridor and being deliberately spurned by a Foreign Service officer . . . simply because that officer does not consider a secretary worthy of being addressed."[41] Many staff personnel believed they were underpaid relative to their private-sector and Civil Service counterparts, and many were frustrated by the lack of opportunities for advancement. Thea de Rouville, who at AFSA had "talked to literally hundreds of staff corps personnel," quoted a management official: "Officers have careers; staff have jobs." De Rouville said she was "infuriated," but she acknowledged the truth in the statement. She also believed staff needed to take responsibility for their own advancement: "We are hired to do a job—we have to make the career," she said.[42]

De Rouville led AFSA's negotiations on staff corps issues, and Ken Bleakley had nothing but praise for her work. "She found solutions to staff corps issues that didn't infuriate the old guard, who couldn't grasp the concept that the staff corps should be seen as professional equals," he said.[43] The 1980 Foreign Service Act improved pay and working conditions for staff personnel. It eliminated the separate Foreign Service staff pay schedule and placed all U.S. citizen-members of the Service on either the Foreign Service schedule or the Senior Foreign Service (SFS) schedule.

The single pay schedule did not eliminate the distinction between officers and staff, who were hired in different ways and, in some areas, operated under different personnel structures. The two categories were retained, Bill Bacchus explained, because "we have people with two distinct types of careers. We hope

**Box 6.3.** Specialists and Generalists

The Foreign Service Act of 1980 eliminated the "staff" designation and did not replace it.[a] The term "specialist" does not appear in the text of the act. The use of "specialist" to refer to what had previously been staff came about gradually, probably at the instigation of the Bureau of Personnel (later the Bureau of Human Resources, now the Bureau of Global Talent Management).

In the postwar history of the Service, the words "specialist" and "generalist" usually described different kinds of Foreign Service officers: specialists whose work required high levels of knowledge or skill in particular areas (such as finance, law, medicine, commerce, or science) and generalists whose work involved more breadth than depth. Socially and professionally, generalists were top dog. As Bill Crockett wrote, "Specialists specialized, but generalists became ambassadors."[b] The word "specialist," however, could also refer to members of the staff corps: communicators, secretaries, or other support staff.[c]

A search of the *Foreign Service Journal* archive shows that "staff corps" remained a part of the Foreign Service vocabulary for a few years after passage of the 1980 Act. The earliest use in the *Journal* of "generalist" and "specialist" in their current meaning seems to be in a "Bicentennial [of the Department of State] Message from the AFSA Board," published in September 1989, which held that keeping up with data management technology "is a daily challenge for Foreign Service generalists and specialists alike." In the 1990s, the Bureau of Human Resources adopted the terms "generalist" and "specialist" as employment categories and began to substitute "generalist" for "officer" in other contexts as well. In time "specialist" replaced "staff," but despite efforts by the department to promote it, the word "generalist" never caught on as a replacement for "officer," and AFSA strongly discourages its use.

a. For the legislative history of the act, see the 1979 hearings before the subcommittees of the House Committee on Foreign Affairs, available for download at https://www.google .com/books/edition/The_Foreign_Service_Act/P5VhD2fz-20C?hl=en.
b. Crockett's quote appears in "Toward a Modern Foreign Service," *FSJ*, February 1964, 22.
c. AFSA President Patricia Woodring wrote in the July 1977 *FSJ*: "There are still elements of second-class treatment for Foreign Service specialists and staff corps." See also Bacchus, *Inside the Legislative Process*, 28.

to . . . maintain the principle that the kind of career you have ought to match the category you're in."[44] Jim Michel, though, said, "We did try . . . to talk about 'members of the Foreign Service' in order to diminish the existing sharp distinction between Foreign Service officers and Foreign Service staff."[45]

At the same time, AFSA struggled with a different conflict involving members of the staff corps. Both WAO and the American Association of Foreign Service Women (AAFSW) pressured the association to improve overseas employment opportunities—often in staff positions—for Foreign Service spouses.[46] And just as many officers struggled to come to terms with affirmative action, many staff personnel, especially secretaries, struggled to accept the changing rules and shifting mores that brought rising numbers of wives into the Foreign Service.[47] AFSA was conflicted on the issue but came down on the side of its staff corps members. At AFSA's insistence, a clause was added to the House bill to make clear that "employment of family members . . . may not be used to avoid fulfilling the need for full-time career positions."[48]

## Retirement and the Senior Foreign Service

Testifying before the Murphy Commission in 1975, AFSA President Tom Boyatt had worried that low pay would deplete the senior ranks. He need not have fretted. Three or four years later, the Service had far too many senior officers—a senior glut.

In 1977, two years after Boyatt's testimony, a federal court in *Bradley v. Vance* threw out the provision of the 1946 Foreign Service Act that made retirement mandatory at age 60.[49] When the State Department appealed to the Supreme Court, AFSA supported the appeal in an amicus brief. AFGE and the Thomas Fund took the other side.

The appeal was successful. The court in 1979 ruled that Congress had a legitimate purpose in treating the Foreign Service and Civil Service differently and restored the original law.[50] In the interim, though, retirements were well below forecast, and the senior ranks swelled. In 1978, according to Bill Bacchus, "as many as 130 senior officers were unassignable, and thus reduced to 'walking the halls' or to make-work special projects." These unemployable, undismissible senior officers were a logjam that blocked promotions all the way down the ranks.[51]

Compounding the problem, mid-level numbers were unusually high. Officer intake had risen in the late 1960s to meet the demands of the Vietnam War. At one point, more than 400 Foreign Service officers were in the field, and another 100 were in Vietnamese-language training.[52] By 1979, these officers were approaching the senior grades, and the logjam increased their risk of dismissal under time-in-class rules. The anxiety that mid-level officers experienced as promotions dwindled and TIC limits approached probably contributed to AFSA's hostile attitude toward affirmative action, one that must have seemed to many to be yet another undeserved obstacle to their retention and advancement.

The 1980 Foreign Service Act did not immediately solve the senior glut, but it did rebuild the senior ranks along the lines of the Senior Executive Service created by the CSRA two years earlier. In addition to creating a separate Senior Foreign Service, it dealt decisively with retirement in an effort to restore the flow-through personnel system that had marked the Foreign Service from the days of the Rogers Act of 1924.

The Supreme Court's 1979 decision had restored mandatory retirement at age 60, but the 1980 Act raised the threshold to 65. Arguing that assignments abroad were increasingly difficult as employees aged, the department favored age 60, as did AFSA. But neither the department nor the association was a match for Rep. Claude Pepper (D-Fla.), chair of the House Select Committee on Aging. Born at the turn of the century, Pepper was a hero to the many elderly in his district and around the country. He opposed all mandatory retirement. Chair of the House Subcommittee on International Operations Rep. Dante Fascell (D-Fla.) represented a district that was also rich in retirees and bordered Pepper's. As Bill Bacchus recalls, when Fascell "approached Pepper with a compromise" of age 65, Pepper agreed. Rep. Pat Schroeder (D-Colo.), chair of the Post Office and Civil Service Committee, then signed on, as did Sen. Claiborne Pell. State and AFSA, when they learned of the agreement on the Hill, accepted the inevitable.[53]

When AFSA surveyed its membership just before Congress took its final votes on the act, it found that the SFS was the new law's least popular, most disliked feature.[54] Provisions on pay were the most popular by far. The survey did not reveal members' thinking, but one can assume that the chance to earn higher pay based on performance, a new benefit, could not overcome concern among mid-level officers that raising the retirement age would mean five more years of senior glut and five more years of severely reduced opportunities for promotion. Management and AFSA hoped to alleviate this problem by weeding the ranks with a revival of selection-out, a prospect that may have alarmed more officers than it mollified.

Especially worrisome to many officers were provisions that required those in Class 1, just below the senior level, to decide when to put themselves forward as candidates for promotion. Those who did so would be considered by selection boards but only for a period of time to be determined by the department. Failure to be promoted within this period—called "the window"—would mean dismissal from the Service. A Class 1 officer who chose to compete for promotion could withdraw but could never again be considered.

AFSA spent many hours negotiating new transition rules before and after the act's passage. Even so, AFSA had to sue to enforce the new act's provisions requiring that base pay be maintained or improved for every officer converting to the Senior Foreign Service.[55] Additionally, a few senior officers, with AFSA support, sued and won the right to a pension if they refused to convert to the

SFS and were therefore dismissed from the Service without having turned 50 or completed 20 years of service.[56]

Representative Schroeder settled another issue with which AFSA had struggled. "We had a real conflict of interest on spousal rights [to a share of an employee's pension] in divorces," said Ken Bleakley. "We could never find a position that satisfied employees who had to share their pensions with ex-spouses, and the AAFSW which looked after the divorcées."[57] Schroeder, then in her fourth term but not yet 40 years old, had no trouble siding with the former spouses and carrying her committee with her. As a result of her work, Section 814 of the act spells out the entitlement to benefits for former spouses of participants in the Foreign Service retirement system.[58] Civil Service spouses enjoy no such protection.

## Labor-Management Relations

Nine years after President Richard Nixon's Executive Order 11636 carved the Foreign Service out of the rules that governed labor unions in the federal workforce, the 1980 Act codified the order and gave the Foreign Service unions a basis in statute. The terminology was revealing: The act replaced the order's "employee-management relations" with "labor-management relations." At about the same time, AFSA lost its reticence about calling itself a labor union. It also abandoned the notion, which it had kept under study since early 1978, of affiliating with a "real" union like the National Treasury Employees Union or the American Federation of State, County, and Municipal Employees to share their political clout and expertise in collective bargaining.[59]

The act endorsed the inclusive view of the bargaining unit that AFSA had championed from the beginning. Management officials remained outside the unit, but management officials were defined as chiefs of mission and principal officers and their deputies, persons appointed to their position by the president (and their deputies), and persons in equivalent positions in the judgment of the Secretary of State. Officials handling labor-management relations and their confidential assistants were also excluded from the bargaining unit, as was the inspector general of the Department of State and the Foreign Service, a new position.[60] The AFGE argument that a manager was any employee who rates the performance of another was rejected.

The act placed responsibility for resolving labor-management disputes with two new institutions: a Foreign Service Labor Relations Board and a Foreign Service Impasse Disputes Panel, both of which are subordinate to the Federal Labor Relations Authority established by the Civil Service Reform

Act. This decision effectively killed the Employee-Management Relations Commission of the Board of the Foreign Service. AFSA had high hopes that the board would nevertheless take on permanent staff and become an important and independent voice on Foreign Service matters,[61] but a staff was never authorized. The board, as a purely advisory body, lost its relevance and over time fell into disuse.

## Grievances

The act reworked the grievance system, not entirely to AFSA's liking. The association resisted what it called an "imposed monopoly": the requirement that the union or "exclusive bargaining agent" represent any grievant who is a member of the bargaining unit, regardless of whether the grievant belonged to the union and regardless of the union's opinion of the merits of the case.[62] A grievant could choose to be represented by an outside attorney or to argue the case on their own, but the union would be guilty of an unfair labor practice if it interfered with the grievant's access to the Foreign Service Grievance Board or with any other right the grievant was entitled to exercise. "I felt we should have a choice about whom we represent," said Bleakley. "Then [Rep.] Pat Schroeder pulled me aside and explained the facts of life to me. 'You want to be a union, you represent all grievants.'"[63]

Sen. Jesse Helms (R-N.C.) offered a series of amendments to the act when it reached the Senate floor. The most viable would have replaced the title on grievances with a version of the bill sponsored by Senator Bayh in reaction to the suicide of Charles Thomas. AFSA had supported the original Bayh bill, which passed the Senate in 1972 and 1975 (see page 72), but the Helms version, in the opinion of AFSA's staff attorney Susan Holik, was vague on critical questions, risking new procedural and jurisdictional disputes.[64] AFGE and the Thomas Fund supported the Helms Amendment, but AFSA now joined the department in opposition. The amendment failed 45 to 36, perhaps (as Bacchus speculates) because Helms, not Bayh, had introduced it.[65]

The final result, said Ken Bleakley, produced "the strongest grievance provisions anywhere in the U.S. government."[66]

## The Crisis at USAID

Labor-management relations at the U.S. Agency for International Development were contentious from the beginning. The Kennedy administration created

USAID in 1961 as an autonomous agency whose director reported to the Secretary of State. Foreign assistance was intended as a temporary policy measure and USAID as a temporary agency. Its Foreign Service personnel were temporary hires, reservists with time-limited commissions. Before 1974, they had no access to the Foreign Service retirement system.[67] In the mid-1970s, with the end of the Civil Operations and Revolutionary Development Support program in Vietnam, USAID let hundreds of its Foreign Service employees go in a massive reduction in force (RIF).[68] The ratio of Civil Service to Foreign Service employees rose. In 1961 almost two-thirds of USAID's workforce were overseas; in 1975, almost two-thirds were in Washington. The Washington staff was very heavily tilted toward the Civil Service, especially in policy positions.[69]

The post–Vietnam War RIF began without consultations with AFSA. Unfair practice complaints multiplied. AFSA Vice President Tex Harris testified before a subcommittee of the Murphy Commission that USAID "is so badly run . . . and is so quickly losing its congressional support that it is on the verge of collapse."[70] President Tom Boyatt, testifying before the full commission, criticized the growth of the Civil Service at USAID, saying it led to an agency "dominated by individuals who know little or nothing about overseas conditions." He sought changes in the relationship of USAID to State and to strengthen State's authority and "eliminate the capacity of the Agency to flout openly the orders of the Foreign Service Grievance Board." He urged that foreign assistance be acknowledged as a permanent feature of U.S. foreign policy and that USAID's Foreign Service personnel (and many of its civil servants) be placed in the career Foreign Service system.[71]

Some of what AFSA had argued for soon came to pass, and some did not. President Jimmy Carter did indeed recognize the permanent nature of foreign aid, but the administration's Reorganization Plan Number 2 placed USAID in a new International Development Cooperation Agency (IDCA) that operated outside the Department of State. The Act of 1980 provided for the conversion of USAID's Foreign Service personnel from reserve to career status, though USAID's management continued to resist providing presidential commissions for its Foreign Service officers. USAID and its parent, IDCA, continued to be dominated by civil servants and political appointees.

Rep. David Obey (D-Wis.) used his position on the Foreign Operations Subcommittee to place an amendment to the International Development and Food Assistance Act of 1978 establishing criteria for designating positions in Washington as Foreign Service or Civil Service, with the intent of making USAID primarily a Foreign Service agency.[72] Convinced that USAID's management was trying to circumvent the Obey Amendment, AFSA put a great deal of work into monitoring USAID's performance, eventually bringing suit against it to enforce the amendment in federal court.[73]

## THE ACT AND AFSA

On September 30, 1980, the Senate adopted the conference report by unanimous consent, Senator Helms being absent from the floor. The House approved it the next day by voice vote. President Carter, who complained about the cost, signed the bill into law on October 17 without ceremony.[74] It was a tribute to all who worked on the bill but especially to Representative Fascell, Representative Leach, and Senator Pell that this major legislation, which benefited no domestic constituency and unleashed not a dime of campaign contributions, was enacted in a presidential election year.

Some years after passage, AFSA Board member Bob Stern listed the goals that AFSA had hoped to achieve in the substance of the act:

- Preserve the historic separateness of the Foreign Service
- Retain the separate Foreign Service retirement system
- Reexamine the up-or-out system
- Realign Foreign Service and Civil Service pay scales
- Halt the erosion in the staff corps
- Codify bargaining rights
- Improve the allowance and benefits package
- Expand the openness of the assignments process[75]

The list is accurate, though it probably could not have been drawn up in 1979 or 1980. The crisp set of goals became more visible in retrospect.

For AFSA, the Foreign Service Act of 1980 marked a coming of age. During the months of debate and legislative maneuver, the association grew in understanding and mastery of its role and potential. AFSA gained expertise, prestige, and power. It learned how to exercise, and insist that State respect, the authority that E.O. 11636 and the union elections of 1973 had given AFSA. It greatly expanded the direct relationship with members of Congress that Bill Harrop and Tom Boyatt had done so much to develop. Members of the Service noticed. AFSA's membership grew, though at the end of 1980 it was still below 1975 levels. Finances began to strengthen.

The act made fundamental changes in the Service; changes within AFSA naturally followed. In the months following passage, AFSA negotiated with management on how to implement the act, with their agreements reflected in revisions to the Foreign Affairs Manual and other regulations. A partial list of topics covered would include the relationship of the Foreign Service and the Civil Service, merit principles, recruitment, the role of the chief of mission, appointments of career candidates and appointments to the Senior Foreign Service, compensation, leave, performance evaluation, the handling of personnel records, promotions, training, titles and ranks, incentives, grievances, medical care, selection-out, separation for cause, and retirement.

As the Foreign Service's union, AFSA became, more than it had been, an authoritative source of advice and guidance for Foreign Service employees regarding agency regulations. To the extent its resources allowed, AFSA's staff grew to meet this need. As the Foreign Service professional organization, AFSA was still the defender of merit and career principles against political assault, the protector of professional integrity against pressure for conformity, and a promoter of professional enhancement through training and education. Union and professional roles overlapped. They occasionally conflicted but more often reinforced each other.

The decision by Congress and the administration to separate the Civil Service and the Foreign Service, together with AFSA's successful assertion of its union role and its attention to the staff corps, put an end to the competition with AFGE. AFSA would soon win representation elections in the Departments of Commerce and Agriculture and would regain its position as the Foreign Service union in USIA (which in 1982 returned to its old name). AFGE continued to represent many of the Civil Service employees in the foreign affairs agencies and throughout the government, but it would never again mount a serious challenge to AFSA in the Foreign Service.

# 7

## Turnover at the Top, 1981–1987

Soon after the 1980 Foreign Service Act was passed, Ken Bleakley answered AFSA's election call. He was ready to run for a second term, heading the unopposed Unity slate. Then came a second call, this one from Ambassador Deane Hinton in El Salvador, looking for a deputy chief of mission. Deane Hinton was a hard man to say no to, and the challenge of El Salvador in the early 1980s could not be turned aside. Bleakley resigned as AFSA's president and withdrew his candidacy in May 1981, in the middle of the campaign.

The Governing Board elected Thea de Rouville to serve out Bleakley's term. On May 9, 1981, Bleakley turned over his gavel, and de Rouville became the first member of the staff corps to serve as AFSA's president.[1] "Thea came on and did a great job" as interim president, Bleakley said, "but it was not the job I intended to do."[2] Bleakley had planned to use committee reports and other legislative history to shape implementation of the Foreign Service Act. He felt he left his work unfinished.

Bleakley's late withdrawal led to a scramble in which Charles Whitehouse won election as a write-in candidate, carrying all four constituencies. Whitehouse, whose father had joined the Foreign Service in 1905 (and whose son Sheldon would be elected to the U.S. Senate), had been a Marine Corps officer in World War II.[3] He was tall and white-haired; one observer said he could have played an ambassador in the movies had he not been one in real life.[4] At the time of his election, he had been several years in retirement after a career of great distinction that included service as deputy ambassador under Ellsworth Bunker in Saigon and at embassies of his own in Laos and Thailand. He held Distinguished Honor Awards from the Department of State and USAID. After

Lars Hydle and Bleakley, he represented a change in background, style, temperament, and thinking.

In the spring of 1981, in an attempt to increase voter participation, the association's membership had changed the bylaws. Members of the Governing Board would continue to serve two-year terms, but the terms were staggered to begin at different times; instead of one election to fill all seats every other year, an election to fill half the seats would be held each year. An election call duly went out in early 1982 for candidates for the presidency and other offices.

Dennis Hays, a past president of the Junior Foreign Service Officers Club then finishing a year at Harvard's John F. Kennedy School of Government in Cambridge, was contemplating a run. "There was a strong feeling that AFSA was stronger on the professional side than on the union side," Hays said. "The secretaries, the communicators, the security guys—AFSA wasn't really taking care of their interests. I had no Friday classes, so I came down to Washington from Boston at my own expense to campaign."

He found plenty of dissatisfaction. The pay raise that followed passage of the Foreign Service Act of 1980 made everyone happy for a while, but different groups (Tex Harris called them "tribes") within the Service felt disadvantaged relative to the others. "The security guys talked about 'black dragons,'" Hays recalls. "They were convinced there was a conspiracy of mid-level and senior political officers to do them in. The secretaries had the September 17 group. Consular and administrative [management] officers thought political officers ran the system and took care of themselves first. Political officers thought the cone system favored administrative officers for promotion."[5]

These divisions gave Hays an opening. "I was too young and too new to the Service to be a black dragon," he said. "I had an inclusive style, and I was willing to delegate."[6] Compared to Whitehouse, Hays was younger (just 28), scrappier, scruffier, and shorter—Tom Cruise to Harrison Ford. Whitehouse did not impress Hays: "I don't know if he was married to a countess, but he should have been. I thought he had nothing in common with the up-and-coming generation of Foreign Service officers. He was a great guy, a nice guy, but independently wealthy, old school, and he didn't understand people who have kids to feed and are living in substandard housing overseas."[7]

Whitehouse had been in office only a few months at the time of the election call. He wanted to run again, but several board members organized a slate to run against him. "Charlie was outraged by this lack of loyalty," Hays recalled. "He was so mad at [the defectors] that he basically released his people to me.

Thea de Rouville . . . and others [also] came over to my ticket."[8] The board members who opposed Whitehouse abandoned their effort, and Hays's Unity slate, now including Ambassador Whitehouse as retiree representative, won an uncontested election.[9] Unity candidates swept the 1983 elections for constituency seats as well.[10]

Hays took office at AFSA on July 15, 1982, the day before George Shultz replaced Alexander Haig as Secretary of State. Shultz, a former secretary of labor, director of the Office of Management and Budget, and secretary of the Treasury, had taught management at Stanford and had run the giant Bechtel Corporation. He took an active interest in management of the department.[11] He installed a new management team, naming businessman Jerry Van Gorkom under secretary for management.

The appointment did not work out. Van Gorkom lacked the patience for Washington, and in less than a year Shultz replaced him with career FSO Ron Spiers. Spiers, ambassador to Pakistan at the time of his nomination, protested that he had no background for the job, but he had impressed Shultz with his thinking about management issues during a chat on the way to the airport in Islamabad, and after Van Gorkom, Shultz wanted a career officer.[12] Spiers entered the position in November 1983 and stayed until his retirement in May 1989.

## IMPLEMENTING THE 1980 ACT

Implementation of the Foreign Service Act of 1980 got off to a slow start. The bill had passed just before an election, and management had almost no time to act before it was thrown into the confusion of a transition—an upheaval, really—from Carter Democrats to Reagan Republicans. AFSA had turmoil of its own, with four presidents (Bleakley, de Rouville, Whitehouse, and Hays) in 14 months.

Different players had different ideas about what was important. One year after the act's adoption, the *Journal* asked representatives of Congress, management, and AFSA to assess it. The staff director for the House Subcommittee on International Operations, Virginia Schlundt, said the key to the act was career development; she awaited "a joint management-labor vision of what career development patterns should be." The deputy assistant secretary of State for personnel, new to his job, dwelled on "conversions of members of the Service from one personnel category to another." And AFSA's Governing Board said only that "implementation has so far not gone well at all" because the "five-agency, two-unions negotiations are . . . cumbersome, unbelievably slow, and perilously close to unworkable."[13]

AFSA and the five agencies approached implementation with fundamentally different outlooks. AFSA, as well as the American Federation of Government Employees' Local 1812 at the U.S. International Communications Agency (the Carter administration's name for the U.S. Information Agency), saw the act as a package deal in which employees assumed responsibilities and risks, and received benefits in exchange. The unions expected implementation to preserve the overall balance that had been negotiated in the act. But management approached implementation piecemeal, proposing regulations on issues such as performance pay, the senior threshold, the interagency selection board for entry into the Senior Foreign Service, personnel conversions, separation for cause, affirmative action, and the grievance system, with each proposal unrelated to the others. The sense of purpose that management had brought to drafting the act and moving it through Congress had been lost with the change of administrations.

Nevertheless, by the beginning of 1983 much had been done. The SFS came into existence on September 28, 1981; by 1983, it had more than a thousand members. The Department of Agriculture introduced the Foreign Service system in the Foreign Agricultural Service (FAS) and the Animal and Plant Health Inspection Service (APHIS), and the Commerce Department adopted the Foreign Service system for its new Foreign Commercial Service (FCS). At USAID, nearly all Foreign Service Reserve personnel converted to career status. Executive orders reconstituted the Board of the Foreign Service and the Grievance Board, and established the Board of Examiners, the Foreign Service Labor Relations Board, and the Foreign Service Impasse Disputes Panel (FSIDP). Regulations had been issued on 28 topics and were under negotiation on 33 more. But management acknowledged that the toughest issues had not been resolved and that negotiations were slowing down.[14] State's new under secretary for management had to agree with AFSA that implementation was "somewhat slower than we would like."[15]

Implementation was especially difficult at USAID. AFSA complained that two years after passage of the act, the agency had neither a time-in-class (TIC) nor an open assignments system; instead, personnel decisions were secretive and ad hoc. And the agency continued to rely heavily on Civil Service personnel and political appointees in its Washington headquarters in defiance of the 1978 Obey Amendment.[16]

## AMBASSADORS

As always, AFSA devoted considerable energy to vetting chiefs of mission. The act urged the appointment of ambassadors with "demonstrated competence" who would "normally" be drawn from the career Service, but the Reagan administration quickly disappointed any expectations that it would be constrained by those provisions. Forty-two of its first 85 appointments were non-career.[17]

The association argued that the increase in non-career appointments to ambassadorships and other senior positions could damage the credibility of a bipartisan foreign policy and destroy "the promotion/attrition model" of the Senior Foreign Service.[18] Charles Whitehouse testified: "I will not quibble over percentages, Mr. Chairman, but I do not believe any reasonable person could affirm that with nominations being about half political and half career at this time, that positions as chief of mission are 'normally' being accorded to career officers."[19]

No reasonable person would call Charlie Whitehouse naive, but his next statement reads as oddly today as it must have in 1982: "Section 304, Paragraph 3 states that contributions to political campaigns should not be a factor in the appointment of an individual as a chief of mission. Given existing limitations on the political contributions an individual may make, Mr. Chairman, this section [is] largely irrelevant. The era of large-scale contributors becoming ambassadors is over."[20]

Not for the first or last time, AFSA called for the creation of a committee to vet ambassadorial nominations, one along the lines of the Standing Committee on the Federal Judiciary that the American Bar Association set up in 1948 to examine candidates for judgeships. A *Journal* editorial urged the Senate Foreign Relations Committee to create a panel of "distinguished former ambassadors" to evaluate career and non-career nominees.[21] Sen. Charles Mathias Jr. (R-Md.), the best friend that career diplomats had on the committee, introduced legislation to limit non-career ambassadors to 15 percent of the total and supported a rating program proposed by the American Academy of Diplomacy. But Mathias had announced that he would leave the Senate at the end of 1986, and his bill attracted no cosponsors and received no hearing.[22] Throughout the decade, AFSA continued to make its case for giving weight to the hortatory provisions of the act with no apparent effect on the president's nominations or the Senate's confirmations.

Hays had a rule of thumb: AFSA would oppose only one ambassadorial nomination a year. "Because we were prepared to do this," Hays said, "it helped the whole system." Some political nominees included AFSA on their get-to-know-me rounds. "Tom Anderson, who was going to Barbados, came to call on me," said Hays. "He said, 'I have great respect for the Foreign Service, I want to work with you guys. I know I need a good DCM [deputy chief of mission]; do you have any suggestions?' He wouldn't have done that if we hadn't objected to those who came before him."[23]

Hays's efforts, like those of his predecessors and successors, had no obvious impact on the raw numbers. By April 1986, only 61 percent of chiefs of mission worldwide were career officers, one point under the previous low of 62 percent recorded in 1962.[24]

## PENSIONS

When the Reagan administration sought to bring the federal workforce into the Social Security system, federal unions, including AFGE and AFSA, mounted a strenuous campaign of opposition. AFSA called the administration's proposals "an unprecedented assault on federal employee benefits."[25] But the administration, which had broken the Professional Air Traffic Controllers Organization (PATCO) after it conducted an illegal strike in 1981, was undeterred.[26] Union objections to Social Security had little impact. Congress brought in new federal hires under Social Security by a lopsided, bipartisan vote.[27]

Over the next three years, AFSA and the Civil Service unions lobbied hard to preserve the most favorable elements of their pension systems. At AFSA, the issue brought a surge in new retiree memberships and in contributions to the Legislative Action Fund, set up in 1983 to support this and other legislative battles. In the end, the unions got most of what they wanted. The Federal Employees' Retirement System (FERS) Act of 1986 established a three-tier system—Social Security, a defined-benefit retirement plan, and a voluntary thrift plan—for all workers hired after December 31, 1983, and open on a voluntary basis to workers hired earlier.[28] The Foreign Service Pension System, established by the same act, matched the three-tier structure of the FERS. The voluntary Foreign Service retirement at age 50 with 20 years' service remained in place, as did an annual cost-of-living adjustment linked to the consumer price index.[29] The unprecedented assault faded from memory.

AFSA took on two other legislative challenges in the 99th Congress. The Senate, on the floor and without hearings, amended the department's authorization legislation for Fiscal Years 1986 and 1987 to remove the Senior Foreign Service from the bargaining unit and drop the requirement in the 1980 Act that the Director General of the Foreign Service be a career officer. The association was caught by surprise, but by its own account, "three AFSA presidents, two congressional liaison officers, and members of the Governing Board waged a well-organized campaign of consultations with Capitol Hill staffers and direct contact with key senators and representatives." An appeal to the membership also produced "scores of cables and calls to legislators." The amendments, absent from the House bill, were dropped in conference.[30]

## GOVERNANCE

Dennis Hays was the first AFSA president to work full time at AFSA in a position funded by the Department of State. With support from management, Hays encumbered a position in the Bureau of Administration and was paid accordingly, but he was effectively detailed to the association. Soon after, an AFSA vice president was funded in a similar manner. The department, Hays said, wasn't just being nice. It feared congressional displeasure if it came up short on carrying out the Foreign Service Act. "The department had brought in a professional labor negotiator, Bob Sherman, to deal with us. Sherman expected to have somebody he could call and deal with any time he needed," said Hays. "It was in his interest, in the department's interest, to make that happen."[31] All presidents since Dennis Hays have worked full time for AFSA under similar arrangements, which were in time expanded to cover the four constituency vice presidents: State, USAID, FCS, and FAS.[32]

In 1984 the association abandoned the staggered elections it had adopted in 1981. Hays served a third year, and in 1985 the membership elected the full AFSA Governing Board to a two-year term, beginning July 15. The 1985 election was the last to choose a first and second vice president.

Hays was sensitive to the need for balance among the different constituencies in the association. He supported changes to the bylaws so that each major active-duty constituency—State, USAID, USIA, and later Agriculture and Commerce—would elect one vice president. Each constituency (later including the International Broadcasting Bureau and APHIS) would also elect one representative for each 1,000 AFSA members or fraction thereof. In 1985 the membership adopted these changes, which took effect after the 1985 elections. The Governing Board gained balance but grew in size and in time became unwieldy.

The need for balance affected AFSA committees as well. Each major constituency had a standing committee of the Governing Board to look after its interests, and the standing committees often reflected the mix of groups within each constituency. When Thea de Rouville headed the State Standing Committee, for example, the committee "had members from almost every cone and almost every grade, from the Senior Foreign Service Association, security officers, junior officers, the Thursday Luncheon Group, the Consular Officers Association, and September 17."[33] Thea told the membership, "We would welcome a representative from any Foreign Service interest group not currently represented."[34]

Unlike the three presidents who preceded him and the three who followed, Dennis Hays finished his elected term. The 1985 election to choose officers and board members for two-year terms was a quiet, even soporific affair. A Unity slate, led by Ambassador Robert "Bob" Keeley for president and the long-serving Thea de Rouville for first vice president, was unopposed in every contest.[35] But Keeley served only a matter of weeks before his nomination and confirmation as ambassador to Greece forced his resignation. The new Governing Board chose newly elected State representative Gerald P. "Gerry" Lamberty to fill out Keeley's term.

## A MORE PERFECT UNION

The Act of 1980 strengthened AFSA's ability to act as a labor union and added to its responsibilities as the exclusive bargaining agent for Foreign Service employees. The act codified the unique framework of Foreign Service labor-management relations, and it did the same with the grievance system. It defined the rights of employees and the rights of management and circumscribed the area open to labor-management negotiations. It established procedures and institutions for resolving disputes that could not be settled at the bargaining table. To carry out its new responsibilities, AFSA had to step up its game.

Membership and money were the keys to a stronger union. Membership, which had declined in 1981 and 1982, recovered in 1983 and 1984. By June 1984, it stood at roughly 7,600, up from 5,900 in June 1980, a gain of nearly 30 percent. Gains were not especially strong among the specialists, who were the focus of Hays's attention, but retirees—perhaps feeling threatened by administration plans for reforming federal pensions—signed up in large numbers, accounting for almost half of the total increase. The association also had success recruiting new officers. "AFSA used to send someone to speak to each A-100 class," said Hays.[36] "We decided to bring the class over to AFSA. We fed them heavy hors d'oeuvres and had a cross-section of our membership talk to them and mix and mingle. There were always two or three leaders in the group, and it usually wasn't too hard to figure out who they were. If we could sign them up, the rest would follow."[37]

More members meant more income. By 1984, total revenues, which in 1982 had been about $615,000, were running at just under $1 million a year (about $2.85 million in 2022 dollars), approximately two-thirds of which came from membership dues. One new source was contributions to the Legislative Action Fund, set up in 1983. By 1986, the fund was taking in over $85,000 a year, enough to put a full-time lobbyist on the association's payroll and cover all the costs of AFSA's work on the Hill.[38] The club and the *Journal*, however, continued to struggle, with the former posting small losses and the latter barely breaking even.[39] The addition of staff, including a new grievance representative and a new legal assistant, kept the budget under pressure. In 1985 with 20 full-time employees, the operating budget ran a small deficit. The membership approved a dues increase.[40]

An audit of the books in 1986 recorded current assets of $1.8 million ($5.1 million in 2022 dollars) and put a value on the building of just under $600,000, or $500,000 not counting the mortgage.[41] The gross numbers were a bit misleading. Fully two-thirds of current assets were locked up in the Scholarship Fund, which, like the much smaller Legislative Action Fund and the AFSA Fund for Programs and Awards, could not be used for general expenses.

## NEW DUTIES, NEW CLOUT

Rising revenues let AFSA exercise the rights it had acquired or consolidated in the 1980 Act. The association represented three times as many grievants in 1985 as it had in 1980, and it engaged in six times as many major legal actions.[42] Most grievances were settled quickly, but those that went to the Foreign Service Grievance Board often ran on for months, sometimes for a year or more.[43] AFSA counseled grievants, edited their submissions, reviewed their documents, and represented them in agency proceedings and before the Grievance Board. About half of the cases involved performance evaluations, and most of those had to do with documents that were missing from the files and never considered by selection boards. Other cases dealt with benefits and allowances, and occasionally with salaries.[44]

Labor-management negotiations often failed, sometimes because management could not coordinate a position among the five Foreign Service agencies. Even when negotiations produced an agreement, compliance did not necessarily follow. "There was little correlation," recalled de Rouville, "between negotiating an agreement and actually abiding by it."[45] AFSA frequently turned to the FSIDP and the Foreign Service Labor Relations Board, the dispute-settlement bodies that the act created. AFSA won some early victories (for example, on the special incentive differential allowance, grievance regulations, family visitation travel, and USAID's failure to advertise open positions), which improved the negotiating climate. "Once we started winning," said Dennis Hays, "they tried harder to work with us."[46]

AFSA's new clout brought negotiated gains for members on shipping and storage allowances, the consumables allowance, performance pay, rest and recreation travel, and Fly America regulations, among many other issues.[47] The association developed, and management accepted, a structure and a set of precepts that allowed officers to compete for promotion across as well as within their areas of expertise (cones). This "multifunctional cone" improved the ability of selection boards to identify officers with the potential to serve as chiefs and deputy chiefs of mission; it also reduced friction among various groups in AFSA's membership.[48] When the department refused to negotiate its determination that danger pay was not owed at any post where dependents were allowed, AFSA was able to persuade Congress to make clear in State's Fiscal Year (FY) 1984 authorization legislation that danger pay and the presence of dependents were unrelated matters.[49]

Congress's sympathy for the professional Service on issues such as danger pay had a grim foundation. When Dennis Hays stepped down as AFSA's president in July 1985, he had presided during his three years in office at ceremonies adding 25 names to the memorial plaque.

## THE SENIOR GLUT

Hays had worked to lift the status of secretaries, communicators, security officers, and others who felt disparaged by the officer elite. Hays's successor, Gerry Lamberty, worried more about that elite, not so much in its relation to other members of the Foreign Service as in its relation to the Civil Service and the other agencies of government.

Lamberty was a mid-level FSO in the economic cone, fluent in Spanish, and a specialist in Latin American affairs. He believed the department's determination to promote only officers who had shown a talent for management came at the expense of the "traditional diplomatic skills, area specialization, and substantive knowledge" that are the heart of the Foreign Service. He wanted a Service smart enough to identify excellence and flexible enough to reward it with stretch assignments and rapid promotions. The efforts of the department's management, supported by many in AFSA, to make a tight connection between personal rank and job classification were, he wrote, "an act of suicide" that could lead to the absorption of the Foreign Service by the Civil Service.[50]

Lamberty was not alone in his concern. Tom Boyatt, looking at the Foreign Service Act five years after its passage, said, "We have been decimating" economic and political officers, weakening the ability of the Service to perform its basic mission. The act "has served to accelerate, if not initiate, these destructive trends."[51] The act's "mechanistic approach" to personnel planning, in conjunction with the loss of a large number of senior positions to political appointees, "has contributed to today's reality: a Foreign Service that is becoming a purveyor of consular services and a provider of administrative support to others who deal with foreign policy."[52]

Boyatt estimated that the administration had increased political appointments above customary levels by about 20 policy positions in Washington and 20 ambassadorships abroad. The loss of 40 promotions to minister counselor and career minister ranks, he said, had a "waterfall effect" that he calculated at about 280 promotions lost to political and economic officers throughout the service.[53] Under Secretary for Management Ron Spiers, in an interview published in February 1987, cited the same ratio. Spiers said that political appointees held a net of 22 more senior positions in State than they had in 1981, a loss of jobs for the Senior Foreign Service that has "a sevenfold cascade effect through the ranks."[54]

The problem that Lamberty and Boyatt saw was the senior glut—an excess supply of senior officers for senior positions (or a shortage of senior positions relative to senior officers), first named in 1967 by one of the department's innumerable commissions.[55] Creation of the SFS provided no relief. A few months after the Foreign Service Act's effective date, about 8 percent of the SFS, roughly 60 of 750 officers, were over complement and had no jobs.[56]

The association placed the blame both on outside appointees filling positions that in the past had gone to career personnel and on a large number of stretch assignments with mid-level officers placed in senior positions. "We can recall," said a 1981 editorial in the *Journal*, "when Dr. Kissinger had 10 to 12 officers on his staff at the NSC [National Security Council]. There are none today. We can recall when an equal number worked in Policy Planning. There is one career officer on that staff today." Outsiders, including senior officials from other agencies, held jobs in intelligence and research, political-military affairs, and international narcotics matters. And "ambitious and capable middle-grade officers" held down a number of senior jobs.[57] Bill Bacchus confirmed AFSA's analysis.

"The problem is not one of absolute numbers," he wrote. "There are always fewer senior officers than . . . senior positions." But "for some senior officers there are no appropriate jobs, either because they do not have needed skills and experience, because jobs are filled from the outside, or because they are filled by more junior officers, who in early 1985 held about 16 percent of senior positions."[58]

As more and more Class 1 officers failed to win promotion and were forced into retirement, positions the association had taken as a professional organization and as a labor union came into conflict. AFSA had argued at least since 1946 that selection-out and a "flow-through" personnel system would strengthen the professional capacity of the Service. But the up-or-out principle was hard for the union to defend when large numbers of officers faced separation before reaching the senior ranks. The idea that a career might end honorably at FS-1 (Foreign Service officer, Class 1), as a military career might end at the rank of colonel, turned out to be less attractive in practice—or in person—than it had been in principle.

The squeeze on promotions divided AFSA against itself. Boyatt's analysis set economic and political officers against their colleagues in the administrative and consular cones. At an open meeting in December 1985, Lamberty said that the department's personnel policies led junior officers to support the forced retirement of Class 1 officers, Class 1 officers to cheer when senior officers were pushed out, and senior officers to fight against stretch assignments for their juniors.[59] Although Lamberty said, "Now we realize we are all in the same boat," divisions in the Service persisted.

Lamberty argued that the senior glut was an artificial construct created by misguided personnel policies. "There is no bulge at the top of the Service," he wrote in 1984, before he became AFSA's president.[60] The senior ranks at the time were about 700 of 4,100 FSOs, or 17 percent, well below the average 21 percent ratio of the previous two decades.[61] Lamberty warned that "exaggerated concern" about unassigned seniors would lead to a rigid assignments system in which rank in person had little meaning, because personal rank would have to match job classification. The Foreign Service would then look like the Civil Service. Flexibility would be gone, with no compensating operational advantages.[62]

Lamberty blamed the large number of unassigned senior officers on the department's fascination, dating from the 1960s, with identifying and promoting officers believed to have a talent for management. The department's purpose, "to put the Foreign Service in charge of the international operations of all the U.S. agencies," was never achieved, but officers' frantic search for the program-direction assignments deemed essential to advancement distorted the personnel system. Officers found it advantageous to be in Washington, "even in over-complement status," rather than overseas, where there were "fewer ticket-punching assignments." Lamberty saw the Foreign Service at risk. The way the act is being administered, he said, "may well lead to its end as a separate corps."[63]

AFSA, obviously conflicted, did not challenge the department on stretch assignments, but it did campaign against the proliferation of non-career appointments, including of civil servants, to Senior Foreign Service positions. These efforts had some effect in USAID, although an AFSA lawsuit challenging the agency's management over its interpretation of the Obey Amendment was unsuccessful.[64]

Money, the root of so many evils, was the root of the personnel crisis. The White House sent tight budgets to Congress, and Congress made them tighter. For FY 1987, President Ronald Reagan requested $3.3 billion ($8.8 billion in 2022 dollars) for the administration of foreign affairs functions. Congress cut that request by $1.2 billion, a 36 percent hit. "We are in a particularly difficult position," said Ron Spiers, "because we are not a program agency. . . . We have to cut people [rather than programs]."[65] To this assertion, AFSA, despite its protests, had no good answer.

Although AFSA fought for flexibility at State, it opposed it at USAID, where agency management wanted to extend the permissible time in class for Class 1 officers from seven to 10 years. "These extensions," said AFSA's USAID Standing Committee, "could cause blockage to promotions and mobility."[66] AFSA's instinct was to oppose any proposal from management at USAID as "yet another in a long line . . . of 11th-hour bad management practices that tend to postpone problems rather than solve them."[67] If USAID's management had pushed for a rigid approach to force more Class 1 officers into retirement, it is possible that AFSA would have taken the opposite position.

Under budgetary pressure, the problem-solving spirit that had led AFSA and management to cooperate on the drafting of the 1980 Act evaporated. At an open meeting that AFSA organized in 1986, Under Secretary Spiers and Director General George Vest argued that thinning the senior ranks was the inevitable and intended result of the 1980 Act that AFSA had supported. More than 100 officers, Spiers said, would be separated in 1987 for exceeding TIC limits. When AFSA President Gerry Lamberty argued for a more flexible approach, Spiers said it had been AFSA, rebelling against alleged cronyism in the old promotion system, that had demanded the "more precise series of hurdles" that were now in place.[68]

The association put its case in a letter to Secretary of State George Shultz. "The department is managing the Foreign Service personnel system to the detriment of our national interest," it said, and made the odd prediction that forcing officers into retirement would raise costs, because the government would have to pay both their pensions and the salaries of their replacements.[69] Shultz brushed the letter aside, saying that "none of the arguments I have heard to date have convinced me that the system has been mismanaged."[70]

## THE 1987 ELECTIONS

Two groups responded to the election call in February 1987, and for the first time since 1981, AFSA held a contested election. The election was the first to take place under the bylaws adopted in 1985 that provided for a vice president from each constituency. Members of Gerry Lamberty's board—with the notable exception of Lamberty himself—formed the Action slate, led by Hartford Jennings as candidate for president and Thea de Rouville as candidate for State vice president. Jennings had served three years on the State Standing Committee, and de Rouville had been on the AFSA Governing Board since 1979. Vice presidential candidates Frank Young of USAID and Steve Telkins of USIA were also current board members, as were several other members of the slate.

Lamberty joined a competing Renewal team—the team did not include candidates for all offices and did not call itself a slate—headed by Perry Shankle, a political officer and, like Lamberty, a specialist in Latin American affairs. Lamberty was standing as a candidate for State representative, the position to which he had been elected in 1985, when he had a chance to go to Guatemala as deputy chief of mission to Ambassador Jim Michel, the State Department lawyer and civil servant who had done so much to put the Foreign Service Act of 1980 together. Ballots had been cast but not counted when Lamberty resigned his AFSA position and dropped out of the campaign. The board chose Frank Young to complete the last two months of what had originally been Bob Keeley's term.

In 1982 Dennis Hays had built a campaign on specialists, junior officers, a balanced ticket, and bread-and-butter issues. Perry Shankle and his Renewal team took the opposite course. The Renewal team was unbalanced—six active-duty State employees, one State retiree, and a USAID officer—and pledged to pay greater attention to professional issues. Shankle singled out Thea de Rouville for attack, saying that she had dominated the board for eight years and had "presided over the reduction in the average grade of Foreign Service officers by about half a grade."[71]

The Action slate ran on its record and boasted of its experience. An independent candidate for president, Paul Molineaux, argued that AFSA's incumbent leadership failed to build consensus and that Perry Shankle "stands for privilege." John Hemenway, who had been elected president in 1975 and had been recalled a few months after taking office, also ran an independent candidacy, declaring in italics that "*AFSA should work to get Ron Spiers fired.*"[72]

The election results were evidence of intense dissatisfaction, even anger, across AFSA's membership. More than a third of the membership voted—a high turnout for an AFSA election. Perry Shankle carried only the State constituency although by a large enough margin to offset—barely—his losses elsewhere. He won with 1,003 out of 3,181 ballots cast, only 31 percent of the vote, and just nine votes more than Hartford Jennings. John Hemenway, whose term in office 10 years before had ended in shame and disgrace (see pages 79–83), carried 22 percent of the total vote and outpolled Shankle at USAID and among retirees. Another frequent independent candidate, John Harter, lost his race for secretary but carried 29 percent of the vote.

Shankle's Renewal team won all but one of the offices for which it competed but in no case by a majority.[73] Thin as it was, the victory proved enduring: AFSA's leadership followed Shankle's "professionalism first" approach for the next six years, through four presidents and two nearly uncontested elections. But as often happens in politics, the changes and results the Renewal team had promised proved hard to deliver.

# 8

## Renewal, 1987–1997

The new approach that Perry Shankle and his renewal team promised in 1987 did not change the budgetary facts. The squeeze was on.

Budgetary authority for the State Department fell by about 6.5 percent between Fiscal Year 1986 and FY1987.[1] The department closed 13 consulates over two years and reduced the number of deputy assistant secretaries by 21. In a downgrading exercise, the number of senior positions in the department in Washington fell by about 130, and many of the remaining positions went to non-career appointees. At the same time, some 70 percent of the senior officers scheduled for retirement were given limited career extensions that allowed them to stay in place. The top of the Foreign Service was full beyond capacity.

The Service had become an up-or-out institution with lots of out and little up. In FY1987, 120 mid-level officers exceeded their time-in-class limits and were pushed into retirement.[2] More than 40 Class 1 officers filed a grievance with the full support of the American Foreign Service Association; the Foreign Service Grievance Board ruled against them on every count.[3]

Secretary of State George Shultz fought hard for resources but did not often win. "We are being brutalized in the budget process," he told a crowd at an open meeting in the Dean Acheson Auditorium. The department planned to cut 1,300 of its 22,000 employees worldwide, cuts that would be especially painful "because State Department employees give taxpayers their money's worth." When the audience applauded at the end of his remarks, he rebuked them and asked for silence, given the nature of his message.[4]

## AFSA'S TWO HATS

New AFSA president Perry Shankle preferred the homburg to the hard hat. From the beginning of his term, Shankle wanted a "renewed emphasis" on professional issues, of which the most important was the budget. He agreed with Under Secretary for Management Ron Spiers that at the State Department, "reductions in funding mean reductions in people"; at the same time, he blamed management policies for "forcing out some of our best officers." To undo budgetary cuts, "we will have to convince both the Congress and the public that the Foreign Service is the first line of defense, and that a well-funded first line is in the national interest."[5]

Shankle asked the Governing Board to give more weight to professional than to union issues.[6] His draft policy statement on the subject read:

> AFSA's role as a trade union is determined by its agreements with the agencies and the Foreign Service Act. AFSA's role as a professional organization, however, is unlimited. . . . Some critical issues for the membership are specifically outside the purview of AFSA as a trade union, but can be dealt with from the perspective of a professional organization. It is primarily through its role as a professional organization that AFSA can influence the public and Congress for the benefit of the membership and the Service.[7]

The board never formally adopted Shankle's draft, but the association followed its ideas and priorities for the next six years.

Shankle's regard for AFSA's professional role recalled in many ways the attitudes of the original Young Turks of 1968 (when AFSA was not yet a union), but his vision of AFSA and the Foreign Service was, in fact, quite different. That became clear when Congress, dissatisfied with the Foreign Service that emerged from its budget cutting, convoked a new Commission on the Foreign Service Personnel System.[8] The commission, chaired by retired FSO John Thomas, a former assistant secretary for administration, called for a legislative overhaul of the Foreign Service Act of 1980 that would remove employees of the Departments of Agriculture and Commerce from the Foreign Service system and build a unified Foreign Service across State, the U.S. Information Agency, and the U.S. Agency for International Development. A unified Foreign Service, the commission said, would need a strong director general who is outside the State Department and no longer serves as the department's director of personnel.

The Young Turks had advocated just such a system, but 20 years later AFSA had abandoned that vision. As Perry Shankle explained, "The Foreign Service Act of 1946 tried to establish a unified Foreign Service, but experience since then has demonstrated this is not possible. . . . The Director General should retain the authority and prestige that come with directing the personnel system of the largest Foreign Service agency as he attempts to coordinate the policies of the other Foreign Service agencies."[9]

The Department of State had always opposed a unified Foreign Service, but now its departing under secretary for management, Ivan Selin, switched sides. In a valedictory talk to members of the Foreign Service in 1991, he argued for one Foreign Service across five agencies, to which all personnel assigned overseas would be seconded.[10]

The Thomas Commission, in another roll-back-the-clock recommendation, argued that "the professional association and the labor union functions should be separate."[11] Perry Shankle, of course, argued the contrary: "AFSA, with its combination of professional and labor union interests, should be a model for public employee organizations."[12]

The Thomas Commission's report, like most of the many similar studies undertaken since 1946, had no discernible effect on the structure or management of the Foreign Service. Partisan differences in Congress, where the chairman and the ranking member of the Senate Foreign Relations Committee—Senators Claiborne Pell (D-R.I.) and Jesse Helms (R-N.C.), respectively—held strong and opposing views of the Service, made legislative action nearly impossible.[13] And administrative action had little support. Indeed, the department undercut the Thomas Commission by convening a commission of its own headed by Ambassador L. Paul "Jerry" Bremer III. The reports of the Bremer and Thomas Commissions were played off against each other, reducing the likelihood that either one would produce much action.[14] The department then assembled a new management task force, which produced a 1992 report titled *State 2000*.[15]

## False Starts

Shankle; State Vice President Evangeline Monroe; her successor, Charles "Chuck" Schmitz; and the Governing Board tried a variety of initiatives to improve the professional reputation of the Foreign Service. Their efforts were hard to launch and harder to sustain.

In one such effort, Shankle and Monroe, after hearing "disparaging comments" on Capitol Hill from members and staff, persuaded the board to "seek to establish" a public relations contract with Washington law firm Arnold & Porter and its new consulting arm, APCO. Monroe reported that the Una Chapman Cox Foundation, a nonprofit public foundation established in 1980 to support a strong Foreign Service, was considering a gift of $50,000 ($121,000 in 2022 dollars) to AFSA for the Arnold & Porter project. Shankle had detailed discussions of the project with William D. Rogers, a senior partner at the firm and a former under secretary of State for economic affairs.[16] But no formal agreement was ever reached, and the relationship withered.

Other efforts also fizzled out. An attempt to develop a "Foreign Service credo" jointly with State's management ended when Under Secretary Spiers, who had initially backed the idea, pulled out.[17] A "professional concerns project," intended to produce a study for the transition team of the winner of the 1988 presidential election, had no result.[18] Shankle told the board in June 1988 that he wanted "to find a way to send AFSA's message into the political world, such as the presidential campaigns and platform committees," but there is no record of any action taken.[19]

The association worked hard at press relations and placed Foreign Service stories in national as well as regional outlets. A *New York Times* story that blamed the Foreign Service Act of 1980 for the large number of up-or-out retirements quoted Shankle: "These numbers go way beyond dropping some of the weaker players off the table. . . . There just aren't enough people of quality with this kind of experience."[20] Shankle told United Press International, a wire service, that the cuts came "at a time when the Central Intelligence Agency is trying to take over foreign policy." According to United Press International, Shankle said that AFSA was coming up with alternative ways to reduce costs, including "doing without some of the latest communications equipment."[21]

## Outreach

Money troubles hampered AFSA's efforts to draw attention to the Foreign Service and build its reputation. All of the outreach programs depended on outside contributions. None of the programs was endowed; AFSA had to scramble constantly to maintain funding. The association was caught in a funding trap: Outreach programs that grew with success became more expensive and harder to sustain.

Chuck Schmitz won the Governing Board's support for an "international associates" program, an unwitting reprise of the "corresponding members" program that U. Alexis Johnson had championed in the mid-1960s. Schmitz planned a series of conferences and events on topics that would attract multinational corporations and international banks as paying international associates of AFSA, with access to Senior Foreign Service personnel and other policy experts. The program would build links between the Foreign Service and the business community and would present the Service as a repository of expertise and a source of creative policy ideas for advancing U.S. commercial interests.

In the first year of the program, AFSA ran conferences on subjects such as climate change (in 1989!), energy, and relations with Mexico. The high point was a splashy, all-day affair cosponsored with the Conference Board and featuring Vice President Dan Quayle. It was here that Deputy Secretary Larry Eagleburger unveiled a "Bill of Rights for U.S. Business," a seven-point list of what American businesses could expect from Foreign Service posts overseas. Eagleburger's speech revived energy and interest across the State Department in commercial promotion for the first time since the Department of Commerce had taken over the function in 1980.[22] But the conference itself lost money. Subsequent events were less ambitious, and participation leveled off. The program staggered on until the end of 2004.[23]

Planning for an AFSA speakers' bureau, to provide speakers "on the challenges and rewards of serving our country abroad" to audiences around the country, began in 1990.[24] The Una Chapman Cox Foundation put up most of the money, and the program reached some 70 audiences in its first year.[25] By 1994, however, funding had run out, and the program temporarily ended.

At the end of 1987, the association hired Dick Thompson for a new position as coordinator for professional issues.[26] Thompson brought fresh energy to the awards programs, which had seen nominations dwindle in quality and quantity. In his first year on the job, the number of nominations rose sharply to 42 for the four principal awards: the Harriman, Rivkin, and Herter Awards and the Avis Bohlen Award, which was introduced in 1982 to honor the Foreign Service family member who has done the most to advance the interests of the United States.[27] Thompson also expanded a program of luncheon speakers, relaunching the series with Larry Eagleburger, then president of the consulting firm Kissinger Associates. At a cost of just $1,100, Thompson put together *Duty and Danger* (1988), a book of stories of Foreign Service personnel performing courageously in perilous circumstances. His work bolstered AFSA's reputation in difficult times.

**Box 8.1.** Foreign Service Showbiz

In 2002 the Fox television network developed a series called *The American Embassy* centered on the adventures of a vice consul in London who joined the Foreign Service to escape her dysfunctional family in Toledo, Ohio. Four episodes aired before the show was canceled.[a]

CBS had more success with *Madam Secretary*, a political drama starring Téa Leoni as Secretary of State that ran for six seasons from 2014 to 2019. Leoni's "Madam Secretary" ran the State Department with a handful of mostly young and handsome aides. The Foreign Service was barely visible.

In 2015 HBO aired *The Brink*, a wild, crude, and deliberately offensive comedy with Tim Robbins as Secretary of State and Jack Black as a junior Foreign Service officer in Pakistan. The show ran for one 10-episode season.

A Netflix dramatic series titled *The Diplomat*, which stars Keri Russell as a career diplomat named U.S. ambassador to London, began a scheduled eight-episode run in April 2023 and was renewed for a second season. The Foreign Service community enjoyed mocking some unrealistic elements of the show but also found that it brought positive attention and new public awareness of the Foreign Service. (An aside: An associate producer told the *FSJ* that AFSA's *Inside a U.S. Embassy* book was a "well-worn" and "daily used" resource on set.)

More seriously, the Public Broadcasting System (PBS) aired "The American Diplomat," profiling three African American diplomats (including career FSO Terence Todman) of the 1950s and 1960s.[b] Like the PBS show "Profiles in Diplomacy," "The American Diplomat" was funded by the Cox Foundation.

*Argo*, a fictionalized account of the rescue of American diplomats hiding in the Canadian embassy in Tehran after revolutionaries seized the American embassy in 1979, won the Academy Award for Best Picture for 2012.

The Foreign Service bloggers called *Two Crabs* have compiled an entertaining list of Foreign Service–related films and TV series from 1939 to 2021.[c]

The Association for Diplomatic Studies and Training (https://adst.org /podcasts/) and the American Academy of Diplomacy (https://www.academyof diplomacy.org/program/podcasts/) present podcasts about diplomacy and the Foreign Service.

a. AFSA News, *FSJ*, May 2002, 9; and "The American Embassy," Wikipedia, last edited January 31, 2023, http://en.wikipedia.org/wiki/The_American_Embassy.
b. "The American Diplomat: First-Class Patriots Abroad, Second-Class Citizens at Home," *American Experience*, directed by Leola Calzolai-Stewart, PBS, February 15, 2022, https://www.pbs.org/wgbh/americanexperience/films/american-diplomat/.
c. "Foreign Service Flicks!," *Two Crabs* (blog), updated September 2022, https://twocrabs .blogs.com/2crabs/2019/06/foreignserviceonscreen.html.

In 1991 the Public Broadcasting System aired a one-hour documentary titled "Profiles in Diplomacy," presenting "a firsthand look at six Foreign Service officers as they fulfill their duties abroad and at the Department of State." Funding for the film came from the Una Chapman Cox Foundation; AFSA shared its mailing list with the foundation at cost for the solicitation of matching funds.[28] (See box 8.1 for other television programs and films that have focused on the Foreign Service.)

## AFSA, Security, and Support for Members

Some of the most senior members of the Service found fault with AFSA, however. Robert Lamb, a career Foreign Service officer, had been confirmed as assistant secretary of State for administration in 1983. In that capacity, he was responsible for the Office of Security (SY). When the bombing of U.S. embassies in Kuwait and Beirut led to heavy loss of life, Congress and the administration recast the Office of Security as the Bureau of Diplomatic Security (DS), with greatly increased resources and responsibilities. Lamb became its first assistant secretary.[29]

AFSA and DS were in frequent conflict. As required by its union status, AFSA often defended employees whose security clearances DS proposed to revoke. The association also had doubts about the efficacy of many of the security measures recommended by the Advisory Panel on Overseas Security led by retired Adm. B. R. "Bobby" Inman and convened after the Kuwait and Beirut bombings.[30] In November 1987, it filed an unfair labor practice complaint with the Federal Labor Relations Authority to force the department to submit security regulations to collective bargaining. But Lamb had full support from Under Secretary Spiers and strong support on Capitol Hill. He publicly criticized AFSA as insensitive to security requirements, even going so far as to call the association "criminally negligent."[31]

After such strong words, Shankle and Monroe met with Lamb to calm things down. The Governing Board set up a committee to examine AFSA's relationship with the employees of Diplomatic Security and talked about establishing an AFSA award for DS members.[32] At first, hotter heads prevailed, and AFSA filed a grievance against the department and the DS Bureau. Lamb then retracted the charge that AFSA was criminally negligent, and AFSA dropped the grievance.[33] The underlying tension remained.[34]

Some other senior diplomats felt that AFSA let them down. Arthur Hartman, ambassador to Moscow, had been attacked in Congress and in the press after Marine guards at the embassy were accused of spying for the Soviets (one was later convicted). According to Monroe, Hartman was "dismayed" at AFSA's lack of support for him.[35] Cuban affairs director Myles Frechette, wrongly accused by the powerful Cuban American National Foundation of supporting a deportation order he had opposed, was left to fight the charges on his own; neither the department nor AFSA stood up for him.[36] Senator Helms placed a hold on the nomination of career FSO Richard Viets, who had served as ambassador to Tanzania and Jordan, to be ambassador to Portugal, and Helms's staff made false allegations against Viets personally. Viets came to believe that AFSA, which offered him no support, opposed his nomination. Shankle told Viets, and members of the Senate Foreign Relations Committee, that AFSA as a matter of policy did not endorse nominees but wished Ambassador Viets every success in his appointment. The appointment, however, was not confirmed; the White House submitted it twice, but the nomination died in the Senate.[37]

For all its struggles, the association had some notable successes. At USAID, historically the agency most hostile to the union, AFSA negotiated an agreement giving employees 25 years from the date of tenure to reach the senior grades, with no TIC restrictions in the intervening grades.[38] The agreement brought USAID into compliance with the Foreign Service Act of 1980, which required that all Foreign Service agencies establish TIC limitations, but it maintained flexibility for management and secured for employees the prospect of a nearly 30-year career. At State, AFSA negotiated an agreement with management on polygraph testing, an issue that in 1985 had led Secretary Shultz to threaten to resign.[39] Under the agreement, testing was voluntary only and limited to a handful of employees under exceptional circumstances.

Negotiation, though, proved less potent than litigation and lobbying. The association joined seven members of Congress in a suit to prevent the Department of State from requiring employees to sign agreements prohibiting the disclosure not of classified but of "classifiable" information. AFSA and the other litigants carried the case to the Supreme Court and won.[40] Litigation and congressional pressure forced the department to abandon a plan to put Foreign Service employees assigned to Soviet bloc countries through psychological testing.[41] An institutional grievance forced USAID to back off a plan to place a non-career employee in a Foreign Service position, and similar litigation compelled the agency to support a paid, full-time vice president at AFSA.[42]

Lobbying on the Hill by AFSA and others defeated a measure sponsored by Senator Helms that would have prevented people leaving government service

**Box 8.2.** AFSA and AFSPA

In 1987 AFSA tried to take control of the American Foreign Service Protective Association (AFSPA), the legally separate organization that offered health and other forms of insurance to members of the Foreign Service. For many years AFSA and AFSPA had not only overlapping memberships but also overlapping boards: Members of the AFSA Governing Board by custom also served as trustees of AFSPA. The two organizations had also been entangled financially, and the financially stronger AFSPA held a $200,000 AFSA mortgage note.

By the 1980s, however, the relationship had changed. AFSA Governing Board members no longer sat on the AFSPA Board, and in 1981 AFSA contracted with underwriters and began to offer certain types of insurance itself. AFSPA, however, had by far the bigger business, including sponsorship of the Foreign Service Benefit Plan (health insurance), under contract to the Office of Personnel Management. AFSA complained that the AFSPA Board was "accountable to no one" because its members were self-selected, not elected. In 1982 AFSA's president wrote to his AFSPA counterpart to urge AFSPA to elect trustees, hold annual meetings, produce an annual report, and set up a consultative committee of members to advise on policy. AFSPA politely rejected this unsolicited advice.

As AFSA's payments on the AFSPA loan came to an end in 1987, AFSPA offered informally to purchase AFSA's insurance programs. AFSA not only said no but also proposed to take over AFSPA, replace its board with AFSA people, and require nonmembers of AFSA who joined the health plan to pay AFSA an annual fee. The proposal was dead on arrival.

In subsequent years, the two associations developed a cooperative relationship, serving many of the same members in different ways.[a] AFSPA broadened its base and by 2022 had 87,000 active-duty and retired members, including civilian employees of the Department of Defense, Civil Service employees of the Department of State, and members of the Civil Service with an overseas mission, regardless of agency. It established the Senior Living Foundation in 1988 to assist retired members of the Foreign Service who are physically or mentally unable to cope with old age.

a. Minutes, AFSA Governing Board meeting, November 25, 1980; AFSA Insurance Program Trust Agreement of January 21, 1981; Hugh Wolff, chairman of the board of AFSA trustees for the insurance program, to AFSA Governing Board, draft memo, August 7, 1987; and Paula Jakub, chief executive officer of AFSPA, interview, October 22, 2013. The AFSA documents are in AFSA's archives. See also the website for AFSPA, https://www.afspa.org.

from working for international organizations for at least 18 months.[43] AFSA's lobbying of the House Civil Service Subcommittee led the administration to drop a plan to deny employees the right to appeal a security clearance decision.[44] Lobbying also killed an amendment, offered by Rep. Trent Lott (R-Miss.), to prevent anyone who negotiates on behalf of the Department of State from belonging to AFSA.[45]

The legal staff in 1988 handled more than 200 employee grievances, up 78 percent from 1985.[46] AFSA hired a second staff attorney for the Labor Management Office and a third grievance counselor for the Department of Member Services in 1992.[47]

The association also took up less noble causes, including an effort to block restrictions on the sales of private property by U.S. government personnel overseas. Such sales, especially of automobiles that diplomatic personnel could bring to a foreign post free of duty, could bring windfall profits to a lucky few. AFSA fought congressional efforts to end the practice and, when an amendment passed anyway, asked the House and Senate Foreign Affairs Committees to reconsider. The association's position, and its tenacity, disturbed some AFSA members. Bill Harrop complained in a letter to the *Foreign Service Journal* that AFSA's stand "will tend to confirm the incorrect perception . . . that we in the Foreign Service are spoiled and self-serving."[48]

## Renewal Renewed

When Perry Shankle looked back on his two years in office, he made the case that without AFSA, things would have been worse. AFSA's lobbying secured from Congress enough funding to prevent a 10 percent reduction in force. Management proposals for widespread use of lie detector and psychological testing were abandoned. But Shankle admitted that on Capitol Hill, "many members and staff do not view us as hard-working professionals." The personnel system, he said, still forces good people into involuntary retirement, leaves people unassigned and positions vacant, and makes ambassadors of unqualified political fundraisers.[49]

The modesty of Shankle's claims did not keep members of his team from sweeping the elections in 1989, but AFSA Secretary Theodore "Ted" S. Wilkinson III led a Continuity and Renewal ticket as candidate for president, and Shankle ran for Wilkinson's position as secretary. Chuck Schmitz, the outgoing State vice president, won election as the retiree vice president, a new position. In 1991 Hume Horan, who had returned from service as ambassador to Saudi

Arabia (his third embassy), led a Continuity and Outreach slate to a sweep of all offices.[50] When Horan resigned to become ambassador to Côte d'Ivoire, the board chose State Vice President William Kirby Jr. to fill out his term. The priorities that had guided the Shankle board remained largely unchanged.

## STATE, USAID, AND USIA

AFSA in 1989 was still very much a State Department organization. Retirees and employees of the department accounted for about 79 percent of the membership.[51] Foreign Service personnel in the Departments of Agriculture and Commerce had yet to choose an exclusive employee representative.

State Department employees, naturally, were the largest consumers of AFSA's services. For example, with a full-time staff of 25, the association provided grievance counseling to 196 State Department employees, 54 USAID employees, and 15 employees of other agencies. About 70 percent of those counseled were AFSA members.[52]

In the spring of 1992, on the earliest date possible under Labor Department rules, AFSA challenged the American Federation of Government Employees for the right to represent Foreign Service employees in the U.S. Information Agency. Even AFSA's supporters in the agency had some doubts about the wisdom of that move. One complained that AFSA was not a labor union but "a professional organization and an elite (even elitist) club" that was "too accommodating," placed too much emphasis on "seeking to influence U.S. foreign policy," and tended to separate "the Foreign Service . . . from our Civil Service colleagues."[53]

The charges had some validity. AFSA's USIA campaigners expected to have a relationship with management that would "obviate the need for loud confrontation." They took public stands against Radio Martí and the proposed Radio Free Asia, and they endorsed stronger efforts to build democracy in the former Soviet Union. They opposed Civil Service "encroachment" on Foreign Service positions in Washington but favored "broadening the opportunities for GS [Civil Service] personnel to serve overseas."[54] AFSA emerged with a solid but not overwhelming win, 358 votes to 267, and AFGE's six-year reign at USIA was over.[55]

## PROFESSIONALISM AND AUSTERITY

Ted Wilkinson shared Perry Shankle's view that professional issues deserved priority over what he sometimes called "militant issues."[56] Wilkinson had high hopes for a positive, cooperative relationship with the new management team that had come into the State Department following the election of President George H. W. Bush. The president, after all, had been ambassador to China and knew the Foreign Service well. Wilkinson also knew the new under secretary for management, Ivan Selin, from undergraduate days at Yale. But old patterns quickly took hold. Within a few weeks of taking office, Wilkinson found himself doing what so many of his predecessors had done: fighting the department on ambassadorial nominations and struggling with cuts in the foreign affairs budget.

## Embassies for Sale

The Foreign Service Act of 1980 required that the president send the Senate Committee on Foreign Relations a statement of qualifications for each nomination of a chief of mission.[57] Sen. Paul Sarbanes (D-Md.) noticed that the statements accompanying the nominations of Melvin Sembler to be ambassador to Australia and Joseph Zappala to be ambassador to Spain were essentially identical. Wilkinson surmised that the White House personnel office did not bother to distinguish between the two big contributors, who were both Florida developers.[58] AFSA sued to gain access to all the statements. "When we saw the texts," said Wilkinson, "it was shameful."[59] In several cases, the amount of the nominees' campaign contributions was prominently featured. AFSA did not fight the Sembler nomination but did oppose that of Zappala, whom the Senate nevertheless confirmed by a vote of 79 to 20.[60]

AFSA had better results opposing the nomination of Joy Silverman to be ambassador to Barbados. Silverman and her husband had given Republican groups some $300,000 (about $716,000 in 2022 dollars) during the election cycle, and she had no substantive qualifications for the job. The Senate, controlled by Democrats and pushed by Sarbanes, did not act on her nomination and returned it to the White House at the end of the session. Wilkinson wrote that "no clearer test of the administration's real intentions could be devised than the decision whether or not to resubmit the nomination. . . . Barbados is a flower in our front garden; we need to cultivate it carefully."[61] Wilkinson got his wish. The administration did not send her name up a second time but gave her a seat on the board of directors of the Kennedy Center instead.[62]

The White House defended the quality of its chief-of-mission nominees. Chase Untermeyer, chief of personnel, accepted AFSA's invitation and told a Foreign Service audience that nominees who had given $100,000 or more were "relatively few."[63]

The fight over ambassadors, said Wilkinson, "is the constant cross that AFSA has to bear. It's one of the less pleasant duties of the AFSA president."[64] A survey of the AFSA membership in February 1990 found strong support for a vigorous and public stand on the issue.[65] And whether due to AFSA's pressure, or Sarbanes's, or the president's proclivities, AFSA was able to report that "nearly all new ambassadorial nominees in 1990 were career officers, and no new case of egregiously unqualified political appointees arose."[66] Indeed, no such case arose for quite some time. In the first 18 months of Bill Clinton's administration, almost 75 percent of ambassadorial appointments went to career officers. The *Washington Post* wrote in June 1993 that "the number of big-money or straight politico ambassadorships is at a record low."[67]

## Protecting the Institution

The more serious threat was continued austerity. Congress and the administration justified lowered spending on defense and international affairs as a peace dividend, made possible by the collapse of the Berlin Wall, the Warsaw Pact, and then the Soviet Union itself.

AFSA called the budget the "transcendent issue" and used "all the influence we could bring to bear" to prevent severe cuts.[68] State's operating budget in FY1991 was smaller in real terms than it had been in 1990. Only the administration's last-minute acceptance of a budget that violated the president's campaign promise of no new taxes avoided a government shutdown and furlough.

AFSA sought ways to stretch agency resources while promoting the interests of its members. Its most successful proposal, first advanced in 1990, was the creation of a roster of retired Foreign Service members willing to return to active service for specific, temporary assignments. Despite verbal support from the highest levels, the State Department dawdled. What came to be called the "Foreign Service Reserve corps," a registry of more than 500 volunteers who pledged to be available at short notice, finally took shape at the end of 1992.[69] A few reservists were called back to duty to staff positions in new posts in the former Soviet Union, but the program did not take off and ended in 1999.[70]

Even the good news in the budget had a bad-news component. The Civil Service and the Foreign Service won a pay raise, intended to bring federal pay into parity with the private sector, but the raise reduced the funds available to the department for other purposes.[71] The Service struggled to staff new posts and responsibilities under rapidly changing conditions across Eastern Europe and the rest of the postcommunist world. When AFSA President Wilkinson

met with Secretary of State James A. Baker in September 1990, he was unsym-
pathetic. Sounding like Secretary Rusk, Baker said that morale in the Foreign
Service was not one of his priorities. He added that he had done enough on the
budget and would not seek additional resources from Capitol Hill.[72]

AFSA, it seemed, was the only organization that tried to see the Foreign
Service whole. Congress, when it paid attention to the Service at all, seemed to
see only the institution's shortcomings: a white male monopoly that had almost
no women or minorities in the upper ranks, weaknesses in management and in
security, and shortages in specific skills—for example, in Arabic and in export
promotion. The leadership of the Department of State seemed unable or unwilling to mount a coherent defense of the Service. It was left to AFSA to explain the
tensions and contradictions between hiring for diversity and the need for special
skills; between telling officers to punch tickets marked "management experience" and helping them acquire language, area, and functional expertise; and
between a smaller Service and one prepared to represent the United States in the
new countries taking shape in Eastern Europe and Central Asia.

The budget squeeze frustrated AFSA's efforts to elevate professional concerns.
Circumstances forced AFSA to devote the bulk of its attention and resources to
protecting jobs and sharing pain equitably. Despite the consistent preference of
Presidents Shankle, Wilkinson, Horan, and Kirby, the union side of the house
grew in importance as the professional organization struggled.

## NEW LEADERSHIP: THE HARRIS YEARS, 1993–1997

The long run of weakly contested elections ended in 1993, when Tex Harris ran
for the presidency. Harris was one of the Young Turks who had worked with Bill
Harrop and Tom Boyatt to secure AFSA's position as a union. He had clear ideas
about what AFSA should be, and he was distressed by what he saw as a lack of
energy and a lack of direction. He organized a Professionalism and Participation slate to challenge a slate headed by the incumbent State, USAID, and USIA
vice presidents. A number of independent candidates, including John Harter for
president, were also on the ballot.

"AFSA's leadership has settled into a comfortable rut," Harris argued, and
AFSA itself had become "little more than an 'ombudsman'" dealing with "mostly
routine administrative issues." The association's "smooth working relationship"
with management at State and USAID was cause for concern, not for satisfaction.
"Attention must be called to the relentless shrinkage of our resources even as . . .
[our] responsibilities proliferate." Harris promised a return to the "creativity and

dynamism" of the early 1970s, and he asked members to raise their participation beyond paying dues and reading the *Journal*.[73]

The incumbents' campaign statement struck a defensive tone that validated many of Harris's contentions. The incumbents pledged "to see that those who do their professional duty in an honest and legal manner not become victims" and that "budget reductions . . . be carried out in a fair manner." They promised to push for "uniform and understandable travel regulations." Like the Harris slate, they also promised "to reinvigorate AFSA," a tacit acknowledgment that even the incumbents thought vigor was in short supply.[74]

Harris squeaked by with just 42 percent of the vote. His slate won only six of the 18 contests for seats on the board.[75] But a win is a win, and Harris made the most of it. He completed his two-year term, ran again, won again, and served two more years.

## Big Government Is Over

AFSA often addressed its membership in hyperbolic and apocalyptic tones. An AFSA annual report credited "massive membership involvement" with stalling an "unprecedented assault on federal employee benefits"—namely, the requirement, already adopted by the time the report was published, that new federal employees be enrolled in the Social Security system.[76] The annual report for 1986–1987 said of the proposed budget for FY1988 that "never in history has the Service faced such severe problems."[77] An October 1995 column by State Vice President Alphonse "Al" La Porta compared involuntary retirements from the Foreign Service with the mass killings in Cambodia.[78] But as Tex Harris took up his position, the Service really was in trouble.

Congress and the administration were determined to show that, in President Clinton's words, "the era of big government is over." Spending on foreign affairs (the Function 150 budget) fell in real terms from 1993 to 2000. In each of those years, the Service brought in too few new officers to replace those who resigned or retired, while senior officers very rarely left before mandatory retirement. The Service became increasingly top-heavy, and staffing gaps in the middle grades became chronic. Vacancies, especially overseas, rose sharply; at some posts, one of every four desks was empty.[79] Training, especially in professional tradecraft, fell into steep decline, with fewer resources expended and fewer people engaged for fewer hours.[80]

Despite AFSA's strenuous lobbying, Congress placed a cap on the number of Foreign Service and SFS personnel in each of the three main foreign affairs agencies and gave agency heads authority to conduct a layoff to stay within the cap.[81] Senator Helms, who replaced Claiborne Pell as chairman of the Senate Foreign Relations Committee after the Republican victory in the 1994 congressional elections, proposed to abolish the Arms Control and Disarmament Agency (ACDA), USAID, and USIA, and transfer their functions to the Department of State.[82] The National Performance Review—a "reinventing government" project led by Vice President Al Gore—urged USAID to bring its Civil Service and Foreign Service employees into a single personnel system, following the model of the Central Intelligence Agency.[83]

Management turned to downsizing with enthusiasm. The new under secretary for management, Dick Moose, announced his intention to reduce the "size and rank structure" of the department's staff, including the Foreign Service, "in significant ways."[84] Moose was a senior vice president at American Express and a former Foreign Service officer who, in a stellar career, had been a Senate subcommittee staff director, a White House aide, an assistant secretary of State, and the deputy under secretary for management for Secretary Cyrus Vance. But AFSA found him hard to deal with. "Dick Moose was a person who would not listen," said Al La Porta. "There were no reasoned arguments that could penetrate him."[85]

Moose could have coined the slogan "Do more with less." He knew he needed to open new posts in the former Soviet Union, and he planned to spend $300 million (about $618 million in 2022 dollars) on infrastructure improvements. He believed, correctly, that operating funds would be cut by 3.5 percent. He knew Congress would demand cuts in staffing, yet he also believed he could handle the situation. "The areas [in personnel] that need work have been identified," he said when he took up his post. Change would be difficult, he acknowledged. "But if I improve my relationship with the people right above me, and the ones right below me, and the ones off to the side, and if everybody starts doing that, then we can move the mountain."[86]

Tex Harris and his board had come into office eager to take on bread-and-butter issues, but the association's room for maneuver was limited. By law, management had the exclusive right to "hire, assign, direct, lay off, and retain" members of the Service. AFSA could negotiate the impact and implementation of any reductions in force, but management could and did ignore AFSA's advice.

Because the association could not weigh in on the criteria for RIFs, its board never had to choose between basing layoffs on performance or on seniority—between what might be called the "professional model" or the "union model." The agencies developed regulations that blended the two models, awarding

Box 8.3.  Labor-Management Partnerships

The Clinton administration knew that job cuts would not be popular with federal workers. Perhaps to mitigate the impact of workforce reductions, or simply to mollify the federal unions, the administration ordered agency heads to "create labor-management partnerships" by forming councils of managers, employees, and union representatives. The partnerships were to "champion changes" stemming from the National Performance Review that would transform the agencies into "organizations capable of delivering the highest quality services to the American people."[a] After contentious negotiations with agency management, AFSA joined labor-management partnerships at the Department of State, USAID, and USIA. But the partnerships did not change the basic rights or responsibilities of labor or management. Their effect on AFSA's relations with management was cosmetic and fleeting.

a. E.O. 12781, October 1, 1993.

points for high ranking by selection boards and points for years of service, and then laying off those with the lowest scores. AFSA tended to favor giving more weight to seniority but generally avoided the debate over whom to cut.[87] Instead, it pressed management to take creative steps to retain personnel—for example, by allowing employees to transfer from overstaffed to understaffed agencies— and to justify any RIFs with transparent workforce planning.

At State, Moose cut staff through attrition, a policy that lasted throughout the 1990s and did deep, long-term damage. The department's Foreign Service was 8,000 strong in 1992. By mid-1997, it was down by 1,000, with specialists accounting for most of the reduction.[88] New hires were cut almost to zero—the entrance exam for officers was not offered in 1995 or 1996—as were promotions into the Senior Foreign Service. Buyouts offered in 1993 and 1994 encouraged early retirement, and TIC rules, which tended to penalize those who had advanced most rapidly, were rigorously enforced. The result was a Service that was cut haphazardly, with no effort to shape the workforce to likely future needs. Al La Porta at first thought that a formal RIF would be "the most damaging thing that management could do." In retrospect, he saw the "stealth RIF" of attrition, and the way Moose carried it out, as "ruining . . . the core capabilities of the Foreign Service."[89]

USIA and USAID underwent real, immediate reductions in force. At USIA, management wanted to cut 31 Foreign Service employees—15 officers and 16 specialists. AFSA argued, with supporting data, that the cuts could be achieved through attrition. Management backed off its original position but did lay off

---

**Box 8.4.** Harris versus Byrne: "The Tiff about the RIF"

AFSA President Tex Harris used every opportunity to contrast USAID's RIF, which would save the agency $20 million, with its new computer system, which cost the agency $60 million and did not work. Larry Byrne, the agency's top management official, ran into Harris at USAID's headquarters (then located at Main State). As Harris reported the encounter, Byrne said, "I'm fed up with your lies," and promised to "get your Foreign Service benefits and that goddamn phony union."[a]

Harris countered with an outdoor employee rally for "Better Management at AID." He also filed an unfair labor practice complaint with the Foreign Service Labor Relations Board, which ordered USAID to post a notice that it would not threaten the union or interfere with, restrain, or coerce employees in the exercise of their rights.

a. AFSA News, *FSJ*, August 1996, 1, 4.

---

nine officers and six specialists. AFSA took credit for saving 16 jobs.[90] At USAID, management laid off 97 Foreign Service employees (mostly officers in grades FE-OC and FS-1) and 103 Civil Service employees (mostly support staff) in the summer of 1996. AFSA's USAID Vice President Frank Miller endured months of fruitless consultations. In the end, he said, he was "happy to report" that the agency promised to provide employees "the best outplacement service available."[91]

## PRIDE AND PROFESSIONALISM

The Foreign Service was already in trouble well before the RIFs began. Sherman Funk, ending a seven-year term as State's inspector general, detected a lack of discipline and a lowering of standards.[92] To that list, Lannon Walker, the old Young Turk just returned from service as ambassador to Nigeria, added a "persistent degradation of skills," a weakening of the career principle in senior assignments, and a failure to change the profile of the Service "so that it represents our nation's diversity."[93]

Harris was determined to use AFSA to restore a sense of pride and professionalism. By 1994, the association could speak for the whole Foreign Service: In that year AFSA won the right to represent Foreign Service employees in the Foreign Agricultural Service and the Foreign Commercial Service. No other union competed.[94] Representation boosted membership, which rose to 10,722 in 1994 and 11,010 in 1995.[95]

Box 8.5.  Mission Statements

The mission statement for the Foreign Service must act as a lantern, an anchor, and, at times, as a conscience.

—*Tex Harris*

The RIFs and budget cuts, and Senator Helms's efforts to shut down USIA, USAID, and ACDA, brought the Foreign Service to a sort of institutional identity crisis, a basic questioning of purpose. Part of its response was drafting a series of mission statements, which are listed below. The statements were not often drawn on after they were written; the greater benefit was in thinking the problem through and finding an expression of purpose that commanded broad support.

AFSA mission statement (*FSJ*, December 1991, 2)
USAID mission statement (*FSJ*, January 1992, 31–35)
Foreign Service mission statement, AFSA draft (*FSJ*, September 1996, 36)
Foreign Service mission statement (*FSJ*, January 1997, 7)
USIA mission statement (*FSJ*, December 1997, 33)

To boost morale, AFSA persuaded the department to restore retirement ceremonies for all State employees, not just those in the Foreign Service. Criteria for AFSA's awards, which had been relaxed to encourage nominations, were returned to their original rigor. The Governing Board approved a new award, for "lifetime contributions to the conduct of American diplomacy," and named U. Alexis Johnson as the first recipient.[96] The Governing Board expanded AFSA's communications with its membership and increased the frequency of surveys and polls on difficult issues. The Professionalism Committee drafted a mission statement and a motto for the Foreign Service and a statement of criteria for the selection of ambassadors—all of which the board adopted and published.[97]

## The Civil Service and the Foreign Service

Budget cuts were not confined to foreign affairs nor were workforce cuts to the Foreign Service. The Civil Service and the domestic agencies were squeezed in roughly equal measure. In its first month in office, the Clinton administration ordered a 4 percent cut in the federal civilian workforce over three years.[98] The National Performance Review aimed at a 12 percent cut over four years and achieved a 15.4 percent cut over five years.[99] Across the government, employment shrank, but agency missions did not. Managers turned to contractors to take up the slack. By 1999, a federal workforce of 1.8 million was outnumbered by an estimated 4.4 million contract employees.[100] The replacement of federal employees by contractors would be especially dramatic at USAID. Like their Foreign Service colleagues, Civil Service employees in the foreign affairs agencies feared for their jobs and their futures.

The National Performance Review led managers at the Commerce Department and USAID to believe they could make gains in efficiency and performance by integrating their Civil and Foreign Services. At USAID, managers drafted a plan to create a new excepted Service (that is, one not subject to Civil Service regulations) that would require its members to be available for assignment worldwide but would not provide them certain benefits and protections of the Foreign Service system. Neither Civil Service nor Foreign Service personnel reacted well to the plan, and when management found it would be costly to implement, it was dropped.[101] The Foreign Service held on to its overseas positions, but contractors, civil servants, and political appointees took a number of Washington positions that under the 1979 Obey Amendment were supposed to go to Foreign Service personnel.[102]

At the Commerce Department, the Foreign Service was an afterthought, with about 200 people among 40,000 civil servants. The department wanted the FCS to operate as the overseas counterpart of the U.S. Commercial Service, which had trade promotion offices in more than 50 U.S. cities. The two services had a single director general, whose stated main goal was to integrate Civil Service and Foreign Service personnel. Integration of the name was easy: the FCS became part of the U.S. and Foreign Commercial Service (US&FCS), which came to be called simply the "Commercial Service."[103]

Integration of the workforce was harder. The department had never made room for its Foreign Service personnel in Washington or in its domestic field offices. So few Foreign Service employees were assigned to headquarters that when the FCS representative left the AFSA Governing Board in August 1994, no one was eligible to replace him.[104] Finding stateside positions for members of the Foreign Service, an essential part of workforce integration, would have required sending significant numbers of civil servants on foreign assignments where few of them wished to go. Management was reluctant to fight that battle.

And management may well have been distracted, first by 1995 legislation to abolish the Commerce Department and then by the death in April 1996 of Secretary Ron Brown and 11 other Commerce Department officials in a plane crash during a trade mission to Croatia.[105] For the rest of the decade, integration made no progress; it was still an abstraction when the director general of the Commercial Service called it her "primary objective" five years later.[106] The department's management never defined "integration" in practical terms, which may explain why AFSA was able to support it as a goal.[107]

Managers at the Department of Agriculture, unlike their counterparts at Commerce, reserved a number of Washington positions for Foreign Service employees returning from overseas. The Civil Service unions—AFGE and the American Federation of State, County, and Municipal Employees—protested, but management, with support from AFSA, held fast.[108]

There was no talk at the Department of State about integrating the two services. But Dick Moose, who had entered the Foreign Service during Wristonization, wanted "excursion tours and stretch tours for people in the Civil Service to do Foreign Service-type jobs, or jobs that have been reserved or traditionally filled by the Foreign Service."[109] Moose thought with this one step he could address Civil Service perceptions of department favoritism toward the Foreign Service and provide technical expertise in areas such as environmental policy, nonproliferation, and narcotics. AFSA came to see the assignment of outsiders to "jobs . . . traditionally filled by the Foreign Service" as a threat to the career principle and a direct challenge to AFSA's effectiveness as a union. An epic row over the issue would break out after Moose's departure.

## Pride in Hard Times

When the government shut down and employees were furloughed at the end of 1995, AFSA's response energized the association and lifted its reputation.[110] Alongside its rival, AFGE, AFSA organized a rally of State, USAID, and USIA employees in what was sometimes called "Foreign Service Park," the small triangle of land outside AFSA's headquarters. The rally showed AFSA's union side in the most public way, with banners, bullhorns, and speeches to the "brothers and sisters" denouncing House Speaker Newt Gingrich and Secretary of State Warren Christopher with bipartisan fervor.[111] The demonstration helped counter the image of AFSA as an officers' club (all but one member of Harris's board were officers) and a tool of management. Even so, when AFGE invited AFSA to join it in a post-shutdown rally on Capitol Hill, the AFSA Governing Board declined.[112]

## Consolidation

Senator Helms's bill to abolish USIA, USAID, and ACDA and to transfer their functions to the Department of State passed in March 1996 as part of the foreign

**Box 8.6.** Larry Lawrence

Pride, as well as professionalism, impelled AFSA to stand up for the career principle in appointments to senior positions and to oppose the worst of the administration's political nominees. Tex Harris challenged the fitness to serve of Larry Lawrence, President Clinton's nominee to be ambassador to Switzerland, in testimony before the Senate Foreign Relations Committee. Lawrence, owner of the Hotel Del Coronado in San Diego, had given the Democrats nearly $200,000 (about $412,000 in 2022 dollars) in the 1992 election cycle and had raised, he said, millions more.

Lawrence was ignorant of foreign affairs, referring to Switzerland in his confirmation hearings as "our ally" and confusing export controls with export promotion. But he was a patriot, he said, who had been wounded in 1945 when his merchant ship, the *Horace Bushnell*, was torpedoed on the Murmansk run.

Democrats controlled the Senate, but with AFSA's opposition, the committee split evenly and sent Lawrence's name to the Senate floor without a recommendation. AFSA's temerity led Sen. Harlan Mathews (D-Tenn.) to place a hold on 27 unfortunate USAID officers whose promotions were then before the Senate.

After some White House pressure, Republicans joined Democrats in confirming Lawrence, 79 to 16. The hold was lifted, and the USAID officers were promoted. Lawrence and his wife, named a delegate to the World Conservation Union with the personal rank of ambassador, arrived in Bern in March. She was in San Diego to greet President Clinton when he arrived for a vacation at the Lawrences' 35-room beach house two months later.

Lawrence was still ambassador when he died in Bern in 1996. Because of his war wound and a request from the White House, the Army allowed his burial at Arlington National Cemetery. A year later, members of Congress investigating Arlington burials discovered that Lawrence had never been in the Merchant Marine; when the *Horace Bushnell* went down, he was a college student in Chicago. Gravediggers, reported the *New York Times*, dug up his remains and "carted away his granite tombstone, which was engraved with lies."[a]

a. *FSJ*, January 1994, 2; *FSJ*, April 1994, 1; *FSJ*, May 1994, 14; Don van Natta Jr., "Army Secretary Denies Political Tie to Burials and National Cemetery," *New York Times*, November 22, 1997; and Don van Natta Jr. and Elaine Sciolino, "Body, and Tombstone of Lies, Are Removed," *New York Times*, December 12, 1997.

relations authorization legislation for that year. The bill had bipartisan support in both chambers (Sen. John F. Kerry [D-Mass.] was one of 82 senators voting aye) and passed easily, only to be vetoed by President Clinton.[113]

The *Journal* gave the Helms bill a great deal of attention, including a nine-page story and a letter from the senator ("I found [Tex Harris's] views very interesting—and helpful") in May 1995.[114] The association's reaction, however, was muted.

AFSA had initially opposed consolidation, not as a union seeking to preserve jobs but out of concern that performance of the agencies' "key functions—information, development, humanitarian response, normal diplomacy, and advocacy"—would deteriorate. When Bill Harrop, who with Tom Boyatt had returned to the board in 1995 as a retiree representative, argued that consolidation could have great advantages, the issue was pushed off to a working group.[115] The Governing Board remained divided, and AFSA played no role in the congressional debate.

Helms persevered, as did his House counterpart, Rep. Benjamin Gilman (R-N.Y.). A consolidation bill, retaining the abolition of USIA and ACDA but modified to preserve USAID (with an administrator "under the direct authority" of the Secretary of State), passed as part of an omnibus appropriations measure in 1998 and was signed into law.[116] With Harris leaning against consolidation and Harrop and Boyatt arguing in favor, the Governing Board was unable to take a position.[117] The association was a bystander as USIA and ACDA passed into history.

## Diversity

If consolidation split the board and rendered the association mute, the issues associated with diversity split the board without silencing it. State Vice President Todd Stewart wrote, "Diversity, merit, fairness: three goals that all Foreign Service members can endorse. But can we pursue these goals simultaneously?"[118]

Hume Horan certainly thought so. During his brief term (1991–1992) as AFSA president, he recruited what he called "the only AFSA board ever that included an equal number of women and minorities, along with an equal number of 'old style' Caucasian males."[119] Management had kept AFSA out of decisions on affirmative action, and that was all right with Horan. "We Americans deserve a Foreign Service that is excellent and representative," he said, "and it is management's job to see that we get it. . . . After 25 years of [equal employment opportunity] efforts, any shortcomings in minority hiring (and retention) are the fault of management, past and present."[120]

Horan argued that a representative and professional Service required energetic, focused recruiting; a hiring process free of bias; and a robust training program.[121] The Foreign Service hiring process had none of those qualities. The State Department's 1992 recruiting budget, including travel and advertising, was just $62,000 ($131,000 in 2022 dollars).[122]

With the arrival of the Clinton administration, the matter gained urgency and intensity. The administration, and Secretary Warren Christopher personally, wanted a quick settlement to the long-running gender and racial discrimination lawsuits against the department. Dick Moose's plans to shrink the Service made changing its racial, ethnic, and gender composition extraordinarily difficult.

In a shift from Horan's approach, the AFSA Board under Tex Harris insisted that management's diversity policies required the union's involvement. AFSA struggled with the tension between protecting jobs and benefits for members and building a Service that would be, as the law required, representative of the American people.

"A lot of white males are discriminated against," said the head of the Merit Systems Protection Board in State's Office of Policy and Evaluation.[123] The number of white males employed in the Foreign Service (officers and specialists) at the Department of State fell by 21 percent, from 5,568 to 4,387, between 1984 and 1992. (The number of white women fell 10 percent, from 1,872 to 1,678.)[124] Yet as the Thursday Luncheon Group pointed out in 1994, Black employees were few in number:

> Only one career assistant secretary, one deputy assistant secretary, six office directors, . . . and three deputy directors are in the department. Fewer than 15 blacks have entered the Foreign Service since 1991. . . . Seven blacks currently serve as ambassador, and only one is posted outside of [Africa or Latin America]. . . . There are only six black deputy chiefs of mission and three black principal officers. Yet many officers believe that their careers are endangered by black officers. This is simply not true.[125]

Indeed, between 1984 and 1992, the number of Black men in State's Foreign Service fell 14 percent, from 253 to 218, and the number of Black women rose by just two, from 147 to 149.[126] There was room in the data to justify everyone's perception of unfairness. "No area," said the Governing Board, "is more controversial among AFSA's members," and on no issue were views so disparate or so passionately held.[127]

Underscoring the lack of progress on this front, in October 1986 Bernard Johns, an African American FSO with 18 years of service, and Walter J. Thomas, who was fired in 1984 after seven years of service, filed a class action lawsuit on behalf of current and former Foreign Service officers who were not promoted or were terminated. Charging that the diplomatic corps kept Black officers from advancing to top positions, the plaintiffs sought back pay and reinstatement for former officers, and asked a U.S. district court judge to bar the State Department from discriminatory practices.[128] The plaintiffs prevailed at last in 1996.[129]

AFSA sometimes tried to avoid alienating large blocs of its membership by sticking to platitudes. Todd Stewart answered his own question: "We continue to believe that it is possible to reconcile merit with diversity—if the task is approached in the spirit of fairness. . . . AFSA looks forward to working with the department in this spirit."[130] General Counsel Sharon Papp produced a 37-page legal memorandum to encourage agencies to "promote diversity . . . compatible with merit principles."[131] President Tex Harris insisted on AFSA's consultation rights. "Without delay," he wrote, "the State Department's management should begin through the partnership process to develop an open and transparent diversity enhancement program."[132]

That process never took place, but AFSA was invited—by the plaintiffs as well as the department—to join negotiations to settle the women's class action suit led by Alison Palmer and Marguerite Cooper. Todd Stewart undertook that unenviable task. "AFSA was historically very wary of taking sides . . . where advantage to one group of employees meant disadvantage to another," he said.[133] And Stewart could see no way by which promotions for female employees would not come at the expense of male employees. "My presence at the table probably moderated demands by the plaintiffs somewhat and probably stiffened the spine of the department to resist terms that would be inequitable," he recalled.[134]

As the exclusive representative of Foreign Service employees, AFSA stood between agency management and organizations such as the Thursday Luncheon Group (for Black professionals), Women's Action Organization, and Gays and Lesbians in Foreign Affairs Agencies (GLIFAA).[135] When GLIFAA asked AFSA to support certain benefits for domestic partners, including accreditation, embassy ID cards, and access to government contract fares when traveling, the board forwarded the proposal to State management with a note that "the AFSA Governing Board takes no position."[136]

Unable to rely on AFSA to advance its case, GLIFAA met separately with the Director General and other management officials, as did other groups with ethnic, racial, or professional affinities.[137] Sometimes those meetings discussed matters over which AFSA had, on paper, exclusive representational rights with regard to members of the Foreign Service. But most affinity groups were not restricted to Foreign Service personnel, and management officials, including the Director General, had responsibilities for Civil Service as well as Foreign Service employees. Exclusivity in such situations proved impossible to enforce.

## THE HARRIS ERA ENDS

In the spring of 1997, as Tex Harris's second term wound down, members of his board organized a Leadership slate, headed by State Vice President Al La Porta as candidate for president. The slate's candidates were unopposed except for a couple of down-ticket independents, one of whom was Tex Harris, who challenged the incumbent secretary. Harris won, carrying every constituency.[138]

AFSA membership had peaked in 1994 at just over 11,000 and then declined as the Foreign Service itself contracted. By 1998, membership had fallen to around 10,400, a drop that hurt the association's finances. The Governing Board was growing stale. When La Porta's board took over in July 1997, most of its 22 members had served on the board before, and three—Harris, Tom Boyatt (treasurer), and Bill Harrop (a retiree representative)—were old lions who had been Young Turks, veterans of the unionization campaigns of the early 1970s. The association had not found its voice on diversity or on consolidation—two issues of acute interest to members of the Service.

But the turning wheel of the Foreign Service brought rejuvenation soon enough. Harris resigned in September 1997 to head for Melbourne as consul general, and La Porta left the following month to become America's first ambassador to Mongolia. The Governing Board then tapped Dan Geisler, newly elected State vice president and a first-time member of the board, to fill out La Porta's term.[139]

Geisler had been a reluctant candidate; when Al La Porta begged him to run for the vice presidency, Geisler agreed on the condition that he not be expected to do more than show up. La Porta's departure and Geisler's elevation to the presidency were a surprise, and the latter insisted on a delay until January 1, 1998.[140] But as soon as Geisler took over, he was fully in charge.

President Andrew Jackson (1829–1837) used the award of federal offices, including diplomatic and consular positions, for political purposes. In time patronage demands became overwhelming: by 1900 the administration had to staff 42 diplomatic and 318 consular posts, as well as 395 consular agencies. Merit systems reforms took hold in the 20th century, but political patronage remains a serious problem for professional diplomacy and the career Foreign Service. *Library of Congress*

Wilbur J. Carr, a civil servant who ran the State Department's consular bureau, is generally regarded as principal author of the Foreign Service Act of 1924. Carr was so wary of AFSA that he insisted on advance approval of every issue of the *(American) Foreign Service Journal*, relenting only when the *Journal* proved to be consistently inoffensive. Carr, who had joined the Department of State as a clerk in 1892, was named ambassador to Czechoslovakia in 1937 and retired in 1939. *Library of Congress*

On March 3, 1933, President Herbert Hoover's last day in office, Secretary of State (and AFSA honorary president) Henry L. Stimson stood next to AFSA Chairman Homer L. Byington and unveiled this tablet in the lobby of the State, War, and Navy Building. Inscribed on the tablet were the names of 65 "diplomatic and consular officers of the United States who while on active duty lost their lives under tragic or heroic circumstances." As of May 2022, there were 321 names on AFSA's memorial plaques in the lobby of Main State. *FSJ Digital Archive*

Loy Henderson used his position as chairman of AFSA's executive committee (1946–1947) to engage AFSA directly with the department in the drafting and implementation of the Foreign Service Act of 1946. Henderson, a four-time ambassador, was the State Department's top management official from 1955 to 1961. *Keystone Press/Alamy Stock Photo*

George F. Kennan, the Soviet expert, was Secretary George C. Marshall's director of policy planning when he served as AFSA president in 1949–1950. Unlike Loy Henderson, Kennan refused to lobby the department. "There is not much to be gained," he said, "by frantically plucking people's sleeves with a view to getting isolated decisions taken in favor of the Service against the better judgment of those who had taken them." Kennan left the State Department in 1950 but returned to public service as ambassador to the Soviet Union (1952) and Yugoslavia (1961–1963). *Library of Congress*

Senator Joseph McCarthy (R-Wisc.), at right, speaks to reporters in 1951. McCarthy and his allies engendered and then exploited a fear of hidden enemies—communists, subversives, and "misfits" and "degenerates" (euphemisms for homosexuals)—that led to the firing or forced resignations of hundreds of State Department employees. The anti-communist Red Scare faded after McCarthy's censure by the Senate in 1954; the anti-gay Lavender Scare (of which McCarthy was not a prime mover) remained virulent at least into the 1970s. AFSA struggled with both. *Everett Collection/Alamy*

Hervé L'Heureux, a consular officer and World War I veteran, led AFSA during the McCarthy era and presided over AFSA's incorporation in the District of Columbia. He was vice chairman (1947–1948) and then chairman (1949–1951) of AFSA's executive committee, and chairman of the board of directors in 1951–1953. *FSJ Digital Archive*

With his signature of E.O. 11491 on October 29, 1969, President Nixon established new rules for labor-management relations across the federal workforce (George P. Shultz, then Secretary of Labor, is seated at Nixon's left). AFSA membership was prepared to seek recognition as a union under the order, but AFSA's leadership was concerned that the order would allow Foreign Service members who had supervisory responsibilities to be excluded as part of management. *Everett Collection/Alamy*

Bill Macomber (at left, with President Gerald Ford, June 1978) was a non-partisan public servant, a political appointee in the administrations of presidents Eisenhower, Kennedy, Johnson, Nixon, and Ford. In 1969–1973 he was deputy under secretary for management, the State Department's top management official. *Courtesy of the Nantucket Historical Association*

The Bray Board, from left: George B. Lambrakis, Alan Carter, Erland Heginbotham, Barbara Good, Richard T. Davies III, Charles W. Bray III, William G. Bradford, Princeton Lyman, William Harrop, and Robert Nevitt. Bray said, "I don't know who speaks for the Foreign Service if AFSA does not." He led the slate that won the AFSA board election that year, taking office in January 1970. When named the department's spokesman, he resigned from the board, passing the leadership to Bill Harrop and Tom Boyatt as chairman and vice chairman in January 1971. The 1970–1971 board, together with AFSA's officers (President Ted Eliot and Vice Presidents John Reinhardt and William Kontos), worked with Bill Macomber to secure a new order, E.O. 11363 of December 17, 1971, that applied only to the Foreign Service. Under these revised rules, AFSA won union elections in 1973 in State, USIA, and USAID. *FSJ Digital Archive*

John E. Reinhardt (right) was elected second vice president of AFSA in January 1968 and first vice president in January 1970. He later served as ambassador to Nigeria (1971–1975) and director of the U.S. Information Agency (USIA), 1977–1980, the first career officer to hold that position. Here he is being sworn in by Vice President Walter Mondale to the post of director of the International Communication Agency (as USIA was briefly called), April 3, 1978. *AP Photo/Charles Harrity*

AFSA president Tom Boyatt (second from left) testified on the State Department Appropriations Authorization Act before the Senate Foreign Relations Committee on March 12, 1974. With him are (from left) AFSA Vice President Tex Harris, AFSA Treasurer Lois Roth, and Hank Cohen, chairman of AFSA's members' interests committee. Boyatt led off with an attack on the sale of ambassadorships to campaign contributors. Boyatt, later ambassador to Burkina Faso and Colombia, and Harris (AFSA president 1993–1997) were elected to positions on AFSA's governing board again and again into the 2010s. Boyatt received AFSA's award for lifetime contributions to American diplomacy in 2008. Cohen, who retired in 1993 with the rank of Career Ambassador, received the same award in 2019. *FSJ Digital Archive*

In May 2010, AFSA President Susan Johnson (left) and U.S. Secretary of State Hillary Clinton unveiled a new memorial plaque at AFSA's annual ceremony honoring Foreign Service employees who lost their lives in the line of duty. *REUTERS/Yuri Gripas*

In March 2019, Ambassador Barbara Stephenson, then AFSA's president, spoke at the *Foreign Service Journal* centennial exhibit opening held in the U.S. Diplomacy Center (now the National Museum for American Diplomacy). This was also the launch of the *FSJ* Digital Archive, which houses 100 years of the *Foreign Service Journal*. *AFSA/Joaquin Sosa*

Marie Yovanovitch—U.S. ambassador to Ukraine from August 2016 to April 2019, when she was recalled by President Donald Trump—takes the oath before testifying in front of the House Permanent Select Committee on Intelligence on November 15, 2019. Yovanovitch was one of several FSOs subpoenaed to testify as part of the first impeachment inquiry into President Trump. At issue was whether Trump used military aid as leverage to pressure Ukraine into investigations that would benefit him politically. A Senior Foreign Service officer and three-time ambassador with a 33-year diplomatic career, Yovanovitch retired in 2020. *UPI/Alamy Live News*

During his farewell event at AFSA headquarters, on July 12, 2023, outgoing AFSA President Eric Rubin (right) shared a moment with incoming AFSA President Tom Yazdgerdi. *AFSA/Nadja Ruzica*

# 9

## Millennium Shift, 1998–2001

Dan Geisler was a 14-year veteran of the Foreign Service, an FS-2 economic officer. He was white haired and ebullient, with a face that lent age to youth and
youth to age. Trained as an engineer, he came to the American Foreign Service Association without a grand vision for the Foreign Service, but he was
determined to strengthen the association and keep a focus on the membership.
Improving communications among the board, the staff, and the members, especially through the recently launched AFSAnet listserv, would build a sense of
common purpose and put AFSA back on a path of growth.

External events quickly set an agenda for the new AFSA president. On
January 29, 1998, Sen. Jesse Helms (R-N.C.) took the floor to denounce "the
numerous moral, ethical, and professional lapses of Foreign Service officers"
and "a [Foreign Service] grievance process that . . . fails adequately to deal with
those who are guilty of such abuses." Helms cited allegations by the Office of the
Inspector General (OIG) of sexual harassment, the sale of visas for sex, and the
diversion and theft of government funds. Because of weak management and a
flawed grievance system, he said, these abuses resulted in punishments no more
severe than brief suspensions from duty. Helms called for changes that would
produce stronger, swifter, and more certain punishment.[1]

While the department tried to defend itself, AFSA defended the Foreign
Service and its members by criticizing the way the OIG operated. Targets of an
investigation were often not so informed until after they had been interviewed,
and even people on the periphery of a case—translators, witnesses, coworkers,
acquaintances—complained of rude treatment, deception, and verbal abuse by
investigators. AFSA insisted on the right to have its labor-management staff
accompany members to OIG investigative interviews, urged the OIG to allow

its interviews to be tape-recorded, and recommended that it set up an internal affairs unit to handle complaints.

AFSA's general counsel, Sharon Papp, noted that OIG investigations sometimes dragged on for years, damaging and in some cases ending the careers of officers eventually proven innocent of any wrongdoing. She issued guidance for members on their rights and responsibilities in OIG and security investigations.[2] She and other AFSA attorneys also secured rulings that the OIG was subject to the jurisdiction of the Foreign Service Grievance Board (FSGB) and to the supervisory authority of the Secretary of State, who could be held responsible for the office's misconduct.[3] In time, Senator Helms's assertions of moral laxity faded from view (it turned out, according to the inspector general herself, that FSOs transgressed at about the same rate as the rest of the federal civilian workforce), but protections for Foreign Service employees emerged stronger than before.[4]

AFSA was able to take on the OIG using its internal resources. Had the challenge required hired support—lawyers or lobbyists, for example—AFSA would have had a hard time dealing with it. The association had no war chest. Its finances were stable but at a low level. Membership dues provided most of its unrestricted revenue, and given flat or declining membership, operating expenses were under steady pressure. Almost all of its assets were in restricted accounts, of which the largest by far was the Scholarship Fund.

AFSA's financial management had been haphazard for years. Even after revenues and expenses came into rough balance in the 1980s, the association's cushion—its liquid, unrestricted assets—was thin. Executive Director Susan Reardon wanted a reserve equal to six months' expenses, which she said was generally considered adequate for a nonprofit organization.[5] But at the end of 1997, unrestricted assets, excluding the value of the headquarters building and the land it stood on, were about $270,000, enough to cover expenses for only 60 days.[6]

Tom Boyatt had become chairman of AFSA's Finance Committee in 1995 and treasurer in 1997. AFSA, he believed, needed to shake off its nonprofit mentality. It needed to bring in revenue above expenses to fund a reserve that would provide both protection from economic downturns or political pressure and freedom to take on projects that might have a slow financial payback or no payback at all.

Geisler had not finished his first week as president when Boyatt took him to lunch to lay out a case for raising dues, the main source of revenue. He won Geisler over, and Geisler won over the board. Informal soundings of the membership—a hallmark of Geisler's deliberate, politically adept leadership—led

to a referendum in which 81 percent of the voters approved a proposal for raising dues and a plan for using the funds.[7] The increased revenues, mainly from
higher dues paid by mid-level officers, allowed an overdue raise in staff salaries,
capital improvements in information technology, and a buildup of reserves.

The board also approved a Boyatt proposal to place the association's reserve
funds under professional management. Returns improved and risk declined. By
2002, AFSA had more than $1 million in unrestricted net assets.[8]

## FOREIGN SERVICE VERSUS CIVIL SERVICE

Tension between the Foreign Service and the Civil Service rose as the agencies in
which they were both employed contracted in size. At the Department of Commerce, the domestic U.S. Commercial Service and the overseas Foreign Commercial Service were merged in name, but the merger meant little more than a
new Commercial Service name and logo. Members of the two organizations had
different ambitions and career paths that rarely crossed.

The relatively few Civil Service personnel who accepted foreign assignments
and Foreign Service commissions rarely wanted to return to Civil Service status. Conversely, members of the Foreign Service generally did not want to be
assigned to the domestic field offices. "How often," one asked, "would I have an
opportunity to use Bahasa Indonesian in Denver or Des Moines?"[9] Management
was frustrated. The Commerce Department representative to the AFSA Governing Board said that the Foreign Commercial Service and the International
Trade Administration, the division of the Commerce Department in which it
was housed, had "an adversarial relationship."[10]

At the Department of Agriculture, management and AFSA had agreed that
members of the Foreign Agricultural Service (FAS) should spend two-thirds of
their careers overseas, as was the case in the Department of State. The Foreign
Service cohort in the FAS had been cut by 10 percent (from 205 to 185 Foreign
Service officers) between 1994 and 1998, but the predominant Civil Service
union, the American Federation of State, County, and Municipal Employees,
pressed for further cuts in the Washington-based FAS and demanded more
overseas postings for civil servants. Management responded by reducing new
Foreign Service FAS hires, while time-in-class limits pruned the upper ranks.[11]
By 1999, civil servants filled 27 percent of the positions in overseas agricultural
trade offices (trade promotion offices often located outside embassy grounds),
perhaps because there were no longer enough Foreign Service personnel
available.[12]

In June 1998, USIA Director Joseph Duffy replaced Foreign Service officers with civil servants in two key senior positions and created a minister counselor position in Vietnam for a political appointee. The agency's AFSA vice president called these three actions, respectively, if not respectfully, a breach of contract, a breach of faith, and a betrayal.[13]

At the Department of State, management assigned a career civil servant, Chief Financial Officer Richard "Rich" Greene, to be consul general in Sydney. Director General Edward "Skip" Gnehm Jr. told the AFSA Board that "by and large" overseas positions go to Foreign Service personnel, but "from time to time" management may do otherwise.[14] The assistant secretary for East Asian affairs fought the appointment, as did Sen. Mitch McConnell (R-Ky.), then chair of the subcommittee handling the department's appropriations. AFSA did little to contest the appointment. Dan Geisler thought the issue was not particularly important—Greene was well qualified, and specialists and mid-level officers didn't care—and the department held its ground.[15]

## EMBASSY SECURITY

While Jesse Helms was denouncing the Foreign Service for its moral laxity, members of al-Qaida were preparing the strikes that would kill more than 200 people in Nairobi and Dar es Salaam on August 7, 1998. The two-pronged attack on the U.S. embassies in Kenya and Tanzania, carried out by suicide bombers, was by one count the 234th attack on U.S. diplomatic installations since 1987.[16] Secretary of State Madeleine Albright named Adm. William Crowe, a former chairman of the Joint Chiefs of Staff and a former ambassador to Great Britain, to head a commission of inquiry into the attacks.[17]

That investigation exonerated personnel at both embassies but pointed out other mistakes, specifically the State Department's failure to learn the lessons taught by the Beirut bombings of 1983 and set forth in the Inman panel's report in 1985. The department and Congress needed to "reprioritize" security improvements and, this time, sustain the effort. Toward that end, the Crowe Commission recommended funding security improvements at $1.4 billion per year for 10 years, of which $1 billion would support a building program and $400 million would fund security upgrades and new hires.[18]

Inexplicably, the Clinton administration requested only about $450 million for FY2000, about 40 percent of what the commission had called for. Dan Geisler testified for AFSA in support of Admiral Crowe's recommendations before the House International Relations Committee (as the Committee on Foreign

Affairs was then called), and Congress came through with an appropriation of $900 million, double the administration's request.[19] The struggle to bring security preparations and funding up to the level recommended by the Crowe Commission seemed likely to follow the course of the struggle over the Inman recommendations a decade earlier until the terrorist attacks of September 11, 2001 (9/11), and then the deaths of Ambassador Christopher Stevens and three other American officials in Benghazi on September 11, 2012, prompted dramatic increases in spending on all aspects of diplomatic security.[20]

## HAPPY 75TH ANNIVERSARY!

Against the somber backdrop of the East Africa bombings, continued budget austerity, and other challenges, retired Ambassador Brandon Grove, an AFSA member and a director of the American Academy of Diplomacy, put together a grand celebration for the 75th anniversary of AFSA and the founding of the modern Foreign Service by the Rogers Act of 1924. Admiral Crowe, speaking at the Foreign Service Day lunch on May 7, 1999, called the Foreign Service "a national asset to be treasured and nurtured."[21] Secretary of State Madeleine Albright and National Security Adviser Sandy Berger spoke at a ceremony adding eight names to the memorial plaque for Foreign Service personnel who died in heroic or tragic circumstances. A departmental memorial plaque unveiled at the same time honored 56 other U.S. government personnel killed in the bombings.[22]

Secretary Albright also attended the anniversary dinner, where she sat at the head table with George Kennan and praised the efforts of "our Foreign Service, Foreign Service Nationals, and Civil Service personnel."[23] She was especially pleased to meet the winner of AFSA's first annual nationwide high school essay contest, which addressed the role of diplomacy in American history.[24]

The essay contest winner was the only AFSA awardee recognized on Foreign Service Day that year. AFSA had presented all its awards for performance and constructive dissent on Foreign Service Day each year from 1988 to 1993, but in 1994 the Governing Board decided the event would have more impact as an occasion of its own, setting a pattern for future years.[25] Grip-and-grin photographs were still numerous, though, thanks to awards from the Diplomatic and Consular Officers, Retired; the Association of American Foreign Service Women (now the Associates of the American Foreign Service Worldwide [AAFSW]); and the Director General. Also announced were some two dozen departmental awards for excellence, almost all of them going to members of the Foreign Service.[26]

The ceremony for the departmental awards, on the eve of Foreign Service Day, was part of Public Service Recognition Week, an event first put together by a coalition of Civil Service organizations in 1985 to honor government employees around the country.[27] Anthony Quainton, Director General from 1995 to 1997, saw the week as a chance to respond to complaints from the department's civil servants about Foreign Service Day. "We held ceremonies which recognized both [the] Civil Service and Foreign Service," he said in an oral history interview. "I think we managed to get the Civil Service and Foreign Service working somewhat better together."[28] That judgment may have been wishful thinking.

## MARSHALL ADAIR AND THE CIVIL SERVICE

By the end of the anniversary celebration, Dan Geisler's term was winding down. He had recruited his successor, Marshall Adair, whose slate was uncontested. Geisler was on the slate and was elected as a State representative, which allowed him to return to active duty. Adair had run for the AFSA Governing Board before, in 1979, as a candidate for State representative on a narrowly defeated slate that opposed drafting a new Foreign Service act.[29]

When Geisler asked him to run for the AFSA presidency, Adair, a political officer, was an aide in the office of the under secretary of State for economic affairs. AFSA seemed a good opportunity for a change. "I came into the presidency eager to build public support for the Foreign Service," he said. "I thought if we applied at home the skills we used in foreign communities, we could build a small constituency for our policies, for our work."[30] Adair hoped to persuade or shame the administration into asking Congress to fund Admiral Crowe's recommendations on embassy security.

Conflicts with the department's management over the Civil Service overtook Adair's positive, outward-looking agenda. The conflicts were long-standing but had recently sharpened. When the Foreign Service began to shrink at the end of the 1980s, the Civil Service in the Department of State, unlike the rest of the federal government, increased in size. In 1988, the year before the Berlin Wall came down, the full-time, permanent workforce of the Department of State included 9,232 Foreign Service members and 4,677 civil servants. Ten years later, the department had cut its Foreign Service staff by 16 percent to 7,724. The number of civil servants, however, had increased by more than 6 percent to 4,977. As a result, the ratio of Foreign Service to Civil Service personnel in the department declined from roughly two to one in 1988 to three to two in 1997.[31]

The change was gradual and may not have been much noticed. It was not reported in the *Foreign Service Journal* or mentioned in the minutes of the AFSA Board. Even so, it surely contributed to a widespread sentiment among members of the Foreign Service that they were unappreciated, if not disdained, by their employers. Civil Service employees held many of the key positions in the department's administrative and human resource bureaus. As a result, the perception grew, more among Foreign Service officers than specialists, that the department had placed decisions affecting their lives and careers in the hands of individuals with no understanding or experience of the Foreign Service and no sympathy for its culture.

The long decade of the loss of jobs and status was the context for AFSA's furious reaction to management's decision in 1999 to assign a civil servant to be deputy chief of mission (DCM) at the embassy in Lima, Peru. The appointee in question, Roberta Jacobson, was undoubtedly qualified for the position. She had served for many years in the Bureau of Western Hemisphere Affairs and had directed the bureau's Policy Planning Office for the past four years. She spoke fluent Spanish, and the ambassador in Lima, a career Foreign Service officer, wanted her.[32] But AFSA's immediate reaction, when it learned of the assignment during a meeting with staff from the Bureau of Human Resources, was negative.

In 1983 AFSA and the department had reached a collective bargaining agreement on limited non-career (LNC) appointments to the Foreign Service. The agreement allowed the department to place a civil servant in a Foreign Service job under a non-career appointment of up to five years but only if the department first notified AFSA, via a formal "certificate of need," that the Director General had failed to find a suitable member of the Foreign Service for the position. The department had not done this in the case of Lima.

The year before, when State assigned a civil servant to be consul general in Sydney, AFSA had let the issue slide.[33] Nonetheless, the 1983 agreement, renewed in 1996, remained valid under a clause that rolled it over annually unless one of the parties sought a change, which had not happened.[34] When General Counsel Sharon Papp brought the agreement to the attention of Marshall Adair, he was determined to hold the department to its terms.

Adair argued the issue with Director General Skip Gnehm. "I said that I and AFSA were all for finding ways to provide Civil Service employees of the Department of State opportunities to serve overseas" but not in "the senior management jobs that Foreign Service officers work for all their careers and need for the acquisition of management experience and credentials."[35] Roberta Jacobson was "good," said Adair, "but she wasn't what you would call unique. There were other people interested [including other women] who were perfectly quali-fied. . . . I told anyone who would listen that AFSA would be happy to support her if the administration wanted to nominate her as an ambassador, but they weren't willing to do that."[36]

AFSA exercised its collective bargaining rights and filed an implementation dispute with the Department of State. When that was denied, AFSA petitioned the Foreign Service Grievance Board (FSGB) to rescind the assignment.[37] The FSGB found for AFSA, but because Jacobson had already left for Peru, it recom-mended that her assignment be curtailed from three years to one.[38] Adair told the Director General, now Marc Grossman, that AFSA would be "compassion-ate" if the department would respect the principle that underlay the case. The department, said Grossman, was not prepared to do so.[39]

The ambassador in Lima announced his resignation from AFSA, and 20 of 49 AFSA members at the post signed a petition asking AFSA to back down.[40] On November 30, Secretary Albright overruled the FSGB on foreign policy grounds, apparently for the first time in 25 years, but agreed to curtail the assignment to two years instead of three.[41] Jacobson, whose position in Washington had been filled by a Foreign Service officer, later rose through the Bureau of Western Hemi-sphere Affairs to become assistant secretary (2012–2016) and served under Presi-dents Barack Obama and Donald Trump as ambassador to Mexico (2016–2018).[42]

AFSA had committed resources and prestige to this fight to block the assign-ment of one outstanding civil servant to a Foreign Service position abroad, and it won no more than half a victory. Some AFSA members were distressed by the fight. "We have all seen Foreign Service DCMs who were real turkeys," wrote one, "so why not give this gifted civil servant a chance?"[43] But most of AFSA's members were delighted. Of 1,375 email responses to an AFSA appeal for com-ment, 1,335 (97 percent) supported AFSA's position.[44]

After the change of administrations, the department exercised its option to renegotiate the 1983 agreement on which AFSA had built its case. The depart-ment's labor negotiator told AFSA that "the department wished to modify . . . obsolete and possible unlawful language" and "develop a system that is most fair to employees in the State Department family."[45] AFSA's response, signed by Mar-shall Adair, was unyielding, referring to "outrage" in the Service over the "illegal" Lima assignment and asserting that "weakening this agreement . . . would cause extreme damage to American diplomacy."[46] The renegotiation of the agreement ended with even tighter restrictions on the department's ability to make LNC appointments to Foreign Service positions.[47]

Adair himself saw a long-term need for "a program that would actually give [members of the Civil Service] the opportunity to serve overseas at different levels, without compromising . . . the integrity and sustainability of the professional diplomatic service." Adair's idea was "to obtain from OMB [Office of Management and Budget] a number of positions, five, 10, 20, . . . and allocate them to the geographic bureaus" to move around at the bureaus' discretion and staff with civil servants. He discussed this and other ideas with a number of the department's Civil Service employees, but they showed little interest. The idea went nowhere. "No one in the department wanted to address a systemic issue," Adair said.[48]

## COLIN POWELL AT STATE

The fight over Lima left a residue of ill will that damaged relations between AFSA and the Bureau of Human Resources, and between the Foreign Service and the Civil Service in the Department of State. AFSA and its members became acutely sensitive to indicators of their status. Bitterness and suspicion affected AFSA's dealings even with a Secretary of State who was a great friend of the Foreign Service, Colin Powell.

A former national security adviser and former chairman of the Joint Chiefs of Staff, Powell had retired as a four-star general. At the earliest possible moment, on Inauguration Day in 2001, the Senate confirmed him as Secretary of State by voice vote.[49]

When Secretary Powell took office, the Foreign Service had suffered a decade of decline. Staffing cuts had left 700 Foreign Service positions vacant, many embassies were housed in "insecure and decrepit facilities," and diplomatic representation was "near a state of crisis." The Service had lost much of its attraction and ability to recruit.[50] Powell recognized this trend and intended to reverse it. At his confirmation hearings, he said, "It is the State Department and its talented and dedicated professionals who are in the forefront of our engagement in the world. While the world has been growing more demanding and more complex, while more and more nations demand and need our attention, we have cut the number of people in the State Department; we have underfunded our facilities; we have neglected our infrastructure. We need to do better."[51]

AFSA prepared his welcome to Main State, where employees greeting him formed a noisy, adoring, and expectant crowd. State was ready for his leadership. He had not been two weeks in office when he received a petition signed by 1,600 State Department employees, both Civil Service and Foreign Service, calling for "a long-term, bipartisan effort" to "modernize and renew our organization [and] transform our outdated culture." The ship of State was, they said, "a rusted-out diplomatic hulk" that was "no longer seaworthy."[52]

The petitioners were an informal group led by a small committee of senior-level members of the Foreign and Civil Services that had taken the name "SOS [Save our State] for the Department of State" (SOS for DOS). They were knocking on an open door. No one in the building was more eager for change than the Secretary of State. Even before his swearing in, Powell had endorsed a plan to add 1,100 people to the Foreign Service over three years at a cost of more than $100 million; he announced the plan at his confirmation hearings. His intent was to fill vacant positions and create a "training float," or an excess of personnel over positions sufficient to allow officers and specialists to undergo periodic training (as in the uniformed services) without leaving desks empty and critical work undone.

Powell had to rely on his personal political standing to push his plan through Congress. His management team—Director General Marc Grossman (soon to be succeeded by Ruth Davis) and Under Secretary for Management Grant Green, a retired Army officer—included no political stars.[53] The Secretary stayed with the plan, soon named the Diplomatic Readiness Initiative (DRI), through budget fights with OMB, during which his predecessors had retreated, and through hearing after hearing. Over the next three years, Congress would fund the creation of 1,069 new Foreign Service positions and more than 200 new Civil Service positions. State also brought in 561 new consular officers and 608 new Diplomatic Security specialists. By 2005, the Service was bigger than it was in 2001 by more than 2,000 people.[54]

Powell intended to revive not just the Foreign Service but also the Department of State. He had a military officer's respect for pageantry and symbolism, and he tried to use these devices to inspire unity among all departmental employees. He often swore in ambassadors personally, and he brought President George W. Bush to the building to attend the swearing in of a new class of FSOs.[55]

Not all of Powell's initiatives were so welcome, however. He announced his intention to rename the Foreign Service Star—a medal Congress had recently created, and for which AFSA had lobbied, honoring civilian employees killed or permanently disabled on official business abroad—the Thomas Jefferson Star for Foreign Service. He rebranded the venerable Foreign Service Lounge as the Employee Service Center. And State Department employees who had almost ritually been described as "Foreign Service, Civil Service, and Foreign Service Nationals" were now homogenized as "international affairs professionals."

In 2001, with Director General Marc Grossman and Assistant Secretary for Administration Pat Kennedy, Powell relaunched Foreign Service Day (which had suffered from poor attendance) as Foreign Affairs Day, bringing civil servants into the celebration.[56] AFSA did not agree with this change and continues to use the original name, Foreign Service Day.

Many in the Foreign Service took the changes as a slight, if not an insult. The demise of the Foreign Service Lounge, a name evocative of old friends, chance encounters, and held mail, hit particularly hard. David Newsom, the country's senior career diplomat when he retired in 1981, wrote that the changes were "insensitive to the special mystique of the Foreign Service" and showed a "lack of respect" for the Service as an institution. AFSA and the Foreign Affairs Council (FAC)—a coalition of 11 organizations (AFSA, the American Academy of Diplomacy, DACOR, the Una Chapman Cox Foundation, the Council of American Ambassadors, and others) supporting a strong Foreign Service—wrote the Secretary to complain that management was "striking the words 'Foreign Service' from the department's lexicon." The letter did not mention another linguistic sore point, the decision in the Bureau of Human Resources to stop calling FSOs "officers" and refer to them instead as "generalists."

In his reply, Secretary Powell agreed to name the medal the Thomas Jefferson Star for Foreign Service, but he rebuked AFSA and the FAC for a lack of team spirit. "Working together we [the Foreign Service and the Civil Service] will be a superb and winning foreign policy team," he wrote. "That is my intention, and it should be your intention, as well."[57]

## JOHN NALAND REACHES OUT

John K. Naland joined the AFSA Governing Board with Marshall Adair in 1999, when he won election as the State Department vice president. Naland would go on to serve two terms as president of the board (2001–2003 and 2007–2009) and—as of this writing—four terms as retiree vice president (2017–2025). Comparing service as AFSA president and vice president, he found the latter more rewarding: "Instead of educating the public about the Foreign Service, which is kind of nebulous, you helped individuals every day."[58]

Naland came to the AFSA Board after 13 years in the Foreign Service. He had served in Colombia, Costa Rica, and Nicaragua; had done a stint in the White House; and had spent a year at Caterpillar under the State Department's Corporate Placement Program. His experience made him a reformer, in the tradition of Lannon Walker, and a pugnacious defender of the Service, in the tradition of Tom Boyatt. This set of qualities brought him strong retiree support: When he became president in 2001, four previous AFSA presidents—Tex Harris, Tom Boyatt, Bill Harrop, and Ted Wilkinson—were members of his board.

At the start of his vice presidency, Naland published a checklist of issues before the association, and at the end of his term, he published a checklist of accomplishments. The first list posed systemic management questions: Should overseas tours be lengthened? Should the TIC limit for mid-level FSOs be reduced? How can the department attract and retain information managers? The second list cited specific members' benefits: a higher entry-level grade for office management specialists, the exemption of certain difficult posts from the four-year-tour policy, an increase in promotion rates in deficit grades, and the help given to 200 members with grievances and 1,000 others with various problems or requests.[59]

Not on either list was a striking and controversial accomplishment. Naland and State representative Lynn Sever had argued for and won the support of the board for 13 specific measures that the affinity group Gays and Lesbians in Foreign Affairs Agencies (now called glifaa) had proposed to improve conditions for its members overseas. The board endorsed the measures against the advice of Marshall Adair, who proposed delay. Secretary Albright adopted eight of the measures as policy in December 2000. These measures changed the treatment of persons whom employees declare to the chief of mission as "members of household" (MOH) who will reside at post with the employee, instructing posts to help MOHs with visa and residency permits, to consider them for employment, and to "work to ensure that the official American community environment is as welcoming as possible."[60]

In retrospect, these policy changes may seem incremental, but at the time, five years after passage of the Defense of Marriage Act, treating gay couples as just couples took political courage. When John Naland raised the issue in a meeting with then Secretary-designate Colin Powell, Powell said, "I do not plan to reverse [the MOH] policy—but I don't want to read about it on the front page of the *Washington Post*." Putting the MOH policy in place, and keeping it there, was (as Naland later said) a big deal.[61]

In an uncontested election, Naland moved from State vice president to president in 2001.[62] More than his predecessors, and using technology they did not have, he sought constant contact with the members, looking for ideas, guidance, and feedback. Like Tex Harris, he used the department's communications system (as AFSA was entitled to do under a collective bargaining agreement) to send weekly messages to all diplomatic and consular posts, always including his email address. He also utilized the AFSAnet, a listserv that grew with the internet in reach and capability, and received responses to email surveys that Steve Kashkett, the State vice president, regularly sent out for an unscientific but revealing sample that reflected the views of those who felt strongly enough to respond.

## THE *FOREIGN SERVICE JOURNAL*

The strongest link between the members and the association remained the monthly *Foreign Service Journal*. Naland and Bob Guldin, editor of the *Journal*, disagreed about the *Journal*'s funding and content. Strong advertising revenue could not keep pace with rising costs. Deficits, around $60,000 a year in 1994, rose to $220,000 in 2001 and became a sore point with the AFSA Board.[63] Content was a sore point as well. "We did a survey," said John Naland, "and the readership wanted at least half the *Journal* to cover professional, in-house issues that no one else wrote about." The AFSA Board rarely interfered with the *Journal*'s Editorial Board, but rarely was not never. "The editor wanted to put out a mini-version of *Foreign Affairs*," Naland said, "and so we parted ways."[64]

Naland and the board put Steven Alan Honley, a former FSO who had been associate editor of the *Journal* for two years, in charge as editor in chief in July 2001. He took the magazine into the digital age, brightening its look and keeping the focus on the Foreign Service, which is what readers wanted.[65] Former FSO Shawn Dorman, the *Journal*'s associate editor and the editor of AFSA's best-selling *Inside a U.S. Embassy*, succeeded Honley in 2014.

Naland's first concern as president was to set a tone and direction for the association itself. The formal expression and adoption of core values was a fairly new management tool in 2001, and Naland, perhaps influenced by his time at Caterpillar, brought the practice to AFSA. On office walls and coffee mugs, staff and visitors could read the list: responsiveness, effectiveness, integrity, efficiency, community, courage, patriotism, empowerment. These values set the tone. The direction had been set by Secretary Powell, and Naland made it AFSA's top priority "to assist the administration in making the case to Congress and the American people for a sustained infusion of additional resources."[66] AFSA stood firmly behind the Diplomatic Readiness Initiative and backed the Secretary's effort in every way.

Naland's second priority for AFSA was to "engage our membership in a discussion of the future of the Foreign Service."[67] AFSA, he said, should "find the value added of the Foreign Service . . . recognize what we do and evaluate

**Box 9.1.** The Independent Voice of the Foreign Service

When the *Journal* began in 1919 as the *American Consular Bulletin*, it made the department jumpy: Wilbur J. Carr, who ran the consular bureau (and pretty much everything else), insisted on clearing every issue.[a] During the McCarthy era, the *Journal* supported John Paton Davies and others against persecution by the department's Security Committee; AFSA's passive leadership did not interfere with the *Journal*'s stand. But at the department's request, AFSA's leadership stepped in to stop the *Journal* from publishing articles or letters critical of Wristonization—the expansion of the Foreign Service through the induction of hundreds of the department's civil servants.[b]

When AFSA became a union in 1973, the *Journal* added AFSA News, a section devoted to the official business and activity of the association. The AFSA Governing Board and staff were responsible for an unsigned column called Association Views, a regular feature added in the 1980s and replaced in the 1990s by a column signed by AFSA's president. Signed columns by agency vice presidents followed. The growth of AFSA News allowed the *Journal* itself to become, in the words of Managing Editor Nancy Johnson, "more *journal*istic."[c] It adopted the slogan "The Independent Voice of the Foreign Service."[d]

The *Journal* is neither an in-house newsletter, like *State Magazine*, nor a policy journal like *Foreign Affairs*. It is a magazine by and for practitioners, providing a unique blend of personal journalism and professional insight into the central problems of American diplomacy, as its multiyear series on the Foreign Service in Iraq (see box 10.2) exemplified.

a. James Barclay Young, "The Origin of the *American Foreign Service Journal*," *AFSJ*, March 1944, 126–28. Young and Wesley Frost were the founders of the *Consular Bulletin* and the American Consular Association.
b. The McCarthy and Wriston issues are covered in chapter 3.
c. Nancy Johnson, "A Stroll through 75 Years of the *Foreign Service Journal*," *FSJ*, May 1994, 38.
d. Ibid., 39.

how well we do it."[68] He saw the connection between professional issues and members' benefits: "If a future 'reform' ever eliminates the features that make us unique, we will inevitably lose the benefits that flow from that uniqueness."[69]

In an echo of the Lima (Roberta Jacobson) case, AFSA Governing Board members argued that AFSA needed to make management understand the value of a separate Foreign Service and the consequences—for morale, retention, and recruitment—of placing outsiders in Foreign Service positions overseas.[70] But the board never collected data to prove its contention, and the department never accepted AFSA's point of view. The argument would recur (for example, in 2006 with regard to a public diplomacy position in Brussels and in 2012 with regard to a principal officer position in Australia), and the issue remained a point of contention between AFSA and management at the Department of State.

## Lobbying Congress

As he had done as AFSA's State vice president, Naland pushed hard on members' benefits, the bread-and-butter issues that resonated with all Foreign Service employees. They included, among others, a capital gains exclusion for Foreign Service members on the sale of a principal residence, enhanced funding for embassy security, and law enforcement availability pay for Diplomatic Security special agents. But the issue of overseas comparability pay (OCP), also known as locality pay, stood out for its importance and difficulty. Securing OCP became (and remains) a typical Washington battle, with success measured in small increments over a long period of time and with no assurance of any permanent victory. It is worth a careful look.

Beginning in 1990, the federal government provided its employees in the United States an additional sum to their base salaries so their pay was comparable to what workers in the private sector in the same geographic area enjoyed. In 2002 the benefit, called "locality pay," added between 8.64 and 19.04 percent to an employee's paycheck depending on the location of the job—unless the job was overseas. The statute that created the benefit, the Federal Employees Pay Comparability Act of 1990, provided a basis for awarding locality pay only in the United States, where comparability surveys could be taken and comparability formulas applied.[71]

Foreign Service and Civil Service employees received no locality pay if they were posted abroad. As locality pay grew over time, the resulting gap became a disincentive for overseas service, since it amounted to a cut in base salary. For employees nearing retirement, the disincentive was especially strong: Losing locality pay would reduce the salary they received in their last years of active duty and thereby reduce the base on which their future pensions would be calculated. Year after year, AFSA members in surveys placed this issue at the top of their priorities.

Ken Nakamura, AFSA's in-house lobbyist, was well prepared and energetic, with excellent access to staff on the authorizing and appropriating committees. But AFSA did not work alone. It had support from two organizations that Tom Boyatt had put together: the Foreign Affairs Council and the AFSA Political Action Committee (AFSA-PAC). AFSA also had essential support from

**Box 9.2.** AFSA-PAC

Tom Boyatt organized AFSA's Political Action Committee in 2002 with the approval of the AFSA Governing Board. Unlike AFSA itself and its Legislative Action Fund, AFSA-PAC was able, under its charter and under the tax code, to make contributions to political candidates and campaigns.

The AFSA Board approved the PAC in February 2002.[a] By June, Boyatt had drafted its bylaws, filed organizational paperwork with the Federal Election Commission, and received more than $25,000 in donations from AFSA members, about 80 percent from retirees.[b] Donations to the PAC, unlike donations to the AFSA Scholarship Fund or the Fund for American Diplomacy, were (and are) not tax deductible.

Under AFSA-PAC's bylaws, the AFSA Governing Board chooses the PAC's officers and names six AFSA members to a committee that runs the PAC. The board appointed Boyatt to the key position of treasurer. The board took the advice of the PAC's organizers and for operational, as well as legal, reasons set up the PAC as an independent, stand-alone organization.

AFSA-PAC, by its own rules, can solicit and accept donations only from AFSA members and cannot access the funds that AFSA members pay to the association in dues.[c]

After some debate, the PAC decided, and the AFSA Board agreed, to restrict itself to contributing only to incumbent senators and representatives running for reelection. (The PAC does not, however, contribute to members who deny the validity of the 2020 presidential election.) The AFSA-PAC's contributions also have to be evenly divided between Republicans and Democrats. With rare exceptions for friends of the Foreign Service, contributions go to members of the foreign affairs authorizing and appropriating committees after an examination of their voting records on issues of concern.[d]

The PAC interlocks with AFSA and its Legislative Action Fund, and with the Foreign Affairs Council and its member organizations, to present a phalanx of support for the Foreign Service and professionalism in the conduct of foreign affairs. AFSA-PAC was not a year old when an appropriations subcommittee chairman asked Boyatt and Naland to stop by for an hour of conversation, validating the connection between money and access that the PAC was formed to exploit.

That connection was still valid twenty years later. AFSA President Eric Rubin (2019–2023) explained, "AFSA-PAC gave Chairman [Gregory W.] Meeks [D-N.Y.] of the House Foreign Affairs Committee $2,000, so I got to sit next to him and spend two hours talking with him at a dinner. Because of the money we give we get invitations, and we take advantage."[e]

a. Minutes, AFSA Governing Board meeting, February 6, 2002.
b. AFSA News, *FSJ*, July–August 2002, 8.
c. Tom Boyatt, interview, February 5, 2014; minutes, AFSA Governing Board meeting, November 6, 2002; and AFSA-PAC Bylaws, September 20, 1917, https://afsa.org/afsa-pac-bylaws.
d. AFSA News, *FSJ*, July–August 2002, 8.
e. Eric Rubin, interview, June 7, 2022.

management in the Department of State and other agencies, which pressed the OMB to include funds for OCP in the international affairs budget.

AFSA's first win on the issue was enactment in the Foreign Relations Authorization Act of 2003 of "virtual locality pay," which calculated the pension due to an employee retiring from an overseas posting based on the salary, including locality pay, that he or she would have earned in Washington, D.C.[72]

AFSA saw virtual locality pay as a bridge to full comparability between pay in Washington and pay overseas, but after many years of effort, it would remain a bridge too far (see pages 190–91 and 206–7).

Overseas service also penalized some homeowners who sold their residence. Under the Taxpayer Relief Act of 1997, homeowners could receive a onetime exemption from tax on capital gains on the sale of a residence in which they had lived for at least two years during the five years prior to the sale. AFSA wanted Congress to allow time on assignment abroad to count toward the residency requirement. Because in this case members of the armed forces faced the same problem, AFSA and the Uniformed Services Coalition worked on the issue together and were successful. Congress amended the law in 2003 to allow Foreign Service and uniformed service members to qualify with two years of residency during the 15 years before the sale.[73]

## Lobbying Agencies

The SOS for DOS group that petitioned for reform at the Department of State had no specific program. One of its leaders, Stephanie Kinney, said the group stayed "at the strategic level" to gain "maximum solidarity and adherence."[74] Separately, former Secretary of Defense (and former Foreign Service officer) Frank Carlucci and a committee of experts put together a reform proposal for the Council on Foreign Relations and the Center for Strategic and International Studies. Carlucci's report, another crag on the Everest of blue-ribbon studies, called on the president to issue a directive laying out a clear division of responsibilities and authorities among the principal national security departments and to declare State Department reform a national security priority.[75] Like SOS for DOS, the Independent Task Force on State Department Reform stayed largely at the strategic level, though it offered a number of specific recommendations on resource management, personnel practices, and public diplomacy.[76]

AFSA played no role in Carlucci's task force or in SOS for DOS, but as a force for reform, it was more effective. AFSA under John Naland approached reform from the viewpoint of its members. The association dealt in specifics and left grand strategy to others.

Some 200 members responded to AFSA's appeal for ideas on reform. A Professional Issues Committee worked with these ideas to produce a list of specific proposals on Service discipline, training and career development, organizational culture, and conditions of service. Many of the proposals were in the mainstream of AFSA thinking going back to the 1960s and aimed to strengthen career principles. To ensure worldwide availability, AFSA proposed a fair-share rule that would require every Service member to serve some time—perhaps two years in 10 or four in 20—in hardship posts as a condition of advancement.[77] To ensure career development, AFSA proposed an in-Service training program with requirements to be met at each career stage.

AFSA opposed the department's efforts to eliminate the requirement, imposed on the initiative of Senator Helms, that selection boards low rank a percentage of officers each year. The AFSA Board—in particular, retiree representatives Bill Harrop and Tom Boyatt—argued that low ranking and selection-out distinguished the Foreign Service from the Civil Service and needed to be maintained.[78] But AFSA also agreed with the department that the 5 percent level required by law led the selection boards to make arbitrary choices. After discussions with the Director General, AFSA and the department worked with Senate Foreign Relations Committee staff and members to reduce the percentage from five to two, but the process took the better part of a decade. The department adopted most of AFSA's proposals, including training requirements, a reduction in nonmedical waivers to the statutory eight-year limit on consecutive years of domestic assignment, increased rotational opportunities for junior officers, and more emphasis on managerial skills in selecting deputy chiefs of mission and other senior officials.[79]

## THE 9/11 ATTACKS

On the brilliant, sunny morning of September 11, 2001 (9/11), Naland and an AFSA delegation of active-duty and retired members, board members, and staff were on Capitol Hill, lobbying for full funding of the administration's budget request for international affairs, including the Diplomatic Readiness Initiative. The day was just beginning, with an early meeting in the hearing room of the Senate Foreign Relations Committee, where staff was telling the AFSA delegation that a member of Congress who spent five minutes a day on foreign affairs was a rarity.[80] The delegation was heading out in small groups to cover the 23 appointments on its schedule when reports flooded in of the disaster at the World Trade Center in New York, soon followed by the horrors from the Pentagon. The Capitol was rapidly evacuated.

The attacks and their aftermath changed AFSA's priorities and emphasis, but did not change its basic goal—a stronger, better-resourced, more professional Foreign Service. When John Naland testified in October 2011 before the Subcommittee on National Security of the House Committee on Government Reform, he called for full funding of the DRI. He did not dispute a recent Government Accountability Office report on staffing shortages at hardship posts. Instead, he repeated well-established AFSA positions: The department should adopt a fair-share rule to ensure tours at hardship posts are part of every Foreign Service member's career; disincentives to hardship tours, such as the lack of locality pay, should be removed; and new staffing requirements should be funded as they arise and not filled by stripping current positions of their incumbents.

The delegation that had heard the news in the Senate hearing room regrouped and returned to the Hill in May 2002 for AFSA's second "Day on the Hill" program. Bill Farrand, a member of the group, wrote, "This time around, the mood was different. There was genuine interest . . . in our message. . . . It was not necessary to remind our Hill interlocutors about the loss of Foreign Service lives in our embassies in Nairobi and Dar es Salaam, and, most recently, in a church in Islamabad."[81]

But the good feeling, if that was indeed what Farrand witnessed, did not last long.

# 10

## The Scapegoat Years, 2002–2009

By the summer of 2002, Congress was hard at work on the legislation that would create the Department of Homeland Security, and finger-pointing over the 9/11 attacks had begun. The U.S. embassy in Saudi Arabia had issued visas to 15 of the 20 hijackers; three of the visas had been issued without an interview. Several members of Congress said the Foreign Service treated visas as customer service, "a device to curry favor with foreign governments," not as an integral feature of national security. Some, including Representatives Dave Weldon (R-Fla.), Dan Burton (R-Ind.), and James Sensenbrenner (R-Wis.), wanted to transfer the visa function, or possibly the entire consular bureau, from State to the new department.[1] The American Foreign Service Association lobbied in defense of State's traditional role but did not testify.[2]

Events moved quickly. In July State's inspector general reported that the embassy in Riyadh had issued 32,000 visas the previous summer, 10,000 of them without a consular interview. After 9/11, said the inspector general, the department should have made "immediate and dramatic changes" in visa policy but did not.[3] The State Department had no coherent response to rising public pressure. The U.S. ambassador said in a cable (leaked to the press) that he was "deeply troubled about the prevailing perception in the media and within Congress, and possibly among the American public at large, that our current practices represent a shameful and inadequate effort on our part." But the embassy seemed to confirm that its policies were faulty when it canceled its Visa Express program, under which certain Saudi travel agencies handled some visa paperwork.

The spokesman for the Bureau of Consular Affairs insisted that "a proper review was done on the hijackers. . . . We would not be able to refuse those people today, in the absence of more information."[4] Even so, Secretary Powell fired the assistant secretary for consular affairs, Mary Ryan, a career Foreign Service officer who had held the job for more than eight years.

AFSA defended the consular bureau. President John Naland held meetings with 14 House staff members, arguing that intelligence agencies had withheld, and continued to withhold, relevant information. He found some sympathy in the House Committee on Foreign Affairs, but he was out in front in a losing cause. The White House had already decided to support those in Congress—a majority of members and nearly all of the president's closest political allies—who were demanding change.[5]

A Government Accountability Office (GAO) report on embassy staffing, published while the visa debate was underway, made AFSA's defense of the Service more difficult. With plenty of numbers to back it up, the report claimed that the vacancy rate for Foreign Service positions at hardship posts was 50 percent higher than in developed countries.[6] Former AFSA President Dennis Hays told the *New York Times*, "People are all too willing to take the comfy job. . . . People look at you as if you're insane if you talk about going to Pakistan or Somalia."[7] The reports of the inspector general and the GAO were validation for those in Congress, the administration, and the public who were prepared to believe that the Department of State was full of incompetents and the Foreign Service full of wimps.

AFSA struggled in this environment to promote professional excellence and fight for members' benefits. It pushed the department to strengthen fair-share rules on assignments, to ensure that all Foreign Service employees serve in hardship posts in the course of a career, and State agreed to make hardship duty a requirement for promotion into the Senior Foreign Service.[8]

On the Hill, whenever the association and the administration were aligned, there was some success. Congress approved nearly all the money and positions requested in the president's budget under the Diplomatic Readiness Initiative. When the association lacked administration backing—for example, in its appeal for overseas comparability (locality) pay—it came up short. But no one could fault the effort to appeal to Congress and the public.

In 2002 AFSA organized 252 speeches on foreign affairs and the Foreign Service, mainly by retired members. Retirees ran 16 one-week programs on the Foreign Service under the auspices of the Elderhostel organization (later renamed Road Scholar). The association placed 31 articles in print and had its statements carried on all four major commercial networks, plus CNN, NPR, and the BBC. By 2004, those numbers had risen to 442 speeches and 82 articles in print.

The second AFSA Day on the Hill, on May 9, 2002, involved some 60 AFSA officers, staff, and retired and active-duty members in meetings with (mostly

**Box 10.1.** *Inside a U.S. Embassy*

AFSA's most successful outreach program is an old-fashioned one: a book. *Inside a U.S. Embassy: How the Foreign Service Works for America* first appeared in 1996 as a 98-page guide to the work of U.S. missions abroad and includes profiles, stories, and day-in-the-life features from six embassies. The first edition was assembled by *Foreign Service Journal* Editor Karen Krebsbach.

The association published a new, 136-page second edition in March 2003 with the original title and format but all-new content and contributors. Former FSO Shawn Dorman, then the *FSJ's* associate editor, put together the 2003 edition.

With input from an advisory committee, Dorman selected and interviewed active-duty Foreign Service members in some two dozen different positions in different U.S. missions for job profiles. She compiled the results into a book of vignettes that capture day-to-day life in the Foreign Service on a personal, as well as professional, level. No book did or does a better job of answering the impossible question, "What do you do?"

AFSA launched the second edition of *Inside a U.S. Embassy* on March 27, 2003, to immediate acclaim and strong sales. The Department of State bought copies by the thousands for use in recruitment and outreach. By the time AFSA published a revised edition two years later, people considering a Foreign Service career knew that it gave the best insight to Foreign Service life. The updated edition included endorsements from former Secretaries of State George Shultz and Madeleine Albright, and from then–Senate Foreign Relations Committee Chair Richard Lugar (R-Ind.) and Ranking Minority Member Joseph "Joe" Biden (D-Del.).

A third, all-new edition in 2011, *Inside a U.S. Embassy: Diplomacy at Work*, expanded the original concept with material on the country team and interagency process, hiring, internships, and fellowships at State and other Foreign Service agencies.

By the end of 2022, more than 250,000 copies of *Inside a U.S. Embassy* had been sold in print and digital formats. The book has been adopted for more than 70 university courses, and U.S. military institutions and U.S. government agencies continue to use it for training courses. It was a *Washington Post* nonfiction bestseller in 2017.[a]

The book's critical and financial success allowed AFSA in 2009 to launch its own publishing imprint, Foreign Service Books, publisher of the history of AFSA you are now reading.

a. "Washington Post Bestsellers: February 19," *Washington Post*, February 19, 2017, https://www.washingtonpost.com/opinions/2017/02/15/89e3a3fe-f391-11e6-9fb1 -2d8f3fc9coed_story.html.

friendly) senators, representatives, and staff. The Coalition for American Leadership Abroad, a group of more than 50 nongovernmental organizations engaged with foreign affairs that AFSA joined in 1997, held a breakfast for congressional staff. The AFSA Fund became the Fund for American Diplomacy and raised $27,000 to support outreach. AFSA also provided expert and technical advice to National Geographic for its documentary *Ambassador: Under Fire Overseas,* shown on the Public Broadcasting System (PBS).[9] Perhaps most important of all, the new AFSA Political Action Committee made $60,000 in campaign contributions "to enable American diplomats," said the *Washington Post,* "to buy the attention of federal lawmakers for whom money speaks with the loudest voice."[10]

John Naland finished what turned out to be the first of two terms as AFSA president in July 2003. He left behind a strong organization, one with over $1 million in unrestricted net assets and a membership whose numbers had finally passed the high point reached in 1995.[11] His successor, John Limbert, running on the Front Line slate, was in Iraq when elected and did not take office until the fall. State Vice President Louise Crane filled in during his absence.

## JOHN LIMBERT RESPONDS TO CHEAP SHOTS

Limbert's life and career gave the lie to the notion that Foreign Service people were soft or that they sought out what Dennis Hays had called the "comfy" posts. "I remember a meeting with a staffer for the Senate majority leader, then Senator [Bill] Frist [R-Tenn.]," Limbert said. "He made some comment about our overprivileged life. I remained polite, though it was hard. I mentioned Iraq and Algeria, and Guinea, and Tehran, and Djibouti, and Mauritania." Limbert had served in all these places. He had been held hostage in Tehran from 1979 to 1981, served as ambassador to the Islamic Republic of Mauritania, and was one of the first civilian officials to enter Iraq after the fall of Baghdad in April 2003. He was fluent in Farsi, held multiple degrees from Harvard, and had taught at the U.S. Naval Academy.

"I didn't mean *you,* of course," the staffer said.[12]

Limbert called 2003 "the year of the scapegoat." Pat Robertson, head of the Christian Broadcasting Network, suggested dropping "a very small nuke" on the State Department.[13] Newt Gingrich, the former Speaker of the House, accused the department of undermining the president's foreign policy (though he also called for increasing the size of the Foreign Service by 40 percent, an idea later adopted by Secretary of State Hillary Rodham Clinton).[14] Louise Crane told the

Governing Board that attacks on the Service had gone beyond strictly conservative media and were appearing in mainstream outlets such as the *New York Times* and *Wall Street Journal*.[15]

Limbert was particularly annoyed by a twice-broadcast PBS program that depicted the U.S. ambassador in Yemen, career FSO Barbara Bodine, as so eager for good relations that around the time of the attack on the USS *Cole* in Aden's harbor in 2000, she had failed to stand up to the terrorist threat. "Nothing," said Limbert, "could have been further from the truth." The department, staying true to a tradition of timidity that reached back at least to the McCarthy era, failed to defend its people or to refute "the distortions and innuendos" the program leveled against Ambassador Bodine.[16]

The struggle to change perceptions—prejudices, really—about the Foreign Service was Sisyphean. By 2004, AFSA's outreach effort had grown to 442 speeches around the country, 82 articles in print, and television coverage on NBC, CBS, ABC, Fox News, Bloomberg News, PBS, NPR, and AP-TV. The effort sometimes seemed to make headway but with no enduring success. Limbert adopted the motto "Let no cheap shot go unanswered," but he had no illusions. He quoted Jonathan Swift: "You can't reason a man out of a thing he hasn't been reasoned into."[17]

Limbert and AFSA had more success with members' benefits, although those efforts, too, had their Sisyphean side. The Governing Board burst into applause when AFSA's congressional lobbyist, Ken Nakamura, announced that Congress passed the Military Families Tax Relief Act of 2003 with a provision making it easier for Foreign Service homeowners on official duty outside the United States to benefit from the tax exclusion on capital gains from the sale of a principal residence.[18] But the much larger issue of locality pay for Foreign Service personnel overseas remained unresolved. Nakamura took to calling locality pay either "pay equity" or overseas comparability pay (OCP) to clarify that what was sought was comparable base pay for Foreign Service employees, whether they served at home or abroad. The AFSA Board scaled back its demands from locality pay at the Washington rate—among the highest in the country—to the rate for the "rest of the United States," the lowest. But neither the change in language nor the change in position brought change on Capitol Hill, where the issue remained hard to explain to dubious staffers.[19] (See chapter 12.)

Because of the linkages between the pay scales for the Senior Foreign Service and the Senior Executive Service, AFSA and State were able to work together to secure the equivalent of locality pay for the SFS under an executive order signed in 2004.[20] Foreign Service employees below the senior grades, however, remained at a disadvantage. By the end of 2004, the gap between base pay in Washington and base pay overseas—the pay cut employees had to take for keeping the *foreign* in Foreign Service—was 16 percent.[21] Despite support from Secretary Powell, and later from Secretary Condoleezza Rice, the administration did not include funds for locality pay in its Fiscal Year 2005 or FY2006 budget requests. The Office of Management and Budget hinted that it would be willing to seek funds for locality pay as part of an overhaul that would place the entire Foreign Service on a pay-for-performance basis. But AFSA's leadership recognized that the proposal would eliminate automatic in-grade step increases without necessarily affecting the evaluation and promotion system.[22] Locality pay for all Foreign Service employees remained AFSA's highest priority and most difficult challenge.

AFSA's success in working with the department on pay for the SFS was not unusual. The association had a strong relationship with management. "We had a very good Director General in Bob Pearson," John Limbert said. "He was one of us." State's support was almost essential on any matter that involved the Hill. Republicans, generally less supportive of the Foreign Service than Democrats, controlled both chambers in the 108th and 109th Congresses (January 2003 to January 2007). Whatever the issue, "What is the department's position?" was the first question AFSA heard on the Hill. "Having Pearson and Powell helped a lot," said Limbert. "Secretary Rice was good too, interested in management, extremely conscientious."[23]

## TWO TESTS: IRAQ AND AFGHANISTAN

Iraq, and later Afghanistan, tested the Foreign Service in many ways. Service members proved willing to go to conflict zones but were hard-pressed to meet the challenges. Even in 2003 and early 2004, before the situation in Iraq had seriously deteriorated, the Foreign Service struggled to supply personnel for the missions they were asked to perform in Baghdad and around the country. Secretary Powell's DRI had brought welcome increases in the junior ranks, but the middle and senior grades were still depleted by the cuts of the 1990s. Posts around the world were stripped to meet the need in Iraq, which was the Service's highest priority.

Moreover, few members of the Service had served in a conflict zone, and even fewer had experience or training in political and economic stabilization. Most had to work through interpreters. Less than 1 percent of the Foreign Service could speak Arabic, and only tiny numbers had Pashto or Dari.

In addition, the mission was unclear. After a January 2003 presidential directive put the Pentagon in charge of the U.S. presence in Iraq,[24] the Defense Department hastily set up an Office of Reconstruction and Humanitarian Affairs (ORHA) under retired Army Lt. Gen. Jay Garner. But in the judgment of its senior State Department member, the office had "no staff, no structure, no recruiting process, and no resources."[25] By May 2003, the Pentagon had disbanded ORHA and established a Coalition Provisional Authority (CPA) in Baghdad, naming retired career Foreign Service Officer L. Paul "Jerry" Bremer to head it. The CPA stayed in place to the end of June 2004, when it turned authority over to an interim Iraqi government, to which an American ambassador, initially FSO John Negroponte, was accredited. His embassy was immediately the largest in the world.

The department's efforts to attract civilian volunteers to Iraq, and later Afghanistan, absorbed AFSA from the beginning. Secretary Powell raised the subject when AFSA's acting president, Louise Crane, met with him and Director General Pearson in March 2004. "There is a problem with 'hard to fill' [positions]," Powell said. "I should be able to send people where I need them." He compared the hectic bidding of the Foreign Service system to open outcry on the Chicago Mercantile Exchange, and he drew a contrast with the military, "where you can indicate preferences" for onward assignments, "and that's it."[26] Louise Crane replied that AFSA supported a fair-share process, not only to make sure hardship posts were staffed but to promote sharing difficult and dangerous service.

The problem Powell raised was not confined to Iraq and Afghanistan. In mid-2004, there were 12 posts with a total of about 400 Foreign Service positions where employees were unaccompanied by dependents and typically served one-year tours. AFSA, as Louise Crane repeatedly emphasized, wanted to reward employees who served in these positions with follow-on assignments to posts "with good schools . . . where there's a chance to restore family life, where the pace won't be so frenetic."[27] The association sent a message to State's bureaus with unsolicited advice: "Do not lock in your favored bidder early. It's against the negotiated rules, anyway. It will make AFSA mad and it violates the transparency the Service needs now more than ever. . . . You will not get the 400-plus bidders you need [for unaccompanied positions] unless there is the expectation their onward bids will be given due consideration."[28]

But AFSA strongly opposed any suggestion or implication that those who served in Iraq, Afghanistan, or other dangerous countries might be given a leg up for promotion. Specifically, it cited Secretary Powell's message to all diplomatic and consular posts that he was "fully confident that service at our posts in Iraq will be recognized in both the promotion and assignment process." This and a follow-up message, said AFSA's State Vice President Louise Crane in a response, "are overselling Iraq service and making promises that cannot be kept." The overselling "corrupts the Foreign Service. It devalues the substantive work you do elsewhere. . . . Promotions must be based on your performance, not your assignment. . . . We recognize service under difficult and dangerous conditions. No more and no less."[29] AFSA President John Limbert sent his own more temperate message to members, offering a different but concurring opinion. "We serve in Iraq for many reasons," he said, "including career advancement." However, the department's suggestion that a tour in Iraq will "lead to promotions and desired assignments" is "false advertising." Limbert found the department's stand "disappointing."[30]

In early 2005, the United States and its allies formally ended their fruitless search for weapons of mass destruction. The installation of a government in Baghdad that had the support of the Iraqi people and posed no threat to neighboring states became, retroactively, the chief purpose for which the war was waged. The U.S. administration began to develop civilian-led teams to work in provincial Iraq to build "a capability in [local] governing bodies to deliver to the people" what governments are supposed to provide.[31] Most of these Provincial Reconstruction Teams (PRTs) were led by U.S. Foreign Service officers (a few were led by civilians from other allied countries) and relied heavily on Foreign Service personnel.

By late 2005, an insurgency against the Iraqi government in Baghdad had taken hold, and levels of violence spiked. President George W. Bush issued National Security Presidential Directive 44, which assigned to the Department of State the lead role in planning, preparing, and conducting all U.S. government efforts to stabilize and rebuild countries and regions "at risk of, in, or in transition from conflict or civil strife," including Iraq and Afghanistan.[32] The new Secretary of State, Condoleezza Rice, turned to the Foreign Service to carry out this new, vast mandate, but additional resources were neither provided nor even sought. The pressures on the Service became overwhelming.

## TONY HOLMES TAKES THE AFSA HELM

AFSA's presidency passed in July 2005 from John Limbert to J. Anthony "Tony" Holmes and the State vice presidency from Louise Crane to Steven Kashkett. Tony Holmes had become active in AFSA at the embassy in Cairo, his first post, in 1980 and had often served as post representative. Like many AFSA leaders, he spent much of his career on African affairs. President Bush named him ambassador to Burkina Faso in 2002, and he came to the AFSA presidency from that assignment in 2005. "I was looking for another mission in Africa," he said, "but [Director General] Bob Pearson told me that none of the 17 ambassadors departing Africa that summer would get a follow-on ambassadorial assignment. The department needed those jobs for people coming out of Iraq." After talking to John Limbert, Holmes decided the AFSA job would be more interesting than anything else he was likely to find, and he agreed to run.

A conversation with Limbert was the incentive for Steve Kashkett as well. Kashkett, a political officer, had spent 20 years in the Service, with overseas tours in Halifax, Beirut, Paris, Port-au-Prince, and Jerusalem. "I was concerned about Iraq and what it was doing to the Foreign Service," he recalls. "I was a member of AFSA but had never paid much attention to it. Then I ran into John Limbert on the street, and he kind of talked me into running for the AFSA job."[33] Holmes and Kashkett were the key figures on the Governing Board that took office in July 2005.

## Sticks and Carrots

From the beginning of the new board's term, Iraq dominated the agenda and colored every issue. An online survey of members found a split on how to entice volunteers to Iraq and Afghanistan, and reward those who served there.[34] According to Steve Kashkett, a "great many" respondents objected to preferential treatment in promotions and assignments, but "a handful" serving in the two war zones argued that "they deserve every possible compensation for living through the hell of being posted in those places." Holmes, Kashkett, and the board agreed that rewards "could and should include" extra pay, rest and recreation, family visits, home leave, and fulfillment of career development requirements. But "promotions are a zero-sum game," and "willingness and ability to go to Baghdad or Kabul for a year, while commendable, tell us little about the skills that should qualify an employee for promotion."[35]

In contrast to his predecessor, Louise Crane, Kashkett also opposed using assignments to reward war zone volunteers. Such service, he said, should not "trump strong qualifications of other bidders" for a particular job. But as pressures from the department rose, he proposed, and the board agreed, that AFSA assent to a management plan to give onward assignment preferences to volunteers serving on PRTs in Iraq.[36] Preferences eventually turned into linked assignments, in which volunteers were paneled simultaneously into Iraq and an onward assignment. The imbalance between the one-year tours in Iraq and the three-year, follow-on tours meant that linked assignments could not be long sustained, but for a time they served their purpose.

The department accepted a long-standing AFSA proposal to increase the maximum hardship-differential and danger-pay bonus to 35 percent each. But in a move it advertised as revenue neutral, it ended the differential at all 5 percent hardship-differential posts. Family members of Iraq volunteers coming out of government housing were allowed to stay in their government quarters, or to keep their housing allowance, during the year of separation. By the spring of 2006, more than 1,000 Foreign Service and Civil Service colleagues had already volunteered, and by the spring of 2007, more than 22 percent of all Foreign Service personnel had served in Iraq or Afghanistan.[37]

Nonetheless, Iraq staffing demands did not abate. Secretary of State Condoleezza Rice's right to order Foreign Service employees, who are available for worldwide service, to Iraq or any other posting was unquestioned; but neither she nor AFSA, nor most Foreign Service employees, wanted to see that authority invoked.

"Up to 2003," said Kashkett, "when a country became a war zone, we shut down the diplomatic mission. In Iraq, for the first time we were not drawing down but ramping up." Some in the Foreign Service, and many outside it, thought the Secretary should simply order people to go where she needed them and be done with it. AFSA disagreed. Kashkett explained: "Directed assignments would have been a disaster. We are not the military. Telling us—single mothers, middle-aged guys with families, unarmed civilians with no military training—that we have to serve in a live-fire zone is not something we should ever be doing. We should do everything possible to get people to volunteer, but service in a war zone should remain voluntary. That was the position of the AFSA board."[38]

AFSA and the department's leadership developed a deep and mutual mistrust. Secretary Rice wrote in her memoir,

> My biggest challenge in taking the reins at State was to ensure the active loyalty of the Foreign Service. I use the modifier "active" because I don't mean to suggest that people were disloyal. But they did sometimes appear less than enthusiastic about the president's policies, and, at worst, some (but not all) kept a kind of psychic distance from the more controversial decisions that had been made. In blunt terms, Iraq had to be the Department of State's war, too—not Bush's war, not the Pentagon's, but *America's* war. And the president's vision for a democratic Middle East had to be more than a slogan that diplomats repeated without believing it to be possible.[39]

**Box 10.2.** The *Journal* and Iraq

The *Foreign Service Journal* dealt with service in Iraq in a way no other publication could, through the eyes of the diplomats and development professionals who were there. From 2004 to 2008, in addition to monthly coverage of the AFSA perspective in AFSA News, the *Journal* focused each March issue on Iraq.

In its July–August 2007 edition, the editors of *Columbia Journalism Review* published an editorial, "Missed Story in Iraq: When Diplomats Are in Danger," highlighting the annual focus on Iraq. They noted, "Every March since the war in Iraq began, the *Foreign Service Journal*—the house organ of the American Foreign Service Association, the professional organization and union for U.S. foreign service employees—has examined the state of diplomacy and nation-building in Iraq. Reading those issues, one thing is apparent: the press has largely ignored an important story about the consequences for thousands of civilian foreign service employees of the administration's disastrous war."[a]

a. "Missed Story in Iraq: When Diplomats Are in Danger," op-ed, *Columbia Journalism Review*, July–August 2007, https://archives.cjr.org/editorial/editorial.php.

She was prepared, she said, "to require Foreign Service officers to serve in Iraq. . . . Ultimately, I didn't have to, because enough people volunteered. But I was prepared to do so and to face down the American Foreign Service Association—a kind of union for U.S. diplomats—before Congress and the American people, if necessary."[40]

The AFSA Board soon came to see the administration as hostile toward the Foreign Service. The belief was widespread in AFSA that the State Department's leadership, including senior career people as well as outside appointees, was quick to bad-mouth the Service to the press, quick to disparage those who questioned the administration's policies, and quick to blame the Service for poor outcomes in Iraq. Tony Holmes, looking back at his time at AFSA, wrote, "The Bush administration's general efforts to stifle dissent and to reward those serving in Iraq with promotions and choice assignments . . . led to the unmistakable politicization of the Foreign Service."[41]

Ill will made ordinary issues difficult and hard issues impossible. The 2005 membership survey had identified winning overseas comparability pay as AFSA's top priority. Secretary Rice expressed support for OCP in meetings with AFSA's leadership, but she did not resist when OMB refused to include it in the president's budget request for FY2006.[42]

For FY2007, the State Department, with the White House's support, proposed to provide budget authority for OCP but linked to the replacement of automatic in-grade pay increases with a pay-for-performance program similar to that in place in the Senior Foreign Service.[43] AFSA was understandably suspicious. It saw the proposed linkage as a maneuver to increase political control over performance evaluations and to use the promise of promotion as an incentive to generate volunteers for duty in Iraq. "The department didn't want to admit that its policies were so unpopular that volunteers were lacking among the professionals who had to implement them," said Tony Holmes. Instead, "they wanted to make promotions dependent on willingness to comply with the demands of the administration, not on actual performance. Legally, they could not do this. So they tried to suborn us" with locality pay.[44] Others believed pay-for-performance was a promise the administration would never keep. When the U.S. Agency for International Development, citing budgetary constraints, refused to award those increases to its SFS, those members who had dismissed pay-for-performance as nothing more than a cover for reducing employee pay felt vindicated.[45]

The lack of comparability pay was no small matter. By 2006, members of the Foreign Service were taking a 17.5 percent cut in base pay when assigned abroad. As a result, the department's proposal attracted many members of the Service. AFSA negotiated changes in a draft Foreign Service Modernization Bill to protect a role for selection boards in determining performance-pay awards, and it hoped to have the modified proposal included in a State authorization bill.[46]

In the end, the House leadership dropped OCP from the bill, ostensibly over concerns about cost.[47] Tony Holmes in retrospect judged that "the Republicans were atavistically against the Foreign Service and the Democrats had a visceral, labor-union reaction to pay-for-performance. It was never going to happen."[48]

## The Brussels Assignment

Mistrust and ill will characterized a dispute between AFSA and the department's management over the assignment in the summer of 2006 of Diane Zeleny, a mid-level (GS-15) civil servant, to a newly created position at the U.S. mission to the European Union in Brussels.[49] The dispute echoed the 1999 fight over the assignment of Roberta Jacobson as deputy chief of mission in Lima, Peru.

Zeleny worked in the office of Under Secretary for Public Diplomacy Karen Hughes. To increase the exposure of foreign media to American policymakers, Hughes had established public diplomacy hubs in Brussels, Dubai, and London, and the department assigned Zeleny to run the hub in Brussels. The SFS position had not been advertised, and as in the Lima case, no certificate of need had been prepared.

"We got wind of this very early on and we warned them," said Tony Holmes, "but they went ahead anyway. Then they lied to us. They told us they had reached out to four FSOs who were technically qualified. We got the names, and every single one said they had never been contacted."[50] He wrote to Secretary Rice in October "with a sense of deep sadness" at the department's "unfathomable" decision and "inexplicable abuse" of its own rules, procedures, and labor-management agreements. The letter called the assignment "pre-cooked" and informed the Secretary that AFSA had filed a grievance to undo it.[51]

The letter and the grievance got the department's attention. In December, Director General George Staples sent a message of apology to the field and invited Tony Holmes to sign on. The letter stated that the assignment would be curtailed and steps taken to ensure that the incident would not be repeated. The grievance was withdrawn.[52]

## THE ELECTION OF 2007

A survey of active-duty State Department AFSA members at the end of 2006 found that two-thirds thought that AFSA should be "more vocal and assertive" in pursuit of members' interests. Nevertheless, by the spring of 2007 some members of the AFSA Board had come to believe that Tony Holmes's aggressive style was an impediment to negotiations with the department. A group coalesced around former President John Naland and formed Team AFSA to run as a slate in the 2007 elections. The slate, which included five incumbent board members, said in its campaign flyer that "the current AFSA president has burned too many bridges with key interlocutors, including the Secretary of State and the Director General of the Foreign Service, to effectively represent AFSA members over the next two years."[53]

Turnout was just 17 percent, about 2,300 voters of nearly 14,000 members. Holmes ran for reelection as an independent, with no slate, as did Steve Kashkett and USAID Vice President Francisco Zamora, whom Team AFSA did not challenge. All members of Team AFSA won, Naland by about two to one.[54] Kashkett and Zamora won second terms.

"Of course," John Naland said later, "once I took office, I saw firsthand what Tony had been up against. Colin Powell [Secretary during Naland's first term as president] treated the Foreign Service as he would his own classic automobile. Secretary Rice treated us like a rented car."[55]

## AFSA AND IRAQ

In 2007 State Department management had little time or attention for any issue but the staffing of Iraq. Columnists, talking heads, and media celebrities who were most fervent in support of the war, and of the president, found the department easy to attack.[56] *New York Post* columnist (and retired Army lieutenant colonel) Ralph Peters in December 2006 wrote of "our self-adoring diplomats," saying, falsely, that "State couldn't get enough volunteers even for its 90-day stints in Iraq," where "every major program that it insisted on running failed."[57] Max Boot, then with the Council on Foreign Relations, used op-ed space in the *New York Times* to complain that "diplomats aren't pulling their weight in Iraq and Afghanistan."[58] Secretary Rice told Congress that State could staff only 87 percent of the positions it needed to fill in Iraq. She asked the Defense Department to fill 129 slots with its personnel, which drew this response from Adm. Edmund Giambastiani, vice chairman of the Joint Chiefs of Staff: "The problem, not surprisingly, is we're used to deploying over there. We send out orders, we execute orders, we deploy our military, and guess what happens? They turn up and do the job."[59]

Although it had trouble staffing the 10 PRTs deployed in Iraq at the beginning of 2007, the department planned to increase the number to 20. Director General Harry Thomas banned extensions of tours in non-hardship posts and cut the maximum consecutive length of service in Washington from six years to five. He changed assignments policy to require that positions be filled in order: Iraq, Afghanistan, and other unaccompanied posts first; followed by other high-hardship and high-danger posts; then posts with critical needs and historically hard-to-staff posts; and only then the rest of the world.[60] Volunteers for service in Iraq were immediately transferred, leaving vacancies that might remain unfilled for months, if not years. By November 2007, 21 percent of Foreign Service positions, overseas and in the department, had no one in them.[61] Steve Kashkett recalls, "Iraq changed everything. Everything became about getting people to serve there. It had a corrupting influence on assignments, incentives, promotions. The idea that when it gets too dangerous for diplomats to function, we evacuate them, that idea went out the window. The Foreign Service, where good work done anywhere was commendable, was transformed. The Service was suddenly all about hardship."[62]

On October 26, 2007, the department notified some 200 people that unless volunteers stepped forward, they would be "prime candidates" to fill some 48 vacant positions in Iraq. Director General Harry Thomas held a town hall meeting, broadcast on the department's internal BNET, on October 31, 2007, to discuss the program.

The meeting broke down in recriminations. John Naland began the question-and-answer period by noting there were "only about 30 spaces left" on the plaque memorializing members of the Service who died abroad under heroic or tragic circumstances. He said that in a poll of AFSA members, only 12 percent "believe that Secretary Rice is fighting for them," and "sometimes, if it's 88 to 12, maybe the 88 percent are correct."

"Eighty-eight percent of the country believed in slavery at one time," said Thomas, who is Black. "Was that correct?" He added, "I really resent people telling me that I do not care about other Foreign Service officers."

In the most widely quoted remark from the event, an officer who identified himself as John Croddy said that assignment to Iraq is "a potential death sentence." "Thanks for your comment," said Thomas, who abruptly closed the meeting.[63]

To the surprise of many officers who attended the meeting, an Associated Press reporter was in the room. Media coverage of the event was extensive, colorful, and negative. Less than three weeks later, the department canceled the "prime candidate" exercise, and the department's spokesman bragged at the daily press briefing that Foreign Service volunteers had stepped up to fill all the remaining vacant positions in Iraq.[64] But the damage had been done. The October 31 meeting, and the press accounts that followed, poisoned relationships between AFSA and management. Members of the public and members of Congress who had never thought well of the Foreign Service felt confirmed in their prejudices. Weblogs, then a fairly new phenomenon, burbled with vituperation. On the department's own *DipNote* blog, FSOs—anonymously—called each other "wimps" and "weenies."

The rancorous exercise had been wholly unnecessary. John Naland blamed "senior officials" who raised "the specter of ordered assignments" to win favor with their "political superiors." In so doing, he wrote, "they undermined congressional and public confidence in the Foreign Service."[65]

Naland knew that the problems of the Foreign Service in Iraq stemmed from a lack of resources and good management, not of courage, talent, loyalty, or duty. A former Army officer and Army War College graduate, he found colorful ways to contrast State and Defense: "The military has more musicians than the State Department has diplomats."[66] He ended his presidency a month early to take an assignment as head of the PRT in Basra, Iraq. The preparation he received for this assignment was the same as that given to nearly all the volunteers for what the department called its most important mission: "Plunk me down in Iraq, no Arabic, never been in the Middle East before, never rebuilt a country before. They just say, hey, do your best."[67]

## Damage Control

The year 2007 was a low point for the Foreign Service and the way it was seen by the State Department's leadership, the White House, the administration's supporters on Capitol Hill, most of the media, and much of the public. AFSA's annual report was succinct: "AFSA's task in 2008 was to stop the damage being done to the career Foreign Service and to prepare for a counteroffensive in 2009 to regain lost ground."[68]

There was much to do. In early 2008, when concerns arose about filling the vacancies that would open in Iraq and Afghanistan in the summer of 2009, AFSA urged State "to simply put out a call for volunteers at an early stage in the process, appealing to our members' sense of duty and patriotism."[69] Department officials did just that, and volunteers came forward to fill every vacancy in Iraq and Afghanistan a year ahead of time. To AFSA's annoyance, the department's leadership, which had done so much damage by hyping the problems in staffing Iraq at the end of 2007, did nothing to publicize the filling of positions in 2008. AFSA issued its own release, appealing to the media to "set the record straight" and report that the Foreign Service and Civil Service colleagues "have stepped forward without hesitation every year to staff the embassies and Provincial Reconstruction Teams of these two war zones." The AFSA release had relatively little impact.[70]

The struggles over war zone staffing and the loss of many positions around the world to that staffing (what became known as "the Iraq tax") had corrosive by-products. Members of the Foreign Service came to believe that assignments and promotions had been corrupted, that the department's leadership and management had given preferential treatment to certain senior officers, staff assistants, and bureau favorites. A 2008 AFSA survey that drew replies from more than 4,000 active-duty members of State's Foreign Service placed unfairness second only to closing the overseas pay gap among members' concerns. Constant appeals from senior department officials would be more believable, respondents said, "if many of those same senior officials had actually volunteered for an unaccompanied war zone tour themselves"—and if not so many careerists were rewarded "for seventh-floor loyalty" with "comfortable ambassadorships" without their having served in Iraq or Afghanistan themselves.[71]

Naland, too, saw toadies at the top. He accused unnamed senior officials of "failing to stand up for the career Service," of acting as "compliant yes-men and yes-women," and of shirking their professional responsibilities for "personal gains such as obtaining . . . a plum assignment" leading to a promotion or a performance-pay bonus.[72] "Have some senior career officials 'sold their souls' over Iraq and other issues in order to advance their careers?" he asked. "I believe they have."[73]

## CLOSING THE OVERSEAS PAY GAP

The single most important issue for AFSA members continued to be OCP. In 2007 the difference between the regular Foreign Service base salary in Washington, which included locality pay, and that in overseas posts, which did not, was 20.88 percent. As AFSA put it in testimony on the Hill, a member of the Foreign Service who spent five years overseas effectively worked one year for no pay at all.

Since 2001, every AFSA president and members of AFSA-PAC had worked to educate lawmakers about the need to close the pay gap. Rather than depending on what had been on-again, off-again support from the administration for inclusion of overseas locality pay, AFSA's strategy shifted in 2008 to securing support for a stand-alone bill linked to pay-for-performance for all Foreign Service ranks. The association's legislative director, Ian Houston, spoke repeatedly to staff and members of the House Foreign Affairs Committee and urged AFSA members to raise the issue with congressional members and staff traveling overseas.

The committee favorably reported a Foreign Service Overseas Pay Equity Act of 2008 that phased in locality pay over three years with no linkage to pay-for-performance and raised the death gratuity benefit for Foreign Service members who die as a result of injuries sustained in the performance of duties overseas. Sen. John Kerry (D-Mass.) sponsored a nearly identical bill in the Senate, which the committee approved by voice vote, but Sen. Tom Coburn (R-Okla.) placed a hold on Kerry's bill and blocked a vote. In the House, as well, the session ended before the bill came to a vote on the floor.[74]

The defeat marked a trail to victory. By 2009, the calumny that the Foreign Service was unwilling to serve in Iraq had lost much of its force. The Democratic Party's sweeping victory in the 2008 elections ended the administration's push to place the entire Service on a pay-for-performance system. Ken Nakamura, now at the Congressional Research Service after years as AFSA's legislative director, produced a report on OCP that allowed congressional staff to cut through the complexities and see the matter of fairness that was at the heart of the issue.[75]

In this new climate, AFSA's years of legislative gardening yielded a harvest at last. A 2009 supplemental appropriations bill, signed into law in June, provided the Department of State temporary authority to pay members of the Service in Class 1 and below at Washington rates when they served abroad.[76] The department intended to implement the change in three tranches, each making up one-third of the gap, in August 2009, 2010, and 2011. (As of March 2023, the third tranche is still pending; see chapter 11 for further details.) Within weeks, members of the Foreign Service around the world saw the first results in their paychecks.[77]

## USAID, THE FOREIGN COMMERCIAL SERVICE, AND THE FOREIGN AGRICULTURAL SERVICE

Over the past half century, perhaps no agency in the federal government had experienced repeated reorganization more frequently than USAID. The agency had not recovered from the reduction in force of the mid-1990s that had cut a third of the Foreign Service and Civil Service staff, leaving the agency with just 2,000 direct-hire employees. As foreign assistance programs increased in number, size, and scope, the staff and its operating budget became increasingly inadequate. Administrators had to find ways to divert program funds to cover operating costs and to use contract employees to perform administrative work in Washington and overseas.

By 2008, USAID was an agency in disarray. Three administrators had come and gone in eight years. Francisco Zamora, the longtime AFSA vice president for USAID, urged the new administration to support the Development Leadership Initiative—a hiring program similar to Colin Powell's Diplomatic Readiness Initiative at State—to increase the agency's Foreign Service staff from 1,200 to more than 2,000 in five years. But AFSA opposed bringing in new Foreign Service employees at middle grades, except as a last resort, and it supported the conversion of USAID's many non-career Foreign Service personnel, whose appointments were limited to five years, to Civil Service status.[78] Management, however, allowed non-career Foreign Service personnel with two years of in-country service to seek conversion to career status at mid-level grades (FS-2).[79]

The Foreign Agricultural Service and the Foreign Commercial Service were similarly stressed. In 2009 FAS faced its third freeze on all hiring, training, and travel since the mid-1990s, and its staffing was fully 22 percent below its authorized level.[80] The Foreign Service Grievance Board and the Foreign Service Labor Relations Board found that FAS management regularly assigned Civil Service employees to overseas positions without advertising the positions to Foreign Service employees, as required by AFSA's collective bargaining agreement.[81] At the Department of Commerce, FCS "froze hiring, international travel, nonessential domestic travel, overtime, training, technology upgrades, and even purchases of some office supplies."[82] At both Departments of Commerce and Agriculture, foreign programs and the Foreign Service people who carried them out were tiny parts of a much larger package. AFSA, trying to make the case for staff and funding, found it hard to get the attention of decision-makers in the agencies, at OMB, and on Capitol Hill.

## A YEAR OF TRANSITIONS

AFSA underwent several transitions of its own in 2009. The renovation of the headquarters building at 2101 E Street Northwest—a $2.2 million project overseen by Executive Director John Mamone, who had succeeded longtime Executive Director Susan Reardon in June 2007—was completed in March, to the great relief of staff members who had been camping out in temporary offices for nearly 18 months. (For most of that period, they occupied rent-free space in a State Department annex.) It was a mark of AFSA's financial strength that the association could finance nearly half the cost with its cash reserves; it borrowed the remainder from the Scholarship Fund at a commercial rate of interest.[83] Legislative Director Ian Houston succeeded John Mamone as AFSA's executive director in January 2009, and John Naland and Steve Kashkett stepped down when a new Governing Board took over in July.

The last six months of Naland's presidency coincided with the start of Barack Obama's administration. Every Foreign Service agency hoped for more resources and better times. Naland testified in support of the Obama administration's first budget, which he hailed as "a multiyear effort to significantly increase the size of the Foreign Service" at State and USAID. "We at the American Foreign Service Association wholeheartedly endorse that," he said.[84]

Naland's testimony cited a study that found "the Secretary of State lacks the tools—people, competencies, authorities, programs and funding—to execute the president's foreign policies."[85] AFSA had taken part in that study, which former AFSA President Tom Boyatt had led for the American Academy of Diplomacy. The study, "A Foreign Affairs Budget for the Future," concluded that State needed to increase staffing by 3,441, and USAID by 1,250, over five years.[86] Many of the ideas and analysis in the study found their way into Secretary Hillary Rodham Clinton's initiative, billed as "Diplomacy 3.0," launched in 2009 to strengthen the Department of State and USAID.[87]

The outgoing board and the incoming Secretary met in March 2009. Naland, Kashkett, and Zamora talked about the demands on U.S. diplomacy, which would require dramatic budget and staffing increases to meet. They also highlighted family issues: Spouses need a chance to work overseas, they said, and domestic partners deserve the same benefits and opportunities as spouses. After asking for an end to the intense focus on Iraq, which had left the perception that other work is not valued, they encouraged the new administration to use the "seasoned career experts" of the Foreign Service as ambassadors, senior officials, and special envoys.[88]

AFSA would have a new Governing Board before the administration's response became clear.

# 11

## Squeeze from the Top, 2009–2015

Over the next six years, the Foreign Service saw growth in its ranks. New hires exceeded attrition—retirements and resignations—by a wide margin. But staffing problems persisted in the upper grades, and for senior personnel, opportunities withered. A hoped-for surge in appointments of career officers as chiefs of mission did not transpire. Senior positions in the Department of State went, in ever larger numbers and ever greater proportions, to political appointees. Career employees found themselves stymied as they sought to move to positions of greater responsibility. AFSA, unable by law to bargain on hiring, promotions, assignments, or many other management prerogatives, was stymied as well.

### DIPLOMACY 3.0

Just four weeks after the 2008 election, Barack Obama tapped Sen. Hillary Clinton (D-N.Y.) as his choice for Secretary of State.[1] Broad approval greeted the nomination, and on the day after the inauguration, the Senate confirmed her by a vote of 94 to two.[2]

The new Secretary proved willing to use her enormous political capital early on. A few weeks after taking office, she announced Diplomacy 3.0, a resource-focused initiative named for the three strands of policy—diplomacy, development, and defense—that she intended to integrate. Diplomacy 3.0 sought to increase the size of State's Foreign Service corps by 25 percent and State's Civil Service by 13 percent by the end of Fiscal Year 2013.[3] A parallel program at USAID, the Development Leadership Initiative (DLI), aimed to double that agency's Foreign Service staff from 1,200 to 2,400 by the end of FY2012.[4] When President Obama announced a National Export Initiative in his January 2010

State of the Union address, expectations rose at the Foreign Commercial Service and the Foreign Agricultural Service that much-needed personnel and budgetary increases would be forthcoming there as well.[5]

The drive for resources had to contend with the financial crash that began with the collapse of Lehman Brothers in September 2008. The crash produced a federal budget deficit of $1.3 trillion in FY2010—almost $1.8 trillion in 2022 dollars—siphoning government resources into economic stimulus packages. Hiring under Diplomacy 3.0 and DLI slowed sharply.

Even so, State and USAID saw dramatic growth in personnel. By the end of Calendar Year 2012, Foreign Service positions at State had grown by 21 percent, and Civil Service positions by 9 percent, above their 2008 levels.[6] When the DLI ended in 2012, the number of Foreign Service personnel at USAID had grown by 40 percent to more than 1,700.[7]

Agencies with secretaries not named Clinton fared less well. The Foreign Agricultural Service began cutting back its overseas presence in 2011. The Foreign Commercial Service, like the Department of State, shifted personnel from low-priority posts in Europe to high-priority posts in fast-growing emerging markets, but the hoped-for increase in personnel did not materialize.[8]

## SUSAN ROCKWELL JOHNSON

The Diplomacy 3.0 initiative coincided with Susan Johnson's two terms as president of AFSA from 2009 to 2013. Johnson was the first woman to be elected to the office; indeed, she was the first to run.[9] She was a double Foreign Service brat: Her mother, as demanded in those days, had given up a Foreign Service career to marry Johnson's father, a Foreign Service officer whose long career included nine overseas tours. Since joining the Service in 1979, Johnson had been posted to every continent except Australia and Antarctica. She had worked on Capitol Hill, in private business, and for nongovernmental organizations (NGOs). She had, as she later said, "experienced the Foreign Service and diplomacy from multiple angles—as a family member, as an FSO, as the spouse of a foreign diplomat, and as an 'insider on the outside' through leave without pay during which I continued to work in the foreign affairs sector and in support of department goals."[10] When she returned to Washington in 2006 from an assignment as deputy high representative for Bosnia and Herzegovina, and supervisor of the Brčko district, no part of her ticket remained unpunched.

Johnson was not an AFSA activist, but as her tour in the Bureau of Democracy, Human Rights, and Labor wound down, she said, "I began to think about the Foreign Service, its role in the department, its quality, its leadership. Bill Far-rand, a former board member and a predecessor as Brcko supervisor, put the AFSA idea in my head. Then Tex Harris approached me and encouraged me to run in the 2009 elections." She consulted other board members, who "grabbed at me like a life raft and urged me to put a slate together."[11] Her Team AFSA slate, which included seven incumbent members of the Governing Board, emphasized strengthening the Foreign Service as an institution with a particular culture, unique values, and high standards. The word "profession" appeared more than a dozen times in the slate's campaign statement. By contrast, the opposing CLEAN slate (for Courageous Leadership and Effective Action Now) emphasized bring-ing AFSA closer to the membership through changes in governance (transpar-ency, term limits, election reforms), with more focus on AFSA as a union.

Voters split their tickets. Ten members of Team AFSA won, including John-son, who won the presidency with 53 percent of the vote. The position of AFSA State vice president went to CLEAN slate's Daniel Hirsch. Candidates from both slates filed complaints about violations of election rules with the Department of Labor's Office of Labor-Management Standards (OLMS), which found probable cause to conclude the election may not have been conducted in accordance with the requirements of the Labor-Management Reporting and Disclosure Act of 1959. Both slates, said the OLMS report, had improperly used state.gov email addresses, AFSA members' email address lists, and the *Foreign Service Journal* to promote their campaigns. AFSA and OLMS agreed that the 2011 election would be run under OLMS supervision.[12]

Depending on one's point of view, the board elected in 2009 was divided or diverse. It included officers and specialists, new recruits and old hands, those concerned mainly with Foreign Service working conditions and those con-cerned mainly with its professional vocation. When the board met on a Saturday in November to draw up its agenda for the year ahead, agreement proved hard to reach. After an all-day meeting, the board settled on 14 priorities grouped under four goals: securing resources for the Service and protecting benefits, increasing cooperation with management, improving the image and outreach of the For-eign Service, and improving AFSA's internal organization.[13] As one participant observed, "We may have spread ourselves too thin."[14]

Professional issues were Johnson's special concern. "I believe," she said, "the Department of State is less and less a healthy environment for the Foreign Ser-vice as a professional cadre. The bureaucratization, the politicization—I mean the patronage—fills positions with short-term appointees with their own agen-das, people who don't know the institution and don't seem inclined to take on the heavy lift that's needed for the reforms that are long overdue."[15] From the start of her first term, she devoted many of her monthly President's Views columns in the *Foreign Service Journal* to the subject. She set up a Committee on Professionalism and Ethics to define and codify the core values and ethical standards that distinguish diplomacy as a profession, and she surveyed active-duty members for their views.[16] When the American Academy of Diplomacy launched a study on professional education and training, AFSA joined in with money, staff time, and other resources.[17]

Union issues did not fade away, of course. Overseas comparability pay, which AFSA polling identified as the association's top priority, had constant attention from AFSA's advocacy staff and support in the Department of State. Efforts on the Hill secured the second OCP tranche in appropriations legislation for FY2010 and cut the pay gap, which had risen to 24 percent, to just 8 percent.[18] A 2009 bill that authorized the third and final tranche passed the House of Representatives, but despite the sponsorship of Foreign Relations Committee Chairman John Kerry, a companion bill in the Senate failed to reach a vote on the floor. By 2014, the pay gap had again begun to widen.[19]

The Labor Management (LM) Office, AFSA's largest with eight of the association's then 28 staff members, had a weekly workload of 350 to 400 inquiries on aspects of Foreign Service employment. In addition to individual cases, AFSA attorneys successfully pursued a grievance on behalf of more than 200 Senior Foreign Service officers and specialists who had been denied an opportunity to compete for performance bonuses; more than 50 of them received retroactive bonuses and pay raises. Similarly, several dozen Diplomatic Security agents received back pay and raises after AFSA showed that the State Department had assigned them too low a pay level when they entered the Service.[20]

## A Second Term

Johnson won a second term—as did Daniel Hirsch as State vice president—in 2011. The low turnout indicated that AFSA's voting membership, which over the previous decade had grown by more than 40 percent, had little interest in the governance of the association. Even though the presidency was contested, only 2,523 of AFSA's roughly 15,100 voting members—less than 17 percent—cast a ballot. Some offices had no candidates. Under the association's bylaws, 10 seats on the board went to representatives of the State Department, one for every 1,000 active-duty AFSA members in the department. But only six candidates were on the ballot, leaving four seats to be filled by the highest vote-getters among the more than 250 individuals who received write-in votes. The four winners received just 18, 16, six, and three votes each. And because none of the dozen AFSA members from the Broadcasting Board of Governors voted, the position of its representative went vacant.[21]

The low percentage of members who voted may have been related to the surge in AFSA's membership, which paralleled the surge in Foreign Service employment under Diplomacy 3.0 at the State Department and under the Development Leadership Initiative at USAID. AFSA membership rose from close to 14,000 at the end of 2008 to more than 16,000 in 2013—a gain of 17 percent.[22] Even if the new members were not fully engaged in AFSA's governance, their membership dues strengthened the association's already healthy finances.

Stronger finances supported internal improvement. Following an outside review of AFSA staff salaries and benefits in 2010, AFSA commissioned a broad review of its operational and board structure in 2012 under the auspices of the AFSA Finance, Audit, and Management Committee chaired by Treasurer Andrew Winter. The study afforded the staff and board an opportunity to discuss and debate how AFSA could build on its strengths and improve its organization.

The review recommended improvements related to staff review policies, general governance, and communications. AFSA responded by holding more frequent and regular meetings of the Executive Committee, establishing a Governance Committee, and creating a new director of communications position, consolidating responsibility for the full range of communications activity—website, social media, events, Foreign Service Books, the *Foreign Service Journal* including AFSA News, Speakers Bureau, Road Scholar program (formerly Elderhostel), editing, marketing, and press relations—in one department.[23]

Separately, in 2012, the *Foreign Service Journal,* largely unchanged in design since 1994, got a new look, a bright, snazzy design with fresh graphics and cleaner fonts. The October 2012 launch issue fittingly celebrated "The New Foreign Service Generation," and a launch party in the State Department's Benjamin Franklin Diplomatic Reception Room drew 200 guests.[24] William Burns and Linda Thomas-Greenfield, then deputy secretary of State and Director General of the Foreign Service, respectively, spoke at the event.[25] In addition to PDF and FlippingBook formats, the *Journal* became available in HTML format on AFSA's website, making it easier to read and share via social media. Traffic to the *Journal*'s page at the AFSA website jumped.[26]

In late 2012, the Foreign Service employees of the Department of Agriculture's Animal and Plant Health Inspection Service voted to select AFSA as their exclusive representative.[27] The first APHIS representative joined the Governing Board in 2014.

## Digging in the Data

Progress on these internal matters occurred while the association struggled to understand and respond to pressures for change in the Foreign Service itself. One point of pressure was the shortage of experienced personnel, a shortage that the surge in entry-level hiring could not quickly relieve. "That's what led me in my second term to start to gather data," Johnson said. "The department doesn't keep good demographic data. They don't share it easily. Sometimes they don't have it. Their analyses are not always neutral or informed."[28]

A June 2012 Government Accountability Office report found that "28 percent of overseas Foreign Service positions were either vacant or filled by upstretch candidates—officers serving in positions above their grade."[29] When management at State and USAID considered relieving the shortage by hiring new members of the Foreign Service at the middle grades, AFSA fought the idea, as it had in the late 1940s and early 1950s. "Where can many new mid-level employees be found?" John Naland wrote in January 2009. "One place not to look is outside the Foreign Service."[30]

Naland's argument—repeated by Johnson, AFSA USAID Vice President Francisco Zamora, and Johnson's successor, Robert J. Silverman—was twofold: Outsiders do not have the knowledge or experience for mid-level Foreign Service jobs, and mid-level hiring would be unfair to those who entered the system at the bottom. AFSA suggested five other ways for agencies to fill shortages: increasing promotion rates, calling back retirees, offering extensions to those facing time-in-class limits, hiring family members, and raising the mandatory retirement age.[31] After AFSA went on record in opposition to mid-level hires, the State Department quietly dropped the idea. The department never explained its decision, but the association's 2010 annual report declared that AFSA's early opposition to mid-level hiring "led to it being dropped."[32]

At senior levels, however, there was no shortage of Foreign Service personnel—quite the contrary—yet Foreign Service officers were a diminishing presence in high-level positions. In the Department of State, high-level jobs went increasingly to political appointees and Civil Service employees; and overseas, the president placed non-career personnel, often political donors, in a rising share of ambassadorships.[33]

These trends worried the AFSA leadership and its counterparts in the Una Chapman Cox Foundation, which supported a strong Foreign Service, and in the American Academy of Diplomacy, an association of former career and non-career officials who have served with distinction in positions of high responsibility in international affairs. In the eyes of these experienced officers and other colleagues, State Department actions and behaviors formed a pattern inimical to the Service, threatening its character and even its existence as America's professional diplomatic service.

The elements of the pattern, visible in trends that went back more than 20 years, included a concerted campaign, contrary to the spirit and letter of the Foreign Service Act of 1980, to homogenize the Foreign Service, Civil Service, and political appointees into a unified foreign affairs workforce under the slogan "One Team, One Mission." Members of the Foreign Service who were commissioned as officers by the president of the United States felt demeaned when the department suppressed the term "officer" in favor of the bland and meaningless "generalist." The academy's chairman, former Under Secretary of State and seven-time Ambassador Tom Pickering, and its president, three-time Ambassador Ron Neumann, joined Johnson as authors of an op-ed piece that appeared in the *Washington Post* on April 11, 2013.[34]

In 1975, said the op-ed, citing State Department data, the department had 18 positions at the level of assistant secretary or above, and FSOs filled 12 of them. In 2013 there were 33 such positions, and FSOs held only eight. The proliferation of political appointees "spawns opportunism and political correctness, weakens [Foreign Service] esprit de corps . . . and emaciates institutional memory." In a statement that proved highly controversial, the three authors said that the department's Civil Service has grown "at the expense of the Foreign Service . . . especially in the policy bureaus" that have functional, not regional, responsibilities. The op-ed was construed by some as offensive to the Civil Service.

*Washington Post* federal workplace columnist Joe Davidson called the column "frank and constructive." A group of nine Senior Foreign Service officers assigned to the State Department circulated an attack on Susan Johnson, rejecting the conclusions of the op-ed without presenting contradictory data or acknowledging that Ambassadors Pickering and Neumann were co-drafters. A defense of Johnson by several former AFSA presidents found its way into the press, but in what may have been an act of retaliation, Johnson, a recipient of multiple meritorious and Distinguished Honor Awards, received no onward assignment and retired soon after the end of her term.

The arguments about the column had no effect on the most important trend the column had identified. The number of active-duty FSOs serving as assistant secretary or above kept falling until it could fall no more. By 2019, in the Trump administration, the number had fallen to zero.

## A NEW TEAM TAKES OVER

Bob Silverman's bid for the presidency of AFSA was a last-minute affair. In the spring of 2013, Silverman, a member of the Senior Foreign Service, was back in Washington after tours in Stockholm and Tel Aviv. He was coming toward the end of an assignment in the bureau of legislative affairs and looking forward to a promised assignment in the Bureau of Near Eastern Affairs (NEA), when in March 2013 he was approached by a former NEA assistant secretary who was an acquaintance but not a mentor. There's concern that a possible candidate for the AFSA presidency isn't up to the job, Silverman was told. Would you consider making a run? A number of groups will support you.

"I had never been particularly involved with AFSA," Silverman said later, "but AFSA had resolved a couple of disputes with the department in my favor, so I had a really good feeling about it. I liked its mission. And running something was attractive to me, so I said, sure enough."[35]

And sure enough, support followed. Silverman put together a slate called "interactive AFSA," or iAFSA, and by May potential opposition had fallen apart. Silverman ran unopposed. Down ballot, members of the iAFSA slate won all the offices for which they competed except State vice president, where independent candidate Matthew Asada, a State representative on the incumbent board, defeated Greg Hicks.[36] The new board took office in July 2013 for a two-year term.

At a retreat in November 2009, the Governing Board led by Susan Johnson had drawn up a program with 14 priorities grouped under four goals (see page 196). The Silverman board followed that example but either aimed higher or scattered its shot, depending on one's point of view. At its November 2013 retreat, the new board adopted a two-year strategic plan with 29 projects in five areas:

1. Internal governance and accountability
2. Member benefits and quality of life
3. Career development and professional capacity
4. Overseas risk management
5. Foreign Service image[37]

The three projects that Silverman chose to highlight in his President's Views column in the *Foreign Service Journal* were, first, the drafting of "guidelines for a successful chief of mission"; second, contributing (via six working groups) to the second Quadrennial Diplomacy and Development Review; and third, preparing for a yearlong celebration in 2014 of the 90th anniversary of both the modern Foreign Service and AFSA. What might be called "union issues" were not a chief concern.[38]

## Chief-of-Mission Guidelines and Certificates of Competency

The project that received the most attention was the preparation, under the rubric of career and professional development, of guidelines for the selection of chiefs of mission. The story of this and related efforts to improve the quality of America's ambassadors illustrates, as few other stories do, the multiple frustrations that AFSA faces in projecting and protecting Foreign Service professionalism.

AFSA had tried before to develop standards that would inform, if not govern, the nomination and confirmation of American ambassadors, but Silverman wanted to try again.[39] He had a clear goal in mind:

> I was comparing it to what the American Bar Association [ABA] does on [rating candidates for] judgeships. I talked to the ABA. It's very transparent. They are a professional association, they have a set of guidelines and criteria, a set of standards that they judge people by. Well, we're a professional association of diplomats. An ambassadorship is one of the highest positions in our profession. Professions have standards. We wanted to say, here are standards for that position. That's what we were aiming for.[40]

He convened a star-studded group of 10 retired ambassadors under Ambassador Charles Ray, a retired career member of the Senior Foreign Service. "It was gender balanced," said Silverman, "it was ethnically balanced, it included a couple of politicals." Debate in the Governing Board focused on the relationship of the guidelines to the Foreign Service Act of 1980, the coordination with other agencies and NGOs, and the extent to which AFSA would endorse non-career appointees—concerns raised chiefly by retiree representatives. In January 2014, the board approved a text that was published in the *Journal* in April.[41] Silverman called the guidelines the "signature achievement" of his term.[42]

This is not the place for a substantive discussion of the guidelines, which focused on four areas: leadership, policy, management, and what might be called "general diplomatic skills"—knowledge of the host country and an ability to promote U.S. interests there.

The guidelines made news, but not because the White House, the Senate Foreign Relations Committee, or the leadership of the Department of State welcomed the advice. Publication of the guidelines coincided with the ambassadorial nominations of several campaign fundraisers. The coincidence gave media outlets an opportunity to contrast AFSA's standards with the paltry résumés of the nominees, and it gave AFSA a chance to make its case for taking ambassadorships seriously. Silverman told the *Washington Post*'s Al Kamen, "We're not going to be satisfied with one or two small victories. We want the system to be fixed; it's broken."[43]

Yet after a brief flurry of activity and attention, all but one of the bundlers were confirmed, and the one who withdrew his nomination was nominated and confirmed to a different country seven years later.[44] Ambassador Ray had written that "the guidelines can only be effective if those involved in the ambassadorial selection process commit to using them as a uniform set of standards against which to assess nominees," a commitment that AFSA had no realistic prospect of securing.[45] The guidelines in time were largely forgotten. They disappeared from AFSA's website and remain accessible only in the *Foreign Service Journal*'s archive.[46]

AFSA had more success in forcing the administration to open ambassadorial "certificates of competence" to the public. The Foreign Service Act of 1980 exhorts the president to appoint as chiefs of mission persons with the "demonstrated competence" to do the job, and it requires the administration to file a report attesting to the competence of each nominee with the Senate Committee on Foreign Relations.[47]

AFSA first sued the department to get its hands on these certificates in 1983, withdrawing the suit after the department agreed to provide the documents.[48] AFSA sued again in 1989, after the department had marked the documents "confidential" and again refused to turn them over.[49] As before, the department gave in rather than risk a court judgment.[50]

When he read the certificates in 1989, AFSA's State Vice President Charles Schmitz reacted strongly. The certificates are "ludicrous," he wrote. They say things like "'Mr. X's impressive business background in real estate combines with his civic activities to qualify him as an excellent candidate.'" Such empty certificates, Schmitz said, demean the function of an ambassador, insult the host country, and arguably violate U.S. law.[51]

The matter then lapsed. At some point, the department stopped providing the certificates to AFSA, and AFSA stopped demanding them until the Silverman board returned to the issue. In 2013 and 2014, AFSA used the Freedom of Information Act (and the threat of potential litigation accompanied by a media campaign) to persuade the department to cough up the certificates, which the association immediately published on its website. AFSA then worked with the Senate Committee on Foreign Relations to secure, at last, legislation that required the department to make the documents public.[52]

A victory, yes, but not much of one. Ambassador Dennis Jett, an authority on ambassadorial appointments, foresaw that making the documents public would have essentially no effect on ambassadorial nominations or confirmations. "The certificates," he wrote, "will not be the smoking gun that proves a nominee's incompetence."[53]

He was right. Presidents continued to nominate individuals whose only real qualification was fundraising prowess, the department continued to write certificates that resemble those so pungently reviewed by Charles Schmitz, and the Senate continued to confirm nominees without regard to "demonstrated competency." Publication of the certificates served chiefly to make visible the hypocrisy and cynicism that had inhabited the process from the beginning.[54]

## But What about Her Emails?

Secretary of State Hillary Clinton's use of a nongovernmental email account and a private server became publicly known in 2013.[55] By 2015, the emails on the private server were the subject of multiple investigations, including by the department's inspector general, the Federal Bureau of Investigation, the intelligence community, and House Select Committee on Benghazi. AFSA assisted, successfully, a number of AFSA members whom the department charged with security violations after it retroactively classified some of the emails.[56]

When the department spokesperson said at a daily press briefing that provisions in the Foreign Affairs Manual (FAM) regarding the use of email were "guidelines" or "policy," not "regulations," Silverman reacted sharply. He wrote to the department to ask whether FAM provisions on conduct and disciplinary standards (3 FAM 4300 and 3 FAM 4500) apply to political appointees as they do to career personnel. Director General Arnold Chacón replied that "3 FAM regulations are much more than 'guidelines'" and that the FAM "applies to Schedule

A and Schedule B appointees. . . . If a Schedule C or other political appointee were to allegedly commit misconduct, then the State Department and the White House would work in concert to review the situation, take action to prevent abuses, and, if appropriate, remove the appointee."[57]

Silverman also sought a commitment from the department to reduce the number of Schedule B appointees serving as deputy assistant secretaries, with a goal of zero by the end of the administration.[58] The department's inspector general later found that from 2013 to 2017 the department often had abused its Schedule B authority.[59]

## Labor Management: Bread and Butter

Successive AFSA presidents may have kept their focus on professional issues, but union matters—primarily compensation, working conditions, and members' rights—received the largest share of AFSA's available resources. In every year from at least 2013 to 2022, the Labor Management Office accounted for

---

**Box 11.1.  A Niche Practice**

Attorneys who specialize in employment and workplace law, even those who deal specifically with the federal workplace, are often unfamiliar with the peculiarities of the Foreign Service. The 2,000,000 members of the federal Civil Service, and the 16,000 members of the Foreign Service, are governed by different laws, regulations, and practices, and are administered by different bureaucracies. Their unions—there are several in the Civil Service—are governed under different titles of the U.S. Code: Title 5 for the Civil Service, Title 22 for the Foreign Service. The two systems have many similarities, but they are not twins and may be no more than distant cousins.

The current head of AFSA's Labor Management Office, Sharon Papp, has mastered the Foreign Service system through more than 30 years with AFSA. "You have to kind of educate yourself," she said. "There's a lot of learning as you go, a kind of on-the-job training."[a]

Labor management has a vocabulary all its own. There is a lexicon of disputes (grievances, cohort grievances, institutional grievances/implementation disputes, unfair labor practices, negotiability disputes, and others) and an alphabet soup of adjudicatory bodies (FSLRB, FSGB, FLRA, FSIDP, EEOC), each with its own rules and procedures. AFSA's website features an excellent guide to the LM world. (Go to afsa.org, click on "Resources" in the menu bar, and then click on "Labor-Management Guidance" in the drop-down list.)

a. Papp, interview, May 20, 2022.

about a third of AFSA's staff, more than any other department. It had direct contact with more than 1,000 AFSA members year after year.[60]

The LM Office is in the Main State building (with an annex in the Reagan Building, where USAID is located), not at AFSA's E Street headquarters. "Many, many years ago," said AFSA General Counsel Sharon Papp, "we negotiated with the State Department for free office space, use of their computers, use of the pouch, things like that. It's more convenient for our members not to have to cross the street to come to us."[61] The physical separation from headquarters can contribute to a certain organizational distance as well; it's up to the AFSA president, who has direct supervisory responsibility for the office, to ensure that LM serves all of AFSA's constituencies and is well integrated with the rest of the association.[62]

## Overseas Comparability Pay

The emphasis in the strategic plan on professional issues did not go unnoticed. A few comments on AFSA's Facebook page contrasted AFSA's attention to ambassadors ("an initiative that benefits a very few") with a perceived lack of attention to overseas comparability pay ("an initiative that will benefit all").[63]

The criticism was in large part misplaced. AFSA, in fact, was active in making its case on OCP to congressional authorizers and appropriators, and the department was strongly supportive.[64] Even so, as Silverman's successor, Barbara Stephenson, would learn, there is a point at which the repetition of unsuccessful arguments becomes counterproductive (see page 211).

As early as 2013, the matter of overseas comparability pay had become what a political officer might call a "frozen conflict." The arguments around the issue remained those laid out in the early 1990s (see pages 169–71). Over the years, the gap between private-sector and federal pay kept rising faster in Washington than in the rest of the country, so the loss of Washington locality pay on overseas assignments kept growing as a source of aggravation and perceived unfairness. By 2022, locality pay added just under 32 percent to the base pay of a federal employee in Washington.

The FY2014 appropriations act included language limiting OCP to no more than two-thirds of Washington, D.C., locality pay.[65] As of this writing (FY2023), substantially identical language has appeared in all subsequent appropriations bills.[66] The details of OCP have been a source of controversy and litigation. AFSA's labor-management team has intervened to secure OCP for Foreign Service members in Washington for long-term training but not assigned to the

Foreign Service Institute, and to force changes in certain calculations by the department that could reduce the two-thirds payout.[67]

But even the most tenacious litigation could not raise OCP to 100 percent of Washington locality pay; that would take action by Congress. While promising to fight for full comparability, AFSA has claimed preservation of the two-thirds cap as a victory over those in the White House or in Congress who would further reduce or eliminate OCP entirely.

*Meritorious Service Increases*

AFSA and the Labor Management Office had more success in the long dispute over meritorious service increases (MSIs, sometimes called "meritorious step increases").

The Foreign Service Act of 1980 allows the department to grant a step increase to any member of the Service "on the basis of especially meritorious service," but it offers no further guidance.[68] For many years, the department routinely awarded MSIs to all individuals whom selection boards recommended for promotion, but who were not in fact promoted, up to a certain percentage that AFSA negotiated with the department and memorialized in the promotion precepts. AFSA challenged the department's actions in 2013, 2014, 2015, and 2016, when the department unilaterally changed the practice. AFSA was successful in its challenges of awards made (or not made) in 2013, 2015, and 2016, and when the last of these cases was resolved in 2021, the wins had put about $6 million in the pockets of those whom the department had wronged.[69]

In the case of the 2014 awards, AFSA won at the Foreign Service Grievance Board, but following the change of administration in 2017, the Foreign Service Labor Relations Board (FSLRB) reversed the decision on appeal. Sharon Papp commented, "You know what? Elections matter. Even in these apolitical bodies, they matter, as we see every day."[70] Following another change in administration, AFSA prevailed before the FSLRB in the 2015 and 2016 MSI cases.

According to Tom Boyatt, AFSA's victory at the FSLRB on the 2013 MSIs established as "settled law" that the department can award MSIs "only under procedures negotiated with the union."[71] AFSA and the department negotiated such procedures in 2016, with effect in 2017. The new procedures took MSI determinations away from the promotion boards and instead created a nomination process with determinations made by new MSI specialist and officer boards. In 2019 AFSA and the department agreed to address "implicit bias" by stripping names and gender indicators from the MSI nominations. The change was generally praised ("We got big kudos," said Ken Kero-Mentz), but some doubted its usefulness: "Since MSI nominators know the employees, any implicit bias is more likely at that stage (including whether to nominate at all). . . . Other than insisting on diversity in judges, trying to tackle bias at the back end will have limited, if any, impact."[72]

## Governance

The new Governing Board, as one of its first steps, convened a subcommittee to review the association's bylaws and in particular to look at the structure of the board itself. The bylaws provided that each constituency (agencies and retirees) be allotted one representative on the board for each 1,000 AFSA members or fraction thereof. As the Foreign Service and AFSA membership grew, so did AFSA's board. In 2013 the board, including the association's officers elected at large, numbered 29. The committee studying governance found that the board, which had numbered just eight in 1974, had become unwieldy and inefficient. To reduce the board's size, the committee proposed amendments to the bylaws that would allot to each constituency one representative on the board for every 2,000 AFSA members or fraction thereof, so long as the fraction was greater than half and so long as each constituency had at least one representative, regardless of the number of its AFSA members.[73]

The board approved the committee's proposal, and in the 2015 election, the association's membership easily approved the amendments by the required two-thirds majority, with 3,216 votes in favor to 504 against.[74]

## No Second Term

Unlike his predecessor, Silverman did not seek a second term. His presidency had been tumultuous. According to a number of AFSA employees, he was given to emotional outbursts that bordered on the abusive. Some members of the Governing Board had considered a motion of censure. Silverman's withdrawal of an official AFSA letter that he had sent to the chairs and ranking members of the House and Senate Foreign Affairs Committees led a senior Hill staff member to refer to AFSA as a "discredited organization." As his term of office wound down, several concerned AFSA grandees went looking for a successor.

# 12

## A Consequential Presidency, 2015–2019

Barbara Stephenson said she "got the adrenaline in my blood" for the Foreign Service at her first post, in Manuel Noriega's Panama in 1985. That adrenaline rush came back to her again and again in the course of her career.

Stephenson had joined the Service in August of that year, just hours after a successful defense of her doctoral thesis. Over the 30 years between her entry on duty and her presidency of the American Foreign Service Association, she served in political hot spots such as Belfast and San Salvador, in seventh-floor line and staff positions, and in positions that honed the managerial skills that Foreign Service officers supposedly don't possess: deputy coordinator for Iraq (administering the largest civilian overseas deployment since Vietnam), deputy chief of mission and chargé in London, ambassador to Panama, and dean of the School of Leadership and Management at the Foreign Service Institute (FSI).

### RECRUITMENT AND CAMPAIGN

She was at FSI in the relative calm of its Arlington campus when her recruitment to the AFSA candidacy began. She was a pretty tough sell. AFSA, she thought, was not much more than a talking shop weakened by internal divisions. It took a succession of Foreign Service luminaries to bring her around.

"There I am at the Silver Diner with Tom Boyatt and I'm like, I don't think that [the AFSA job] is right for me. Then Brother Harrop had me at the Metropolitan Club or the Cosmos Club or somewhere, talking me into this." She was willing to serve, she told Bill Harrop, "if and only if I can recruit a board unified around a vision, so we can win and carry out a governing plan. . . . I have no interest in spending two years squabbling." But first she wanted another assignment: "I need to do what I'm going to do next," she said.

Boyatt and Harrop had softened her up. Then Tom Pickering weighed in. Pickering, for whom she had worked as special assistant during his time as under secretary for political affairs, was then retired, but his pitch was irresistible. "'It has to be you,' he said, 'because they will follow your lead.'" She couldn't say no.

Her campaign bore some similarities to the effort of early AFSA reformers Lannon Walker and Charlie Bray (see chapter 3). Stephenson noted,

> Recruiting a slate was difficult, but we had a unified slate all the way down. Bill Haugh [candidate for secretary] came up with the name of our slate, "Strong Diplomacy." We met at my house regularly, we had whiteboard sessions, we did campaign positions. It was a central idea that it would not be just about the union side, which can sometimes feel like protecting poor performers who ruin our reputation, but explicitly about breathing new life into the professional association.[1]

She pledged to take no position on any issue without consulting the membership and to act always to make the Foreign Service stronger.

Angie Bryant, the slate's candidate for State vice president, liked the balance: "As she [Stephenson] outlined her vision of a stronger Foreign Service, taking the lead in foreign policy, I began to envision what AFSA could be . . . an organization with the potential to represent the Foreign Service to Congress, the media, and the American people; uphold the provisions of the Foreign Service Act . . . and help our less-experienced colleagues develop the skills to build the Foreign Service of the future."[2]

Stephenson faced competition. Matthew Asada, the incumbent State vice president, headed a rival Future Forward slate that fielded candidates for retiree vice president and eight of the 11 State representatives but contended for no other positions. Tex Harris ran an independent campaign in which he charged that "AFSA is neither trying, nor able to protect the Foreign Service profession" and "lacks direction and effective governance."[3] When the results were announced, Stephenson had 2,032 votes, just over 50 percent of the 4,034 valid ballots cast. Down ballot, the Strong Diplomacy slate swept the board.[4] The new board took office in July 2015. Voters also approved the bylaw amendment, developed and introduced by the Silverman board, that reduced the size of the Governing Board from 29 to 19 members; it was to take effect with the 2017 elections.

## TROUBLE ON THE HILL

Every AFSA president since 1973 has faced the challenge of managing an organization with competing union and professional mandates. Stephenson's explicit tilt toward AFSA's obligations as a professional association caused some friction with AFSA's staff, fully a third of which worked on labor-management issues. But her first visit to Capitol Hill as AFSA president confirmed her in her position and filled her with urgency:

> Tom Boyatt, who ran the AFSA-PAC [AFSA Political Action Committee, see page 170], took me to a fund-raiser for Senator [Bob] Corker [R-Tenn., chairman of the Committee on Foreign Relations]. After the event I ran into Corker on the street, waiting for his car, and he started in on me about overseas comparability pay [OCP] and about how all the Foreign Service did was whine about this and didn't tell the truth about it. We were always saying that Foreign Service officers wouldn't serve overseas if they didn't get that third tranche, but Corker said that's not what members hear on Codels [congressional delegations]. What we hear, he said, is that it costs less to live overseas than to pay for Washington housing, so no, they're not considering not serving overseas. So, he told me, you don't have any credibility, and I'm going to start a review of your housing benefits, all your benefits. And I thought, we're in trouble.
>
> I was determined that they would come to see us in a better light. We were losing the larger picture. The point we needed to make to Congress . . . is that we are chosen through an extraordinary process and make extraordinary sacrifices in the name of our country, and we do it willingly. Don't start off with allowances, talk about how proud we are to serve. I convinced my board to shut up about OCP—we could come back to it later, when we had gained more respect.[5]

## INTERNAL AFFAIRS

Stephenson organized her administration around three pillars: inreach, outreach, and workforce planning. All three were closely linked.

"Inreach," or consultation with members, was key to understanding the problems in the workforce from the members' point of view and to developing specific goals for the association. "Outreach" meant making friends and allies, explaining and defending the work of the Service. And "workforce planning" involved building the Service for the future.

Stephenson initiated a series of what she called "structured conversations," essentially focus groups without the sociological scaffolding. "We had box lunches with different cohorts, FS-1 econ officers, FS-2 consular officers, specialists in different categories, and so forth, and I'd say, 'I'm going to eat and shut up because I want to hear from you.' It was very open-ended. What I heard was, they still loved the mission, but bureaucratic processes that had become ever more complicated got in the way."

Stephenson heard about bidding rules that were almost impossible to meet, endless and seemingly punitive obstacles facing Service members with special-needs children, nearly universal opposition to lateral entry, anger from entry-level officers at the prospect of two or even three tours on a visa line, distress from specialists about the operation of linked assignments, and plenty of complaints about "a bunch of cranky old white guys running the place for their benefit. . . . People were just so annoyed, feeling that the Service didn't value them.

"My predecessor [Bob Silverman] wrote a really great piece about the obstacles that block a Foreign Service career path," she said. "It asked how we can find the next Bill Burns. Well, here's part of the answer. To find the next Bill Burns, we need to stop doing all this crap we do to ourselves."[6]

AFSA weighed in on some of these issues. Stephenson said,

> We heard from entry-level officers in the A-100 class who heard from HR [human resources] or the Director General that they would do their first and second tours and maybe a third tour on the visa line, and they were like, wow, this is not what I signed up for. There was a shortage of [limited non-career appointee] consular adjudicators, and we learned that HR required candidates to have a college degree in order to apply. We persuaded HR to require a degree to be accepted, not to apply. Then they could go to college campuses and recruit. A simple tweak, but it made a big difference.[7]

Mid-level economic officers complained that promotions were blocked, leading to dismissals as time-in-class limits came into play. Economic sections in much of the world had been stripped of personnel to supply the need for FSOs in Iraq, and staffing levels had never recovered. And then, when (as happened in many posts) the economic and political sections were merged in the name of efficiency, Stephenson said, the top job went "to a political officer. So when we downsized in Iraq, many of the billets for FS-1 and FS-2 economic officers had just vanished, and the econ officers leaving Iraq had no place to go. HR would solve this problem by offering the econ officers leave without pay—it would cost too much to put these officers back in the field, they said. And this was at a time when we really needed to be upping our game against China."[8] State Vice President Ken Kero-Mentz pointed out that "as of June 2018, there were roughly 1,550 State FS [Foreign Service] economic officers, but only 700 econ positions by grade." No surprise, then, that economic officers were the least likely to be promoted.[9]

Frustrated at the department's approach to the issue, AFSA went directly to the Hill. Stephenson again: "I worked the Senate staff, Paul Grove on [Sen.] Lindsey Graham's staff and others, and they put $600,000 in a budget line item to cover overseas deployment costs. That was a big one. After ten years of erosion in the cone, of course we didn't solve the problem, not close, but we made our point in an important way. The department took notice."[10]

## TRANSITION TO TRUMP

Stephenson's presidency was upended on election day in November 2016. Most of the Foreign Service, like most pollsters and journalists, expected Hillary Clinton to win. Her defeat was a surprise, a shock. (Perhaps it should not have been. Service as Secretary of State had jinxed many a candidate; no former secretary had made it to the White House since James Buchanan won the election of 1856.[11])

Every change of administration is a difficult period for government professionals, and one that involves a change of parties and policies is especially hard. No previous transition, however, resembled the passage from Barack Obama to Donald J. Trump.

The president-elect, the first to come to the White House with no experience of public office or military service, was profoundly ignorant of the workings of the government. He harbored as well a deep suspicion, bordering on paranoia, of the motives and intentions of the entire federal establishment.

AFSA tried to allay those suspicions. As the title of her January 2017 column in the *Foreign Service Journal*, Barbara Stephenson chose "You Can Count on Us." "I want to get this right," she said, "and encourage the new administration to rely heavily on us, the career professionals, to advance American interests."[12] Senior FSO Keith W. Mines, writing in the same issue, was plainer and more forceful: "We are here for you, Mr. President, and we are in this together."[13]

And for a brief moment, it seemed that the career Service and the new leadership could rise together. When Rex Tillerson, retired after 11 years as chief executive officer at ExxonMobil, was named Secretary of State, many in the building welcomed the prospect of a skilled manager taking charge. And Tillerson, who would make a "redesign" of the department central to his tenure, had a good pitch. He arrived at the department on February 1, 2017, to greet State Department employees gathered at the C Street entrance. "If we stay focused on the work before us," he said, "I promise I will work to ensure you achieve your own personal success and your professional satisfaction in what you are doing." These were welcome words.[14]

But the honeymoon, if that's what it was, had really ended before it began. Treating government professionals as political enemies and likely saboteurs was a feature of the 2016 campaign that the victorious administration had no interest in abandoning. Writers in *Foreign Policy* magazine noted the campaign's "aggressive villainization" of career public servants, along with other members of a supposed intellectual elite.[15]

An early public attack on administration policy by hundreds of foreign affairs professionals seemed to justify the administration's attitude. A few days after his inauguration, the president issued an order titled "Protecting the Nation from Foreign Terrorist Entry into the United States." The order, an attempt to carry out the president's campaign promise of a "total and complete ban of Muslims entering the United States," provoked widespread opposition.[16] In the State Department, career professionals used email to circulate a "Dissent Channel" message that quickly gathered about 1,000 signatures, most from FSOs.

The term "Dissent Channel" appears here in scare quotes because the message was not, and seemed never intended to be, confidential.[17] On the contrary, it leaked to the press in draft even before it was formally submitted. White House press secretary Sean Spicer, who had begun his brief and ignominious stint in the job with obvious lies about the size of the crowd at the inaugural ceremony, denounced the message and the messenger from his podium: "These career bureaucrats have a problem with it?" he said. "They should either get with the program or they should go."[18]

Spicer's snarl found an echo in the public. A cab driver passing the State Department told his passenger, "You see that building? Every one of them should be fired, for being disloyal to the president."[19] In the Foreign Service, too, there was concern. "Political leaders must trust that our advice and implementation will be expert and unbiased," FSO Matt Tompkins wrote in the *Foreign Service Journal*. "Public advocacy destroys that trust."[20]

## THE TRUMP BUDGET

Hard evidence of the administration's low regard for the State Department, with its "radical leftist officials" and "Obama holdovers," appeared in March with the release of the budget request for Fiscal Year 2018. The administration sought a one-third cut in spending on State and U.S. Agency for International Development, from about $57 billion in FY2017 (the last fiscal year of the Obama administration) to $40.2 billion.[21] In April a freeze on civilian hiring that the administration had imposed across the federal government in January came to end—except at the Department of State, where it remained in place until May 2018.[22] Career officers found the department "adrift and listless." One told a journalist, "I used to love my job. Now, it feels like coming to the hospital to take care of a terminally ill family member. You come in every day, you bring flowers, you brush their hair, paint their nails, even though you know there's no point. But you do it out of love."[23]

Even though the president's party controlled both houses of Congress, a 33 percent cut in the foreign affairs budget was White House overreach. At a June hearing, Senator Corker schooled the witness, Secretary Tillerson: "The budget that's been presented is not going to be the budget that we're going to deal with. It's just not."[24]

The budget debate gave Stephenson and AFSA a chance to drive home that the Foreign Service is sacrifice, service, and love of country, a change in approach that went far to repair a frayed relationship with Congress. In September, Senate appropriators, led by committee chairman Lindsey Graham (R-S.C.), reported out a bill at $51.3 billion for FY2018, less than the $57 billion of the previous budget but close to $11 billion more than the administration had requested.[25] Senator Graham later wrote in the *Foreign Service Journal*, "Our diplomats and development specialists have [for 75 years] been on the front lines, all too often in the crosshairs of the enemy. The knowledge and experience of these dedicated public servants are unparalleled."[26]

At the end of the day, actual FY2018 funding was just over $54 billion.[27]

## A SECOND TERM

Barbara Stephenson had not planned on running for a second term, but as the administration's approach to the Service took shape, she came to believe that walking out would be irresponsible.[28] Many of the "Strong Diplomacy" board members followed her lead and stood for a second term, and new candidates were recruited to the slate where incumbents did not run. The presidency and most other offices were uncontested. Members of the Strong Diplomacy slate were elected as president, secretary (Tom Boyatt), treasurer (retired ambassador E. Anthony "Tony" Wayne), State vice president (Ken Kero-Mentz), and all State and retiree representative positions. The position of retiree vice president, however, went to former AFSA president and State vice president John Naland, who ran as an independent. Naland was the only candidate to defeat a member of the Strong Diplomacy slate (Bill Haugh).[29] The new board took office in July 2017.

Stephenson's second term would prove to be quite different from her first and not only because of the Trump budget. Her determination to give the professional stature of the Foreign Service priority over union issues involving pay (including overseas comparability pay and preserving the annuity exception), working conditions, and particular grievances faced a rising level of resistance.[30] Within the board, Ken Kero-Mentz and John Naland pushed for more attention to union matters. The unified board that was so important to her model for managing the association came under strain.

## AFSA SHAKE-UP

Stephenson was nevertheless determined to fulfill her slate's campaign promise and continue breathing new life into AFSA's professional side. When her staffing plans ran into budgetary constraints, she looked for ways to free up funds from existing resources. She consulted principals at other nonprofits about best practices and sought ways to reduce AFSA's expenses. The Scholarship Fund, she found, had a substantial endowment, but its administrative expenses as a share of income were far higher than the industry standard. With support from the Finance, Audit, and Management Committee, she took steps to reduce the fund's expenses by redirecting fundraising efforts, away from the Scholarship Fund toward the Fund for American Diplomacy, for outreach and constituency-building. The director of the Scholarship Fund, who had been in that position since 1993, left AFSA and was not replaced. As a result, said Stephenson, "we were able to give out lots more money in actual scholarships."[31]

Stephenson reorganized some departments and established (in 2016) a new department for professional policy issues, charged among other duties with compiling a database that could be used to parse, challenge, and expand on the often opaque information provided by the department's Bureau of Human Resources.[32] She updated the AFSA employee handbook. She revised the way minutes of Governing Board meetings were recorded so that differences within the board were minimized or not reported at all. Also, she replaced the Executive Committee, which included the secretary, the treasurer, and the constituency vice presidents, with a management committee that included only herself and two retired ambassadors, Secretary Tom Boyatt and Treasurer Tony Wayne. When, unsurprisingly, the vice presidents pushed back, Stephenson relented, and five vice presidents (State, USAID, FCS, FAS, and retirees) returned to the committee. The vice presidents then engineered a change in the bylaws, approved in 2019, to restore the Executive Committee with its former membership.[33]

Some of AFSA's past presidents asked Stephenson to replace Executive Director Ian Houston, who had been with AFSA for more than a decade, first working on legislative affairs and later as executive director. Houston took the matter out of Stephenson's hands by deciding to leave. "It was difficult to break away," he said, "because I cared so much for the organization and the people around it, but in retrospect I'm glad I did. I'm a strong believer that staff should move on and fresh energy be given an opportunity to innovate."[34]

Stephenson may have shared that sentiment. During her tenure, several AFSA employees left, office portfolios were shuffled, and new departments created. Up until then, AFSA had experienced very little turnover; the changes were not all well received by remaining professional staff. "Fixing all these governance issues was a thankless task," Stephenson said. "It's some of the most painful things I've ever done."[35]

Despite any friction that Stephenson's management style and priorities created within the board, there was united support for her response to the administration's attacks on the Service, the department, and diplomacy itself. Stephenson was, said Ken Kero-Mentz, "so eloquent a speaker, so good at pulling data into her brain and then pushing it out in a way that makes sense to any listener.... Having her as our spokesperson during those Trump years was absolutely critical, and I will sing her praises on that all the time. Even her detractors will."[36]

## PUSH COMES TO SHOVE

Becoming the face of a challenge to the administration and the secretary was not a role that Stephenson sought. Her messaging and AFSA's had stressed a desire to work with the new administration, to give it space to succeed. When it became clear that the administration would make cooperation impossible, she stood up for the Foreign Service.

On May 3, 2017, Secretary Tillerson addressed a subdued but respectful audience of department employees gathered in the Dean Acheson Auditorium. After a review of the administration's "America First" foreign policies, he turned to his plans to "redesign" the State Department: "There's nothing easy about it," he said, "and I don't want to diminish in any way the challenges I know this presents for individuals, it presents to families, it presents to organizations." He repeated what he had said when he first came to the building three months earlier: "I can promise you that when this is all done, you're going to have a much more satisfying, fulfilling career. . . . You will know exactly how what you do every day contributes to our delivery on mission."[37]

The redesign, which Tillerson and his staff often described as "employee-driven," was then cloaked in an obscurity from which it never emerged. Individual AFSA members and AFSA itself shared their thoughts with the redesign team but were never engaged in an exchange of ideas. The secretary never articulated a broad vision for the redesign, later named "the impact initiative," and the entire exercise became mired in consultants' reports, congressional pushback, and the mutual lack of confidence between Secretary Tillerson and the president.[38]

Stephenson could have responded to Tillerson's remarks with a challenge to the secretary to reconcile the department's mission with the administration's budget. Instead, in an interview on the Federal News Network, she did not mention the budget but spoke only of the desirability of change: "I saw an awful lot of potential in what Secretary Tillerson laid out. I'm encouraging all of our folks to make the most of this opportunity" to support reform.[39]

That interview took place at 9:00 a.m. on May 5, Foreign Service Day.[40] A few hours later, a brief, unpleasant incident occurred that led to a sharp change in the narrative. Secretary Tillerson had agreed to attend the memorial plaque ceremony in the State Department's C Street lobby. He and Stephenson met in a holding room before the ceremony, but when she tried to brief him on what was about to happen, he physically shoved her aside.

Stephenson had known *New York Times* columnist Roger Cohen for many years, and in what she thought was a casual conversation, she mentioned the incident to him. She was appalled when, two months later, Cohen used the incident in a column on the state of the Foreign Service: "That shove captured the rudeness and remoteness that have undermined trust at Foggy Bottom," he wrote. "Stephenson began to understand the many distressed people coming to her 'asking if their service is still valued.'" Cohen went on to quote senior Foreign Service officers on what they saw: "a slow unraveling of the institution" (Ambassador Jake Walles); "a toxic, troubled environment and organization" (Ambassador Nancy McEldowney); and "utter disdain for our expertise" (Ambassador Dana Shell Smith).[41]

Stephenson's distress about the column was misplaced. In retrospect, the piece freed her to speak her mind. It was "the tipping point . . . when everybody in Washington realized it was really dangerous to have him [Tillerson] at the helm, and that we've all got to organize and make a counter-case, or he will take down American diplomacy."[42]

In November, AFSA released an advance copy of Stephenson's President's View column, "Time to Ask Why," slated for publication in the December *Foreign Service Journal*. Here were the numbers on staffing cuts under Tillerson, compiled by the Professional Policy Issues Department AFSA had set up the year before, that gave weight to what had been just anecdotes: "The Foreign Service officer corps at State has lost 60 percent of its Career Ambassadors since January. Ranks of Career Ministers, our three-star equivalents, are down from 33 to 19. The ranks of our two-star Minister Counselors have fallen from 431 right after Labor Day to 359 today—and are still falling." And here was the confrontational tone that had been absent:

> Why such a focus on decapitating leadership? . . . [N]ine in 10 Americans favor a strong global leadership role for our great country, and we know . . . that such leadership is impossible without a strong professional Foreign Service deployed around the world. . . . Where then, does the impetus come from to weaken the American Foreign Service? Where is the mandate to pull the Foreign Service team from the field and forfeit the game to our adversaries?[43]

The column resonated in the media. Stephenson appeared on the PBS *NewsHour*.[44] So as not to "look like just a bunch of politicized left-wing Democrats," she declined an invitation to appear on the *Rachel Maddow Show*, but even without her, the show did a 19-minute segment on the column.[45] Future Secretary of State Antony Blinken, then–managing director of the Penn Biden Center for Diplomacy and Global Engagement, quoted her in a column in the *New York Times*.[46] She was cited in the *Washington Post*, *Foreign Policy*, *Time*, *Vox*, and other outlets.[47] Many months later, Stephenson was still being cited, notably by the *Economist* and in a powerful report by the Senate Foreign Relations Committee minority (Democratic) staff.[48]

Stephenson outlasted Secretary Tillerson, whom President Trump fired (famously, by tweet) on March 13, 2018. Relations between the president and the secretary were never close and had been deteriorating for some time.[49] The president never explained the firing, but Tillerson often disagreed with the president

**Box 12.1. The President's Views**

Although some AFSA presidents (U. Alexis Johnson, Charles Whitehead, and Dennis Hays among them) contributed occasional signed columns to the *Foreign Service Journal*, a presidential opinion piece or editorial became a regular *Journal* feature only with Perry Shankle's Association Views column, which started its run in September 1987. The name changed to President's Views with the first column from Tex Harris, published in September 1993, and it has remained the same ever since.

The President's Views column, like nearly all of the material in the *Journal*, must be put into final form at least six weeks prior to publication. Because of this lag, presidents have usually used the column to discuss issues of long-standing, not breaking news.

Barbara Stephenson's columns were, as *Journal* Editor Shawn Dorman said, "forward policy documents." Starting with "Dear S: You Can Count on Us" (January–February 2017) to "Time to Ask Why" (December 2017) and "Staying Constructive in Trying Times" (March 2019), they trace the arc of AFSA's response to the stark challenges posed by the Trump administration.

Stephenson's decision to release "Time to Ask Why" ahead of its formal publication ensured that the column, which she knew was newsworthy and provocative, received wide media attention. By choosing her monthly column (rather than, say, a press release) as her format, she brought enhanced stature to both AFSA and the *Foreign Service Journal*.

and was never able to represent him credibly abroad.[50] Tillerson's successor, Central Intelligence Agency (CIA) Director and former congressman Michael "Mike" Pompeo, was confirmed on April 26.

Tillerson's redesign did not so much collapse as simply fade to black. The *Foreign Service Journal* commented, "It's as if that most recent reform project never happened."[51]

## POMPEO

Michael Pompeo was a California native transplanted to Kansas. He was a West Pointer, first in his class of 1986; an attorney; a businessman who ran and later sold an aircraft parts manufacturing enterprise in Wichita; and a Republican member of Congress, elected in 2010 and three times thereafter. On the House Select Committee on Benghazi, he was a prominent, hyper-aggressive interrogator of Secretary of State Hillary Clinton.

In light of subsequent events, it is worth recalling that the Benghazi committee after two years of investigation found no evidence of wrongdoing. Pompeo and Rep. Jim Jordan (R-Ohio), however, issued a 51-page report of their own that implied a politically motivated cover-up. Secretary Clinton had appeared before the committee and endured 11 hours of largely hostile questioning.

Pompeo resigned his seat in Congress to become President Trump's first director of Central Intelligence. He held that position for 14 months before his appointment as Secretary of State. The Senate confirmed him on April 26, 2018, by a vote of 57 to 42.

During his time at the CIA, Pompeo was rarely in the headlines. Perhaps that is why he outlasted so many others—a White House chief of staff, a chief political strategist, a press secretary, and two national security advisers, plus a couple of cabinet secretaries and scores of subcabinet officials—who had joined the new administration but quit or were fired before Pompeo finished his stint in Langley.[52]

At his swearing in, Pompeo declared, "I want the State Department to get its swagger back." And in words that tracked Stephenson's own columns, he said, "We need our men and women out at the front lines executing American diplomacy with great vigor and energy. . . . The United States diplomatic corps needs to be in every corner, every stretch of the world, executing missions on behalf of this country."[53]

Barbara Stephenson wrote that on hearing these words, she felt "a surge of optimism."[54] And she added later, "We now see signs of rebuilding, of restoring the strength of the Foreign Service."[55] Within days of his confirmation, Pompeo lifted the hiring freeze and—of great importance to the Foreign Service—he restored the ability of overseas posts to hire eligible family members, including spouses and partners of employees on permanent assignment.

A year into his term, Pompeo was able to testify that "by end of this year, we'll have at or near more FSOs than ever," and Stephenson was able to report that "there were more officers in each of the mid-ranks—FS-1, FS-2 and FS-3—in December 2018 than in December 2016." (The senior ranks, she added, remained seriously depleted.)[56]

To some extent, Stephenson's expressed sentiments were a ploy, intended to encourage Pompeo to match his actions to his words.[57] But any surge of optimism was bound to collide both with the president's insistence that a "deep state" conspiracy of federal employees was out to undermine him and his presidency, and with the secretary's unwillingness to defend his people if it meant challenging the president.[58]

Despite his expansive vision for American diplomacy, Pompeo did not push back against repeated White House budget requests for deep cuts in spending on international affairs.[59] In June 2018, the press exposed what many members of the Foreign Service already knew: Certain political appointees in the Department of State were conducting a campaign of harassment and vilification against career professionals they considered insufficiently loyal, not to the United States but to President Trump.[60] Even when the press stories were confirmed in reports by the department's inspector general (whom he later fired), Pompeo did not address the issue.[61]

Pompeo's first year as Secretary of State coincided with the last year in office of the AFSA Governing Board elected in 2017, but his impact on AFSA was less than might be imagined. The Tillerson era had created some new problems and exacerbated many others, but the end of that era solved none of them.

Although gross numbers looked better, the workforce in its structure and skills had hardly improved. Barbara Stephenson offered this analysis:

> With the hiring freeze, civil servants in State could only get promoted by moving to another agency. So the Bureau of Human Resources [which is staffed in large part by members of the Civil Service] was left with a lot of vacancies and talent siphoned off by the time the freeze was lifted. I don't think that HR has ever recovered. There's no one with the skills to manage the intake and the other stuff that needs to be done. Workforce generation is not a typical skill in the Foreign Service. Look to fix HR and then you'll be able to fix what's wrong with the Service.[62]

## HOLDING THE LINE

AFSA's first priority remained the defense of the joint State-USAID budget against the administration's proposed deep cuts.

Stephenson used her monthly column in the *Foreign Service Journal* to make the point that in the decade from 2008 to 2016, spending on core diplomatic functions, adjusted for inflation, fell by 23 percent. True, she wrote, budgets increased over that period, but spending on security enhancements, including the Worldwide Security Protection Program, absorbed more than 100 percent of the increases in appropriations for ongoing operations at State and USAID.[63] Pointing out that under-resourcing of diplomacy was a long-term, bipartisan affair helped AFSA press for better funding from a clearly nonpartisan stance.

To build a constituency and make the case to Congress for greater resources, the Governing Board asked the *Foreign Service Journal* to devote an issue to commercial diplomacy, export promotion, and other forms of economic statecraft. The staff and editorial board of the *Journal* were not accustomed to input from the Governing Board on what to print, but in this case there was no pushback. Almost all 104 pages of the *Journal's* January–February 2019 issue dealt with the subject featured on the cover: "Economic Diplomacy Works."

AFSA's emphasis on economics, and on the contrast between the shrinking U.S. diplomatic footprint and China's expanding worldwide presence, helped to secure in the FY2020 budget an increase in appropriations for core diplomatic functions, even as the administration sought a cut from FY2019 appropriated levels.[64] So effective was the work of Julie Nutter, Kim Greenplate, and their staffs in AFSA's Professional Policy Issues and Advocacy Departments that "AFSA emerged as the lead content creator for the US Foreign Service on Capitol Hill."[65] Their work inspired as well the formation of a Foreign Service caucus in the Senate, led by Senators Chris Van Hollen (D-Md.) and Dan Sullivan (R-Alaska).[66]

## MEMBER BENEFITS

In all this turmoil, stressed members of the Service looked to AFSA to defend the collective and individual rights of its members. A zealous defense of employee rights is the normal work of a labor union, but as Ken Kero-Mentz pointed out, the work was different in the Trump administration: "Even during the mid-to-late 1990s when the State Department hired very few officers and specialists, the impetus [behind conflicts with management] was budgetary, rather than disdain for who we are and the work we do."[67]

The atmosphere of confrontation and hostility did not prevent AFSA from gaining some hard-won victories. Here are some examples.

### Non-career Hires at USAID

In 2015 when USAID brought health officers on board using its authority under the Foreign Service Act of 1980 to hire non-career personnel on Foreign Service limited (FSL) appointments, AFSA cried foul. AFSA acknowledged the agency's right to hire, but it insisted on its own right as a union to negotiate the procedures under which such hiring would occur. The discussions took two years, but in 2017 AFSA and USAID reached a formal agreement that required USAID to inform AFSA before advertising an FSL position so that qualified career Foreign Service employees would have a chance to respond and be considered first.[68]

The agreement was at best only a partial success; USAID continued to make FSL appointments, often in contravention of its own stated policies. In June 2020, the agency notified AFSA of its intent to withdraw from the agreement. By then, the agency had hired hundreds of FSL personnel to positions that, in AFSA's view, should have gone to career personnel. AFSA filed an implementation dispute in August 2020 that was still pending before the Foreign Service Grievance Board as of this writing in early 2023.

## Children with Special Needs

Members of the Foreign Service with children who have special needs—for health care (including mental health care), for physical accommodations, and especially for education—have long struggled to manage their careers and their families in responsible ways. The *Foreign Service Journal* highlighted this problem in its June 2016 issue and published a letter describing long-standing struggles with the Bureau of Medical Services (MED) in its December 2016 issue.[69] The *Journal*'s efforts caught the eye of the *Washington Post*, which brought national attention to the subject. The *Post*'s story, based in part on an interview with Ken Kero-Mentz, ran under the headline "State Department Support for Diplomats with Children with Disabilities Is Contracting."[70] AFSA repeatedly petitioned MED and brought pressure on the department from friends on the Hill as well.[71]

By the end of the Governing Board's 2017–2019 term, the department had named a special-needs implementation coordinator and adopted a new Foreign Affairs Manual provision (FAM 3280) that "offers a supportive regulatory framework for the Special Needs Education Allowance and protects Foreign Service families against the subjective interpretations previously employed, often to their detriment."[72] In 2020 AFSA President Eric Rubin was able to report that "what many saw as a 'gotcha' approach from the Bureau of Medical Services is, we hope, now being replaced with a 'How can we help you serve overseas?' attitude."[73]

## Security Investigations

Service members involved in security investigations, including clearance-revocation investigations, often come to AFSA for advice and help. An adverse decision by the Bureau of Diplomatic Security can affect one's assignments, promotions, and entire career. AFSA as a union needs to protect its members, but AFSA has no interest in urging measures that weaken national security. (AFSA amended its bylaws in 2019 to require that active-duty candidates for president or constituency vice president hold valid security clearances.[74]) Sharon Papp said, "The law says all doubts shall be resolved in favor of national security. The person who decides whether you should have a security clearance has broad discretion, and there are very, very limited grounds to challenge this decision in court."[75]

Since the late 1970s, pursuant to a memorandum from Secretary of State Cyrus Vance (1977–1980), the Bureau of Diplomatic Security has not been allowed to record employees without their permission. "Over the years, there's been a chipping away" of that protection, Papp said. In June 2016, however, the Diplomatic Security Service/Office of Special Investigations (DSS/OSI) began to record interviews conducted in the United States of employees who were the subjects of investigation without being required to get their consent. Papp said,

> Security is a management right, which means we can't bargain over it, but we can bargain over the impact and implementation of management's exercise of its rights. In this case, AFSA negotiated a number of safeguards for employees: the posting of signage to indicate a recording is in progress, a private room for AFSA to confer with employees, the right to get a copy of the recording at an appropriate time.
>
> Employees get access to the recordings if they are proposed for discipline or if their clearance is revoked. In addition, if the investigators want a second interview, and the employee calls AFSA, we have access to the recording before the second interview. That's very important—we don't know what was said the first time, and we don't want the employee in a second interview to be called out for lying, or for a lack of candor.

Papp continued, "That's an example of how negotiations over procedures can provide members, or in this case employees, with a measure of protection," even in an area where management is in control.[76]

## TRUMP AND THE FEDERAL WORKFORCE

The administration, or at least a good portion of it, seemed to believe that the professional workforce in the federal government functioned as a resistance movement, eager and able to confound the policies the people had elected

President Trump to carry out. The White House was determined to assert itself against this so-called deep state.

On May 25, 2018, President Trump issued three executive orders intended to "ensure transparency, efficiency, and accountability" in the federal workforce by strengthening management and weakening employee unions:

- E.O. 13836 set guidelines intended to accelerate the negotiation of collective bargaining agreements and narrow their scope.
- E.O. 13837 imposed new controls and restrictions on "union time" (during which employees continue to receive their usual pay and benefits while engaged in collective bargaining and certain other union activities) and on union use of government facilities or resources.
- E.O. 13839 gave management greater power to fire employees by removing a number of employee procedural protections.[77]

Civil Service unions, led by the American Federation of Government Employees, sued to block implementation of the orders and won significant but not total victories.

The executive orders referred to Title 5 of the U.S. Code (governing Civil Service employees and unions) rather than Title 22 (governing the Foreign Service). AFSA, not wishing to draw attention to its exclusion from the orders, decided not to join the lawsuit.[78]

The president's next swipe at government employees came in the waning days of the administration with the issuance of an executive order intended to expand political patronage appointments at the expense of career professionals. Executive Order 13957 of October 21, 2020, required agency heads to identify "positions of a confidential, policy-determining, policy-making, or policy-advocating character not normally subject to change as a result of a Presidential transition." Those Schedule F positions would then lose Civil Service protections, their occupants could be dismissed without cause and without recourse, and their replacements appointed without competitive examination.[79] Schedule F would have affected an estimated 50,000 federal employees.[80]

The order said civil servants in policy positions should possess "appropriate temperament, acumen, impartiality, and sound judgment," and stated, more problematically, that presidential—that is, political—oversight is required to ensure that outcome. Secretary of State Pompeo told *Axios*, "We need to do more to hold the D.C. bureaucracy accountable. Great employees need to be rewarded and underperformers shown the door."[81]

The *Lawfare* blog offered this rebuttal: "The U.S. government is able to take on high-risk, high-cost ventures—nuclear security, pandemic response, environmental clean-up, food safety, and more—because civil servants are hired based on qualifications, not party affiliation; give advice based on data and integrity, not fear of reprisal; and owe allegiance to the Constitution, not the president."[82]

President Biden revoked all four executive orders immediately upon taking office.[83]

## FINAL MONTHS

Two episodes in the final months of the 2017–2019 board exemplified the discord and dysfunction into which the government had fallen and the delight the administration took in vainglorious display.

### Discord and Dysfunction

Seven cabinet-level agencies, including the Departments of State, Commerce, and Agriculture, shut down on December 21, 2018. They had run out of money.

The closure, which lasted 35 days, stemmed from the president's sudden demand that Congress appropriate at least $5 billion for construction of a wall on the U.S.-Mexico border. Democrats, then in the minority in both chambers but able to block Senate action with the threat of a filibuster, offered to provide $1.5 billion for border security measures that did not include a wall. Not good enough, said the president. And with no deal, no appropriations.[84]

Eight hundred thousand federal employees were affected. For many, the weeks without a paycheck were a real hardship. The shutdown disrupted diplomacy around the globe, although most consular services, which are funded by visa, passport, and other fees, were able to continue. Medevac requests were delayed.[85] AFSA staff—employees of the association, not the government—continued to work as best they could, but their counterparts in the departments were unavailable.[86] Secretary Pompeo, traveling in Abu Dhabi with his wife, insisted that morale was good, but Foreign Service employees "who work for an organization that consistently understaffs and overworks its team" felt differently. Some asked AFSA to sue the government.[87] "This was one of the roughest patches I can remember in my more than 33 years in the Foreign Service," said Barbara Stephenson.[88] The closure cost the economy an estimated $11 billion.[89]

The pony in this pile of manure, such as it was, was the eventual enactment of the Government Employee Fair Treatment Act, which provided back pay for federal workers on furlough and guaranteed that back pay would be awarded should the government once again shut itself down.[90]

## Display

On the first anniversary of his arrival at the State Department, Secretary Pompeo, to the strains of Pharrell Williams's "Happy" and Bruno Mars's "Uptown Funk," entered the department's C Street lobby to unveil and read out loud a "professional ethos" statement inscribed on a two-story banner. The "all-hands pep rally," as one writer called it, celebrated the Department of State as "the premier agency delivering on behalf of the President of the United States."[91]

It was widely believed that in its original conception and early drafts, the ethos statement was far more hostile. Eric Rubin, soon to become AFSA's president, said, "The language was essentially: You shall not leak, you shall not be disloyal to the president. Thanks to some pushback from career people, it got to a somewhat better place, but it was still seen as insulting and superfluous and unnecessary." His view was shared by the New Yorker's Susan Glasser: "An early draft was seen as a loyalty oath aimed at leakers."[92]

The display was also seen as condescending; some of Rubin's friends called it "the Burger King customer service pledge."[93] Retired Senior Foreign Service

---

**Box 12.2.** Department of State Professional Ethos

I am a champion of American diplomacy.
My colleagues and I proudly serve the United States
and the American people at the Department of State,
America's first executive department.
We support and defend the Constitution of the United States.
We protect the American people and promote their interests and
values around the world by leading our nation's foreign policy.
As a member of this team, I serve with unfailing professionalism
in both my demeanor and my actions, even in the face of adversity.
I act with uncompromising personal and professional integrity.
I take ownership of and responsibility for my actions and decisions.
And I show unstinting respect in word and deed for my colleagues
and all who serve alongside me.
Together, we are the United States Department of State.

Source: U.S. Department of State, "Our Professional Ethos," 2017–2021 Archived Content, https://2017-2021.state.gov/about/professional-ethos/index.html.

members William Burns and Linda Thomas-Greenfield, later appointed in the Biden administration as director of Central Intelligence and ambassador to the United Nations, respectively, put the ethos in a larger context. "No amount of empty rhetoric about ethos and swagger," they wrote, "can conceal the institutional damage" to the Foreign Service resulting from decades of neglect and "relentless attacks by the Trump administration."[94]

And then things got worse.

# 13

## Which Side Are You On? 2019–2023

Tom Boyatt, the first president of AFSA after its triple victory in union elections, was more than confident—he was *certain*—that AFSA with its new powers would stand as a bulwark against political intimidation of the Service and its members. Writing in the Watergate year of 1974, he said, "We have indicated . . . our willingness to undergo tremendous sacrifice for this nation, but we will never again permit McCarthyism or any other threat to impinge upon our integrity or to silence our dedication to serving the national interest."[1]

Forty-five years later, that resolve would be tested.

### A NEW PRESIDENT

Near the end of her second term, Barbara Stephenson started looking for a possible successor. She admired Eric Rubin, who had followed her before as special assistant to Under Secretary for Political Affairs Tom Pickering. Rubin, a career minister with 34 years in the Foreign Service, was finishing his tour as ambassador to Bulgaria when Stephenson approached him about contending for the AFSA presidency.

Rubin recalled,

> I had been three and a half years in Sofia. I had made the transition from President Obama's ambassador to President Trump's ambassador, a conscious decision to stay in. I'm not sorry I did it, but it was a challenge. When I thought about running for the presidency of AFSA, that was a major factor, helping to get the Service through this difficult time. And it wasn't just

Barbara, it was John Naland, Ken Kero-Mentz, other members of the board. In the end, it was an easy sell. I thought it was a great opportunity.[2]

Unlike Stephenson, who tilted away from the union side of the job, Rubin was all in. He said,

> I grew up in a union family, a family with a history of strong support for the labor movement. As a kid, I sang "Which Side Are You On?" and "Joe Hill" and the other union songs. My wife and I were members of the Newspaper Guild, an AFL-CIO [American Federation of Labor and Congress of Industrial Organizations] union—we met at the *New York Times*, where I was a reporter trainee. I'm a believer in unions, as well as in diplomacy and all that it stands for.

He put together a partial slate—candidates for several offices ran as independents, and some offices had no candidates—under the same "Strong Diplomacy" name that Stephenson had used. "I thought continuity made sense, and people I talked to just liked the name." He won election with no opposition.[3]

Rubin and the new Governing Board took office on July 15, 2019. Neither Rubin nor his colleagues were then aware of the chain of events, already underway, that would soon engulf the Foreign Service.

## A PERFECT CALL

Three months before the new board took office, President Trump and Secretary Pompeo forced the American ambassador to Ukraine, career FSO Marie Yovanovitch, to leave her post. The president and his political allies—former New York Mayor Rudy Giuliani and others—intended to induce or coerce Ukraine to announce investigations into alleged Ukrainian interference in the 2016 U.S. elections and into the activities of former Vice President Joe Biden and his son Hunter, a board member at a Ukrainian energy company. Ambassador Yovanovitch knew Giuliani's Ukrainian contacts were thoroughly corrupt, and in accordance with stated U.S. policy and her long-standing instructions, she used every opportunity to encourage Ukraine's government to fight corruption.

To President Trump and Rudy Giuliani, however, she was in the way, so she had to go. The White House demanded her recall, Secretary Pompeo offered no defense, and she was told to pack her bags. As she recounts in her memoir, she boarded the plane and was en route to Washington just as Pompeo was presenting his "ethos" in the State Department lobby—perhaps as he was reading aloud his pledge to "show unstinting respect in word and deed for my colleagues and all who serve alongside me."[4] (Pompeo later wrote, falsely, that "Yovanovitch was the quintessential example of a leftist, progressive, activist Foreign Service officer who behaved in ways that would have made our Founders cry."[5])

In July President Trump put a hold on $391 million of military assistance to Ukraine.[6] He then called Ukraine's new president, Volodymyr Zelensky. When Zelensky said, "We are almost ready to buy more Javelins" (a U.S. anti-tank weapon), Trump did not address the issue but replied with the memorable phrase, "I want you to do me a favor though." He then asked explicitly that Ukraine open the investigations. He added, "The former ambassador from the United States, the woman, was bad news and the people she was dealing with in the Ukraine were bad news. . . . [S]he's going to go through some things."

The first public account of the call was a readout from the Ukrainian side. Though sketchy and ambiguous, the Ukrainian account was enough to provoke the leadership of the House of Representatives, then under Democratic control, to open an investigation into the "Trump-Giuliani Ukraine scheme." Ten days later, on September 18, the news broke that the Ukrainian readout had been corroborated and amplified by a report to Congress from a whistleblower who had been in on the call at the White House. The White House then released a summary transcript of that call—a "perfect call," in the president's telling. The preceding quotes come from that White House transcript.[7]

To House Democrats, the transcript confirmed that the president had abused his office. Their investigation became an "impeachment inquiry," raising the stakes on all sides. Ambassador Yovanovitch—along with members of the Foreign Service, the Civil Service, and the armed services, and others whose testimony was sought—was trapped between the rock of a legislative branch with subpoena power and the hard place of an executive branch that demanded silence.[8]

The choice was painful but clear: As a legal matter, failure to comply with a congressional subpoena would be a felony.[9] As a professional matter, Ambassador Yovanovitch understood her duty: "I wasn't being asked to opine on whether the president's actions constituted impeachable offenses; I was being called as a fact witness to share what I knew. I was continuing to be what I always had been: a nonpartisan professional."[10]

The same choice faced other career Foreign Service members sought by the committee: Ambassador Michael McKinley, David Holmes, Jennifer Williams, and George Kent. All testified under oath as nonpartisan professionals. So did Ambassador William Taylor, a member of the Civil Service; Lt. Col. Alexander Vindman, U.S. Army; Fiona Hill, then with the National Security Council; and others.

At AFSA, President Rubin and the board felt the weight of history. "We knew," Rubin said, "that we had failed to adequately support our members during the McCarthy period, the Lavender Scare, some other times. The feeling on the board was, this is a moment of testing, we've got to be worthy of it."[11]

In a series of *Foreign Service Journal* columns that recalled this history, Rubin offered a credo for the Service in difficult political times: "We don't take sides in political or policy battles. We support the fundamental vision of a Foreign Service that is committed to the success of the policies established by our elected leaders." The credo came with a corollary: "There are, however, two sides to that coin: We expect our elected and appointed leaders to respect the career professionals.... [We ask] that our patriotism, sacrifice and dedication be recognized ... that our commitment to nonpartisan, nonpolitical service be taken for what it is: a solemn oath to duty, honor and country."[12]

For witnesses who were members of the Service, AFSA's moral support was welcome. AFSA's financial support, however, was a lifeline.

It wasn't initially clear, however, what help AFSA or anyone else could offer. The rules regarding AFSA's Legal Defense Fund, established in 2007 at the initiative of Sharon Papp and named later that year in honor of late AFSA labor-management counselor Richard Scissors, were complex and open to interpretation.[13]

Eric Rubin explained:

Under existing precedents, federal employees could not accept *pro bono* legal representation. It was considered a gift of services by the Office of Government Ethics and therefore not allowed. We knew of course that to go before Congress, you had to have a really good lawyer, one who knows the score. So we went into an off-site huddle with our labor-management team to see what we could do.

We lobbied really hard. The career employees in L [the office of the State Department's legal adviser] were sympathetic to the fact that we had these members of the Foreign Service who were facing financial ruin through no fault of their own. They were not charged with anything. They were witnesses. We succeeded in making the case that AFSA members should be able to get help from their union.[14]

The State Department lawyers made a distinction between a gift, which would have been problematic, and a benefit of AFSA membership. The Labor Management Office got it in writing from the Office of the Legal Adviser at State: AFSA members could receive support from a legal defense fund that AFSA controlled.[15] Rubin said, "So we went out and did a public call for donations. We raised $750,000 in three months."[16] Other groups joined the appeal, including the American Academy of Diplomacy, the Association of Black American Ambassadors, and a group of former diplomats led by Anthony Lake, the FSO who served as national security adviser to President Bill Clinton.[17] As of mid-2022, no AFSA member was out a single penny, and the Legal Defense Fund still had more than $300,000 remaining.[18] Witnesses who were not AFSA members did not have access to AFSA's fund. "You had to be a member for six months to get full services," Rubin explained. "We did have to turn down some people."[19]

Ambassador Yovanovitch found her lawyers through the oft-maligned old boy network. John Herbst, with whom she had served during his time as ambassador to Ukraine in 2003–2006, connected her to his childhood friend Larry Robbins, now "a top Washington lawyer experienced in high-profile congressional investigations." Even with a strong legal team, Yovanovitch still turned to AFSA for its unique expertise. "AFSA told us that the administration would have a hard time disciplining or firing me if I testified. Most importantly, they assured me that my pension was safe." AFSA, she wrote, "had been my first stop when I was recalled . . . and it had stood by me ever since."[20]

The congressional inquiry led the House of Representatives on December 18, 2019, to impeach President Trump for abuse of power and obstruction of Congress. The inevitable acquittal in the Republican-controlled Senate came on February 5, 2020.

Ambassador Yovanovitch retired on January 31, 2020. In her March 2020 Editor's Letter, "Going Through Things," Shawn Dorman, editor in chief of the *Foreign Service Journal*, wrote, "While the Service lost another outstanding senior diplomat, it also gained a hero."[21]

## PANDEMIC

A week after the February acquittal of President Trump, the World Health Organization (WHO) gave a name to a mysterious disease that had sickened thousands of people in Wuhan, China: COVID-19. By then the virus-borne disease had already been confirmed in Thailand, Japan, and Washington State. In March, the WHO declared COVID-19 a pandemic, and President Trump urged "medical doctors" to examine whether it could be treated by exposing affected organs to light or injecting them with disinfectant. By April, the United States was leading the world in the number of reported cases and deaths, a distinction it continued to hold for the next two years. The April unemployment rate reached 14.7 percent.[22]

The U.S. government and those sectors of the economy fortunate enough to have computers, broadband access, and indoor work could operate remotely.[23] Much of the rest of the country shut down, voluntarily or under official compulsion, or worked with high levels of stress and risk. Air travel came to a halt. Americans overseas were stranded.

The Service responded in heroic fashion. The *Foreign Service Journal* devoted its July–August issue to pandemic diplomacy, including a selection of first-person accounts of rescues and evacuations of American citizens from distant places where the disease raged, among them South Sudan, Ecuador, Guinea, Peru, Pakistan, Liberia, and Wuhan, China.[24] Between January and June 2020, Foreign Service posts managed the repatriation of more than 100,000 Americans from 137 countries.[25]

## COVID and AFSA

AFSA closed its doors on March 16, 2020; they stayed closed for the next 14 months. The association continued to function, however, using Zoom and Microsoft Teams to conduct its business. The *Foreign Service Journal* continued to be published on time every month throughout the pandemic. Rubin said,

> We did the classic union stuff, advocating for our members. We did things we're proud of. We won on a whole bunch of fronts.
>
> For one thing, we said people need time because they've got kids at home who are not in school. They've got elderly parents. So we won [from the Department of State] 10 hours per week, 20 hours per pay period, of administrative leave for all our members who were teleworking. We were very strong in advocating for what became known as virtual onboarding, so that hiring did not have to stop because offices were closed.[26]

AFSA won that battle as well.

## ELECTIONS

A history of the American Foreign Service Association does not need to recount the extraordinary events that followed the U.S. elections of November 3, 2020. President Trump's rejection of the election results, and his encouragement of the January 6, 2021, attack on the Capitol by his supporters, led to a second impeachment and a second acquittal. In those shattering events, AFSA and the Service, so heavily involved in what became impeachment number 1, were bystanders. When President Biden took his oath of office on January 20, they turned their attention to serving the new administration.

Just days before the inauguration of President Biden, AFSA issued its call for nominations for the Governing Board that would take office in July. President Eric Rubin declared his intention to run for a second term. His campaign statement was aimed squarely at the new administration:

> We will insist on the nomination and appointment of our most talented senior colleagues to a much larger share of ambassadorships and assistant secretary-level positions than we saw in the previous administration. We will also insist that political appointees to such positions be truly qualified, and not selected in reward for campaign donations—a practice prohibited by the Foreign Service Act of 1980.
>
> We will work with the new administration and with Congress on critically needed reforms to the 41-year-old Foreign Service Act, which must be brought up to date, while maintaining the core tenets of a non-partisan, merit-based service. We will seek to reexamine every aspect of our profession: recruitment, training, assignments, evaluations, promotions, and retirement. We are not satisfied with the status quo in any area of our careers.[27]

Rubin was joined on the ballot by four incumbent vice presidents: Tom Yazdgerdi (State), Jason Singer (USAID), Jay Carreiro (Foreign Commercial Service), and John Naland (retirees). All ran unopposed and returned to the board. Of AFSA's 16,667 members, only 3,169 (19 percent) cast ballots.[28]

## BREAKTHROUGH

The continuity in leadership at AFSA supported continuity of policy and continuity of effort, resulting at last in legislative breakthroughs. Rubin said,

We were part of the coalition that pushed for paid family leave—[Retiree Vice President] John Naland was very active in the coalition of federal unions that won parental leave in a Republican congress—I still can't believe that happened. We won in-state college tuition for members of the Foreign Service serving abroad. We won protections for Foreign Service members like those available to the military, in terms of breaking leases, car loans, cell phone contracts, and so forth when there are transfers. . . . The administration has been no help at all. We do it ourselves on the Hill.[29]

Bills to accomplish these goals (and many others) were introduced in the 116th Congress (2019–2021) and reintroduced in the 117th Congress (2021–2023). They finally passed because "AFSA took the initiative to get them attached to a must-pass piece of legislation," the Fiscal Year 2022 National Defense Authorization Act. President Biden signed the act, incorporating the Foreign Service Families Act, the Department of State Authorization Act (the first such act to pass in 20 years), and provisions to improve the government's response to "anomalous health incidents" (also known as "Havana syndrome"), into law on December 27, 2021.[30]

With that signature, AFSA achieved what AFSA's director of congressional advocacy called "goals that have been part of AFSA's legislative agenda for years, if not decades. . . . The resulting positive effects on FS [Foreign Service] life, are already [March 2022] reverberating throughout our community."[31]

What led to the breakthrough? Certainly, the distractions and divisions that had blocked the passage even of legislation with bipartisan support diminished with the end of the Trump administration. More important, however, was Foreign Service performance. During the pandemic, "members of Congress and their staffs were dealing directly with overseas posts to get constituents safely back to the United States. . . . This personal, direct interaction with posts overseas brought the importance of the international affairs budget and the work of the Foreign Service to the forefront."[32]

## A RACIAL RECKONING

On May 25, 2020, while America was reeling from the spreading pandemic, Darnella Frazier took out her cell phone and recorded Derek Chauvin, a white Minneapolis police officer, slowly murdering George Floyd, a Black man arrested for buying cigarettes with a phony $20 bill. Her video of Floyd, pinned to the ground and choking to death under Chauvin's knee while other officers assisted or stood by, inspired massive protests in the United States and worldwide. In July a *New York Times* headline read, "Black Lives Matter May Be the Largest Movement in U.S. History."[33]

The protests brought a rare moment of national introspection that reached into almost every American institution. The Foreign Service, with its history of exclusionary whiteness and maleness, found space on the bandwagon. The American Academy of Diplomacy issued a press release: "Rebuilding after the Violence: State Must Improve on Diversity."[34] The Government Accountability Office issued reports that reflected none too favorably on diversity at USAID and State.[35] An AFSA roundtable with three retired ambassadors associated with Harvard's Belfer Center for Science and International Affairs highlighted this statistic: "President Trump appointed 189 ambassadors over the last four years. Five of them have been African American. During President Obama's administration with Joe Biden, 46 of their ambassadors were African Americans. During George W. Bush's administration, 44 of his ambassadors were African American."[36] The Association of Black American Ambassadors proposed the adoption of 21 specific measures to "make diversity and inclusion real" at State and USAID.[37]

AFSA has no control over hiring, promotions, assignments, retention, or any of the other determinants of the demographic composition of the Service. But AFSA, as the title of this book proclaims, is the voice of the Foreign Service and is able as an employee union and professional society to speak for the Service and to the Service as well.

In contrast to its hesitation in the 1990s (see pages 143–46), AFSA's Governing Board and staff moved aggressively to address issues of diversity and inclusion across the foreign affairs agencies. The board and staff undertook two surveys of the membership—the first on diversity and inclusion, the second on retention—and followed up with extensive consultations with employee affinity and resource groups. Diversity was a topic at seven town halls that AFSA held in February 2021 alone. Based on these conversations, the Professional Policy Issues Department and an ad hoc board committee produced a set of recommendations on "retention, diversity, equity, inclusion, and accessibility" to guide AFSA's advocacy work and outreach in the Biden administration.[38]

The *Foreign Service Journal* spoke to its readership. Issues of race, diversity, and inclusion, which had received only occasional attention in the *Journal's* pages, saw a concentrated push after the murder of George Floyd in May 2020. The *FSJ* made sure that the issues that the George Floyd protests had placed before the country would remain a center of attention in the Foreign Service. A bold Speaking Out column from Ambassador Michael McKinley, "Changing

Mindsets on Race at State" (*FSJ*, July–August 2020) led the way to expanded and continuous coverage of diversity and inclusion issues in the *Journal*. The theme for five of the *Journal's* editions between July 2020 and July 2023 focused on diversity and inclusion with more than 25 articles, not counting readers' letters or coverage of the issue in AFSA News. Other Speaking Out essays and feature articles in additional editions also put the spotlight on diversity, equity, inclusion, and accessibility. In the twenty-first century at least, no other subject has received such intensive coverage in the *Journal*.

## THE *FOREIGN SERVICE JOURNAL* IN THE DIGITAL AGE

For most of the first 100 years of its existence, the *Foreign Service Journal* was very nearly the only way for AFSA's officers, and later its staff, to communicate with the membership and the public.[39] In recent years, the communications environment in which the *Journal* operates has become much richer, and the *Journal*, which is at its heart a print magazine, has changed, grown, and adapted.

The purpose of the *Journal*, defined in its bylaws, is "to advance the goals of AFSA and serve the interests of the Foreign Service community." The *Journal* is to be "a forum for lively debate" and a "record of the activities of AFSA," with balanced coverage of issues specific to the Foreign Service and issues of foreign policy, tilting somewhat toward the former.[40]

Shawn Dorman, who replaced the retiring Steven Honley as editor in chief in January 2014 and who also serves as AFSA's publications director, sees a larger purpose:

> We're woven into the AFSA mission . . . aiming to tell the story of the Foreign Service in a way that works for a dual audience, those inside the Service as our primary audience, but also those outside who can learn about the role and value of the Foreign Service on our pages. The *Journal* editor is part of the management team. Working with the Editorial Board, we're independent, doing our own thing, but very much trying to be tuned in to AFSA priorities and what AFSA is doing. We're working in that context. It's helpful when the president and the Governing Board care about what the *Journal* is doing, not that they want to mess with it, but that they see it as a vehicle, an important outlet.[41]

A subscription to the *Journal* used to be the one tangible benefit of AFSA membership, a constant reminder of the association's presence and value.

Membership still brings the print edition by mail but the identical content online is free to all, members and nonmembers alike, at afsa.org/fsj. Since May 2017, that site has included a searchable digital archive of every *Journal* issue back to 1919. Citations from the *Journal* are appearing more regularly in articles and books on diplomatic history, international affairs, and public administration.[42]

Free access helps to tell the story of the Foreign Service to readers outside the world of AFSA members. "When the *Journal* puts something out there that gets attention," Dorman says, "it can lead to change."[43] The media attention and political responses to Barbara Stephenson's December 2017 *FSJ* President's Views column "Time to Ask Why" (see page 219) are one example. And after *Foreign Policy* picked up a May 2022 Speaking Out column on the shortcomings of State's Bureau of Medical Services in the area of reproductive health, the bureau suddenly became responsive.[44]

The *Journal* relies on the Governing Board for its budget. "More than half of the *Journal*'s costs are covered by advertising," said Dorman. Most of the rest comes from the portion of member dues going toward the subscription, which has been listed as $20 a year since about 2012.[45] From 2004 to 2011, the member subscription was listed at $13.

To make sure the *Journal* reaches a wide audience, AFSA staff distributes content through all major social media outlets, including LinkedIn, Facebook, Twitter, and Instagram, and by email to tailored lists of journalists, researchers, bloggers, newsletters, scholars, and others. A weekly email newsletter, the *FSJ* Insider, created in 2021, had close to 2,000 subscribers by early 2023. Google analytics track readership and response, allowing continuous refinement of distribution methods.

Even while expanding the *Journal*'s reach, Dorman has kept a steady focus on the *Journal*'s primary audience: members of the Foreign Service, past and present. Her monthly Letter from the Editor (introduced by Steve Honley as an occasional feature) frames the contents of each issue and regularly appeals for reader involvement: letters, opinion pieces (she calls the Speaking Out column "the most significant space in the magazine"), personal stories, feature articles. "This is *your* magazine," she writes.[46]

Should the *Journal*, like many other publications, move toward more frequent online updates of its content and away from reliance on its ten-issues-a-year print edition? AFSA President Eric Rubin was a staunch supporter of the *FSJ* print edition during his two terms, as were the AFSA presidents before him. The hard copy of the *FSJ* remains one of few tangible, delivered-to-you benefits of membership. For many reasons, including the challenge and cost of upgrading the website, and the conviction that the *Journal* is not and should not be in the breaking news business, the Governing Board and the *Journal's* Editorial Board were not planning any major changes as of this writing. But the *Journal* is always evolving, and if readers demand change, change will likely happen.

## MORALE

As this is written, two years after the end of the Trump administration, those who expected rapid change have felt a letdown. "The beatings have stopped," John Naland said, "but morale has not improved."[47]

"Are things better than they had been?" said Eric Rubin.

Well, of course they are. But there are disappointed people, dashed expectations.

Times are tough and resources are limited. The damage the Trump administration did was intentional. They did not like senior career people, they did not like alternative views, they did not like people who talked back. So now, after the purges and the push to get senior people to leave under the Trump administration, we really have a deficit of senior leadership. It's made worse by the demographic challenges at the end of the baby boom. The Senior Foreign Service is not what it was. It may never be again.

There's a loss of confidence. The Europeans and other allies, they're not sure we won't go back [to Trump administration policies]. The Foreign Service isn't sure either. Can you count on a long career, or are you at risk? To some extent, people are thinking, should I stay or should I go?

Another factor, where we're not doing better at all, is the amount of crap that people have to put up with. One example—we had people who paid their own way home, because under Fly America rules that was the only way they could bring their pets. Unbelievable. And it's hard to put your finger on it, but people are less willing to put up with stuff than they used to be.

---

**Box 13.1.** Morale

**Morale,** *n.* The state of spirits of a person or group as exhibited by confidence, cheerfulness, discipline, and willingness to perform assigned tasks.

—*American Heritage Dictionary,* 5th ed.

Rubin also observed, "The work culture is changing."[48] Because of "extensive exposure to the U.S. military in combat conditions," there's been "a slow militarization of Foreign Service culture, with less room for constructive debate and dissent in policy recommendations. When I joined in 1985, I would have been laughed at if I called [my boss] 'ma'am' or 'sir.' A small thing perhaps, but one that reflects broader cultural change."[49]

He continued,

> We've done some polling—that's part of our job, to try to track what people are feeling and thinking. Most of what we get is not very positive. A lot of people feel they have bad bosses, abusive work environments. Attrition in the career service has been markedly higher, you can track it.
>
> It's just not as much fun as it once was to be on the front lines of American diplomacy. It's not so much fun now, you know, to work in a desperately understaffed embassy in Africa and try to catch up with the Chinese, who are better staffed and better resourced. We're just not in a good place on resources and funding, we've got many people doing two or three jobs. We've got all these jobs in Washington that should be overseas—the biggest domestic footprint in the history of the Service.
>
> And two years in, there are so many vacancies at the top. Of course nominees get jammed up in the Senate, but that doesn't explain why there has been no nominee for under secretary of public diplomacy, none for inspector general, and none for some 20 ambassadorships.
>
> Then there's diversity. We can't say progress is slow because we're going backward. The Senior Foreign Service is the least diverse it's been in more than 30 years. The Senior Foreign Service now is two-thirds male and more than 80 percent white.[50] When this administration says, we'd like to appoint more career people, but so many left there isn't enough talent, and not enough diverse talent, they have a point.[51]

## REFORMING THE FOREIGN SERVICE

The American Foreign Service Association was not alone in this somber assessment of the state of the Foreign Service. Even before the Trump administration left office, retired members of the Senior Foreign Service, working from places such as the Council on Foreign Relations, the Belfer Center, the Truman Center for National Policy, and the American Academy of Diplomacy, had begun to publish proposals for major reforms.[52] Some called for replacing the Foreign

Service Act of 1980 with new legislation that would "make reforms durable."[53] By the fall of 2022, much of this work (particularly the Belfer Center report) had been distilled into *Blueprints for a More Modern U.S. Diplomatic Service*, a 200-page report put together with the substantive, financial, and logistic support of the American Academy of Diplomacy, the Una Chapman Cox Foundation, and Arizona State University.[54]

AFSA had some issues with the original Belfer Center report, particularly with proposals to improve demographic diversity in the Foreign Service through greatly expanded mid-level hiring. Those proposals were dropped from the *Blueprints*, a move that AFSA (according to Eric Rubin) agreed to support.[55]

The Biden administration had its own ideas. In an October 2021 address at the Foreign Service Institute, Secretary Blinken outlined "our plan to modernize the purpose and institution of American diplomacy." Although he stressed that "some of our proposals are already being implemented," he laid out a program that was more aspirational than specific: build diplomatic capacity and expertise, elevate new policy voices, build and retain a diverse workforce, modernize the department's technology and analytic capability, and reinvigorate in-person diplomacy and public engagement.[56]

Coordination between the department's management and the retired officers was sketchy and haphazard, to the extent it existed at all. Of course, neither the retired officers nor the universities and think tanks with which they were affiliated had any formal claim on the department's attention. AFSA's situation was quite different. But the department, despite its long and formal relationship with AFSA, also kept the association on the sidelines.

In April 2022, the department announced that "to meet the Secretary's modernization goals," it would change the process for admitting new officers by eliminating the written exam—the Foreign Service Officer Test (FSOT)—as a pass-fail exercise. Instead, a panel of examiners would judge the FSOT in conjunction with the rest of a candidate's file to decide whether the candidate should be invited to an oral assessment. And the essay portion of the FSOT would not be read by humans but would be scored by a computer using artificial intelligence.[57]

AFSA was caught by surprise. It issued a statement: "AFSA was completely unaware of the effort to revise and modernize the Foreign Service intake process, which appears to have been going on for more than a year. We were not given any briefing or notification before this week's changes were announced online and posted by the State Department Press Office. . . . AFSA remains concerned that these unilateral changes risk being seen as excessively subjective and subject to partisan influence."[58]

AFSA in time came to terms with the substance of the changes. "We had a tough board meeting," Rubin said, "but we don't have bargaining rights on recruitment, so we're not going to lie down on the railroad tracks about this. We're going to consider this a pilot project whether or not they do. And we're going to ask for information on how it's going, and we're going to evaluate it."[59] In an inaugural occasional feature, "Straight from the Source," the *Foreign Service Journal* gave the department space to explain the changes, which appeared to be less dramatic than initially believed.[60] But the department by its action incurred a serious loss of trust, if not in its good intentions, then in its competence and commitment to its own promises.

As Eric Rubin noted, "There are little things [the administration has done] that we're very happy with. The dissent channel, the revival of the Open Forum, that's really positive and important." But large-scale reform—the sort of change the retired senior officers were talking about—would "require the administration to engage with the Hill, and they're not really willing to engage much." AFSA, by contrast, has taken a practical, pragmatic, and incremental approach to strengthening the Foreign Service and improving the lives and working conditions of its members: "We've gotten a lot of nuts-and-bolts victories out of Congress with no help from the administration whatsoever."[61]

⇥

In the late spring of 2023, outgoing State Vice President Tom Yazdgerdi won the AFSA presidential election. He and the new Governing Board took office in July 2023.

# Epilogue

## AFSA Strong

The American Foreign Service Association has been the professional society for the Foreign Service for 100 years and its labor union for more than 50.

As a professional society, AFSA promotes excellence throughout the Service, building among its members a shared sense of mission and history; recognizing their courage, integrity, and ability; protecting their right of independent thought and responsible dissent; defending the career principle against the encroachment of patronage; and promoting professional enhancement through training and education.

As a union, AFSA represents members of the Service in six agencies, including those members who do not pay dues to the association. AFSA's union rights and responsibilities are defined, and limited, by law. The association bargains on personnel policies and practices that affect the conditions of employment of those it represents, but its bargaining power does not extend to salaries or to any agency's mission, budget, organization, or internal security practices. AFSA may negotiate procedures for assignments, promotion, and discipline, but management retains the right to hire, assign, direct, punish, and lay off employees; to determine the number of promotions; to strike names from a list of those recommended for promotion, at least temporarily; and to hire contractors. In collective bargaining, AFSA does not represent Service members in management positions: chiefs of mission, deputy chiefs of mission, assistant secretaries and their equivalents.

In both its union and professional roles, AFSA defends the unique characteristics of the Foreign Service, including worldwide service, merit-based competition for advancement, and an acceptance of hazards and hardships not faced by those who serve at home.

When AFSA and management work together to educate the public, the administration, and Congress about American diplomacy and the need to support it, they carry weight. The more people know about the Foreign Service, the more favorably they see it.[1]

That kind of cooperation was impossible during the Trump administration. Secretary Pompeo had no interest in promoting the career service, which he regarded with contempt and considered a political enemy.[2] Secretary Blinken, like nearly all of his predecessors, treats the department's career staff, Foreign Service and Civil Service, with respect. By all accounts, he is appreciative of their loyalty and eager to draw on their expertise. But rebuilding a Service damaged and depleted during the Trump administration, and then equipping the Service with the numbers, skills, and technology to meet the challenges of the current moment, is a mammoth task for which no clear plan seems to exist.

A Foreign Service marked by independence of thought, loyalty in service, and excellence in performance cannot be taken for granted. As this history has shown, AFSA has called on successive administrations at least since the 1960s to forgo patronage, to strengthen in-service training and education, to protect dissent, and to take other steps needed to build and maintain an elite corps. Progress in many areas has been disappointing, and the Trump administration proved that much that had been achieved could be undone.

Happily, even before the arrival of the Trump administration, AFSA recognized its own shortcomings and took steps to address them. Ásgeir Sigfússon, who took an AFSA internship in 2001 and is now the association's executive director, offers a long view: "My first impression when I walked into AFSA was that it felt very much like a mom-and-pop shop. The staff was small, maybe 20 people, the building was a bit dilapidated." In 2023, with a staff of 40, "it's just a much more modern organization than it used to be. . . . We're doing a lot more. We're addressing things that we weren't able to even 10 years ago."[3] Membership since 2001 is up more than 50 percent, to around 16,500; the budget is up about 75 percent, to about $5.5 million.

Across all agencies, close to 80 percent of active-duty members of the Foreign Service belong to AFSA. Its services are popular; its publications well regarded and well read. It owns its building, free of liens. The association is financially sound, with liquid reserves exceeding eight months' expenses, a positive cash flow from operations, and net assets of $21.4 million at the end of 2022. AFSA is a now mature organization. The skill and dedication of AFSA's professional staff have grown along with its numbers. AFSA is stronger than it has ever been.[4]

The question for AFSA's leadership, and even more for AFSA's membership, is how to bring that strength to bear to achieve the association's goals: to promote the career Foreign Service as the institutional backbone of American diplomacy; to enhance its effectiveness and protect the rights and interests of its members; to maintain high professional standards for all American diplomats, career and non-career; and to be a strong advocate for the Foreign Service with the management, the administration, the Congress, and the public.

AFSA is the voice of the Foreign Service. With energy, imagination, courage, and wisdom, this voice will be heard.

# Appendix A

# AFSA'S LEADERSHIP

The American Foreign Service Association was an unincorporated association from its founding in 1924 to its incorporation in the District of Columbia in 1951. Following incorporation, the Executive Committee became a Board of Directors, and the Articles of Association were replaced by Articles of Incorporation and bylaws.

Until 1973, AFSA members voted for an electoral college that met to elect the Executive Committee (after 1951, the Board of Directors), which then elected the association's president as well as its own chairman and other officers.

In September 1973, AFSA replaced the electoral college and the Board of Directors with direct elections of a Governing Board, headed by a directly elected president and other association officers. If the presidency or other office should fall vacant, the board can name a person to fill the remainder of the term.

Terms of office:

| | |
|---|---|
| 1925–1947 | One-year term beginning July 1 |
| 1947–1969 | One-year term beginning October 1 |
| 1969–1974 | Two-year term beginning January 15 |
| 1974– | Two-year term beginning July 15 |

| Year | President | *Chairman* <br> *of the Executive Committee, 1924–1951* <br> *of the Board of Directors, 1951–1973* |
|---|---|---|
| 1924–1925 | | Evan R. Young |
| 1925–1926 | | Francis White |
| 1927–1928 | Evan R. Young | William Dawson |

| Year | President | Chairman<br>*of the Executive Committee, 1924–1951*<br>*of the Board of Directors, 1951–1973* |
|------|-----------|---------------------------------------------|
| 1928–1929 | Horace Lee Washington | Arthur Bliss Lane |
| 1929–1930 | George T. Summerlin | Arthur Bliss Lane |
| 1930–1931 | George T. Summerlin | Ralph J. Totten |
| 1931–1932 | Arthur Bliss Lane | Homer Byington |
| 1932–1933 | Leo J. Keena | Homer Byington |
| 1933–1934 | Norman Armour | Thomas M. Wilson |
| 1934–1935 | Homer Byington | Thomas M. Wilson |
| 1935–1936 | John Campbell White | Thomas M. Wilson |
| 1936–1937 | Coert Du Bois | Thomas M. Wilson |
| 1937–1938 | Ray Atherton | G. Howland Shaw |
| 1938–1939 | Ray Atherton | G. Howland Shaw |
| 1939–1940 | John K. Davis | Joseph W. Ballantine |
| 1940–1941 | Joseph E. Jacobs | George L. Brandt |
| 1941–1942 | Herschel V. Johnson | Howard Bucknell |
| 1942–1943 | Nathaniel Davis | Howard Travers |
| 1943–1944 | Joseph C. Grew | Edwin P. Stanton |
| 1944–1945 | Joseph C. Grew | H. Merle Cochran |
| 1945–1946 | John Erhardt | Loy Henderson |
| 1946–1947 | Robert Woods Bliss | Ellis O. Briggs |
| 1947–1948 | Edwin C. Wilson | William E. DeCourcy |
| 1948–1949 | Norman Armour | George M. Butler |
| 1949–1950 | George F. Kennan | Hervé L'Heureux |
| 1950–1951 | H. Freeman Matthews | Hervé L'Heureux |
| 1951–1952 | H. Freeman Matthews | Hervé L'Heureux |
| 1952–1953 | John F. Simmons | Hervé L'Heureux |
| 1953–1954 | John D. Hickerson | Tyler Thompson |
| 1954–1955 | John D. Hickerson | Andrew B. Foster |
| 1955–1956 | Robert D. Murphy | Outerbridge Horsey<br>Henry Villard |

| Year | President | Chairman of the Executive Committee, 1924–1951 of the Board of Directors, 1951–1973 |
|------|-----------|-----------|
| 1956–1957 | C. Burke Elbrick | E. Allan Lightner Jr. |
| 1957–1958 | Edward T. Wailes | E. Allan Lightner Jr. |
| 1958–1959 | Joseph C. Satterthwaite | J. Graham Parsons |
| 1959–1960 | G. Frederick Reinhart | Thomas S. Estes |
| 1960–1961 | Livingston T. Merchant | William L. Blue |
| 1961–1962 | Charles E. Bohlen | William Boswell |
| 1962–1963 | Lucius D. Battle | Elbert G. Mathews |
| 1963–1964 | Charles E. Bohlen | Elbert G. Mathews |
| 1964–1965 | Samuel D. Berger | W. T. M. Beale |
| 1965–1966 | U. Alexis Johnson | John H. Stutesman Jr. |
| 1966–1967 | Douglas MacArthur II<br>Foy D. Kohler | David H. McKillop |
| 1967–1968 | Foy D. Kohler<br>Philip Habib | Lannon Walker |
| 1968–1969 | Philip Habib | Lannon Walker |
| 1970–1972 | Theodore L. Eliot Jr. | Charles W. Bray III<br>William C. Harrop |
| 1972–1973 | David H. McKillop<br>(vacant) | William C. Harrop<br>Thomas D. Boyatt |
| 1974–1975 | Thomas D. Boyatt | |
| 1975 | John D. Hemenway<br>Lars Hydle, Acting<br>Patricia Woodring | |
| 1977 | Patricia Woodring<br>Lars Hydle | |
| 1977–1979 | Lars Hydle | |
| 1979–1981 | Kenneth Bleakley<br>Anthea S. de Rouville | |
| 1981–1982 | Charles S. Whitehouse | |
| 1982–1985 | Dennis K. Hays<br>Robert Keeley | |

| Year | President | *Chairman* of the Executive Committee, 1924–1951 of the Board of Directors, 1951–1973 |
| --- | --- | --- |
| 1985–1987 | Gerald Lamberty Frank Young | |
| 1987–1989 | Perry Shankle | |
| 1989–1991 | Theodore Wilkinson | |
| 1991–1992 | Hume Horan William A. Kirby Jr. | |
| 1993–1995 | F. A. "Tex" Harris | |
| 1995–1997 | F. A. "Tex" Harris | |
| 1997 | Alphonse F. La Porta Willard A. De Pree | |
| 1998–1999 | Daniel F. Geisler | |
| 1999–2001 | Marshall Adair | |
| 2001–2003 | John K. Naland | |
| 2003–2005 | John W. Limbert | |
| 2005–2007 | J. Anthony Holmes | |
| 2007–2009 | John K. Naland | |
| 2009–2011 | Susan R. Johnson | |
| 2011–2013 | Susan R. Johnson | |
| 2013–2015 | Robert Silverman | |
| 2015–2017 | Barbara Stephenson | |
| 2017–2019 | Barbara Stephenson | |
| 2019–2021 | Eric Rubin | |
| 2021–2023 | Eric Rubin | |
| 2023– | Tom Yazdgerdi | |

# Appendix B

# CHRONOLOGY

| | |
|---|---|
| 1789 | President George Washington signs bill creating the Department of State on September 15. |
| 1791 | Secretary of State Thomas Jefferson establishes separate diplomatic and consular services. |
| 1856 | Organic Act regulates diplomatic and consular posts and sets salary cap of $17,500, which stays in place for 90 years. |
| 1869 | Appointment of first Black diplomat, Ebenezer Don Carlos Bassett, as minister resident and consul general in Haiti. |
| 1870 | Secretary of State Hamilton Fish organizes department into nine bureaus and two agencies, with one translator and one telegrapher. Sets office hours as 9:30 a.m. to 4:00 p.m. |
| 1895 | President Grover Cleveland places most consular positions within merit system. |
| 1909 | President William Howard Taft extends merit system to all diplomatic positions below ministerial rank and prohibits consideration of candidates' political affiliation. |
| 1918 | American Consular Association formed. |
| 1919 | *American Consular Bulletin* begins publication. |
| 1922 | First woman, Lucile Atcherson, appointed to diplomatic service. |
| 1924 | Foreign Service Act of 1924 (Rogers Act) unifies the diplomatic and consular services, creating the Foreign Service of the United States. |
| 1924 | The American Consular Association reconstitutes itself as the American Foreign Service Association (AFSA) "for the purpose of fostering an esprit de corps" among Foreign Service |

|      | employees. The *American Consular Bulletin* becomes the *American Foreign Service Journal*. |
|------|---|
| 1926 | Elizabeth Harriman gives AFSA $25,000 to establish scholarship fund in honor of her late son Oliver, a Foreign Service officer. |
| 1927 | Foreign and Domestic Commerce Act of 1927 establishes the Foreign Commerce Service. |
| 1929 | Foreign Service clerks and non-career vice consuls at Embassy Paris form National Federation of Federal Employees Local 349, called the "Foreign Service Local." |
| 1929 | Incorporation of the American Foreign Service Protective Association, set up to provide group insurance for AFSA members. |
| 1930 | Foreign Agricultural Service Act of 1930 establishes the Foreign Agricultural Service. |
| 1931 | Moses-Linthicum Act regulates Foreign Service ranks and retirement. |
| 1933 | Ruth Bryan Owen, minister to Denmark, is first woman appointed as chief of mission. |
| 1933 | Secretary of State Henry L. Stimson unveils AFSA's Roll of Honor, a memorial plaque honoring "those in the American Foreign Service who . . . have died under tragic or heroic circumstances." |
| 1933 | AFSA confers its first scholarship. |
| 1939 | Congress closes Foreign Commerce and Foreign Agricultural Services as an austerity measure. Functions are transferred to the State Department and personnel to the Foreign Service. |
| 1941 | State Department suspends recruitment into the regular Foreign Service. Congress creates the Foreign Service Auxiliary, which outnumbers regular Foreign Service personnel by the end of the war. |
| 1945 | The Office of War Information (propaganda) and Office of Strategic Services (intelligence operations) are closed, and their functions and personnel transferred to the Department of State. |
| 1946 | Rogers Act replaced by Foreign Service Act of 1946, which creates a Foreign Service staff corps and a Foreign Service Reserve corps, and provides detailed regulation of personnel management, compensation, and allowances. AFSA does not accept members of staff or reserve corps as active members of AFSA until 1949. |

| | |
|---|---|
| 1947 | National Security Act creates the National Security Council and Central Intelligence Agency (CIA). Intelligence functions pass from State to CIA. |
| 1947 | Hoover Commission on Reorganization of the Executive Branch recommends merging the Foreign Service and Civil Service within the State Department to correct what it calls a "cancerous cleavage." However, no action is taken. |
| 1950–1953 | During McCarthy era and Lavender Scare, State fires more than 500 employees as security risks. Most were dismissed on suspicion of being gay, not disloyal. |
| 1951 | The *American Foreign Service Journal* renamed the *Foreign Service Journal,* beginning with the August 1951 issue. |
| 1951 | AFSA incorporates in the District of Columbia. Articles of Incorporation and Bylaws replace Articles of Organization. AFSA replaces its Executive Committee with a Board of Directors, chosen annually by an electoral college of 18 members. AFSA has about 2,000 active-duty and 500 associate members out of a pool of 12,000 eligible people. |
| 1953 | Congress restores the Foreign Agricultural Service in the Department of Agriculture. |
| 1953 | Congress creates the U.S. Information Agency (USIA). Press and information functions, cultural diplomacy, and international exchange programs pass from State to USIA. |
| 1954 | In what becomes known as "Wristonization," State opens the Foreign Service to about 1,500 Civil Service employees and makes a similar number of domestic positions available to Foreign Service officers (FSOs). |
| 1955 | International Cooperation Agency created within Department of State. |
| 1956 | Junior FSOs at State form the Junior Foreign Service Officers Club (JFSOC). |
| 1961 | Foreign Assistance Act of 1961 reconstitutes International Cooperation Agency as U.S. Agency for International Development (USAID). |
| 1962 | President John F. Kennedy signs Executive Order (E.O.) 10988, authorizing federal employees to unionize. |
| 1964 | AFSA forms a Committee on Career Principles. |
| 1965 | AFSA; Diplomatic and Consular Officers, Retired (DACOR); and State Department organize first Foreign Service Day to promote |

exchanges among career diplomats, academicians, journalists, and businesspeople.

1965     AFSA and department back legislation (Hays bill) to bring nearly all employees of State, USAID, and USIA into one personnel system. Bill passes House but not the Senate.

1967     AFSA buys building at 2101 E Street Northwest in Washington, D.C., for its headquarters.

1967     AFSA elections give reformist "Young Turks," led by Lannon Walker and Charlie Bray, all 18 seats in the electoral college. Lannon Walker chosen to lead Executive Committee.

1967–1968     AFSA sets up awards for constructive dissent that are funded by donations from the Harriman, Herter, and Rivkin families and named for the donors.

1968     AFSA publishes *Toward a Modern Diplomacy,* a 185-page manifesto based on report of Committee on Career Principles. It calls for a unified Foreign Service operating in State, USIA, USAID, and the Commerce and Labor Departments under an independent director general.

1969     President Richard Nixon signs E.O. 11491, setting new rules for labor-management relations within the federal government.

1970     State and AFSA negotiate the Foreign Service's exemption from E.O. 11491.

1970     Women's Action Organization formed to address treatment of women in foreign affairs agencies.

1971     President Nixon signs E.O. 11636, setting labor-management rules for the Foreign Service. AFSA resolves to seek recognition as the Foreign Service union.

1971     FSO Alison Palmer files antidiscrimination suit against the Department of State.

1972     State issues "Policy on Wives," asserting that "the wife of a Foreign Service employee who is with her husband at a foreign post is an individual, not a government employee."

1972     Bill Harrop and Tom Boyatt lead AFSA in representation contest with the American Federation of Government Employees (AFGE). Contest hinges on legal issue of who is labor and who is management.

1973     AFSA wins representation elections at State, USIA, and USAID. New AFSA bylaws replace the association's chairman and directors with a president and Governing Board, effective the next year.

1973    Hundreds attend AFSA luncheon honoring the "China hands," Foreign Service officers purged during the McCarthy era as dissenters of questionable loyalty.

1973    "Thursday Luncheon Group" of Black officers in foreign affairs agencies holds first meeting.

1974    Foreign Service personnel at USAID brought into the Foreign Service retirement system. A reduction in force at USAID results in dismissal of hundreds of Foreign Service employees.

1976    AFSA's membership votes to recall President John Hemenway after nine months in office. Governing Board chooses Pat Woodring to complete his term. She becomes AFSA's first female president.

1976    Alison Palmer refiles lawsuit against State as a class action suit, claiming discrimination against women in hiring, promotion, and assignments. AFSA does not join.

1976    AFSA and State reach agreement on regulations to implement grievance legislation passed in 1975.

1976    USIA rejects AFSA in favor of AFGE in a second representation election.

1978    Civil Service Reform Act of 1978 establishes the Senior Executive Service, the Office of Personnel Management, and the Equal Employment Opportunity Commission.

1979    Iranian revolutionaries seize U.S. Embassy Tehran. More than 60 members of the Foreign Service and armed services are taken hostage.

1979–1980    Pursuant to congressional action and the administration's Reorganization Plan 3, commercial functions and 129 overseas positions transferred from State to the Department of Commerce.

1979    Legislation introduced to replace the Foreign Service Act of 1946. AFSA is heavily involved in shaping the bill, which becomes the Foreign Service Act of 1980.

1980    The Foreign Service Act of 1980 regulates appointments, compensation, classification of positions and assignments, promotion and retention, training, career development, retirement and disability, travel, leave, benefits,

|      | labor-management relations, personnel grievances, and relations with other agencies. It establishes the Senior Foreign Service. |
|------|------|
| 1981 | Tehran hostages released on President Ronald Reagan's Inauguration Day, January 20. |
| 1982 | The Mary Harriman Foundation funds a new, annual Avis Bohlen Award, honoring the Foreign Service family member who has done the most to advance U.S. interests overseas. |
| 1983 | Despite opposition from AFSA and other unions, Congress brings new federal employees into the Social Security system. |
| 1983 | Terrorist attacks on American embassies in Beirut and Kuwait inflict heavy loss of life. |
| 1983 | The Department of State funds the AFSA presidency as a full-time position. |
| 1983 | AFSA establishes a Legislative Action Fund. |
| 1985 | New bylaws provide for an AFSA vice president to represent each constituency. |
| 1985 | Black Foreign Service employees bring an antidiscrimination suit against the Department of State. |
| 1986 | Foreign affairs budgets enter period of austerity that will last until 2001. |
| 1987 | About 130 State Department senior positions are cut. Thirteen consulates close. |
| 1989 | Court decisions favor plaintiffs in women's class action suit filed in 1976. |
| 1989 | AFSA establishes program of conferences with Senior Foreign Service officers that are intended to attract international businesses as paying "international associates." |
| 1992 | AFSA wins election challenging AFGE's representation of the Foreign Service in USIA. |
| 1992 | Gays and Lesbians in Foreign Affairs Agencies (GLIFAA) is established. |
| 1994 | AFSA wins uncontested representation elections in the Foreign Agricultural Service and the Foreign Commercial Service. |
| 1995 | AFSA joins AFGE in a State-USAID-USIA rally protesting a government shutdown and furlough of employees. |
| 1995 | AFSA publishes first edition of *Inside a U.S. Embassy: How the Foreign Service Works for America*. |
| 1996 | Court decisions favor plaintiffs in 1985 suit brought by Black employees against the State Department. |

| | |
|---|---|
| 1997 | Department of State employs about 7,000 Foreign Service members, compared to about 8,000 in 1992. Specialists account for more than half of decline. |
| 1998 | Al-Qaida attacks on American embassies in Nairobi and Dar es Salaam kill more than 200. |
| 1999 | AFSA conducts first annual high school essay contest. |
| 1999 | Congress closes USIA, transferring personnel and functions to Department of State. The Broadcasting Board of Governors remains outside State, and its Foreign Service employees keep AFSA representation. |
| 1999 | AFSA fights assignment of State Department Civil Service employee to deputy chief of mission position on which qualified Foreign Service officers had bid. Foreign Service Grievance Board sides with AFSA, but Secretary of State Madeleine Albright overrules decision on national security grounds. |
| 1999 | Congress extends law enforcement availability pay to Diplomatic Security special agents. |
| 2000 | Delavan Foundation funds Tex Harris Award honoring specialists for constructive dissent. |
| 2001 | Secretary Colin Powell launches Diplomatic Readiness Initiative, adding 1,049 Foreign Service and 200 Civil Service positions in Department of State over three years. |
| 2001 | AFSA objects as Secretary Powell makes several name changes: Foreign Service Day to Foreign Affairs Day, Foreign Service Lounge to Employee Service Center, and Foreign Service Star medal to Thomas Jefferson Star for Foreign Service. |
| 2001 | September 11 attacks bring surge of registrations for Foreign Service exam. |
| 2002 | Governing Board approves creation of AFSA-PAC, a political action committee. |
| 2002 | Congress authorizes award of retirement credit to eligible family members who performed part-time, intermittent, temporary services abroad between 1989 and 1998. |
| 2003 | AFSA publishes new edition of *Inside a U.S. Embassy: How the Foreign Service Works for America.* |
| 2003 | Military Family Tax Relief Act provides exclusion from taxation on capital gains from the sale of a primary residence for Foreign Service members who served abroad for at least two of the previous 15 years. |

| 2005 | AFSA publishes revised edition of *Inside a U.S. Embassy*. |
|---|---|
| 2005 | National Security Decision Directive 44 assigns the State Department to lead responsibility for contingency operations, including in Iraq and Afghanistan. |
| 2007 | AFSA establishes Legal Defense Fund. |
| 2007–2008 | AFSA renovates its headquarters, first time in 40 years. |
| 2008 | Lehman Brothers' bankruptcy (September) precipitates global financial crisis. |
| 2009 | Diplomacy 3.0 and Development Leadership Initiative increase funding and positions in State and USAID, respectively. |
| 2009 | Overseas comparability pay (OCP) adjusts base pay of Foreign Service members serving abroad by two-thirds of locality-pay adjustment for federal employees in Washington, D.C. |
| 2009 | AFSA establishes Foreign Service Books imprint. |
| 2010 | Publication of State's first Quadrennial Diplomacy and Development Review (QDDR), *Leading through Civilian Power*. |
| 2011 | Foreign Service Books publishes third edition of *Inside a U.S. Embassy*, with subtitle *Diplomacy at Work*. |
| 2013 | AFSA wins uncontested election to represent Foreign Service employees of Animal and Plant Health Inspection Service at the Department of Agriculture. |
| 2013 | AFSA President Susan Johnson coauthors *Washington Post* op-ed highlighting the lack of Foreign Service professionals in senior positions at Department of State. |
| 2014 | OCP capped by law at two-thirds of Washington, D.C., locality pay. |
| 2015 | Second QDDR, *Enduring Leadership in a Dynamic World*, is published. |
| 2018 | President Donald Trump issues executive orders restricting use of government resources by public-employee unions. |
| 2018 | Failure to enact appropriations forces 35-day partial government shutdown from December 18, 2018, to January 25, 2019. State, USAID, and most diplomatic functions are affected. |
| 2019 | House of Representatives opens impeachment inquiry into President Trump's conduct toward Ukraine. AFSA's Legal Defense Fund disburses more than $485,000 to AFSA members called to testify. |
| 2020 | Onset of COVID-19 pandemic (January). Foreign Service manages repatriation of more than 100,000 Americans from 137 countries. AFSA offices closed from March 2020 to May 2021. |

| 2020 | President Trump in October issues "Schedule F" executive order to enable replacement of as many as 50,000 Foreign and Civil Service professionals by political appointees. November election of Joseph "Joe" Biden renders order moot. |
| 2021 | Ambassador Gina Abercrombie-Winstanley named State's first chief diversity and inclusion officer. |
| 2021 | Fiscal Year 2022 National Defense Authorization Act incorporates long-sought AFSA goals: family leave, in-state college tuition during overseas duty, parity with military in financial protection during transfers, improved response to anomalous health incidents ("Havana syndrome"), and so on. |
| 2022 | State revises the Foreign Service Officer Test process. |
| 2024 | The Foreign Service and AFSA celebrate 100 years of service. |

# A NOTE ON SOURCES

The principal sources for this book are the *Foreign Service Journal*, minutes of meetings of the governing bodies of the American Foreign Service Association, and interviews with participants in the events described.

The American Foreign Service Association began publishing the *Foreign Service Journal* in October 1924 as the *American Foreign Service Journal*, a name it kept until August 1951. The *Journal* was published in a printed edition at least eleven times a year until 2014, when it began publishing 10 issues per year with combined January–February and July–August issues. The *Journal* is identified in citations as *FSJ*. All issues of the *Journal* may be accessed at https://afsa.org/publications.

The paper minutes and other records of the association are stored in AFSA archives in Woodbridge, Virginia. Minutes from January 1992 on are available in electronic format.

A list of interviews conducted by the author appears on page 265. The author also made use of interviews conducted for the oral history project of the Association for Diplomatic Studies and Training and posted on its website, www.adst.org.

Short works, including material from the online archives of the *New York Times* and the *Washington Post*, are cited only in the endnotes. Longer works are noted in the bibliography.

Links were active as of May 2023.

# INTERVIEWS

Marshall Adair — May 15, 2013

Matthew Asada — March 10, 2022

Kenneth W. "Ken" Bleakley — August 9, 2013

Thomas D. "Tom" Boyatt — January 11 and January 31, 2013; December 23, 2013; February 5, 2014; May 13, 2022

Herman "Hank" Cohen — May 29, 2013

Shawn Dorman — June 22, 2022

Dan Geisler — January 27, 2014

Perri Green — October 17, 2013

Kim Greenplate — July 6, 2022

Bruce Gregory — January 8, 2013

F. Allen "Tex" Harris — January 23 and January 25, 2013; April 18, 2014

Dennis K. Hays — September 5, 2013

Bernard M. "Bud" Hensgen — February 7, 2013

J. Anthony "Tony" Holmes — April 1, 2014

Ian Houston — April 14, 2022

Lars Hydle — February 2, 2013

Paula Jakub — October 22, 2013

Susan Rockwell Johnson — April 16, 2014

Steve Kashkett — April 7, 2014

Ken Kero-Mentz — April 20, 2022

Alphonse F. La Porta — May 16, 2013

John W. Limbert — March 3, 2014

| | |
|---|---|
| Richard H. "Rick" Melton | May 30, 2013 |
| John K. Naland | June 4, 2013 |
| Julie Nutter | June 23, 2022 |
| Sharon Papp | February 5, 2013; May 20, 2022 |
| Eric Rubin | June 7 and November 8, 2022 |
| Ásgeir Sigfússon | July 11, 2022 |
| Robert Silverman | March 22, 2022 |
| Jason Singer | July 14, 2022 |
| Barbara Stephenson | March 9 and March 23, 2022 |
| Lannon Walker | January 24, 2013 |
| Theodore S. "Ted" Wilkinson III | February 12, 2013 |
| Richard L. "Rick" Williamson | February 25, 2013 |

# NOTES

## 1. Diplomats and Consuls, 1789–1924

1. The full texts of the act and the implementing regulations issued by executive order appear in the July 1924 issue of the *American Consular Bulletin*, available online at https://afsa.org/fsj-archive.

2. See Barnes and Morgan, *Foreign Service*, 205; and George V. Allen, "A Half Century in Perspective," *Foreign Service Journal (FSJ)*, March 1969, 30.

3. "Improving the Foreign Service: Committee Finds Increase in Morale," *New York Times*, August 24, 1924.

4. *American Foreign Service Journal (AFSJ)*, October 1924, 37. The *AFSJ* became the *FSJ* with the August 1951 issue.

5. Barnes and Morgan, *Foreign Service*, 17.

6. Hunt, *Department of State*, 12.

7. Barnes and Morgan, *Foreign Service*, 18.

8. Hunt, *Department of State*, 2–13.

9. Jefferson was the first Secretary of State. John Jay, a holdover in the office from the Articles of Confederation, was secretary of the Department of Foreign Affairs during that agency's brief existence and continued to serve through the transition until Jefferson could take up the post of Secretary of State in 1790. Ibid., 54–96; and Barnes and Morgan, *Foreign Service*, 39.

10. Barnes and Morgan, *Foreign Service*, 48–52.

11. The war powers of Congress are in Article I, Section 8. Treaty-making and appointment to offices are in Article II, Section 2. For Jefferson's decision to challenge the pirate principality in Tripoli, see Parker, *Uncle Sam in Barbary*, 135. For an account of executive-legislative clashes regarding the Louisiana Purchase, see Adams, *History of the United States*, 319–35. Jefferson did submit the treaty of purchase to the Senate, which narrowly approved it.

12. Washington did not publicly deliver his farewell address. It first appeared on September 19, 1796, in the Philadelphia *Daily American Advertiser* and then in papers around the country. U.S. Senate, "Washington's Farewell Address," 26–27.

13. Barnes and Morgan, *Foreign Service*, 43. In practice, the highest grade was minister plenipotentiary. The United States did not appoint an ambassador until 1893.

14. Ibid., appendix 4.

15. Ibid., 60, 198; and Stuart, *American Diplomatic and Consular Practice*, 311–12.

16. Barnes and Morgan, *Foreign Service*, 56–59.

17. Ibid., 74–80.

18. Stuart, *American Diplomatic and Consular Practice*, 21.

19. The patent office was gone by 1836, the census by 1850, and copyrights by 1859. The administration of interior territories passed to the Department of the Interior in 1873, and the administration of presidential pardons became a function of the Department of Justice and the White House in 1893. After President Theodore Roosevelt transferred custody of historical records from State to the Library of Congress in 1903, the administration of immigration, which did not shift to the Justice Department until 1940, became the department's only major domestic responsibility. Some vestigial tasks remained. The department continued to service the reports of presidential electors until 1984, and it still retains responsibility under eighteenth-century statutes for receiving the resignations of the president and vice president, and for keeping custody of the Great Seal. The laws and orders dealing with these matters are catalogued in Plischke, *U.S. Department of State*.

20. Werking, *Master Architects*, 15.

21. Porter (O. Henry), "The Phonograph and the Graft," in *Cabbages and Kings*, 108.

22. Barnes and Morgan, *Foreign Service*, 107.

23. See White House, "Table 4.2—Percentage Distribution of Outlays by Agency, 1962–2028," Historical Tables, https://www.whitehouse.gov/omb/budget/historical-tables/.

24. Barnes and Morgan, in *Foreign Service*, cite Thomas Aspinall, consul in London from 1815 to 1853; John March, consul in Madeira from 1817 to 1859; and Alexander Hammett, consul in Naples from 1809 to 1861.

25. Quoted in ibid., 125. The inspector was DeB. Randolph Keim.

26. Andrew Jackson, "December 8, 1829: First Annual Message to Congress." This text is taken from the version published at the University of Virginia's Miller Center, https://millercenter.org/the-presidency/presidential-speeches/december-8-1829-first-annual-message-congress.

27. Bierce, *Devil's Dictionary*, 18.

28. Adams, *History of the United States*, 1080. Hay and Adams had adjacent houses at 16th and H Streets Northwest, on what is now the site of the Hay-Adams hotel.

29. Goodwin, *Team of Rivals*, 703.

30. See Edward Devol, "Chapter and Verse in American Diplomacy," *FSJ*, August 1976. Nathaniel Hawthorne, consul at Liverpool from 1853 to 1857, left a rare firsthand description of the duties and conduct of the office in that period in *Our Old Home: A Series of English Sketches* (New York, 1906). See also Arthur Frost, "Nathaniel Hawthorne, Consul at Liverpool," *FSJ*, August 1958, 10–13. James Weldon Johnson, a novelist, essayist, poet, and force in the Harlem Renaissance, entered the consular service via examination after having first received assurances that he would receive an appointment. He served as consul in Puerto Cabello, Venezuela (1906–1908), and in Corinto, Nicaragua (1910–1913). He left an account of his service in his autobiography *Along This Way*, first published in 1933 and still in print.

31. Mattox, *Twilight of Amateur Diplomacy*, 42–45.

32. Diplomat Huntington Wilson, "The American Foreign Service," 1906, cited in Werking, *Master Architects*, 15. According to Werking, correspondence "was filed by kind and not by subject.... Diplomatic correspondence was arranged in four series: instructions to United States diplomats, dispatches from them, notes to foreign embassies

or legations in the United States, and notes from them . . . bound chronologically by country." Most consular correspondence was arranged chronologically regardless of consulate. Miscellaneous correspondence was arranged chronologically as incoming or outgoing.

33. Quotes appear in Stuart, *Department of State*, 193–94.

34. Cited in Werking, *Master Architects*, 11.

35. Stuart, *American Diplomatic and Consular Practice*, 94; and Smith Simpson, "Perspectives on Reform," *FSJ*, August 1971, 17.

36. Stuart, *American Diplomatic and Consular Practice*, 96.

37. Barnes and Morgan, *Foreign Service*, 155–56.

38. Simpson, "Perspectives on Reform," 19.

39. U.S. Congress, House of Representatives, Committee on Foreign Affairs, Hearings on H.R. 17 and H.R. 6357, 68th Cong., 1st sess., 11, 40.

40. Hugh Gibson, "Foreign Service Rickety," *New York Times*, January 27, 1924.

41. Barnes and Morgan, *Foreign Service*, 205.

42. Minutes, American Consular Association meeting, August 4, 1924.

## 2. The Birth of AFSA, 1924–1946

1. *American Consular Bulletin*, September 1924, 317, 347–48. Allen Dulles resigned from the Foreign Service in 1926 to join the law firm of Sullivan and Cromwell in New York. *AFSJ*, November 1926, 360. For a history of the American Consular Association, see the digital archive of the *AFSJ*, March 1929, 74.

2. *American Consular Bulletin*, September 1924, 317.

3. *AFSJ*, October 1924, 10.

4. Clerks, secretaries, and other staff were employees of the department but were not members of the Foreign Service until passage of the Foreign Service Act of 1946. See pages 28–29.

5. *AFSJ*, October and November 1924. Articles were adopted June 8, 1927, and amended January 22, 1931, and April 21, 1931.

6. *AFSJ*, August 1925, 248.

7. Minutes of special meeting of the association, December 6, 1926.

8. James Barclay Young, "The 25th Anniversary of the Foreign Service Association," *AFSJ*, March 1943, 135. Cushman's is gone, but the facade of the building has been preserved.

9. Report of the AFSA Executive Committee for 1926–1927 [AFSA archives]. "No luncheons were held during the summer months owing to the heat."

10. The *Journal* published sample questions, but not answers, from tests given in training classes for new consular officers. For example, "The master [of an American vessel] has not obtained his clearance from the local port authorities, who have advised you that he intends to sail without clearing. What action will you take?" *AFSJ*, March 1927. In December 1924, AFSA's Executive Committee had debated whether to post questions from consular officers with answers in the columns of the *Journal*. The committee decided that doing so would cause confusion and could lead to neglect of consular instructions provided through official channels.

11. *AFSJ*, October 1924, 10.

12. A general meeting of the association on January 22, 1931, by unanimous vote amended Section V of the Articles of Association to eliminate the distinction between consular and diplomatic officers.

13. The agreement was reached in August 1933. The text of the press release of August 25, 1933, was published in "Washington Items," *AFSJ*, October 1933, 381–82.

14. The Foreign Commerce Service (FCS) and the Foreign Agricultural Service (FAS) were closed by the Reorganization Act of 1939. Personnel were transferred under Reorganization Plan II, approved June 7, 1939. The president nominated officers in those services (113 from the FCS and nine from the FAS) to be officers in the Foreign Service on June 30, 1939. The Senate confirmed the nominees on July 6. See *AFSJ*, August 1939, 429; and "Report of the Executive Committee of the Foreign Service Association, 1938–1939," *AFSJ*, December 1939, 649. The FCS and FAS officers acquired status as FSOs without examination and without loss of salary, and their numbers did not count against the limits set in law on the percentage of FSOs allowed in each of the top six grades. The overseas employees of the Bureau of Mines were consolidated with the Foreign Service in 1943. See Jones, *Personnel Systems*, 30.

15. Minutes, AFSA Governing Board meeting, June 15, 1929.

16. "Important Announcement," *AFSJ*, December 1929, 406–7.

17. *Foreign Service Employee* (FSE) 1, no. 8 (January 1930): 4. The *FSE* closed in September 1931 and was replaced by the *Foreign Service Record*, which published its first edition as vol. 4, no. 1 in October 1931. The *Foreign Service Record*, like its predecessor, was identified as "the official organ of the Federal Employees Union No. 349."

18. *FSE*, October 1930, 11; and *FSE*, June 1931, 9.

19. *AFSJ*, July 1931, 266–68.

20. *Washington Herald*, June 11, 1931, cited in the *AFSJ*, July 1931, 268.

21. Economy Act of June 30, 1932. Post and representation allowances were eliminated, and the allowance for rent, heat, and light was cut by 65 percent. Additionally, official personnel lost the exemption from U.S. income tax available to nonofficial U.S. citizens resident abroad. See "Conditions in the American Foreign Service," a statement by Rep. Edith Nourse Rogers (R-Mass.) [widow of Rep. John J. Rogers] before a subcommittee of the House Appropriations Committee, in *AFSJ*, February 1934, 63–65.

22. "Arrangement to Reduce Loss by Exchange," *AFSJ*, September 1933, 323.

23. "A Short History of the Department of State: The Rogers Act," Office of the Historian, Department of State, http://history.state.gov/departmenthistory/short-history/rogers.

24. *AFSJ*, January 1929, 22.

25. "Report of the Executive Committee of the American Foreign Service Association for the Year July 1, 1920 to June 30, 1930," *AFSJ*, March 1931, 282.

26. *AFSJ*, September 1932, 362; *AFSJ*, April 1933, 130–31; and *AFSJ*, September 1933, 330.

27. Secretary of State Christian Herter, former Secretary Dean Acheson, and Secretary-designate Dean Rusk were all present at the C Street unveiling. See Gwen Barrows, "Washington Letter," *FSJ*, February 1961, 30.

28. See "The Foreign Service Honor Roll," *FSJ*, May 2020, 44–49; "AFSA Renovates and Expands Memorial Plaques," *FSJ*, June 2021, 47; and AFSA, "Memorial Plaques," https://afsa.org/memorial-plaques. The June 2021 entry in the *Journal* and the text on the web page are unsigned, but Naland confirmed in conversation with the author that they are his work.

29. Notes, AFSA Executive Committee meeting, December 12, 1926; and George H. Butler, "Group Insurance in the Foreign Service," *FSJ*, June 1956, 19.

30. Notes, AFSA Executive Committee meetings of December 12, 1926; November 19, 1929; and April 6, 1931.

31. Dawn Cuthell, "Something for the Good of the Service," *FSJ*, February 1981, 4; and "Mrs. J. L. Harriman Dies in Baltimore," *New York Times*, March 6, 1934. Tuition at an Ivy League school in 1926 was about $400 a year. See "Tuition and Mandated Fees, Room and Board, and Other Educational Costs at Penn, 1920–1929," Penn Libraries (https://archives.upenn.edu/exhibits/penn-history/tuition/tuition-1920-1929/). Mrs. Harriman's gift of $25,000 is equivalent to about $400,000 in 2022 dollars.

32. *AFSJ*, March 1927, 90–92; and *AFSJ*, September 1933, 330.

33. See, for example, comments of Education Committee Chair Roberta Merriam: "It continually surprises the Foreign Service Association that there are so few applicants for the scholarships that we have" (*AFSJ*, January 1941, 38–39).

34. AFSA, "2016 AFSA Annual Report," 38, https://afsa.org/sites/default/files/flipping_book/ar2016/files/assets/basic-html/page-1.html#.

35. AFSA, "2019–2021 AFSA Governing Board Term Report," *FSJ*, July–August 2021, 63. The executive director was Ásgeir Sigfússon.

36. John K. Naland, "AFSA's Good Works: Scholarship Program," *FSJ*, January–February 2023, 48.

37. *AFSJ*, October 1938, 590; *AFSJ*, May 1940, 258; and Lilian Grosvenor Coville, "Education of Foreign Service Children," *AFSJ*, June 1940, 316–17.

38. *AFSJ*, August 1940, 438.

39. The first remark is noted in Henry Stimson's diary, which cites a conversation he had with President-elect Roosevelt on January 6, 1933. Stimson, who later served as Roosevelt's secretary of war, was then the outgoing Secretary of State. See Morgan, *FDR*, 368–69. See also Smith, *FDR*, 417.

40. Trask, *Short History*, 29.

41. Smith, *FDR*, 417–18.

42. Moskin, *American Statecraft*, 666–67.

43. Cited in ibid., 417. See also Nasaw, *Patriarch*, 508–9.

44. Moskin, *American Statecraft*, 418. See also Andrew Meier, "'The God-Damnedest Thing': The Plot to Thwart U.S. Aid to Europe's Jews and the Man Who Exposed It," *Politico Magazine*, September 23, 2022, https://www.politico.com/news/magazine/2022/09/23/henry-morgenthau-roosevelt-government-europes-jews-00058206.

45. Moskin, *American Statecraft*, 419. Some sources use the spelling "Miles Standish."

46. Ellen Rafshoon, "Harry Bingham: Beyond the Call of Duty," *FSJ*, June 2002, 18–25; and Francis Almeida Luzzatto, "Thank You, Myles Standish," *Washington Post*, November 25, 1997, https://www.washingtonpost.com/archive/lifestyle/1997/11/25/thank-you-myles-standish/6cb1801b-30fc-4f9e-ab3e-a8479deb895d/.

47. In June 1943, the *Journal* published a defensive editorial that protested against those "who persist in affecting to believe that the Foreign Service is a foppish career providing for its members an unending sequence of cocktail parties, dinner parties, night clubs, and boudoirs, and exemption from military service" (294). The editorial stated that one-third of Foreign Service officers were military veterans, and 16 percent had been or were still interned in enemy territory. The numbers on prior military service by Foreign Service officers come from a letter to the *Journal* from FSO Carl M. J. von Zielinski, who examined the records of the 883 officers listed in the Department of State's *Biographic Register* (*AFSJ*, October 1943, 533–34). An anonymous letter published in the *Journal* in November 1945 complained that to appease public opinion, "over a score"

of FSOs were released from the Service in 1944 for induction "as buck privates or the equivalent" in the armed forces (25).

48. In 1937 the Foreign Service had 703 officers, of whom 49 (7 percent) were assigned to the department and another 16 (2 percent) were in Washington for training. See the text of a speech by G. Howland Shaw, chief of the division of Foreign Service personnel, delivered at Forest Park High School in Baltimore, December 3, 1937 (*AFSJ*, January 1938, 10).

49. *AFSJ*, April 1943, 182.

50. In June 1944, 172 of 380 auxiliary officers (45 percent) were engaged in economic analysis. Another 76 (20 percent) worked as vice consuls. Walton C. Ferris, "Concerning the Auxiliary," *AFSJ*, July 1944, 356.

51. Extract from speech delivered in New York on October 26, 1943 (*AFSJ*, December 1943, 622).

52. *AFSJ*, December 1943, 630. This view was fairly common. A November 1945 letter to the *Journal* complained about the assignment of agricultural, labor, and mining attachés to the legation in South Africa, saying that "there is scarcely a thing that they as specialists will report on that we experienced Foreign Service officers could not do just as well" (*AFSJ*, March 1946, 25).

53. Barnes and Morgan, *Foreign Service*, 245–47.

54. Departmental Order 1218, January 15, 1944. See also John C. Ross, "The Reorganized Department of State," *AFSJ*, March 1944, 118; and Monnett Davis, "Foreign Service Planning," *AFSJ*, January 1945, 7.

55. G. Howland Shaw, "Post-War Problems of the Foreign Service," *AFSJ*, February 1944, 65.

56. Letter to the *Journal* dated February 6, 1944 (*AFSJ*, March 1944, 149).

57. *AFSJ*, December 1942, 666–70.

58. Minutes, AFSA Executive Committee meetings, October 1943 to January 1944.

59. Minutes, AFSA Governing Board meeting, October 17, 1944, and subsequent undated minutes.

60. Draft, no date [AFSA archives].

61. Draft, March 5, 1945 [AFSA archives].

62. Ibid.

63. Letter, March 19, 1945 [AFSA archives]. See also *AFSJ*, April 1945, 22, 33, 53. The percentage limitations, set in the Rogers Act of 1924, allowed no more than 6 percent of officers in Class 1, down to no more than 14 percent in Class 6 (Jones, *Personnel Systems*, 34). The Bloom Bill of May 3, 1945, named for the chairman of the House Foreign Affairs Committee, Rep. Sol Bloom (D-N.Y.), ended these restrictions.

64. Public Law (P.L.) 48, 79th Cong., 1st sess.; *AFSJ*, June 1945, 10; and Jones, *Personnel Systems*, 33–34.

65. Berhard G. Bechhoefer, "1946 Revisited," *FSJ*, November 1966, 28. Bechhoefer, a State Department (not Foreign Service) officer, was a member of the planning staff.

66. Minutes, AFSA Executive Committee meetings, April 15, 1945, to September 30, 1945.

67. Minutes, AFSA Executive Committee meetings, October 8, 1945.

68. Merle Cochran and Edwin Stanton headed the outgoing committee, which included Andrew Foster of the Office of Foreign Service. Loy Henderson and John Carter Vincent headed the incoming committee.

69. Before the fall 1945 exam for members and veterans of the armed forces and Merchant Marine, the department had offered a special exam in the spring for departmental

Civil Service and non-career Foreign Service employees, bringing in 125 new junior officers. See Jones, *Personnel Systems*, 42.

70. To qualify under the Manpower Act, an applicant had to be at least 31 years of age, to be a citizen for at least 15 years, and to have served in the armed forces or Merchant Marine, or to have two years' responsible experience in any branch of the federal government. The act gave the department authority to hire lateral entries during a two-year period. Of some 2,500 applicants, 800 qualified for an oral examination, and eventually 166 were appointed. See Jones, *Personnel Systems*, 41–42.

71. The *Washington Post* wrote on July 2, 1945, the day Byrnes's appointment was announced, "It is to be hoped that the new administration will not be content with anything less than a complete overhaul and radical expansion of the State Department. The State Department is the Department of Peace in a world which for years is bound to find peace uneasy. . . . Audacity is required, and we feel sure that Mr. Byrnes would get the backing of both the president and Congress for a program of real reorganization based upon the democratization of the Foreign Service."

72. Bureau of the Budget, "The Organization and Administration of the Department of State," August 1945, 6, cited in Jones, *Personnel Systems*, 36.

73. Jones, *Personnel Systems*, 36–39.

74. Julian F. Harrington, "How the Legislation Developed," *AFSJ*, September 1946, 7; and "1944 Contest Draws 60 Essays," *FSJ*, September 1995, 40. The top prize of $500 (about $7,500 in 2022 dollars) went to James Orr Denby.

75. Jones, *Personnel Systems*, 40–41. Sentiment favoring a career Foreign Service was not universal, and the Bureau of the Budget was not the only skeptic. Foreign Service Officer George V. Allen, soon to be named ambassador to Iran, wrote in January 1946 that "a career Service has a tendency to become an end in itself, and the purpose of its establishment—to serve the government and the people of the United States—to be obscured" (*AFSJ*, January 1946, 14). The *American Foreign Service Journal* in March 1946 outlined the work being done in the Office of the Foreign Service in an unsigned article with the (premature) title "The Principal Features of the Foreign Service Act of 1946."

76. Harrington, "How the Legislation Developed."

77. Julian F. Harrington, "The Birth of the Foreign Service Act," *AFSJ*, November 1946, 22–25. Harrington writes that Chapin and his drafting colleagues envisioned "an elite corps in the Department similar to that of the Marine Corps in the Navy Department," while the Bureau of the Budget "insisted on a vertical chain of command stemming down from the Secretary of State" (25). AFSA took up Chapin's vision in the Committee on Career Principles' 1968 report *Toward a Modern Diplomacy*, 68–73.

78. Jones, *Personnel Systems*, 42–50.

79. Ibid., 49.

80. *AFSJ*, October 1949, 33.

81. Minutes, AFSA Executive Committee meetings, October 22, 1943, and January 4, 1944.

82. Minutes, AFSA Executive Committee meetings, January 4, 1944.

83. Minutes, AFSA Executive Committee meetings, April 13 to September 30, 1945.

84. Under current (2023) criteria, Consul General Meily, killed in a plane crash en route to his post, is eligible for inclusion on the honor roll and was added to the Virtual AFSA Memorial Plaque at https://afsa.org/virtual-afsa-memorial-plaque.

85. Minutes, AFSA Executive Committee meetings of April 13 to September 30, 1945; January 10, 1946; and March 10, 1948. See also minutes, AFSA general meeting, April 21, 1948.

86. AFSA Committee on Career Principles, "The Foreign Service of the United States; Whatever Became of It?," *Toward a Modern Diplomacy*, 4. https://afsa.org/foreign -service-journal-november-part-2-1968.

87. Ibid., 6.

## 3. Growth and Turmoil, 1946–1967

1. P.L. 80-253, July 27, 1947. Dean Acheson, then under secretary of State, blamed the loss of the intelligence function on "gross stupidity. . . . The State Department had abdicated not only leadership in this field but any serious position." Acheson, *Present at the Creation*, 127.

2. The Economic Cooperation Administration was created by the Economic Cooperation Act of 1948 (P.L. 472, April 3, 1948, 62 Stat. 138). Charles Mee wrote, "To be young, to be American, were wonderful things in the late Forties; to be one of Averell Harriman's aides—or an aide to one of his aides—was transcendental. By 1952, 2,500 people would come to work for the American embassy in Paris; with their wives and children they would form an American community of some 7,500. Of them all, only 129 were Foreign Service officers. . . . They filled the Hotel Talleyrand, and seven large office buildings, and seven grand residences for special dignitaries, and stored $15 million worth of desks and teletype machines and radio equipment and stationery in a warehouse" (Mee, *Marshall Plan*, 249–50).

3. Executive Order (E.O.) 10477, August 1, 1953; and Reorganization Plan No. 8 (63 Stat. 203), effective August 1, 1953.

4. P.L. 83-690, August 28, 1954.

5. The Trade Agreements Act of 1979 (P.L. 96-39, signed July 26, 1979) and Reorganization Plan 3, which took effect on April 1, 1980, transferred the commercial function from State to Commerce, which established the Foreign Commercial Service in the International Trade Administration. In 1981, Commerce joined the FCS with its domestic export-promotion arm to create the U.S. and Foreign Commercial Service. See U.S. General Accounting Office, "Problems Hamper Foreign Commercial Service's Progress," October 18, 1982, https://www.gao.gov/assets/id-83-10.pdf.

6. Trade Expansion Act of 1962, P.L. 87-794, October 11, 1962.

7. The reports are Hoover, *U.S. Commission*; Rowe, Ramspeck, and DeCourcy, *Improved Personnel System*; Brookings, *Administration of Foreign Affairs*; White House Task Force, unpublished (see Jones, *Personnel Systems*, 101–3); and Department of State (Wriston Committee Report), *Toward a Stronger Foreign Service*. The Hoover Commission's Task Force on Foreign Affairs—headed by Harvey Bundy and James Grafton Rogers, both assistant secretaries under Hoover's Secretary of State Henry Stimson—published its report separately.

8. Hoover, *U.S. Commission*, 24 (emphasis in the original).

9. Acheson, *Present at the Creation*, 244.

10. Jones, *Personnel Systems*, 67–70 (emphasis added).

11. Ibid., 69n25.

12. George Kennan from minutes of the general meeting, *AFSJ*, August 1950, 9.

13. Rusk, *As I Saw It*, 131.

14. Jones, *Personnel Systems*, 71–74; and U.S. Department of State, "Directive to Improve."

15. *AFSJ*, April 1951, 24.

16. Jones, *Personnel Systems*, 71–74.

17. Acheson, *Present at the Creation*, 245.

18. Kahn, *China Hands*, 175.

19. Frederick R. Barkley, "FBI Seizes 6 as Spies," *New York Times*, June 7, 1945. Service had provided a journalist with copies of a small number of reports he had written on conditions in China. Despite the prosecutor's recommendation, a grand jury refused to indict him.

20. U.S. Department of State, *Diplomatic Security*, 80. Service, one of the China hands, fought the charges through a series of clearances and new accusations but was terminated in 1950. He sued the department over his dismissal, finally prevailing with a Supreme Court ruling in 1956 that the department had violated its own procedures. He was reinstated in 1957 and retired in 1962. See Kahn, *China Hands*.

21. U.S. Department of State, *Diplomatic Security*, 79, 87.

22. McCarthy's speech was not recorded, and no transcript was taken down. This quote is from the account published the day after the event by a journalist who was there, Frank Desmond of the *Wheeling Intelligencer*. See also James M. Lindsay, "TWE Remembers: Joseph McCarthy's Wheeling Speech," Council on Foreign Relations (blog post), February 9, 2011, https://www.cfr.org/blog/twe-remembers-joseph-mccarthys-wheeling-speech.

23. Cited in Acheson, *Present at the Creation*, 365.

24. U.S. Department of State, *Diplomatic Security*, 124.

25. This story is told in detail in Kahn, *China Hands*.

26. Nathan and Oliver, *Foreign Policy Making*, 17.

27. Cited in William Lenderking Jr., "Dissent, Disloyalty, and Foreign Service Finkism," *FSJ*, May 1974, 13 (emphasis added).

28. *AFSJ*, July 1951, 23–24. FSO Avery F. Peterson was chairman of the Editorial Board.

29. *FSJ*, November 1952, 28; and "Herve L'Heureux, Diplomatic Aide, Dies; Consul General of Montreal Since 1955," *New York Times*, July 10, 1957, 27.

30. Minutes, AFSA general business meeting, September 20, 1951, as published in *FSJ*, October 1951, 58–59.

31. Minutes, AFSA general business meeting, June 26, 1952, as published in *FSJ*, August 1952, 38.

32. Minutes, AFSA general business meeting, September 20, 1951, in *FSJ*, 58.

33. Membership numbers from minutes of AFSA general business meeting, June 26, 1952, in *FSJ*, 38. Eligible pool from George H. Butler, "Why Association Membership," *FSJ*, December 1952, 9–10. Beginning in August 1951 and continuing until June 1963, the *Journal*'s masthead page included a statement describing AFSA as "an unofficial and voluntary association of the members, active and retired, of *The Foreign Service of the United States and the Department of State*" (*FSJ*, December 1952, 3, italics in original). Active-duty personnel were eligible for active membership; others were eligible for associate membership. The figure of 12,000 is Butler's estimate of those eligible for active or associate membership.

34. Minutes, *FSJ*, August 1952, 38.

35. Butler, "Why Association Membership," 10.

36. *FSJ*, April 1953, 4–10, 10–12, 50–51. The *Journal* titled the letter "Constructive Criticism" and published Thompson's reply in the same issue.

37. Minutes, AFSA general business meeting, September 20, 1954, as published in *FSJ*, November 1954, 46.

38. Jones, *Personnel Systems*, 103–4.

39. "Secretary Dulles Accepts Wriston Committee Report," letter, June 15, 1954, *FSJ*, July 1954, 33, 46, 52.

40. P.L. 759 of August 31, 1954, and P.L. 22 of April 5, 1955, provided authority for additional lateral entries. P.L. 828 of July 28, 1956, further eased lateral entry and replaced the six numbered Foreign Service ranks with eight. It also raised pay for chiefs of mission and created the rank of career ambassador. Jones, *Personnel Systems*, 112–14.

41. "Henry Wriston Speaks to the Foreign Service on Personnel Problems," a summary of comments at a luncheon meeting of the Foreign Service Association at the Officers Club at Fort McNair on March 30, 1954, in *FSJ*, May 1954, 35.

42. Jones, *Personnel Systems*, 115.

43. Ibid.

44. George Kennan, "The Future of Our Professional Diplomacy," *Foreign Affairs* 33, no. 4 (July 1955): 370. At the time of publication in July 1955, Kennan was on extended leave from the Foreign Service.

45. Minutes, AFSA Board meetings, August 4 and September 15, 1954 (meeting with Saltzman and agreement to pass letters to him); and minutes, AFSA Board meeting, April 9, 1958 (decision to stop publishing letters critical of the Wriston program).

46. Minutes, AFSA Board meeting, August 18, 1954.

47. "The Lesson of 'The Ugly American,'" *FSJ*, December 1958, 25. Marlon Brando starred in the 1963 movie version of the novel.

48. Minutes, AFSA Board meeting, December 8, 1958.

49. Minutes, AFSA Board meeting, February 24, 1959.

50. Minutes, AFSA Board meeting, April 20, 1959.

51. *FSJ*, November 1959, 49–50.

52. Postal workers were an exception. They formed the National Association of Letter Carriers in 1889. Nevin and Nevin, *Federal Union*, 6.

53. The amendment was cited on the masthead of the *Foreign Service Employee*, the publication of Local 349 of the National Federation of Federal Employees (the "Foreign Service Local" mentioned in chapter 2, formed by a group of employees at the American embassy in Paris): "The right of persons employed in the Civil Service of the United States, either individually or collectively, to petition Congress or any member thereof, or to furnish information to either house of Congress, or to any committee or member thereof, shall not be denied of interfered with."

54. Franklin D. Roosevelt, letter to Luther C. Steward, August 16, 1937, at John Woolley and Gerhard Peters, The American Presidency Project, www.presidency.ucsb.edu/ws /index.php?pid=15445#axzz1Jy35UQb9.

55. E.O. 10988, 3 CFR 521 (1959–1963), issued January 17, 1962. The order defined an employee organization as "any lawful association . . . having as a primary purpose the improvement of working conditions among federal employees." The definition also excluded any association that "asserts the right to strike" against the government or a government agency.

56. Shultz, *Turmoil and Triumph*, 144.

57. *FSJ*, June 1962, 54.

58. Gregory, "Union Representation," 1.

59. The Kennedy transition reports are cited in Schlesinger, *Thousand Days*, 410–13. The Kennan quote comes from "Diplomacy as a Profession," a speech he delivered to AFSA on March 30, 1961; text in *FSJ*, May 1961, 23–27. Kennan was appointed ambassador to Yugoslavia on March 9, 1961; see "George Frost Kennan (1904–2005)," Office of

the Historian, Department of State, https://history.state.gov/departmenthistory/people
/kennan-george-frost.

60. Cited in *FSJ*, October 1967, 31.

61. Cited in Schlesinger, *Thousand Days*, 408–9. Schlesinger writes that "the report pointed out that, if Kennedy himself had entered the Foreign Service instead of politics, he could at this point barely qualify for appointment to Class 2," roughly equivalent to today's FS-2.

62. *FSJ*, January 1963, 4.

63. *FSJ*, March 1962, 58.

64. *FSJ*, November 1963, 4.

65. A note to that effect appears on the masthead page of the *FSJ* in every issue from August 1951 to June 1963.

66. In September 1961, AFSA's active-duty members numbered 3,598; associate members numbered 1,602 (Joan M. Clark, "Report of the Secretary-Treasurer," *FSJ*, November 1961, 53). At year's end 1960, active-duty Foreign Service employees of the Department of State, including officers, reserve officers, and members of the staff corps, numbered 8,350 (Barnes and Morgan, *Foreign Service*, 307). No count of retirees is available.

67. *FSJ*, June 1963, 2.

68. According to the *Oxford English Dictionary*, the first use of "generation gap" was in a July 28, 1962, headline in the *Daily Record* of Stroudsburg, Pa.: "Generation Gap Affects Parent-Child Relations." The phrase and others like it (for example, "credibility gap"—may derive from the phrase "missile gap," which figured prominently in the 1960 presidential campaign.

69. *FSJ*, June 1964, 44 (emphasis in the original). The Committee on Career Principles was set up in 1964 but did not begin to function until 1965.

70. The JFSOC was formed in the spring of 1956. Dwight Ambach was its first president. See minutes, AFSA Board meetings, March 28 and June 19, 1956.

71. *FSJ*, August 1964, 45.

72. *FSJ*, September 1967, 42–43, 48–49.

73. *FSJ*, June 1964, 44–46; *FSJ*, August 1964, 45; *FSJ*, March 1966, 4; and *FSJ*, December 1966, 38–39.

74. The AFGE had 108,000 members in 1962, according to the union's website. See "Part 4: The Griner Era (1962–1972)," AFGE Time Capsule, March 15, 2010, https://web .archive.org/web/20130609070729/http://www.afge.org/index.cfm?page=TimeCapsule &Fuse=Content&ContentID=2243.

75. Legislation along these lines was sponsored by Rep. Wayne Hays (D-Ohio) and Sen. Stuart Symington (D-Mo.); see "Foreign Affairs Academy," *1963 Congressional Quarterly Almanac*, 88th Cong., 1st sess., https://library.cqpress.com/cqalmanac/document .php?id=cqal63-1317122. Similar legislation had been introduced in 1951 by Rep. Russell Mack (R-Wash.), whom the *Journal* quoted: "If we had specially trained career men and women who are free from politics staffing the Department of State, the Foreign Service, in my opinion, would be greatly improved and our chances of becoming involved in wars decreased" (*AFSJ*, January 1951, 24). The reference to women is noteworthy.

76. P.L. 89-308 (HR-4170). See "Good Work, DACOR," *FSJ*, February 1966, 29.

77. Board Chairman Dave McKillop's report, *FSJ*, October 1967, 53.

78. *FSJ*, September 1965, 49; and *FSJ*, November 1965, 41.

79. *FSJ*, March 1966, 4.

80. Results of membership drive in *FSJ*, October 1967, 30. Number of those eligible for membership in *FSJ*, October 1966, 27.

81. Minutes, AFSA Board meeting, May 5, 1967. The American Foreign Service Protective Association provided a 20-year loan of $200,000 ($1.4 million in 2013 dollars) at 5 percent interest, and AFSA borrowed another $50,000 from its own Scholarship Fund on the same terms. The seller covered $15,000 of the price by making a gift in that amount to the Scholarship Fund. The 1967 board may not have been aware that in January 1956, a real estate broker named Frederick Hunt of Walker and Dunlop had spoken to AFSA Board member David Key to propose that the association purchase the lot, then vacant, at 21st and E Streets Northwest. He estimated the price would be about $180,000 (9,000 square feet at $20 per square foot).The association did not pursue the proposal (undated memo, David Key to the files, AFSA archives).

82. William J. Crockett, Association for Diplomatic Studies and Training Oral History Project (ADST OHP) interview, June 20, 1990.

83. William Crockett, "'The Foreign Service That Could Be,' Speech Delivered to the [American] Foreign Service Association, October 29, 1964," *FSJ*, December 1964, 46 (emphasis in the original). Crockett's remarks were out of step with departmental behavior. In fact, the Secretary of State was never willing to give the Director General of the Foreign Service the independence that the 1946 Act envisioned and that would be needed if the Service were to respond to the needs of all agencies.

84. "The Hays Bill," *FSJ*, June 1965, 30. The reform board elected in 1967 favored a unified Foreign Service across all agencies but wanted the Foreign Service kept separate from the Civil Service in each agency. See AFSA Committee on Career Principles, *Toward a Modern Diplomacy*; and an open letter from Board Chairman Lannon Walker to Director General John Burns: "We believe we need a home service [Civil Service] in addition to a unified Foreign Service." *FSJ*, August 1969, 32–34, 48.

85. Crockett, ADST OHP interview; and U.S. Department of State, "Notes of Telephone Conversation between Under Secretary of State [Elliot] (Richardson) and Representative Wayne Hays, July 15, 1969," in *Foreign Relations of the United States*, vol. 2, *Organization and Management*, ed. Humphrey and Keefer, document 305, http://history .state.gov/historicaldocuments/frus1969-76v02/d305.

86. Daalder and Destler, *In the Shadow*, 51. The text of NSAM 341, March 2, 1966, is available at Office of the Historian, Department of State, http://history.state.gov /historicaldocuments/frus1964-68v33/d56. The authority of the SIG and the IRGs did not extend to the activities of U.S. military forces under an area military commander.

87. The Foreign Service Institute (FSI), established by the Foreign Service Act of 1946, opened in March 1947 at 2115 C Street Northwest, near the future (and present) headquarters of the Department of State. Prior to the opening of FSI, a division of training in the department provided new officers with instruction and orientation in a basement room in the State, War, and Navy Building, now the Eisenhower Executive Office Building. The room number, A-100, came to identify both entering Foreign Service classes and their course of instruction.

88. Lannon Walker, interview, January 24, 2013.

89. "After the Hays Bill—What?," undated memorandum provided to the author by Lannon Walker, 1. See also Charles W. Bray III et al., "1966: Are We Obsolete?," *FSJ*, November 1966, 26–27, 45.

90. "Prospectus for the Future," editorial, *FSJ*, November 1967, 36.

91. Bray et al., "Are We Obsolete?," 27 (emphasis in the original).

92. "Interim Report of the Committee on Career Principles," *FSJ*, November 1967, 30A–30D; and "Principal Officers and Chiefs of Mission Alphabetical Listing," Office of the Historian, Department of State, https://history.state.gov/departmenthistory/people/by-name.

93. All members of the Group of 18 were white male Foreign Service officers. See *FSJ*, November 1967, 38–41.

94. Foy Kohler, "AFSA: The Days to Come," *FSJ*, November 1967, 34.

95. The campaign appeal bore the French title "*Un Peu de Zèle*" (a bit of zeal), after Talleyrand's advice to eighteenth-century diplomats: "*Et surtout, pas trop de zèle*" (above all, not too much zeal). The citations in the text come from a copy of the appeal that Lannon Walker supplied to the author.

96. *FSJ*, October 1967, 43.

## 4. Transformation, 1968–1973

1. Walker, interview. "We wanted someone who would be tough and articulate on the role of the ambassador," Walker said, "and we got what we paid for." Walker later endured painful service under Ambassador Graham Martin during the final months of the Saigon embassy.

2. AFSA Committee on Career Principles, *Toward a Modern Diplomacy*, v.

3. The *Foreign Service Journal* published *Toward a Modern Diplomacy* in full as a special section of its November 1968 issue. It is available online to read or download at https://afsa.org/foreign-service-journal-november-part-2-1968.

4. Ibid., 2–3.

5. Ibid., 2–3, 5–6, 9, 63–72.

6. These recommendations come from the appended working papers of the subcommittees on personnel systems, manpower utilization and planning, training, openness, organization and leadership, technology and systems analysis, and remuneration and benefits.

7. Krogh was then an associate dean at the Fletcher School of International Affairs at Tufts University. He became dean of the School of Foreign Service at Georgetown University in 1970, a position he held until his retirement in 1995.

8. Walker, interview.

9. Report, AFSA secretary-treasurer, December 20, 1968.

10. Ibid.

11. The Mary W. Harriman Foundation, named for the mother of Averell Harriman, funded the Harriman Award for entry-level officers. Enid Long, widow of William Rivkin, President Kennedy's ambassador to Luxembourg and President Johnson's ambassador to Senegal and Gambia, funded the Rivkin Award for mid-level FSOs. Mrs. Christian A. Herter funded the award named for her late husband, the former Secretary of State, and given to an FSO at the senior level. The awards of $2,500 each were funded with annual gifts and were not endowed. Perri Green, interview, October 17, 2013.

12. AFSA Committee on Career Principles, *Toward a Modern Diplomacy*, iii; and Charles A. Kennedy, "An Interview with Charles W. Bray III," *FSJ*, April and May 1969.

13. Walker, interview.

14. "Republican Party Platform of 1968, August 5, 1968," at https://www.presidency.ucsb.edu/documents/republican-party-platform-1968. See also Kennedy, "Interview," *FSJ*, May 1969.

15. Kennedy, "Interview," May 1969.

16. *Washington Post*, October 21, 1968, A21.

17. "Diplomats Open Drive for Reform," *New York Times*, October 21, 1968; "Foreign Service Group Hopes to Gain," *New York Times*, December 6, 1968; and "New Life in Old State," *New York Times*, December 10, 1968.

18. Idar Rimestad, ADST OHP interview, June 22, 1990.

19. Walker, interview.

20. Rimestad, ADST OHP interview.

21. Cohen, "AFSA Becomes a Union: Bread-and-Butter Issues," *FSJ*, June 2003, 35–36.

22. "Un Peu de Zèle," from a copy of the appeal that Lannon Walker supplied to the author.

23. *FSJ*, November 1968, 25–27.

24. Letter dated March 6, 1969, *FSJ*, April 1969, 25–26. Walker complained to Under Secretary Richardson in August about the lack of a reply. See also Minutes, AFSA Board meeting, August 29, 1969.

25. "William Macomber, Diplomat and Met Chief, Dies at 82," *New York Times* obituary, November 22, 2003, www.nytimes.com/2003/11/22/nyregion/william-macomber -diplomat-and-met-chief-dies-at-82.html. See also Tex Harris, "AFSA Becomes a Union: The Reformers' Victory," *FSJ*, June 2003, 20–21.

26. Minutes, AFSA Board meetings, February 12 (Draper), August 29, and September 19, 1969.

27. Shimabukuro, "Collective Bargaining," 5.

28. E.O. 11491 generally barred union activity by supervisors but contained a savings clause that permitted supervisors who were union members to retain their membership.

29. See "FG 261 (Federal Labor Relations Council)," Richard Nixon Presidential Library, www.nixonlibrary.gov/forresearchers/find/textual/central/subject/FG261.php; and "Executive Orders: E.O. 11491—Labor-Management Relations in the Federal Service," Section 2, "Definitions," https://www.nixonlibrary.gov/finding-aids/fg-261-federal -labor-relations-council-white-house-central-files-subject-files.

30. Macomber's views were expressed in open hearings before the Federal Labor Relations Council on November 16, 1970 (AFSA News, *FSJ*, December 1970). E.O. 11491 excluded the military and such national security agencies as the Federal Bureau of Investigation (FBI) and Central Intelligence Agency (CIA). The Department of State was not considered a national security agency for purposes of the order.

31. U.S. Department of State, "Editorial Note," in *Foreign Relations of the United States*, vol. 2, *Organization and Management*, ed. Humphrey and Keefer, document 312, http:// history.state.gov/historicaldocuments/frus1969-76v02/d312. For the text of Macomber's speech, see *Department of State Bulletin*, February 2, 1970, 130–41.

32. U.S. Department of State, "Editorial Note," document 312. The task forces were (1) career management and assignment policies under function specialization; (2) performance appraisal and promotion policies; (3) personnel requirements and resources; (4) personnel training for the Department of State; (5) personnel perquisites: non-salary compensations and allowances; (6) recruitment and employment; (7) stimulation of creativity; (8) role of the country director; (9) openness in the foreign affairs community; (10) reorganization of the Foreign Service Institute; (11) roles and functions of diplomatic missions; (12) management evaluation system; and (13) management tools.

33. Macomber's dubious authority was P.L. 90-494 of August 20, 1968, which established the Foreign Service Information Officer Corps in 1968 and provided authority to

convert Foreign Service Reserve officers with limited appointments to Foreign Service Reserve officers with unlimited tenure. See Gregory, "Union Representation," 6–8; and Bacchus, *Inside the Legislative Process*, xi–xii.

34. Kennedy, "Interview," April 1969.

35. Minutes, AFSA Board meeting, April 18, 1969. The committee—a subcommittee of the Members' Interests Committee—consisted of Frank Wisner, Robert "Bob" Pfeiffer, and Paul Hare.

36. "Report of the Sub-Committee on Employee-Management Relations to the Board of Directors," AFSA News, *FSJ*, July 1969.

37. Minutes, AFSA Board meetings, August 29 and September 19, 1969.

38. "Message from the Board," *FSJ*, February 1970, 2.

39. Minutes, AFSA Board meetings, January 27, March 24, April 14, June 2, August 4, December 1, and December 9, 1970. AFSA's comments were largely the work of the Committee on Career Principles, chaired by Ambassador Margaret Tibbets.

40. Bruce Gregory, interview, January 8, 2013.

41. Minutes, AFSA Board meetings, May 5, June 16, and June 30, 1970.

42. Board member Donald Easum performed the analysis of E.O. 11491.

43. Minutes, AFSA Board meeting, September 8, 1970.

44. Bradford's letter is in the *FSJ*, November 1970, 35. The January 1971 *Journal* published a number of letters reacting to Bradford's resignation.

45. Minutes, AFSA Board meetings, January 5, January 12, and February 16, 1971.

46. Minutes, AFSA Board meetings, January 12, 1971; and F. Allen "Tex" Harris, interview, January 25, 2013.

47. Harris, "AFSA Becomes a Union," 24. Ted Eliot was then the department's executive secretary and well known to Secretary Rogers.

48. Full text in "Stormy E.O. Meeting," AFSA News, *FSJ*, March 1971.

49. Ibid. See also a letter to the editor from former AFSA Board Chairman J. Graham Parsons, *FSJ*, March 1971, 51.

50. Minutes, AFSA Board meeting, February 9, 1971.

51. Minutes, AFSA Board meeting, March 16, 1971.

52. *FSJ*, May 1971, 54 (referendum results). The AFSA website uses the number 86 percent, as does Harris, "AFSA Becomes a Union," 25.

53. Minutes, AFSA Board meeting, April 6, 1971.

54. Thomas D. "Tom" Boyatt, interview, January 11, 2013.

55. Harris, "AFSA Becomes a Union," 25.

56. E.O. 11636, Sections 8, 10.

57. The Executive Order provided for a three-person commission, with a chairman from the Office of Management and Budget and members from the Department of Labor and the Civil Service Commission. In the *FSJ*, EMRC was often referred to as the "Employee-Management Relations Committee" (and sometimes as the "Council"); the Executive Order, with confusing nomenclature, created the commission "as a committee of the Board of the Foreign Service." The Board of the the Foreign Service, established by Section 211 of the Foreign Service Act of 1946, by statute had as its chair an assistant secretary of State, so at least on paper the State Department was in a strong position to influence EMRC decisions.

58. The Participation slate also included Tom Boyatt (first vice president), Barbara Good (second vice president), Hank Cohen, Jim Holmes, Bill Lenderking, David Loving, Linda Lowenstein and Samuel Thornburg of USAID, and John Tuohey of USIA. The

Members' Interest slate included Len Baldyga (USIA), John Ivie (an incumbent board member), Ed Peck, Roz Ridgway, Matt Ward (JFSOC), James Wilson, and others. Richard Haga, Paul A. Toussaint, and John Harter ran as individuals. See AFSA News, *FSJ*, November 1971, 49–52; AFSA News, *FSJ*, December 1971, 34–35; and *FSJ*, February 1972.

59. Minutes, AFSA Board meetings, January 11, January 17, and January 31, 1972; and AFSA executive session, February 7, 1972.

60. Quoted in *FSJ*, November 1972, 31.

61. Gregory, "Union Representation," 2. Gregory is quoting the AFGE's submissions to the Federal Labor Relations Council in November 1970, in connection with hearings on what became E.O. 11636.

62. Tom Boyatt, correspondence with the author, February 8, 2014.

63. *FSJ*, July 1972, 29; *FSJ*, August 1972, 32, 35; and William C. Harrop, ADST OHP interview, August 24, 1993, 38.

64. Richard H. "Rick" Melton, interview, May 30, 2013.

65. Boyatt, interview; and Melton, interview.

66. *FSJ*, July 1972, 29; and *FSJ*, August 1972, 35.

67. *FSJ*, June 1972, 53. JFSOC had about 300 members, of whom 127 voted.

68. *FSJ*, January 1973, 27, 30; *FSJ*, February 1973, 34; *FSJ*, April 1973, 33; and *FSJ*, May 1973, 44.

## 5. The New AFSA, 1973–1979

1. Minutes, AFSA Governing Board meeting, January 15, 1974.

2. *FSJ*, November 1967, 36.

3. Harris, "AFSA Becomes a Union," 18.

4. This account is based in large part on documentation in the Ford presidential library, described in note 8 below.

5. The term "selection-out," once applied only to dismissal for failure to meet the standards of the class, came to be used in cases of dismissal for time in class as well. It is used here to cover both grounds for dismissal.

6. Gregory, interview.

7. Gregory, "Union Representation," 7–8; and *FSJ*, February 1974, 39. The case is *Lindsey v. Kissinger*, 367 F. Supp. 949 (D.D.C.).

8. Gregory, "Union Representation," 7.

9. A private bill providing the Thomas family financial relief became law on January 2, 1975 (P.L. 93-108, S 2446). At the urging of Chief of Staff Donald Rumsfeld, following his signature of the bill President Ford sent a personal letter of condolence and appreciation to Cynthia Thomas. See Gerald Ford to Cynthia Thomas, Letter, Box 19, Folder "12/31/74 HJR1178 Continuing Appropriations for FY 1975," White House Records Office, Gerald R. Ford Presidential Library, 11, https://www.fordlibrarymuseum.gov/library/document/0055/1668881.pdf.

10. Harris, interview, January 23, 2013; *FSJ*, November 1971, 46; and Harris, "AFSA Becomes a Union," 19.

11. S. 2023 was introduced on June 8, 1971. See Gregory, "Union Representation," 4; and Harris, "AFSA Becomes a Union," 19.

12. The interim procedures, announced in October 1971, anticipated Section 10 of E.O. 11636.

13. P.L. 94-141, Foreign Relations Authorization Act of 1976, November 29, 1975.

14. Lawrence Eagleburger, then deputy under secretary for management, signed the agreement for the department. "He saw me at the ceremony," said Harris, "and flashed me the bird." Harris, interview, January 23, 2013.

15. A discussion at the AFSA Board meeting of February 23, 1971, indicates a belief that grievance procedures were not well adapted to handling selection-out problems, which tended to be problems of a group and not of an individual.

16. John Harter, ADST OHP interview, July 22, 1997.

17. Ibid. Harter was dismissed from the Foreign Service in 1983 in an episode that became the subject of a second grievance and a lawsuit that Harter fought to the Supreme Court, which declined to hear the case. He was elected to the AFSA Governing Board in 1989 as a retiree representative and organized a number of conferences under AFSA's auspices in the early 1990s.

18. Elinor Constable, ADST OHP interview, May 30, 1996.

19. The department reversed these policies in the 1972 "Policy on Wives of Foreign Service Employees," a message sent to all posts on January 22, 1972. See U.S. Department of State, "Airgram from the Department of State to All Posts," in *Foreign Relations of the United States*, vol. 2, *Organization and Management*, ed. Humphrey and Keefer, document 341, https://history.state.gov/historicaldocuments/frus1969-76v02/d341. William Macomber was the principal author. Rick Williamson, who later became AFSA's counselor and then its executive director, helped develop the draft as chairman of the department's Open Forum.

20. McGlen and Sarkees, "Gender and the Foreign Policy Institutions," in Wilson, *Diversity*, 330–31; and Benjamin Welles, "Woman Winning State Department Case," *New York Times*, February 28, 1972, 4. AFSA Chairman Harrop testified before the Senate Foreign Relations Committee on the Mace nomination, but he neither opposed nor endorsed the appointment. It was AFSA's first testimony on an ambassadorial nomination. Howard Mace was later assigned as consul general in Istanbul, where he served under his old boss, Ambassador William Macomber.

21. An account of the Palmer case and related litigation is at Andrea Strano, "Foreign Service Women Today: The Palmer Case and Beyond," *FSJ*, March 2016, 24–28.

22. AFSA sought to affiliate with an ad hoc committee of women that became the Women's Action Organization, but the committee chose to remain independent. Fenzi, *Married to the Foreign Service*, 178–79.

23. Quoted in Shapiro, "A House Divided," in Wilson, *Diversity*, 95. The year was 1994.

24. The 1989 judgment and 2002 consent decree are summarized in the July 11, 2005, order of the federal district court for the District of Columbia in *Palmer v. Rice*, No. 76-1439 (HHK/JMF), https://ecf.dcd.uscourts.gov/cgi-bin/show_public_doc?1976cv1439-649.

25. *FSJ*, August 1974, 35.

26. "Hard Cases Make Bad Law," editorial, *FSJ*, April 1972, 4.

27. Melton, interview.

28. Editorial, *FSJ*, February 1952, 20.

29. Minutes, AFSA Board meetings, October 31 and December 5, 1969.

30. U. Alexis Johnson, "Caught in the Nutcracker," *FSJ*, September 1984, 32.

31. Nancy Johnson, "From Striped Pants Set to White Collar Union," *FSJ*, May 1999, 70–71.

32. "Penalties Barred for Protesting Diplomatic Officials," *New York Times*, June 17, 1970.

33. *FSJ*, March 1973; and Eric Pace, "Honor Came a Bit Late: Old China Hands," *New York Times*, February 4, 1973.

34. Patricia Sullivan, "Charles Bray III: Career Diplomat, Resigned over Nixon-Era Wiretaps," *Washington Post*, July 29, 2006. Bray returned to government as deputy director of USIA (later the U.S. International Communication Agency) in the Carter administration.

35. Kissinger, *Years of Upheaval*, 119.

36. *FSJ*, August 1974, 34.

37. Thomas D. Boyatt, ADST OHP interview, March 8, 1990, 34. Boyatt did not go to Chad, but in 1978 he did serve as President Jimmy Carter's ambassador to Ouagadougou (Upper Volta, now Burkina Faso).

38. *FSJ*, September 1974, 33.

39. *FSJ*, August 1974, 35.

40. *FSJ*, October 1974, 61.

41. Stuart Taylor Jr., "Libel Suit Is File against 'Missing,'" *New York Times*, January 11, 1983.

42. Minutes, AFSA Governing Board meeting, January 4, 1975. Agencies could appeal to the Employee-Management Relations Commission of the Board of the Foreign Service to decide whether an issue was "consultable" (i.e., whether management was obliged under E.O. 11636 to discuss it with the employee representative).

43. Boyatt, interview, January 31, 2013.

44. Richard L. "Rick" Williamson, interview, February 25, 2013.

45. William Greider, "Kissinger Foe Wins Election in State Department," *Washington Post*, July 12, 1975.

46. Minutes, AFSA Governing Board meeting, November 19, 1975: "During discussion of this [grievance] issue, Mr. Hydle asked Mrs. Thomas to refrain from constantly interrupting him. Mrs. Thomas threw a glass of ginger ale at Vice President Hydle."

47. Letter, Hydle to Hemenway, April 5, 1976 [AFSA archives].

48. Minutes, AFSA Governing Board meeting, May 4, 1976.

49. Minutes, AFSA Governing Board meeting, November 17, 1976. About 57 percent of AFSA's 5,689 members cast ballots: 3,279 ballots were submitted, of which 208 were disqualified and not opened, and 138 were opened and discarded under challenge. John Harter and Tom Foltz observed the count as Hemenway's representatives.

50. Minutes, AFSA Governing Board meeting, December 21, 1976.

51. Minutes, AFSA Governing Board meeting, December 20, 1977. Hemenway continued to pursue a suit against Lars Hydle and other board members in connection with an incident involving the mailing of circulars and a libel suit against six AFSA members in connection with the recall. Both suits failed.

52. Minutes, AFSA Governing Board meeting, August 11, 1975; and "AFSA Board: Hostility Reigns," *Federal Times*, August 27, 1975.

53. P.L. 90-494, August 20, 1968.

54. Gregory, "Union Representation," 6–8; and Bacchus, *Inside the Legislative Process*, xi–xii, 24n61. Gregory was himself a civil servant who joined the foreign affairs specialist program.

55. Email from Bruce Gregory to author, July 12, 2013. Gregory cites a "News & Views" newsletter issued by AFGE Local 1812, the unit serving USIA, on January 9, 1976.

56. Letter, Will Sutter, USIA representative on AFSA's board, January 11, 1976.

57. Certification signed by Edward Preston, chairman, in author's possession.

58. Minutes, AFSA Governing Board meeting, March 6, 1977; and AFSA president's annual report, June 30, 1978.

59. Minutes, AFSA Governing Board meeting, December 7, 1976.

60. Report, AFSA Finance Committee to AFSA Governing Board, May 10, 1977.

61. Active membership was 6,784 on July 15, 1975, when Hemenway took office, and just 5,656 on November 15, 1976, at the time of the recall. Attachment to minutes, AFSA Governing Board meeting, November 30, 1976.

62. Bacchus, Staffing for Foreign Affairs, 145.

63. AFSA ballot tally sheet.

64. Memo to AFSA Governing Board, August 2, 1976.

65. Letter, AFSA President Ted Eliot to Martin Herz, November 7, 1969. Martin Herz was then minister counselor in Saigon. Eliot had misgivings about the committee. At a board meeting on December 5, 1969, he wondered about the propriety of "one set of presidential appointees"—meaning commissioned Foreign Service officers—passing judgment on another. Herz's was the first AFSA committee to be chaired from overseas.

66. See, for example, George Crile, "Our Man in Jamaica," *Harper's Magazine*, October 1974, 88. The scandal resulted in bipartisan legislation, which AFSA supported, to require that ambassadorial nominees disclose their political contributions.

67. Letters to Senator Fulbright and Secretary Rogers, June 29, 1973, in *FSJ*, October 1973, 49–50.

68. Carter, *Why Not the Best?*, 169.

69. Austin Scott, "Carter Names Advisory Committee, Headed by Askew, on Envoy Selection," *Washington Post*, February 4, 1977, C7; and AFSA press release, February 4, 1977.

70. Letter, Lars Hydle to John D. Scanlan, February 15, 1977. *The Plum Book*, or *United States Government Policy and Supporting Positions* (published every four years alternately by the Senate and House Committees on Governmental Affairs), uses this definition: "Schedule C positions [are] excepted from the competitive service by the president, or by the director, Office of Personnel Management, because of the confidential or policy-determining nature of the position duties." Schedule C positions do not require Senate confirmation and are normally at the GS-15 pay grade or lower.

71. Letter, Pat Woodring to Secretary Vance, January 28, 1977.

72. Letter, Lars Hydle to Senator Ribicoff, November 16, 1977.

73. AFSA press release, November 19, 1977; and "Annual Report of the AFSA Governing Board," *FSJ*, July 1979, 30.

74. Statement of Lars H. Hydle, president of the American Foreign Service Association, at the Tenth Annual AFSA Awards Ceremony on December 9, 1977, 2, 3–4; and Graham Hovey, "Brzezinski, U.S. Diplomats' Guest, Is Told White House Ignores Them," *New York Times*, December 11, 1977.

75. P.L. 95-465, October 17, 1980, Section 304.

76. Carter and Ford numbers from AFSA, "Appointments—Jimmy Carter," Ambassador Tracker, https://afsa.org/ambassadorscarter.aspx; and AFSA, "Appointments—Gerald Ford," Ambassador Tracker, https://afsa.org/ambassadorsford.aspx. Johnson and Nixon numbers are from William B. Macomber Jr., "Memorandum from the Deputy Under Secretary of State for Administration (Macomber) to the President's Assistance (Flanigan), December 29, 1970," U.S. Department of State, *Foreign Relations of the United*

*States*, vol. 2, *Organization and Management*, ed. Humphrey and Keefer, document 328, https://history.state.gov/historicaldocuments/frus1969-76v02/d328.

77. *FSJ*, December 1977, 35. The Secretary of State is not included in the count.

78. Reorganization Act of 1977, P.L. 95-17, April 6, 1977.

79. Even after the Department of State had accepted the transfer of the commercial function to Commerce, AFSA maintained its opposition. In testimony, AFSA Governing Board member Bob Stern asked Congress to "reverse this folly" and suggested prophetically that "the 'separate commercial promotion function' will atrophy rather than prosper." Statement of Robert H. Stern of AFSA before the Senate Subcommittee on Arms Control, Oceans, International Operations, and Environment, December 14, 1979, 6.

80. Bacchus, *Inside the Legislative Process*, 14–15, 19n32.

81. Civil Service Reform Act of 1978, P.L. 95-454, October 13, 1978.

82. "Annual Report of the AFSA Governing Board," 4.

83. Bacchus, *Inside the Legislative Process*, 31.


## 6. The Foreign Service Act of 1980

1. Kenneth W. "Ken" Bleakley, interview, August 9, 2013.

2. Election results were published in the *FSJ*, August 1979, 40. In the balloting for president, Bleakley won 1,185 votes to 711 for Rogers, 703 for Pfeiffer, and 122 for John D. Hemenway.

3. *FSJ*, May 1979, 24F.

4. Ibid.

5. Wolfgang Saxon, "Benjamin H. Read Is Dead at 67; a Leading Foreign Affairs Scholar," *New York Times*, March 19, 1993; and Jimmy Carter, "Department of State Nomination of Benjamin H. Read to Be Deputy Under Secretary, July 25, 1977," at John Woolley and Gerhard Peters, The American Presidency Project, www.presidency.ucsb.edu/ws/index.php?pid=7863.

6. Bacchus, *Inside the Legislative Process*, iii; William I. Bacchus and Thomas Stern, ADST OHP interview, February 19, 1990; and *Washington Post*, February 4, 2013 (obituary).

7. James Michel, ADST OHP interview, October 21, 2005.

8. Bleakley, interview; and Bacchus, *Inside the Legislative Process*, 47.

9. Bacchus, *Inside the Legislative Process*, 47.

10. Bob Stern, a member of the AFSA Board, looked back on this process and summarized the results in a letter to the *Journal*. See "Implementation, Not Law," *FSJ*, June 1986, 12–13.

11. "Toward a Unified Personnel System" was the title of Management Bulletin #8, February 1971, establishing the foreign affairs specialist corps in the Foreign Service and providing for the voluntary conversion of civil servants to foreign affairs specialists. The word "specialist" has a long, confusing history in the Foreign Service. In the 1950s and 1960s, the word denoted a Foreign Service officer with particular skills and knowledge (e.g., Japanese, economics, maritime law). After the 1980 Act, the word came to refer to a member of the Service hired for a specific position and employed in one of 22 job specialties.

12. Bacchus, *Inside the Legislative Process*, 23.

13. Mattox, "Report of the [Murphy] Commission," 13.

14. Statement of Tom Boyatt, president of AFSA, April 28, 1975, in *FSJ*, July 1975, 29–34. The testimony also supported a single personnel agency for the Foreign Service in State, USIA, and USAID.

15. Pell's proposal borrowed from a recommendation of the Murphy Commission favoring the establishment of a high-level foreign affairs executive service that would tap into the expertise of civil servants in State and other agencies. Mattox, "Report of the [Murphy] Commission," 13.

16. Ibid., 14–15.

17. Statement before the Subcommittee on International Operations of the House Committee on Foreign Affairs and the Subcommittee on the Civil Service of the House Committee on the Post Office and Civil Service, July 17, 1979, 2 [AFSA archives].

18. Transcript of open meeting, Acheson Auditorium, Department of State, October 23, 1980, 8–9 [AFSA archives].

19. The AFGE secured an amendment that allowed some 900 foreign affairs specialists at USICA (the U.S. International Communications Agency, the name given to USIA under the Carter administration's reorganization) to opt to retain that status if they so chose. Bacchus, *Inside the Legislative Process*, 116–17.

20. Ibid., 107.

21. Carol Laise, ADST OHP interview, April 17, 1989.

22. Ben Read told an open meeting with State Department employees on October 28, 1980, "When the Congress approved the president's Trade Reorganization Act, and I sat down with others from here with Secretary [of Commerce Philip] Klutznick and Deputy Secretary [of Commerce Luther H.] Hodges [Jr.], it was quite apparent that the intent of the Department of Commerce was to create yet another new Civil Service entity abroad, somewhat on the model of . . . the Foreign Agricultural Service. We persuaded them . . . that there was far more to be gained to bring the Foreign Commercial Service within the new community of foreign affairs agencies that would have the common legislative base which this Act now provides" (transcript, 24).

23. *FSJ*, July 1979, 29; and Bacchus, *Inside the Legislative Process*, 38–39.

24. Bacchus, *Inside the Legislative Process*, 50–51, 84.

25. AFSA cable to all posts, September 26, 1980.

26. The Congress that enacted the 1946 Act had 11 white women and two Black men in a House of 435 members; in the Senate, every one of the 96 members was a white male. Race and gender were not uppermost on their minds. They were more concerned about reversing the dominance of Ivy Leaguers, who accounted for a third of the officer corps.

27. Moose, a former Foreign Service officer, served only briefly in this position before being named assistant secretary for African affairs. He left the department at the end of the Carter administration and returned in the Clinton administration as under secretary for management (1993–1996).

28. Quoted in "Report on Minority Progress Still 'Distressing,'" *New York Times*, June 28, 1983.

29. *FSJ*, June 1979, 43.

30. AFSA Red Top, January 20, 1978, published as the editorial "Equal Opportunity, Affirmative Action, and the Foreign Service," *FSJ*, February 1978, 2.

31. *FSJ*, March 1978, 17, 35. According to Barbara Good, she and Jean Joyce founded the Ad Hoc Committee to Improve the Status of Women in the Foreign Affairs Agencies in July 1970. The ad hoc committee became the WAO in November 1970. Barbara Good, ADST OHP interview, May 25, 1993, 10.

32. James Doyle, "Taking Exception," Letters to *FSJ*, *FSJ*, April 1978, 45.

33. C. J. Quinlan, "Affirmative Action," Letters to *FSJ*, *FSJ*, May 1978, 4.

34. John Treacy, "Affirmative Action," Letters to *FSJ*, *FSJ*, May 1978, 4.

35. *FSJ*, June 1979, 43–45.

36. "Annual Report of AFSA Governing Board," *FSJ*, July 1979, 30. The board called these groups "an institutionalized chip on the shoulder."

37. Marguerite Cooper King, letter to the editor, *FSJ*, August 1979, 39; and outgoing AFSA President Lars Hydle, reply, *FSJ*, August 1979, 39.

38. Bleakley, interview.

39. Section 101(4). Among the 100 senators in the 96th Congress (1979–1981) there was one woman and no Black senators. Among the 435 members of the House, there were 16 women and 15 Black members. See Brookings Institution, *Vital Statistics on Congress*, tables 1-19 and 1-16, respectively, https://www.brookings.edu/wp-content/uploads/2021/02/Chpt-1.pdf.

40. Statement of James R. Washington, president of the Thursday Luncheon Group (State, USAID, USICA), before the House Foreign Affairs Subcommittee on International Operations and the House Post Office and Civil Service Subcommittee on Employee Ethics and Utilization, on the Foreign Service Act of 1979, September 20, 1979, 5 [AFSA archives]. Section 105(d) requires the department to have minority recruitment and affirmative action plans and to report annually to Congress on their effectiveness.

41. Pauline Slavik, *FSJ*, May 1983, 20. Slavik was interviewed in 1981 by John Harter.

42. Anthea de Rouville, "Don't Dismiss the Secretarial Task Force," *FSJ*, September 1983, 33 (emphasis in the original).

43. Bleakley, interview.

44. Transcript of open meeting of State employees, 68.

45. James Michel, ADST OHP interview, September 10, 1991, 7.

46. Eileen Quinn, "Problems with the New Secretarial Task Force: A Staff Corps Member's View," *FSJ*, May 1983, 27.

47. The first married couple with both members in the Foreign Service assigned to the same post appears to be John W. "Jock" Shirley and Katherine H. Shirley, who were assigned to Warsaw in 1971. See Katherine Horberg Shirley, "Another Ambassador" (letter to the editor), *Wellesley Magazine*, Fall 2019, 3, https://repository.wellesley.edu/object/wellesley23875.

48. "American Foreign Service Association Section-by-Section Analysis of the Bill to Promote the Foreign Policy of the United States by Strengthening and Improving the Foreign Service of the United States and for Other Purposes," in U.S. Congress, *Hearings on H.R. 4674*, 127. The clause appears in Section 333 (b) of the act.

49. The case began as *Bradley v. Vance* and was appealed as *Vance v. Bradley*.

50. Ted Wilkinson, "AFSA and the Courts: The Bradley Case," *FSJ*, June 2003, 40.

51. Bacchus, *Staffing for Foreign Affairs*, 201; and Bacchus, *Inside the Legislative Process*, 32, gives the number of unassigned senior officers as "more than 100 out of 900 or so."

52. Kopp and Gillespie, *Career Diplomacy*, 18.

53. Bacchus, *Inside the Legislative Process*, 59n4.

54. Survey of AFSA members, reported in *FSJ*, September 1980, 24–26.

55. *FSJ*, January 1982, 16B.

56. Judge Gerhard Gesell decided *Meresman et al. v. Haig* for the plaintiffs in federal district court for the District of Columbia, June 8, 1981.

57. Bleakley, interview. The AAFSW kept its initials but took the name "Associates of the American Foreign Service Worldwide" in December 1999. AFSA News, *FSJ*, February 2000, 2.

58. Section 814, 22 USC 4054.

59. The board set up an ad hoc union affiliation committee in 1977. The committee concluded that affiliation would be unpopular with retirees and that the general membership would probably not support the increase in dues that affiliation would require. In the 1980 membership survey, 77 percent of respondents preferred the union/professional association combination over other forms of representation. See minutes, AFSA Governing Board meeting, April 11, 1978; and survey results in *FSJ*, September 1980, 26.

60. Chapter 10 of the act covers labor-management relations. Section 209 established the position of inspector general.

61. "Section-by-Section Analysis," in U.S. Congress, *Hearings on H.R. 4674*, 125–26.

62. At the time, AFSA was the exclusive bargaining agent for the Foreign Service in State and USAID, while AFGE represented the Foreign Service cohort in the USICA (later the USIA). Members of the Foreign Service in the Commerce and Agriculture Departments, also covered by the act, had not chosen a bargaining agent.

63. Bleakley, interview. The grievance provisions are in chapter 11 of the act.

64. Memo, Holik to AFSA Governing Board, "Comparison of Chapter 11 of H.R. 6790, the Foreign Service Act of 1980 and S. 2712, Foreign Service Grievance Legislation (Bayh Bill)," undated.

65. Bacchus, *Inside the Legislative Process*, 74–75.

66. Transcript of open meeting, Acheson Auditorium, Department of State, October 23, 1980, 14.

67. USAID Foreign Service personnel were brought into the Foreign Service retirement system by the Foreign Assistance Act of 1973, P.L. 93-189, December 17, 1973.

68. In the federal workplace, a reduction in force is a cut in the number of authorized positions in an agency that requires laying off employees.

69. Bacchus, *Staffing for Foreign Affairs*, 54.

70. Testimony before the Public Diplomacy Subcommittee of the Murphy Commission, April 3, 1975, 15 [AFSA archives].

71. *FSJ*, July 1975, 31–32.

72. Bacchus, *Staffing for Foreign Affairs*, 54–55.

73. See, for example, *FSJ*, January 1980, 23; *FSJ*, March 1980, 25; *FSJ*, September 1980, 21; *FSJ*, June 1981, 20C; and *FSJ*, October 1981, 16A–C. See also Frank D. Corell, ADST OHP interview, September 29, 1998, 70.

74. Bacchus, *Inside the Legislative Process*, 90–93.

75. "Implementation, Not Law," letter to the editor, *FSJ*, June 1986, 12–13.

## 7. Turnover at the Top, 1981–1987

1. *FSJ*, July–August 1981, 18A. Patricia Woodring, whom the board had appointed as president in December 1976 after that office had fallen vacant, had entered the Foreign Service as a staff officer but was a Foreign Service Reserve officer at the time of her appointment. She joined the reserve through the Mustang program (see *FSJ*, January 1977, 38). As of 2022, Thea de Rouville remains the only member of the staff corps (specialist) to serve as AFSA's president.

2. Bleakley, interview.

3. Charles Whitehouse, ADST OHP interview, November 28, 1989, 11. Sheldon White-house, a Democrat, was elected to the Senate from Rhode Island in 2006 and reelected in 2012 and 2018.

4. Schaffer, *Ellsworth Bunker*, 178.

5. Dennis K. Hays, interview, September 5, 2013; and Harris, interview, January 23, 2013.

6. Hays, interview.

7. Dennis K. Hays, ADST OHP interview, November 28, 2008, 17.

8. Ibid.

9. *FSJ*, July–August 1982, 2; and *FSJ*, September 1982, 18A.

10. *FSJ*, September 1983, 41.

11. Shultz was secretary of labor (1969–1970), director of the Office of Management and Budget (1970–1972), and secretary of the treasury (1972–1974). After leaving government, he taught at Stanford and was president of Bechtel, a global construction and engineering firm.

12. Jerry Van Gorkom resigned in October 1983 after just over 10 months in office. Shultz, *Turmoil and Triumph*, 16–17, 34–35; and Ronald Spiers, ADST OHP interview, November 11, 1995, 4. The new management team included Bill Harrop, former AFSA chairman, as inspector general.

13. "One Year after the Act," *FSJ*, May 1982, 26–32. The staff director was Virginia Schlundt; the deputy assistant secretary for personnel was Andrew Steigman. The comments by the AFSA Governing Board were not attributed to any individual.

14. "Report to the Speaker of the House of Representatives and the Committee on Foreign Relations of the Senate concerning Implementation of the Foreign Service Act of 1980, February 1, 1983" (Section 2402 report), I-1–II-7 [AFSA archives].

15. "Statement on the Implementation of Foreign Service Act of 1980 before the House Subcommittee on International Operations, June 3, 1982," 3 [AFSA archives]. The under secretary was Richard Kennedy.

16. AFSA comments on the USAID portion of the 1982 Section 2402 report, February 1983, 1, 12–13. The association's lawsuit against USAID on the Obey Amendment was still in federal court.

17. Charles Mathias, "Politics or Merit," *FSJ*, April 1982, 30. Mathias, citing testimony by Assistant Secretary of State Richard Fairbanks, added that at the end of 1981, 41 career ambassadors had been retained at their posts, so 65 percent of all serving ambassadors were career Foreign Service officers.

18. AFSA comments on the State Department portion of the 1982 Section 2402 Report, May 28, 1982, Summary, 2.

19. Testimony of Charles W. Whitehouse, president of the American Foreign Service Association, before the Subcommittee on International Operations, March 1982, 6 [AFSA archives]. The percentage of non-career chief-of-mission (COM) appointments tends to be highest in the first year of a president's term. Later in the Reagan administration, the non-career share of COM appointments fell to 40 percent and then to around 35 percent.

20. Ibid., 7. Ambassador Whitehouse was likely referring to the $1,000 limit on individual contributions imposed by the Federal Elections Campaign Act of 1974, one of the post-Watergate reforms.

21. *FSJ*, July–August 1982, 18.

22. S. 1886, introduced November 23, 1981 (97th Congress). See also *FSJ*, September 1986, 25. The American Academy of Diplomacy, founded in 1983, is a self-selected society of former career and career U.S. government officials who have served with distinction in international affairs (see www.academyofdiplomacy.org).

23. Hays, interview.

24. Bureau of Management, Department of State, cited in *FSJ*, September 1986, 25.

25. *FSJ*, May 1983, 40.

26. "Transcript of President Reagan's News Conference," *New York Times*, August 14, 1981; "U.S. Moves to Hire New Controllers," *New York Times*, August 18, 1981; and "PATCO Decertification Vote Is Switched from 2–1 to 3–0," *New York Times*, November 5, 1981.

27. The Social Security Amendments of 1983 passed 282 to 140 in the House and 88 to 9 in the Senate, and were signed into law as P.L. 98-21 on April 20, 1983. Federal employees, including members of the Foreign Service, had already been brought under Medicare by the Tax Equity and Fiscal Responsibility Act of 1982.

28. P.L. 99-335, signed into law on June 6, 1986.

29. The effect of the law on the Foreign Service is described in *FSJ*, July–August 1986, 52; *FSJ*, October 1986, 60; and *FSJ*, December 1986, 51.

30. *FSJ*, October 1985, 46. The authorization bill was signed into law on August 17, 1985, as P.L. 99-93.

31. Hays, ADST OHP interview, 27.

32. Active-duty agency representatives to AFSA are not detailed to AFSA but receive a reasonable amount of official time to attend meetings on labor-management issues. But a 2019 State-AFSA collective bargaining agreement included a provision to allow a negotiation to create an additional full-time position, which AFSA would assign to its Labor Management Office and use to improve coverage of issues affecting specialists. After some delay, the position was created and was filled on a two-year trial basis in July 2023 by one of the active-duty State representatives on the Governing Board. Continuation of the position is subject to later negotiations between State and AFSA.

33. AFSA 1982–1983 Annual Report, *FSJ*, December 1983, 41.

34. Ibid.

35. Bob Keeley, a career officer, had been ambassador to Mauritius (1976–1978) and Zimbabwe (1980–1984). Keeley carried 2,566 of the 2,831 ballots cast. See *FSJ*, September 1985, 56.

36. A-100 is the designation of the orientation program for newly hired Foreign Service officers. The name comes from the number of the room in the old State Department building (now the Eisenhower Executive Office Building) where the first such class was held in 1947.

37. Hays, interview.

38. Executive Director Robert Beers left his position to become the association's first full-time congressional liaison in January 1983. He was paid out of general revenues until the Legislative Action Fund was able to cover his salary. A second lobbyist, Rick Weiss, was added in 1985. See *FSJ*, November 1985, 51.

39. Profit and loss accounting for the *Foreign Service Journal* is a murky business. The *Journal* is distributed to AFSA's dues-paying members at no additional cost to them, so some portion of AFSA's revenue from dues should be credited to the *Journal*. What that amount should be is open to debate.

40. AFSA 1983–1984 Annual Report, *FSJ*, September 1984, 55–59; AFSA 1984–1985 Annual Report, *FSJ*, November 1985, 51–56; and Letter from the Treasurer, *FSJ*, January

1985, 42. The new dues structure ran from a low of $30 per year for retirees with annuities under $20,000 to a high of $143 per year ($420 in 2022 dollars) for members of the Senior Foreign Service. See *FSJ*, December 1984, 41. Closing the Foreign Service Club was rejected in a 1982 membership referendum.

41. AFSA and associated organizations, audited combined financial statements for the year ended June 30, 1986, *FSJ*, November 1986, 58–59. Coopers & Lybrand performed the audit.

42. Letter from the Treasurer, *FSJ*, January 1985, 42.

43. *FSJ*, December 1983, 43.

44. Ibid.; *FSJ*, September 1984, 59; *FSJ*, November 1985, 55; and *FSJ*, October 1986, 46.

45. *FSJ*, December 1983, 41.

46. Hays, interview.

47. AFSA 1982–1983 Annual Report, 40–44; and AFSA 1983–1984 Annual Report, 55–60.

48. Hays, interview. The multifunctional cone was abolished in 2004. See Minutes, AFSA Board meeting, August 18, 2004.

49. *FSJ*, January 1984, 41.

50. Gerald Lamberty, "An Act of Suicide," *FSJ*, February 1986, 25. At the time Lamberty's article was published, for example, 55-year-old Tom Pickering had served as ambassador to Jordan, Nigeria, El Salvador, and Israel, and as assistant secretary for oceans and international environmental and scientific affairs; Steve Bosworth was 47 and had been ambassador to Tunisia, director of policy planning, and ambassador to the Philippines; and Tom Enders, then ambassador to Spain, was 55 and had served as assistant secretary for economic and business affairs, assistant secretary for American republic affairs, ambassador to Canada, and ambassador to the European Economic Communities (now the European Union).

51. AFSA interview of Thomas D. Boyatt and William I. Bacchus, "Five Years after the Act: The Fate of the Service," *FSJ*, February 1986, 19.

52. Ibid., 20.

53. Ibid., 22.

54. "Managing Adversity: The State of State," *FSJ*, February 1987, 32.

55. The Heineman Commission, cited in Bacchus, *Staffing for Foreign Affairs*, 92–93.

56. *FSJ*, December 1981, 13.

57. Ibid.

58. Bacchus, *Staffing for Foreign Affairs*, 92–93n; and Ronald I. Spiers, "Thinning the Soup," *FSJ*, March 1985, 35.

59. *FSJ*, April 1986, 38.

60. *FSJ*, December 1984, 27.

61. Spiers, "Thinning the Soup," 35.

62. *FSJ*, December 1984, 27.

63. Lamberty, "Act of Suicide," 25.

64. "AFSA Stops AID from Politicizing Deputy Directors," *FSJ*, February 1982, 18A. For the Obey Amendment lawsuit, see *FSJ*, December 1983, 42.

65. *FSJ*, February 1987, 30.

66. AFSA 1985–1986 Annual Report, *FSJ*, October 1986, 42.

67. Ibid.

68. *FSJ*, May 1986, 41.

69. *FSJ*, March 1986, 3; and *FSJ*, June 1986, 49.

70. *FSJ*, June 1986, 49.

71. *FSJ*, May 1987, 51.

72. Election section, *FSJ*, May 1987, 52 (emphasis in the original).

73. *FSJ*, September 1987, 58.

## 8. Renewal, 1987–1997

1. Office of Management and Budget, "Historical Table 5.2."

2. George Gedda, "Cutbacks at State Department Outlined," Associated Press dispatch, September 18, 1987, 1 [AFSA archives]; Barbara Gamarekian, "23 in the Foreign Service Fight to Retain Jobs," *New York Times*, October 4, 1987, 1; and Barbara Gamarekian, "Washington Talk: The Foreign Service—New Rules on Retirement," *New York Times*, September 3, 1988, 1.

3. *FSJ*, January 1991, 59. The grievants claimed the department had misled them about their chances for promotion, inducing them to open the six-year window of competition for promotion into the Senior Foreign Service. When the period expired, the officers were to be separated from the Service, but they remained on active duty while their grievance was under review. Their careers ended when the Grievance Board ruled in favor of the department.

4. Gedda, "Cutbacks at State Department," 1.

5. "Demanding Views," *FSJ*, September 1967, 3; "President's Overview, Annual Report of the Governing Board, 1986–1987," *FSJ*, December 1987, 54; and Perry Shankle, "The Importance of Professionalism," *FSJ*, October 1967, 56.

6. President's Overview, *FSJ*, December 1987, 54.

7. Minutes, AFSA Governing Board meeting, September 2, 1987.

8. The Commission on the Foreign Service Personnel System was mandated by the Foreign Relations Authorization Act of 1989–1990.

9. AFSA President Perry Shankle, Statement Submitted to the Subcommittee on Civil Service of the Post Office and Civil Service Committee, House of Representatives, June 21, 1989, 5–6 [AFSA archives].

10. *FSJ*, July 1991, 50. Selin spoke on May 16; he left the department July 1 to become chairman of the Nuclear Regulatory Commission.

11. Report of the Commission on the Foreign Service Personnel System [Thomas Commission], June 1989, executive summary, 6 [AFSA archives].

12. Shankle, Statement to House of Representatives, 4.

13. Nearly but not totally impossible. When the Thomas and Bremer Commissions' reports were done, Congress in a bipartisan vote mandated a new commission on Foreign Service personnel chaired by retired Ambassador Nick Veliotes.

14. The two reports are analyzed and compared in Ann Luppi, "Studies Aim at Personnel Reform," *FSJ*, July–August 1989, 29–34.

15. U.S. Department of State, *State 2000*.

16. Minutes, AFSA Governing Board meetings, November 1, December 16, 1987. William D. Rogers, not to be confused with former Secretary of State William P. Rogers, was assistant secretary for inter-American affairs (1974–1976) and under secretary for economic affairs (1976). For the history of the Una Chapman Cox Foundation, see uccoxfoundation.org.

17. *FSJ*, February 1988, 64; and minutes, AFSA Governing Board meeting, February 10, 1988.

18. Minutes, AFSA Governing Board meeting, February 10, 1988.

19. Minutes, AFSA Governing Board meeting, June 8, 1988. There is a contrast with the efforts of AFSA officers John Reinhardt and Charlie Bray, who went to the Republican National Convention in Miami in 1968, met with members of the platform committee, and secured a statement in the platform supporting a strong Foreign Service.

20. Gamarekian, "Washington Talk."

21. United Press International wire dispatch, October 2, 1987 [AFSA archives].

22. Eagleburger spoke on November 30, 1989. See Kopp, *Commercial Diplomacy*, 122.

23. AFSA internal document, "International Associates: Outline of Program," May 10, 1989; Theodore S. "Ted" Wilkinson, interview, February 12, 2013; and *FSJ*, January 1990, 52–53. Forty-five companies participated as international associates in the early 1990s; see AFSA 1992 Annual Report, *FSJ*, January 1993, 1; AFSA 1993 Annual Report, AFSA News, *FSJ*, March 1994, 6; AFSA 1994 Annual Report, AFSA News, *FSJ*, March 1995, 15; and minutes, AFSA Governing Board meeting, December 15, 2004. The *Journal* called the November 1989 program "AFSA's first major conference on international affairs." One of the program's goals was to polish State's image as a supporter of American business overseas, despite the impending transfer of the commercial function to the Department of Commerce.

24. *FSJ*, June 1990, 55.

25. AFSA 1992 Annual Report, 7. The Cox Foundation, established by a legacy from a U.S. citizen rescued from distress by a consular officer in India in 1949, supports a strong U.S. Foreign Service.

26. Minutes, AFSA Governing Board meeting, October 14, 1987. Thompson was hired at the beginning of January 1988. See minutes, AFSA Governing Board meeting, January 8, 1988.

27. Funds for these awards had to be raised annually. Avis Bohlen was the wife of Charles "Chip" Bohlen, a career diplomat and ambassador to the Philippines, France, and the Soviet Union. Funds for the Avis Bohlen Award, like those for the Harriman Award, came from the Mary Harriman Foundation. The Harrimans and the Bohlens were friends and colleagues. The exception to the requirement for annual funding is the Matilda W. Sinclaire Award for proficiency in hard languages, endowed by a bequest from Ms. Sinclaire in 1982.

28. Theodore S. Wilkinson, "Casting a Longer Shadow," *FSJ*, June 1990, 55.

29. The transformation of the Office of Security into a full-fledged bureau followed a review of diplomatic security by a panel headed by retired Adm. B. R. "Bobby" Inman. U.S. Department of State, Bureau of Diplomatic Security, *History* gives much credit also to David Fields, who became head of SY after the 1983 Kuwait bombings (285–89).

30. U.S. Department of State, "Overseas Security."

31. The phrase "criminally negligent" is quoted from Lamb's speech to DS personnel on November 2, 1987. See *FSJ*, February 1988, 3.

32. Minutes, AFSA Governing Board meeting, November 18, 1987.

33. Minutes, AFSA Governing Board meeting, January 20, February 8, and June 8, 1988.

34. Minutes, AFSA Governing Board meeting, July 6, 1994.

35. Minutes, AFSA Governing Board meeting, September 16, 1987. The Marine guard convicted of espionage was Sgt. Clayton Lonetree. Hartman, who had been assistant secretary for European affairs and ambassador to France, held the rank of career ambassador. In 1995 Hartman sought and won election to AFSA's Governing Board as a retiree representative, but with a heavy travel schedule he attended no board meetings and resigned after six weeks.

36. Myles Frechette, "Nothing Personal," *FSJ*, August 1995, 19.

37. Minutes, AFSA Governing Board meeting, December 16, 1987; Richard N. Viets, ADST OHP interview, April 6, 1990, 91–92; and "People: Richard Noyes Viets (1930–)," Office of the Historian, Department of State, http://history.state.gov/departmenthistory /people/viets-richard-noyes.

38. *FSJ*, November 1988, 53.

39. Shultz, *Turmoil and Triumph*, 801. When the White House in National Security Decision Directive 196 proposed random polygraph testing of all government employees with access to sensitive information, Shultz told a reporter he would take such a test only once, because "[t]he minute in this government I am told that I'm not trusted is the day that I leave."

40. *FSJ*, December 1989, 59.

41. *FSJ*, November 1988, 54; and *FSJ*, December 1989, 60.

42. *FSJ*, December 1989, 60; and *FSJ*, January 1991, 59. The Foreign Service Impasse Disputes Panel required USAID to pay for a full-time AFSA vice president in a ruling of July 11, 1992, issued after a year of litigation. See AFSA News, *FSJ*, October 1992, 1.

43. Ibid. The bill was the Integrity in Post Employment Act of 1988, S. 237.

44. Ibid.

45. Minutes, AFSA Governing Board meeting, October 14, 1987.

46. *FSJ*, May 1989, 57.

47. AFSA 1992 Annual Report, 1.

48. *FSJ*, September 1988, 6. The amendment in question was part of the Foreign Relations Authorization Act of 1988–1989.

49. *FSJ*, July 1989, 2.

50. Campaign statements in *FSJ*, May 1991, 61–67; voting results in *FSJ*, August 1991, 47. A notable loser in that race was John Naland, who later served twice as AFSA's president. In a field of six to elect five Department of State representatives, Naland, who did not join the slate and was sharply critical of AFSA's performance, came in last. He later married the woman who defeated him, Barbara Reioux.

51. Total membership in 1989 was 9,621, of which 6,155 (64 percent) were active duty and 2,796 (29 percent) were retirees. Another 7 percent were recorded as associate, life, or jubilee members. Of the active-duty members, 4,773 (77 percent) were employed at State and 1,153 (19 percent) at USAID. See "Annual Report of the AFSA Governing Board, 1988–1989," *FSJ*, December 1989, 57.

52. Figures for calendar year 1988. Memo to the Governing Board from Chris Bazar, director of member services, attachment to the minutes of the AFSA Governing Board meeting of February 27, 1989.

53. Letter to AFSA from USIA officer Christopher Midura, AFSA News, *FSJ*, April 1992, 6.

54. AFSA News, *FSJ*, April 1992, 7; AFSA News, *FSJ*, September 1992, 4–5; and AFSA News, *FSJ*, January 1993, 9. Radio Martí had been broadcasting to Cuba since 1985. Radio Free Asia began broadcasting in 1996. AFSA opposed Radio Free Asia as "duplicative" of Voice of America and a threat to USIA jobs and funds.

55. *FSJ*, January 1993, 9; and AFSA 1992 Annual Report, 3. There were 905 persons in the bargaining unit. Turnout was 69 percent.

56. Wilkinson, interview.

57. Section 304(a)(4) requires that nominations as chief of mission include "a report on the demonstrated competence of that nominee to perform the duties of the position in which he or she is to serve."

58. Theodore Wilkinson, ADST OHP interview, January 11, 1999, 106.

59. Wilkinson, interview. The statements were handed over on October 2, 1989; see *FSJ*, December 1989, 68.

60. For AFSA's opposition, see Wilkinson, interview. For the Senate vote, see *Congressional Record*, 101st Cong., 1st sess., October 3, 1989, S-12403.

61. *FSJ*, February 1990, 68.

62. "Nation: Bush Ally Gets Arts Post after Senate Rejects Ambassadorship," *Los Angeles Times*, February 1, 1990. Joy Silverman later became the central figure in a 1992 tabloid story as a victim of blackmail and extortion by the chief judge of the New York Court of Appeals, Sol Wachtler.

63. *FSJ*, October 1989, 59. Untermeyer spoke at the AFSA luncheon series that Dick Thompson organized.

64. Wilkinson, interview.

65. *FSJ*, August 1990, 59.

66. AFSA 1990 Annual Report, *FSJ*, December 1990, 42.

67. Al Kamen, "In the Loop," *Washington Post*, June 25, 1993, A23.

68. *FSJ*, January 1991, 53; and AFSA 1990 Annual Report, 42.

69. AFSA 1990 Annual Report, 43; AFSA 1991 Annual Report, *FSJ*, December 1991, 3; *FSJ*, March 1992, 2; and AFSA 1992 Annual Report, 5.

70. AFSA News, *FSJ*, September 1993, 1; and AFSA News, *FSJ*, October 1999, 5. Bureaus and posts needing temporary help likely found it more convenient to hire willing retirees under the When Actually Employed program.

71. AFSA News, *FSJ*, October 1999, 5.

72. Minutes, AFSA Governing Board meeting, October 3, 1990.

73. AFSA News election insert, *FSJ*, May 1993, 2–3.

74. Ibid., 4.

75. The results were Harris, 1,416 (42 percent); Joe Melrose, 1,161 (35 percent); John Harter, 742 (22 percent). See AFSA News, *FSJ*, August 1995, 1.

76. *FSJ*, December 1983, 40.

77. *FSJ*, December 1987, 53–54.

78. AFSA News, *FSJ*, October 1995, 2.

79. Kopp and Gillespie, *Career Diplomacy*, 33–35.

80. Training expenditures dropped from $47.5 million in 1990 to $40.3 million in 1991. Wilkinson's testimony before the Senate Foreign Relations Committee's Subcommittee on Terrorism, Narcotics, and International Operations, March 12, 1991, cited in *FSJ*, May 1991, 55. The number of people engaged in professional training fell by 19 percent, and the number of hours in all training fell by 17 percent between 1983 and 1987 (U.S. General Accounting Office [GAO], "Professional Development," 14–15).

81. Foreign Relations Authorization Act, Fiscal Years 1994 and 1995, P.L. 103-236, enacted April 30, 1994, Sections 121, 128, 171. For AFSA's lobbying efforts, see AFSA News, *FSJ*, July 1993, 1.

82. Foreign Relations Revitalization Act of 1995, S. 908, introduced June 9, 1995.

83. "Agency for International Development, Part 1: Overhaul the AID Personnel System," September 7, 1993, 19–27, National Archives Clinton Presidential Materials Project, https://govinfo.library.unt.edu/npr/library/reports/aid03.html. The report describes the CIA's personnel system as based on the Civil Service system and with required availability for service abroad and rank in person.

84. Quoted in *FSJ*, September 1993, 2.

85. Alphonse F. La Porta, ADST OHP interview, February 11, 2001, 149.

86. Quoted in Don Oberdorfer, "It Starts with People: Don Oberdorfer Interviews Richard Moose," *FSJ*, November 1993, 31–34.

87. Minutes, AFSA Governing Board meeting, April 5, 1995.

88. *FSJ*, November 1997, 5.

89. AFSA News, *FSJ*, October 1996, 2; and La Porta, ADST OHP interview, 150.

90. AFSA News, *FSJ*, July 1996, 7; and AFSA News, *FSJ*, May 1997, 1.

91. Minutes, AFSA Governing Board meeting, June 19, 1996; and AFSA News, *FSJ*, July 1996, 3.

92. *FSJ*, March 1994, 18–23. State representatives on the AFSA Governing Board in 1994 noted that "there is a great deal of anger by [junior] officers who did not receive their first choice" of assignment and that the department is "even having trouble finding political officers to serve in nicer West African posts." See minutes, AFSA Governing Board meetings, August 24, September 14, 1994, e-archives.

93. *FSJ*, December 1993, 13–17.

94. AFSA News, *FSJ*, July 1994, 1; and AFSA News, *FSJ*, September 1994, 1. The votes were 129 to 17 at FAS (May 1994) and 120 to 8 at FCS (August 1994). FAS had a representative on the board but under the bylaws was not allotted a slot for a vice president until it had maintained a minimum of 100 members for three consecutive months, a target it reached in June 1996 (minutes, AFSA Governing Board meeting, June 19, 1996). Foreign Service employees at the Animal and Plant Health Inspection Service in the Department of Agriculture were not part of the bargaining unit and did not take part in the election. AFSA Governing Board minutes from April 8, 1998, indicate some APHIS interest in joining AFSA, but a serious effort, which would have required a show-of-interest campaign, did not take place. Foreign Service employees of APHIS finally chose AFSA as their employee representative in 2013.

95. AFSA 1994 Annual Report, 9.

96. Minutes, Governing Board meetings of December 12, 1994, and March 1, 1995. Ambassador Johnson received the award from former Secretary of State Alexander Haig at a ceremony in the department on June 29, when all AFSA awards were presented.

97. Sources for the mission statement and motto are AFSA News, *FSJ*, September 1996, 4; and minutes, AFSA Governing Board meetings, September 11 and December 4, 1995. The text is in *FSJ*, January 1997, 5. AFSA members wanted a statement of just three or four lines, but the final version was about 450 words. The motto was "America's Advocate to the World." Sources on the criteria for ambassadorial nominations are the minutes of the AFSA Governing Board meeting of February 12, 1997; and text in AFSA News, *FSJ*, June–July 1997, 12.

98. E.O. 12839, February 10, 1993.

99. Coalition for Effective Change, "A Study of the Long-Term Effects of Federal Workforce Reduction in the 1990s," March 2013, 1, https://federalnewsnetwork.com/wp-content/uploads/pdfs/Cuts_in_the_1990s_and_Effects_Today_3-2013.pdf.

100. Estimate of contract workers from Paul Light, "The Real Crisis in Government," *Washington Post*, January 12, 2010. The same article estimates 7.5 million contract workers at the end of Fiscal Year 2005.

101. Minutes, AFSA Governing Board meetings, March 30, June 8, and June 22, 1994; and minutes, AFSA Governing Board meeting, March 15, 1995.

102. AFSA News, *FSJ*, October 1995, 3.

103. Report of the FCS representative, minutes, AFSA Governing Board meetings, June 22 and August 24, 1994.

104. Minutes, AFSA Governing Board meeting, August 22, 1994.

105. Rep. Dick Chrysler (R-Mich.) introduced H.R. 1756 to abolish the Commerce Department in June 1995 (104th Congress). The bill had 74 cosponsors and received a hearing and press attention but not a vote. The bill would have transferred the FCS to the Office of the U.S. Trade Representative. Ron Brown died in an airplane crash while leading a trade mission to Croatia in April 1996. See R. W. Apple Jr., "Crash in the Balkans," *New York Times*, April 5, 1996.

106. Peter Frederick, "Commercial Service: V.P. Voice," AFSA News, *FSJ*, December 1999, 4.

107. Ibid. The director general of the US&FCS was Lauri Fitz-Pegado.

108. Minutes, AFSA Governing Board meeting, April 12, 1995.

109. Quoted in Oberdorfer, "It Starts with People," 34. The Civil Service perception of favoritism was documented in a report by the State Department's Civil Service ombudsman in 1995.

110. A failure to enact timely appropriations led to shutdowns of much of the federal government and furloughs of most federal employees for five days in November 1995 and again from December 16, 1995, to January 6, 1996. Employees were later paid retroactively for the days they were on furlough.

111. Anthony Quainton, ADST OHP interview, November 6, 1997, 165.

112. Minutes, AFSA Governing Board meeting, January 17, 1996.

113. H.R. 1561, Foreign Relations Authorization Act for Fiscal Years 1996 and 1997, passed the House 222 to 192 on June 8, 1995, and the Senate 82 to 16, on December 14, 1995. The conference report passed the House 226 to 172 on March 12, 1996, and the Senate 52 to 44 on March 28. After President Clinton's veto, the House failed to override, 234 to 188 (282 needed) on April 30, 1996.

114. *FSJ*, May 1995, 7, 36–45.

115. Minutes, AFSA Governing Board meeting, August 16, 1995.

116. P.L. 105-277, Omnibus Consolidated and Emergency Supplemental Appropriations Act, 1999.

117. Minutes, AFSA Governing Board meeting, February 12, 1997.

118. AFSA News, *FSJ*, January 1994, 3.

119. Hume Horan, ADST OHP interview, November 3, 2000, 138. Twenty-one people served on the 1991–1992 board; 10 were white men, and 11 were women or minorities. See *FSJ*, June 1992, 2.

120. First sentence from testimony before the House Foreign Affairs Subcommittee on October 31, 1991, cited in *FSJ*, December 1991, 54. Second sentence from signed column in *FSJ*, May 1992, 2.

121. *FSJ*, January 1990, 54; and *FSJ*, April 1990, 2.

122. *FSJ*, May 1992, 2.

123. Keith Bell, quoted in *FSJ*, November 1996, 33.

124. GAO, "Equal Employment Opportunity," appendix I, 83.

125. Letter to the editor, *FSJ*, August 1994, 8–10. The signatories, all officers of the Thursday Luncheon Group, were Fannie Allen, president; Carolyn Coleman, USAID vice president; Donald Q. Washington, USIA vice president; and Harry Thomas, State vice president. Thomas would later serve as Director General of the Foreign Service.

126. GAO, "Equal Employment Opportunity," 83.

127. AFSA 1993 Annual Report, AFSA News insert. The quoted sentence is from a section of the report signed by AFSA President Tex Harris.

128. Francine Modderno, "The Issue of Race, Ethnicity," *FSJ*, November 1996, 20–27.

129. "Selected Highlights," AFSA Timeline, May 2014, https://afsa.org/timeline.aspx.

130. AFSA News, *FSJ*, May 1994, 2.

131. AFSA 1994 Annual Report, AFSA News, 13.

132. Tex Harris, "Diversity, Yes, but with Grand Rules," *FSJ*, March 1994, 4.

133. John Todd Stewart, ADST OHP interview, October 25, 1999, 99.

134. Ibid., 100.

135. The group replaced the name "Gays and Lesbians in Foreign Affairs Agencies" with the acronym "GLIFAA" in 2014. At least since January 2020, the organization has used the lowercase "glifaa" as its official name. Glifaa, "Gliffa By-Laws," September 2022, https://glifaa.org/resources/by-laws/.

136. Minutes, AFSA Governing Board meeting, May 15, 1996.

137. Quainton, ADST OHP interview, 166.

138. The results were Harris, 1,847; Aury Fernandez (incumbent), 1,398. Except for the posts of secretary, USIA vice president, and USIA representative, La Porta and his slate were unopposed. See AFSA News, *FSJ*, August 1997, 5.

139. Willard De Pree, a retiree representative, served as interim president from October 21, 1997, to January 1, 1998, when Dan Geisler took over.

140. Dan Geisler, interview, January 27, 2014.

## 9. Millennium Shift, 1998–2001

1. U.S. Government, *Congressional Record*, Senate, January 29, 1998, 225–26.

2. See *FSJ*, August 1997, 5; *FSJ*, March 1998, 29; AFSA News, *FSJ*, July–August 1998, 8–9; and AFSA News, *FSJ*, October 1998, 2.

3. AFSA News, *FSJ*, February 2001, 1, 3.

4. Inspector General Jacquelyn Williams-Bridgers compared misbehavior in the Foreign Service and the federal workforce in a report to Congress discussed in Eva-Lotta Jansson, "The IG Issue Reaches the Hill," *FSJ*, March 1998, 29.

5. Minutes, AFSA Governing Board meeting, February 12, 1997.

6. AFSA News, *FSJ*, September 1998, 5–8.

7. AFSA News, *FSJ*, January 1999, 2.

8. *FSJ*, May 8, 2002.

9. Minutes, AFSA Governing Board meeting, January 14, 1998; and AFSA News, *FSJ*, March 1998, 4.

10. AFSA News, *FSJ*, March 1998, 4.

11. AFSA News, *FSJ*, May 1998, 2.

12. AFSA News, *FSJ*, November 1998, 2.

13. AFSA News, *FSJ*, July–August 1998, 4. USIA was merged into the State Department and ceased to exist on October 1, 1999. The merger brought enough AFSA members into the State Department to add one more State representative to the AFSA Governing Board. The board chose the outgoing USIA vice president, Riley Sever, to fill it, and the Director General agreed to keep Sever's position and salary in place for one transitional year.

14. Minutes, AFSA Governing Board meeting, March 11, 1998. Jim Michel had made the same point at an open meeting on October 23, 1980, to discuss the Foreign Service Act of 1980. A transcript of the meeting is in the AFSA archives.

15. Geisler, interview. It is not clear how Senator McConnell became involved. Al Kamen reported in the *Washington Post* that Assistant Secretary Stanley Roth appealed

to Gnehm to reverse the appointment, which had been approved by the Deputy Chiefs of Mission (DCM)/Principal Officers Committee ("In the Loop," February 18, 1998, A19). According to Kamen, Senator McConnell also wrote to Gnehm in protest of what he called an "unprecedented decision." Kamen said McConnell's letter raised the issue of the presence on the DCM/Principal Officers Committee of Greene's boss, Under Secretary for Management Bonnie Cohen, whose "outspoken endorsement" of Greene could place "undue and inappropriate pressure" on committee members who were her subordinates. AFSA's State Vice President John Naland wrote in the *Journal* in his April 2000 VP Voice column that AFSA "raised a ruckus" about the appointment, but there is no record of any active opposition. Dan Geisler, then AFSA's president, thought Greene was well qualified for the post and called on him to tell him so. Tex Harris told the author that AFSA did not fight the Greene appointment (interview, January 23, 2013). Rich Greene served two years in Sydney and went on to become principal deputy assistant secretary for population, refugee, and migration affairs, and then deputy director of foreign assistance in the George W. Bush administration.

16. The count was that of the Crowe Commission. The list appears in its report, cited in note 19 of this chapter.

17. The commission served as the accountability review board required by the Omnibus Diplomatic Security and Antiterrorism Act of 1986.

18. The Crowe Commission's report, formally the "Report of the Accountability Review Boards [on the] Bombings of the U.S. Embassies in Nairobi, Kenya, and Dar es Salaam, Tanzania, on August 7, 1998," January 1999, is available in State Department archives online at http://1997-2001.state.gov/www/regions/africa/accountability_report.html.

19. U.S. House of Representatives, 106th Cong., 1st sess., Conference Report to accompany H.R. 3194, 972; and AFSA 1999 Annual Report, *FSJ*, March 2000, AFSA News insert.

20. Appropriations to the Department of State for embassy security, construction, and maintenance reached nearly $1.5 billion by FY2012 and were nearly $2 billion in FY2022. See U.S. Department of State, *Congressional Budget Justification*, 1, 35; and Gill, Lawson, and Morgenstern, "Department of State," 5.

21. *State Magazine*, July–August 1999, 22.

22. Ibid. The department had asked AFSA to include these 56 names, but AFSA decided they did not meet the plaque's criteria. The separate departmental plaque was a negotiated solution.

23. Ibid., 2.

24. The winner received a cash prize of $2,500. AFSA now conducts the contest in partnership with Semester at Sea, an accredited shipboard educational program, that gives the winner a fully funded semester voyage. An additional sponsor is the U.S. Institute of Peace. Green, interview.

25. AFSA 1994 Annual Report, AFSA News, *FSJ*, March 1995, 13.

26. These included one Foreign Service national from each regional bureau and many functional awards: outstanding DCM, distinction in public finance, and excellence in trade promotion, international economic affairs, management, reporting and analysis, reporting in science and technology, global affairs, personnel management, consular affairs, office management, information management, administration, and others.

27. See Partnership for Public Service, "Public Service Recognition Week: May 7–13, 2023," https://ourpublicservice.org/wp-content/uploads/2023/03/PSRW23_guide_how tocelebrate.pdf.

28. Quainton, ADST OHP interview, 168.

29. See chapter 5. Bob Pfeiffer, a labor officer, headed the losing ticket. In the contest for State representative, 10 candidates competed for three seats. Adair came in fourth, falling short by 85 votes of 5,741 cast. *FSJ*, August 1979, 40.

30. Marshall Adair, interview, May 15, 2013.

31. *State Magazine*, April 1998, 12. During this period, the number of full-time permanent employees who were Foreign Service nationals rose from 9,455 to 9,508.

32. The ambassador was John Hamilton.

33. Marshall Adair and Dan Geisler, cited in minutes, AFSA Governing Board meeting, February 9, 2000; and John Naland, cited in minutes, AFSA Governing Board's offsite meeting, July 20, 2001. Geisler said that in 1998 the department had assigned a civil servant under an LNC appointment as DCM in Lagos, but no member of the Foreign Service had bid on the job.

34. Minutes, AFSA Governing Board meeting, March 7, 2001. The collective bargaining agreement, in a memorandum of understanding, was codified in volume 3 of the State Department's Foreign Affairs Manual (FAM) at https://fam.state.gov.

35. Marshall P. Adair, ADST OHP interview, September 1, 2011, 197.

36. Adair, interview.

37. Minutes, AFSA Governing Board meeting, March 8, 2000. The motion to file the grievance passed unanimously.

38. AFSA-State Implementation Dispute, FSGB Case No. 1000-017, in Foreign Service Grievance Board, *Annual Report for the Year 2020*, 10, https://www.fsgb.gov/sys_attachment.do?sys_id=e9d93d05dbabf2000b87f4b40f9619e7.

39. Minutes, AFSA Governing Board meeting, September 6, 2000.

40. Ibid.

41. Foreign Service Grievance Board, *Annual Report for the Year 2020*, 10; and Minutes, AFSA Governing Board meeting, December 14, 2000. The Secretary has authority under Section 1106(d) of the Foreign Service Act of 1980 to overrule the FSGB for reasons of national security or foreign policy.

42. "Roberta S. Jacobson," Office of the Historian, Department of State, https://history.state.gov/departmenthistory/people/jacobson-roberta-s. In his "Remarks at the Launch of the 100,000 Strong in the Americas Partnership" on January 17, 2014, Secretary of State John F. Kerry called Roberta Jacobson "the best of the best" (https://2009-2017.state.gov/secretary/remarks/2014/01/220027.htm).

43. Anonymous comment cited by John Naland in AFSA News, *FSJ*, April 2000, 4.

44. AFSA News, *FSJ*, January 2001, 1, 4.

45. Letter from Chief Labor Negotiator Susan Morse, cited in AFSA News, *FSJ*, May 2001, 1.

46. Ibid., 6.

47. The regulations are at State Department, 3 FAM 2290: Limited Non-Career Appointments under Section 303 of the Foreign Service Act, https://fam.state.gov/FAM/03FAM/03FAM2290.html. See in particular 3 FAM 2294: Filling Positions under "Exceptional Circumstance," revised April 18, 2014.

48. Adair, ADST OHP interview, 198, 199.

49. See "Presidential Cabinet Nominations: President Jimmy Carter through President George W. Bush," Virtual Reference Desk, updated November 28, 2017, www.senate.gov/reference/resources/pdf/cabinettable.pdf.

50. Vacant positions from Niels Marquardt, "The DRI Rides to the Rescue," *FSJ*, April 2004, 21; decrepit facilities and near state of crisis from U.S. Department of State, *America's*

*Overseas Presence*, 5; and how the Service has lost its attraction from *War for Talent: Maintaining a Strong Talent Pool*, an April 1999 report by McKinsey & Company commissioned by the Department of State and cited in John Naland, "The War for Talent," AFSA News, *FSJ*, November 1999, 3.

51. Confirmation hearing by Secretary-designate Colin L. Powell before the Senate Committee on Foreign Relations, January 17, 2001, http://2001-2009.state.gov/secretary /former/powell/remarks/2001/443.htm.

52. Shawn Dorman, "Are State Employees Ready for Reform?," *FSJ*, May 2001, 34.

53. Grant Green, like Frank Carlucci, Tom Boyatt, and a number of other military, Foreign Service, and government veterans, was a former employee of Sears World Trade, a division of Sears, Roebuck & Co. that opened in Washington in 1982 and failed in 1986.

54. Kopp, *Commercial Diplomacy*, 35–37.

55. Christopher M. Jones, "The Other Side of Powell's Record," *American Diplomacy*, March 2006, https://americandiplomacy.web.unc.edu/2006/03/the-other-side-of -powells-record/.

56. Poor attendance referred to in minutes of AFSA Governing Board meeting, May 10, 2000.

57. Sources for the linguistic dispute are AFSA News, *FSJ*, May 2001, 1, 5; AFSA News, *FSJ*, June 2001, 5, 9; AFSA News, *FSJ*, July–August 2001, 1, 5; AFSA News, *FSJ*, September 2001, 7; Steven Mufson, *Washington Post*, June 19, 2001; and William Safire, *New York Times*, July 22, 2001. The Foreign Service Star was authorized by P.L. 106-115 of November 29, 1999. The founder and chairman of the Foreign Affairs Council was Tom Boyatt, who signed the letter with Marshall Adair and the chief executives of eight other organizations.

58. John K. Naland, interview, June 4, 2013.

59. AFSA News, *FSJ*, September 1999, 4; and AFSA News, *FSJ*, June 2001, 3.

60. Minutes, AFSA Governing Board meetings, November 3, 1999, and January 10, 2001; and memorandum for the author from John Naland, December 21, 2012. For the controversy, see Dale V. Slaght, "The Foreign Service and Gay Rights: One FSO Speaks Out," *FSJ*, September 2001, 14, 16; Brook Hefright, "The Foreign Service and Gay Rights: A Gay FSO Responds," *FSJ*, September 2001, 15, 17–18; and Bob Guldin, "Not Quite Family: 'Members of Household' at State," *FSJ*, June 2004, 17.

61. The Defense of Marriage Act, P.L. 104-199, September 21, 1996, defined marriage (for the federal government) as between one man and one woman, and allowed states to refuse to recognize same-sex marriages performed in states where such marriages were legal. The act was rendered void by later Supreme Court decisions, particularly *Obergefell v. Hodges* 135 S. Ct. 2584 (2015). Naland note to author, February 23, 2022.

62. AFSA News, *FSJ*, April 2001, 1. Only about 25 percent of AFSA members voted.

63. For budget numbers, see auditor's report for 1994, AFSA News, *FSJ*, July 1995, 13; and AFSA 2001 Annual Report, AFSA News, *FSJ*, March 2002, 6. The fact that no portion of membership dues was allocated to the *FSJ* (as subscription revenue) gave the impression that the *Journal* was in deficit.

64. Naland, interview. A similar debate took place in 1967, with positions reversed. A Planning Committee of the AFSA Governing Board proposed to turn the *Journal* into a professional quarterly for "those with a serious interest in foreign affairs," relegating in-house material to a nonsubscription newsletter. *Journal* staff opposed the idea, and the full board let it die. See *FSJ*, September 1967, 42–43, 48–49.

65. "Letter from the Editor," *FSJ*, January 2002, 9.

66. *FSJ*, August 2001, 5.

67. Ibid.

68. Minutes, AFSA Governing Board and staff off-site meeting, July 20, 2001.

69. *FSJ*, August 2001, 5.

70. Minutes, AFSA Governing Board and staff off-site meeting.

71. See Office of Personnel Management, "Federal Employees Pay Comparability Act of 1990," H. Rept. 101-730, https://www.congress.gov/bill/101st-congress/house-bill/3979?s=1&r=67. The act did not apply to military personnel. The Central Intelligence Agency, the Defense Intelligence Agency, and the National Security Agency all paid Washington, D.C.–level salaries to their overseas civilian employees.

72. P.L. 107-208, September 30, 2002.

73. AFSA News, *FSJ*, January 2004, 3.

74. Dorman, "Are State Employees Ready?," 33

75. Carlucci and Brzezinski, "State Department Reform."

76. Frank Carlucci, "What State Needs: Resources for Reform," *FSJ*, May 2001, 17–20.

77. Information available to AFSA indicated that about 15 percent of Foreign Service personnel and family members had medical restrictions on availability (Minutes, AFSA Governing Board meeting, October 2, 2002). The fair-share proposal did not address this problem.

78. Minutes, AFSA Governing Board meeting, August 8, 2001.

79. AFSA News *FSJ*, March 2002, 12.

80. Bill Farrand, "Warm Welcome on the Hill," AFSA News, *FSJ*, June 2002, 8.

81. Ibid. Grenades thrown into the Protestant International Church near the American embassy in Islamabad on March 18, 2002, killed five people, including embassy employee Barbara Green and her daughter, high school senior Kristen Wormsley. Barbara Green's husband, diplomat Milton Green, and their young son were injured.

## 10. The Scapegoat Years, 2002–2009

1. Susan Schmidt and Bill Miller, "Homeland Security Department to Oversee Visa Program; Move Would Limit Role of State Dept.," *Washington Post*, August 6, 2002.

2. Minutes, AFSA Governing Board meeting, July 2, 2002.

3. James Dao, "Consuls Lax in Screening for Visas, Report Says," *New York Times*, December 22, 2002.

4. Schmidt and Miller, "Homeland Security Department."

5. Ibid.

6. GAO, "Staffing Shortfalls," 5.

7. Christopher Marquis, "More Say Yes to Foreign Service, but Not to Hardship Assignments," *New York Times*, July 22, 2002.

8. Minutes, AFSA Governing Board meeting, May 7, 2003.

9. AFSA 2002 Annual Report, AFSA News, *FSJ*, March 2003, 1; and AFSA News, *FSJ*, July–August 2002, 8.

10. "A Foreign Service PAC," editorial, *Washington Post*, December 4, 2002, A22.

11. Net assets from consolidated financial statement, minutes, AFSA Board meeting, May 8, 2002; and membership from AFSA 2002 Annual Report, 1.

12. John W. Limbert, interview, March 3, 2014.

13. Cited in Kralev, *America's Other Army*, 44.

14. Newt Gingrich, "Transforming the State Department: The Next Challenge for the Bush Administration," speech at the American Enterprise Institute, Washington, D.C., April 22, 2003, cited in Kopp and Gillespie, *Career Diplomacy*, 116, 120.

15. Minutes, AFSA Board meeting, August 7, 2002.

16. Limbert's quote from *FSJ*, November 2004, 5. Limbert's President's Views column did not identify Barbara Bodine by name. The program was a *Frontline* episode, "The Man Who Knew," an encomium to FBI agent John O'Neill, which was first broadcast in October 2002 and repeated in September 2004.

17. Limbert, interview.

18. Minutes, AFSA Governing Board meeting, November 5, 2003; and Military Family Tax Relief Act of 2003, P.L. 108-121, November 11, 2003. Nakamura had been working on securing this provision at least since 1997.

19. Minutes, AFSA Governing Board meeting, March 5, 2003.

20. E.O. 13325, January 23, 2004. For the full story, see Halchin, "Senior Executive Service," 15–16.

21. AFSA 2004 Annual Report, AFSA News, *FSJ*, March 2005, 1. The reduced level of base pay also affected the calculation of retirement and allowances, such as post differentials linked to base pay.

22. AFSA 2005 Annual Report, AFSA News, *FSJ*, March 2006, 1.

23. Limbert, interview.

24. George W. Bush, National Security Presidential Directive (NSPD) 24, January 20, 2003. The 2003 directive was declassified and made public in 2011 (https://irp.fas .org/offdocs/nspd/nspd-24.pdf). See Halchin, "Coalition Provisional Authority," CRS-1, CRS-5.

25. Bodine, "Preemptive Post-Conflict Stabilization," in Miklaucic, *Commanding Heights*, 37.

26. Minutes, AFSA Governing Board meeting, April 7, 2004; and AFSA News, *FSJ*, June 2004, 7.

27. Louise Crane, AFSA News, *FSJ*, September 2004, 3.

28. Ibid.

29. State cables 207935 and 239051 (November 2004), and response from State Vice President Crane, cited in AFSA News, *FSJ*, January 2005, 7.

30. Ibid.

31. Maj. Gen. Eric T. "Rick" Olson, interviewed by Marilyn Green for the United States Institute of Peace and the Association for Diplomatic Studies and Training on March 12, 2008, www.usip.org/sites/default/files/file/resources/collections/histories/iraq _prt/5.pdf. General Olson was director of the national coordination team in Baghdad that provided guidance to the Provincial Reconstruction Team in Iraq in 2006 and 2007.

32. George W. Bush, NSPD-44, December 7, 2005: "The Secretary of State shall coordinate and lead integrated United States government efforts, involving all U.S. departments and agencies with relevant responsibilities, to prepare, plan for, and conduct stabilization and reconstruction activities" (www.fas.org/irp/offdocs/nspd/nspd-44.html).

33. Steve Kashkett, interview, April 7, 2014.

34. AFSA News, *FSJ*, November 2005, 6–7.

35. Ibid., 3; and minutes, AFSA Governing Board meeting, September 14, 2005.

36. Minutes, AFSA Governing Board meeting, May 3, 2006. At the same meeting, Retiree Representative Gil Sheinbaum noted that in 1965, then–Under Secretary for Management Bill Crockett directed that all Foreign Service personnel serving in Vietnam receive a promotion. Although the order was not made officially, Sheinbaum said it was understood by all and carried out.

37. The figure of 22 percent includes those on temporary duty of 90 days or more. See Kopp and Gillespie, *Career Diplomacy*, 114–15.

38. Kashkett, interview.

39. Rice, *No Higher Honor*, 303 (emphasis in the original). The phrase "active loyalty" recalls the "positive loyalty" that John Foster Dulles demanded during the purge of the China hands.

40. Ibid., 466.

41. Holmes, "Where Are the Civilians?"

42. When AFSA lobbyists told Rep. Frank Wolf (R-Va.) that Secretary Rice supported overseas comparability pay for the Foreign Service, Wolf asked for a call from Rice as evidence of that support. She never made the call, and her chief of staff told AFSA that she would not go against the White House on the issue. Minutes, AFSA Governing Board meeting, November 2, 2005.

43. *FSJ*, September 2006, 69.

44. J. Anthony "Tony" Holmes, interview, April 1, 2014.

45. Minutes, AFSA Governing Board meeting, July 5, 2006.

46. Ibid.

47. The statement by floor manager Rep. Chris Smith (R-N.J.) appears in *FSJ*, February 2007, 56.

48. Holmes, interview. John Naland reported that "Congressional Democrats are unwilling to go forward with a bill [H.R. 3202] that would include pay-for-performance provisions" (Minutes, AFSA Governing Board meeting, April 2, 2008).

49. AFSA was careful not to use Zeleny's name, which never appeared in the *Foreign Service Journal* or in the minutes of Governing Board discussions of the issue. Tony Holmes did not use her name in his letter to Secretary Rice, and neither he nor Steve Kashkett used her name in conversations with the author. But her name was well known at the time of the dispute and appeared in the *Washington Post*. See Al Kamen, "A Diplomat's Plum Post, Plucked Away," December 22, 2006.

50. Holmes, interview.

51. Letter, October 24, 2006 [AFSA archives].

52. AFSA News, *FSJ*, February 2007, 55. The AFSA News report carries the text of the joint message, State 199798 of December 15, 2006.

53. AFSA News Special Election Edition, March 2007, 2.

54. Election results memo, Election Committee to AFSA candidates, June 4, 2007.

55. John Naland, correspondence with author, April 22, 2014.

56. Some analysts got the story right. Andrew Exum, writing under the pseudonym Abu Muquwama, posted the following blog entry on October 27, 2007: "Folks in the Department of Defense like to blame things in Iraq on State and the other agencies, but there are two big problems with the State Department. One, it's too darn small. It is no accident that the 2008 presidential candidates are echoing Newt Gingrich's call to triple the size of the department—or at least increase the number of officers. Two, unlike the U.S. military, State has no real expeditionary history. When a soldier is ordered to war, he goes. State, meanwhile, does not 'mobilize' and 'deploy' its personnel. Neither, for that matter, does the Department of Justice, the Department of the Treasury, or any of the other agencies that need to partner with Defense in an effort like that in Iraq and Afghanistan" ("Prime Candidates for Iraq," *Small Wars Journal* blog, http://smallwarsjournal.com/blog/prime-candidates-for-iraq-updated). David Kilcullen in the same post noted that the U.S. armed forces employ about 1.68 million uniformed members. "The Department of Defense is about 210 times larger than USAID and State combined."

57. "Strip for Action," *New York Post*, December 26, 2006.

58. Max Boot, "Send the State Department to War," *New York Times*, November 14, 2007.

59. Helene Cooper, "Few Veteran Diplomats Accept Mission to Iraq," *New York Times*, February 8, 2007. The Secretary made her comments, and revealed her request to the Department of Defense, at a hearing before the House International Relations Committee on February 7, 2007.

60. Kopp and Gillespie, *Career Diplomacy*, 113. The maximum number of years of consecutive service in Washington was restored to six in 2013.

61. Ibid., 116.

62. Kashkett, interview.

63. This account is based mainly on the following sources: Muquwama, "Prime Candidates for Iraq"; Helene Cooper, "Foreign Service Officers Resist Mandatory Iraq Postings," *New York Times*, October 31, 2007; Karen DeYoung, "Envoys Resist Forced Iraq Duty; Top State Officials Face Angry Questions," *Washington Post*, November 1, 2007, A-1; Glenn Kessler, "Rice Reaffirms Plan to Force Diplomats to Fill Iraq Posts," *Washington Post*, November 3, 2007, A-6; Sean McCormack, Daily Press Briefing, Department of State, November 1, 2007, http://2001-2009.state.gov/r/pa/prs/dpb/2007/nov/94478.htm; and Shawn Dorman, "Iraq 'Prime Candidate' Exercise Canceled," AFSA News, *FSJ*, January 2008, 57, 64.

64. Sean McCormack, Daily Press Briefing, State Department, November 19, 2007, http://2001-2009.state.gov/r/pa/prs/dpb/2007/nov/95334.htm. The "prime candidate" exercise was canceled on November 16, 2007.

65. John Naland, "Professional Responsibility," *FSJ*, November 2008, 5.

66. "Bench Strength," *FSJ*, January 2008, 5.

67. Naland, interview. Department spokesman McCormack said of assignments to Iraq, "The Secretary feels and the management of this department feel as though that there isn't really any higher priority for the Foreign Service and the State Department in terms of our foreign policy and national security" (daily press briefing, November 19, 2007).

68. AFSA 2008 Annual Report, AFSA News, *FSJ*, March 2009, 59.

69. Steve Kashkett, "War Zone Assignments: Lessons Learned," AFSA News, *FSJ*, November 2008, 77.

70. AFSA News, *FSJ*, December 2008, 69.

71. Kashkett, "War Zone Assignments."

72. Naland, "Professional Responsibility."

73. John Naland, "A Professional Issue," *FSJ*, October 2008, 5.

74. See House report 110-877, 110th Cong., 2nd sess., September 24, 2008, https://www.congress.gov/congressional-report/110th-congress/house-report/877/1?s=1&r=66. Senator Kerry's bill was S.3426. See also AFSA News, *FSJ*, December 2008, 59, 65.

75. Nakamura, "Proposals."

76. P.L. 111-32, Supplemental Appropriations Act of 2009, June 24, 2009, Section 1113.

77. GAO, "Overseas Comparability Pay," 2011. Implementation was delayed at the International Broadcasting Bureau, whose employees received OCP retroactive to August 2009 in April 2010. See minutes, AFSA Governing Board meeting, April 7, 2010.

78. Francisco Zamora, "Advice for the New USAID Administrator," *FSJ*, January 2009, 58–59.

79. Minutes, AFSA Governing Board meeting, May 7, 2008.

80. Allan Mustard, "FAS at a Crossroads: Reshaping Ag Diplomacy," *FSJ*, May 2009, 31; and Minutes, AFSA Governing Board meeting, March 4, 2009.

81. AFSA 2009 Annual Report, AFSA News, *FSJ*, March 2010, 51.

82. Shawn Zeller, "Hoping for a Break: Foreign Trade Agencies under Pressure," *FSJ*, May 2009, 16.

83. Minutes, AFSA Governing Board meeting, February 4, 2009.

84. Testimony of John K. Naland, president, American Foreign Service Association, before the House Appropriations Subcommittee on State, Foreign Operations, and Related Programs, 111th Cong., 1st sess., March 26, 2009, www.gpo.gov/fdsys/pkg/CHRG -111hhrg55310/html/CHRG-111hhrg55310.htm.

85. American Academy of Diplomacy and Stimson Center, "Foreign Affairs Budget," 1.

86. Ibid., 5.

87. "Diplomacy 3.0" was shorthand for "diplomacy, development, and defense," which Secretary Hillary Rodham Clinton identified as three interrelated components of U.S. foreign policy.

88. AFSA News, *FSJ*, May 2009, 45, 49.

## 11. Squeeze from the Top, 2009–2015

1. Katherine Q. Seelye, "Live Blog: Presenting the National Security Team," *New York Times*, December 1, 2008, at www.nytimes.com.

2. Kate Phillips, "Senate Confirms Clinton as Secretary of State," *New York Times*, January 21, 2009. The two opposing votes were Sen. Jim DeMint (R-S.C.) and Sen. David Vitter (R-La.).

3. U.S. Department of State and USAID, *2010 QDDR*.

4. USAID, Office of the Inspector General, USAID Management Challenges, Information Memo for the Administrator, October 23, 2008, 6.

5. State of the Union Address, January 27, 2010; and E.O. 13534, March 11, 2010.

6. Linda Thomas-Greenfield, "Direct from the DG," *State Magazine*, July–August 2013, 9.

7. AFSA 2013 Annual Report, 1, https://afsa.org/sites/default/files/flipping_book /ar2013/files/assets/basic-html/page-4.html. Beginning in 2013, the annual reports were published separately. Beginning in 2017–2019, the "annual" report was replaced by a biennial report that covers the two-year term of a Governing Board. Links to all annual reports since 2003 are at https://afsa.org/AFSA-annual-report.

8. "Agriculture Secretary Vilsack Announces Blueprint for Stronger Service," U.S. Department of Agriculture press release 0003.12, January 3, 2012; and International Trade Administration, "Budget Estimates, Fiscal Year 2012, Congressional Submission," ITA-96, www.osec.doc.gov/bmi/budget/12CJ/ITA_FY_2012_Congressional _Submission.pdf.

9. Patricia Woodring and Thea de Rouville, presidents in 1977 and 1981, respectively, were named to the position by the AFSA Governing Board.

10. Remarks at AFSA Awards Ceremony (AFSA Achievement and Contributions to the Association Award), October 19, 2022; text provided to the author. The spouse referred to is Riaz M. Khan, retired Pakistani diplomat and former foreign secretary of Pakistan. For biographic information, see "Biography of Susan Rockwell Johnson," Office of the High Representative, August 20, 2004, http://www.ohr.int/?ohr_archive =biography-of-susan-rockwell-johnson; and Association for Diplomatic Studies and Training, "ADST Staff," https://adst.org/about-adst/staff/.

11. Susan Rockwell Johnson, interview, April 16, 2014; and email to the author, October 30, 2022.

12. Office of Labor-Management Standards, "Voluntary Compliance Agreements 2010," last updated January 4, 2011, http://www.dol.gov/olms/regs/compliance/volun _agree_2010.htm.

13. AFSA News, *FSJ*, January 2010, 37.

14. Keith Curtis, FCS vice president, *FSJ*, January 2010, 41.

15. Johnson, interview; and email to the author, October 30, 2022.

16. See, for example, the 2010 columns "Seeing Diplomacy as a Profession," May; "AFSA's Role as a Professional Association," September; and "Professional Ethics and Codes of Conduct," November.

17. As in the case of the "Foreign Affairs Budget for the Future" and a subsequent budget study, "Diplomacy in a Time of Scarcity," the academy retained the Stimson Center to prepare the draft and final product. The study was released in February 2011 as "Forging a 21st-Century Diplomatic Service for the United States through Professional Education and Training," https://www.academyofdiplomacy.org/publication/forging-a -21st-century-diplomatic-service-for-the-united-states-through-professional-education -and-training/. AFSA's financial contribution was about $70,000.

18. Consolidated Appropriations Act, 2010, P.L. 111-117, December 16, 2009; and AFSA 2010 Annual Report, *FSJ*, March 2011, 26.

19. S. 2971, Foreign Relations Authorization Act, Fiscal Years 2010 and 2011. A similar measure, the Foreign Service Overseas Pay Equity Act of 2009, had already passed the House. As of this writing (April 2023), Congress has not acted on the third tranche.

20. AFSA 2010 Annual Report, 25.

21. Ambassador George Jones, Chairman, Elections Committee, "Election Results, 2011–2013 AFSA Governing Board," cited in Kopp, *Voice of the Foreign Service* (2015 edition), 297n19; and number of eligible voting members from David T. Jones, "Unionization, AFSA and the Foreign Service," *FSJ*, April 2013, 17.

22. Membership figures from the 2008 AFSA Annual Report and the AFSA 2012 Annual Report, *FSJ*, March 2013.

23. AFSA 2013 Annual Report, 2, 15, https://afsa.org/sites/default/files/flipping_book /ar2013/files/assets/basic-html/page-4.html.

24. AFSA 2012 Annual Report, *FSJ*, March 2013, AFSA News, 62.

25. "*Foreign Service Journal* Redesign Launch Event," AFSAtube, October 11, 2012, https://www.youtube.com/watch?v=Sd1kFNO_se4.

26. AFSA 2013 Annual Report, 15.

27. AFSA 2012 Annual Report, AFSA News, 67.

28. Johnson, interview.

29. U.S. Government Accountability Office, "Foreign Service Midlevel Staffing Gaps Persist despite Significant Increases in Hiring," Report no. GAO-12-721, June 2012, 8, http://www.gao.gov/assets/600/591595.pdf.

30. *FSJ*, January 2009, 59.

31. Ibid. See also Francisco Zamora, "Developing Your People," *FSJ*, December 2010, AFSA News, 54; Susan Johnson, "Strategic Planning, Part II," *FSJ*, December 2011, 5; and Robert Silverman, "Righting the Personnel Balance at State," *FSJ*, November 2014, 7.

32. *FSJ*, March 2011, 23.

33. According to AFSA's website, the share of ambassadorial appointments going to career personnel was 69 percent in the G. H. W. Bush administration, 72 percent

in the Clinton administration, and 70 percent in the G. W. Bush administration. As of October 24, 2014, the share of ambassadorial posts held by career personnel was just 59 percent.

34. Print editions used the title "Bring Back the Professional Diplomats." The online edition, and the online archive edition quoted here, had the title "Presidents Are Breaking the U.S. Foreign Service." See http://www.washingtonpost.com/opinions/presidents -are-breaking-the-us-foreign-service/2013/04/11/4efb5afe-a235-11e2-82bc-511538ae90a4 _story.html.

35. Robert Silverman, interview, March 22, 2022.

36. Ibid. Silverman believes that Hicks's candidacy was damaged by his high-profile congressional testimony on Benghazi, which challenged on a number of points the administration's account of the September 11, 2012, attack.

37. AFSA, "2013–2015 Governing Board Strategic Plan," November 6, 2013, https:// www.afsa.org/strategicplan.aspx.

38. Robert Silverman, "New Ideas from AFSA," *FSJ*, December 2013, 7.

39. See pages 84–86.

40. Silverman, interview.

41. Governing Board minutes, December 4, 2013, and January 8, 2014; and "Guidelines for Successful Performance as a Chief of Mission," *FSJ*, April 2014, 49–51. The published guidelines include a list of the members of the working group.

42. Silverman, interview.

43. Al Kamen, "State Department Employees Union Demands Documents on Embattled Ambassador Nominees," *Washington Post*, March 5, 2014.

44. The fundraisers confirmed in the spring of 2015 included Robert C. Barber to Iceland, Noah Mamet to Argentina, and Colleen Bell to Hungary. Denise Campbell Bauer was confirmed to Belgium in August 2013 before the guidelines had been completed. George Tsunis withdrew from consideration as ambassador to Norway in 2015 but in 2022 was nominated and confirmed as ambassador to Greece.

45. *FSJ*, July–August 2014, 52.

46. *FSJ*, April 2014, 49–51.

47. Section 304(a)(1) and (4).

48. "AFSA Sues to Force Release of Envoy Competency Reports," *FSJ*, May 1983, 37.

49. "AFSA Contests Classification of Certificates," *FSJ*, November 1989, 56.

50. "Annual Report of the Governing Board, 1988–1989," *FSJ*, December 1989, 57–59.

51. "Does the State Department Respect Ambassadors?," *FSJ*, September 1989, 65.

52. Email from Tex Harris to Carlos Osorio, March 14, 2014, copied to author; and Matthew W. Asada, interview, March 10, 2022. See also Susan Crabtree, "Under Legal Fire, State Dept. Hands over Docs on 'Competence' of Ambassadors," *Washington Examiner*, March 7, 2014, https://www.washingtonexaminer.com/under-legal-fire-state-dept -hands-over-docs-on-competence-of-ambassadors; and Ali Weinberg, "Foreign Service Pros Threaten to Sue over Ambassadors' Competence," March 5, 2014, http://abcnews.go .com/blogs/headlines/2014/03/foreign-service-pros-threaten-to-sue-over-ambassadors -competence. Section 712 of the Department of State Authorization Act for Fiscal Year 2017, P.L. 114-323 of December 16, 2016, requires publication of the certificates "in a conspicuous manner and location" on the Department of State's website within seven days of their submission to the committee. The certificates for nominees of the current administration are online at state.gov, along with links to archived certificates back to 2017. Ryan Scoville used Freedom of Information Act requests and lawsuits to obtain

what appears to be all the certificates of competency produced by the department from 1980 to 2014. See Ryan Scoville, "Unqualified Ambassadors," *Duke Law Journal* 69 (June 2019): 71–196, https://dlj.law.duke.edu/article/unqualified-ambassadors-scoville-vol69 -iss1/; and Ryan Scoville, "Certificates of Competency for Nominees to Be Chiefs of Mission: 1980–2014," February 13, 2019, https://ryanscoville.com/2019/02/13/certificates-of -competency-for-nominees-to-be-chiefs-of-mission-1980-2014/.

53. "How to Get Better Ambassadors," *FSJ*, July–August 2014, 17–18. Among other studies, Ambassador Dennis Jett is the author of *American Diplomats: A Guide for Aspiring Diplomats and Foreign Service Officers* (Handel, Switzerland: Palgrave Macmillan, 2014 and 2022).

54. See, for example, the following certificates of competency from the U.S. Department of State: "Blanchard Lynda—Republic of Slovenia—February 2019," May 15, 2019, https://www.state.gov/blanchard-lynda-republic-of-slovenia-february-2019/; "Sands Carla—Kingdom of Denmark, September 2017," September 15, 2017, https://www.state .gov/sands-carla-kingdom-of-denmark-september-2017/; "Thornhill, Barbara Hale— Republic of Singapore—October 2019," October 18, 2019, https://www.state.gov/thornhill -barbara-hale-republic-of-singapore-october-2019/; and many others.

55. Casey Hicks, "Timeline of Hillary Clinton's Email Scandal," CNN, November 7, 2016, https://www.cnn.com/2016/10/28/politics/hillary-clinton-email-timeline.

56. See Elias Groll, "Hillary Clinton and Schrödinger's Cat: What Does It Mean to 'Retroactively Classify'?," *Foreign Policy*, July 24, 2015, https://foreignpolicy.com /2015/07/24/hillary-clinton-and-schrodingers-cat-what-does-it-mean-to-retroactively -classify/; Krishnadev Kalamur, "Some Clinton Emails Were Retroactively Classified," National Public Radio, May 22, 2015, https://www.npr.org/sections/thetwo-way/2015/05 /22/408774111/state-department-to-release-more-clinton-emails-today; and Michael S. Schmidt and Matt Apuzzo, "Inquiry Sought in Hillary Clinton's Use of Email," *New York Times*, July 23, 2015, https://www.nytimes.com/2015/07/24/us/politics/inquiry-is-sought -in-hillary-clinton-email-account.html?searchResultPosition=7.

57. Jen Psaki, Daily Press Briefing, March 9, 2015, https://2009-2017.state.gov/r/pa/prs /dpb/2015/03/238679.htm; and Chacón-Silverman letter of April 17, 2015, provided to the author. Schedules A, B, and C are excepted personnel categories that include presidential appointees not confirmed by the Senate (Schedule A); persons with special scientific, technical, or professional expertise (Schedule B); and persons appointed to positions of a confidential or policy-determining nature (Schedule C).

58. Silverman email to Jonathan Finer (Secretary Clinton's chief of staff), Jennifer Stout (Secretary Clinton's deputy chief of staff), and Patrick Kennedy (under secretary for management), June 16, 2015, provided to the author. The email states, "I appreciate the Secretary's commitment to continue reducing the hiring of Schedule B appointees in DAS [deputy assistant secretary] positions, now down to three such positions, with the goal of reducing it to zero by the end of the administration."

59. Office of the Inspector General, Office of Evaluations and Special Projects, "Evaluation of the Department of State's Use of Schedule B Hiring Authority," ESP-19-03, February 2019, https://www.stateoig.gov/report/esp-19-03.

60. See AFSA's Annual Reports at https://afsa.org/afsa-annual-report and the masthead page of the *Foreign Service Journal*.

61. Sharon Papp, interview, May 20, 2022.

62. Ibid. Sharon Papp explained that until 2021, her direct boss had been the State vice president.

63. Cited in a March 16, 2014, post on diplopundit.net (no longer active, captured March 10, 2022). The criticism was misplaced. The department's FY2014 budget request had in fact included $81.4 million to make base pay for Foreign Service personnel stationed abroad comparable to pay in Washington, including 100 percent of locality pay. AFSA supported the request in letters to the authorizing and appropriating committees. See Susan Epstein, Alex Tiersky, and Marian Lawson, "State, Foreign Operations, and Related Programs: FY2014 Budget and Appropriations," Report R43043 (Washington, D.C.: Congressional Research Service, January 16, 2014, https://sgp.fas.org/crs/row/R43043.pdf); and *FSJ*, November 2014, 89.

64. The department included full funding of OCP in its budget requests. As a senator, Secretary Kerry had introduced the Foreign Service Overseas Equity Pay Act of 2008, which became the basis for the authorizing language appearing in the 2009 supplemental appropriations act. Secretary Kerry and USAID Administrator Gayle Smith included an appeal for full funding of OCP in budget testimony (*FSJ*, April 2016, 47). On behalf of AFSA, Silverman wrote detailed letters on OCP to the chairs and ranking members of the committees of jurisdiction and, with other members of the Governing Board, made face-to-face appeals to members. See *FSJ*, November 2014, 82; and *FSJ*, June 2015, 55.

65. P.L. 113-235, Consolidated and Further Continuing Appropriations Act, 2015, December 16, 2014, Section 7034(l).

66. P.L. 115-141 of March 23, 2018; P.L. 116-260 of December 27, 2020; and P.L. 117-103 of March 15, 2022.

67. *FSJ*, November 2014, 82; LM Office annual report to Governing Board, January 27, 2015; AFSA Annual Report 2017–2019, 65, https://afsa.org/sites/default/files/2017-2019-afsa-governing-board-term-report.pdf; and *FSJ*, January–February 2018, 64.

68. Section 406(2)(b).

69. "AFSA Celebrates Win on Meritorious Service Increases," *FSJ*, April 2021, 59; and Tom Yazdgerdi, "2021: A Year of Unrealized Potential?," *FSJ*, December 2021, 66.

70. Papp, interview.

71. AFSA, "2016 AFSA Annual Report," 16, https://afsa.org/sites/default/files/flipping_book/ar2016/files/assets/basic-html/page-1.html.

72. "Kudos": Ken Kero-Mentz, "AFSA [State] VP Briefing Memo" [to Tom Yazdgerdi], undated, 5, provided to the author. "Since MSI nominators . . .": Alex Karagiannis, "Evaluation Reform at State: A Work in Progress," *FSJ*, April 2020, 30.

73. "Proposed Bylaw Amendment to Rightsize AFSA Governing Board," *FSJ*, December 2014, 42–43, 54.

74. AFSA, "Results: 2015–2017 AFSA Governing Board Election," https://afsa.org/results-2015-2017-afsa-governing-board-election.

## 12. A Consequential Presidency, 2015–2019

1. This quotation and Barbara Stephenson's recollections in the previous paragraphs are drawn from interviews with the author on March 9 and March 23, 2022.

2. See "2015–2017 AFSA Governing Board Election Candidates' Statements," AFSA News Special Election Issue, April 2015, 5, https://www.scribd.com/document/260660216/2015-AFSA-Candidate-Statements; and "AFSA Governing Board Election Town Hall at Foreign Service Institute, March 30, 2015," video, https://www.youtube.com/watch?v=sN5NrV2xNtU.

3. "Candidates' Statements," 4; and AFSA Town Hall.

4. AFSA, "Results: 2015–2017 AFSA Governing Board Election." Just under 25 percent of AFSA's 16,288 members voted (membership data from AFSA's 2015 Annual Report), https://afsa.org/sites/default/files/flipping_book/ar2015/files/assets/basic-html/page-1 .html#.

5. Stephenson, interview, March 9, 2022. Bob Corker did not run for reelection and left the Senate on January 3, 2019, but his idea survived his departure. The FY2021 State authorization bill, the first to pass in 20 years, calls for a study of Foreign Service allowances. The State authorization was incorporated as Division E of the National Defense Authorization Act for FY2022 (P.L. 117-81, December 27, 2021). The relevant provision is Section 5302. Text at https://www.congress.gov/bill/117th-congress/senate-bill/1605/text.

6. Stephenson, interview. In his column, "How to Find the Next Bill Burns" (*FSJ*, April 2015, 7), Bob Silverman pointed out that several of the jobs that Bill Burns filled on his way up were taken by political appointees and lost to the Foreign Service.

7. Stephenson interview.

8. Ibid.

9. "Where Does the Econ Track Lead?," *FSJ*, January–February 2019, 60.

10. Stephenson, interview. Senator Graham (R-S.C.) was chairman of the subcommittee on appropriations for the Department of State, Foreign Operations, and Related Programs (SFORP). Paul Grove is the son of the late Ambassador Brandon Grove, a founder of the American Academy of Diplomacy.

11. Six early presidents—Thomas Jefferson, James Madison, James Monroe, John Quincy Adams, Martin Van Buren, and James Buchanan—served as Secretary of State before winning the presidency. James G. Blaine, Henry Clay, Elihu Root, Daniel Webster, and Hillary Clinton served as Secretary of State before unsuccessfully seeking the presidency. Clay, Blaine, William Jennings Bryan, Charles Evans Hughes, Edmund Muskie, Alexander Haig, Hillary Clinton, and John Kerry served as Secretary of State after unsuccessfully seeking the presidency.

12. "Dear S: You Can Count on Us," *FSJ*, January–February 2017, 7.

13. Keith D. Mines, "Mr. President, You Have Partners at State to Help Navigate the World's Shoals," *FSJ*, January–February 2017, 22.

14. Tamara Cofman Wittes, "What Tillerson Got Right—and Wrong—in His Speech at State," Brookings Institution, February 7, 2017, https://www.brookings.edu/blog/order -from-chaos/2017/02/07/what-tillerson-got-right-and-wrong-in-his-speech-at-state/.

15. Whitney Kassel and Loren DeJonge Schulman, "Donald Trump's Great Patriotic Purge," *Foreign Policy*, April 26, 2017, https://foreignpolicy.com/2017/04/26/donald -trumps-great-patriotic-purge-state-bureacracy-civil-service/.

16. Associated Press, "Trump Reaffirms Urge to Halt Muslims," December 7, 2015, https://www.nytimes.com/video/us/100000004080249/trump-reaffirms-urge-to-halt -muslims.html?searchResultPosition=1. The video shows Donald Trump reading a statement he had released to the press earlier that day. To comply with court orders, including a decision of the Supreme Court, the original E.O. 13769 of January 27, 2017, was superseded by E.O. 13780 of March 6, 2017. See the latter's text, "Protecting the Nation from Foreign Terrorist Entry into the United States," https://www.federalregister.gov /documents/2017/03/09/2017-04837/protecting-the-nation-from-foreign-terrorist-entry -into-the-united-states. President Joe Biden revoked E.O. 13780 on January 20, 2021.

17. The literature on the Dissent Channel is extensive. See, for example, Hannah Gurman's book *The Dissent Papers: The Voices of Diplomats in the Cold War and Beyond* (New York: Columbia University Press, 2012); Harry Kopp, "The State of Dissent in the

Foreign Service," *FSJ*, September 2017; and Tom Boyatt, "What if I Disagree? Dissent in the Foreign Service," in AFSA, *Inside a U.S. Embassy*, 94–96.

18. Mark Landler, "State Dept. Officials Should Quit if They Disagree with Trump, White House Warns," *New York Times*, January 31, 2017; Jeffrey Gettleman, "State Dept. Dissent Cable on Trump's Bank Draws 1,000 Signatures," *New York Times*, January 31, 2017; and Shawn Dorman, "State's Dissent Channel Lights Up," *FSJ*, March 2017, 18. Spicer's term as press secretary lasted just six months (Glenn Thrush, "Sean Spicer Resigns as Press Secretary," *New York Times*, July 21, 2017).

19. The passenger was Ambassador Marcie Ries, who told this story to Barbara Stephenson (Stephenson, interview, March 23, 2022).

20. Matt Tompkins, "The Golden Rule of Professionalism," *FSJ*, June 2017.

21. Congressional Research Service, "Department of State, Foreign Operations, and Related Programs: FY2018 Budget and Appropriations," Report R44890, updated April 13, 2018, 1, https://crsreports.congress.gov/product/pdf/R/R44890. The administration's attacks on the State Department were amply tracked and documented in the press and elsewhere. The following citations are a sample: Nahal Toosi and Andrew Restuccia, "Federal Staffers Panicked by Conservative Media Attacks," *Politico*, March 22, 2017, https://www.politico.com/story/2017/03/government-employees-conservative-media -236321; Julie Hirschfield Davis, "Rumblings of a 'Deep State' Undermining Trump? It Was Once a Foreign Concept," *New York Times*, March 6, 2017, https://www.nytimes.com /2017/03/06/us/politics/deep-state-trump.html; and House Committee on Oversight and Reform, "Engel and Cummings to State Department Inspector: Address Alleged Political Retribution against Career Employees," January 29, 2018, https://oversightdemocrats .house.gov/news/press-releases/engel-cummings-to-state-dept-inspector-address -alleged-political-retribution.

22. U.S. Department of State, Office of Inspector General, "Review of the Effects of the Department of State Hiring Freeze, ISP-I-19-23," August 2019. The freeze was partially lifted at the end of 2017 to allow the hiring of eligible family members.

23. Julia Ioffe, "The State of Trump's State Department," *The Atlantic*, March 1, 2017, https://www.theatlantic.com/international/archive/2017/03/state-department-trump /517965/.

24. Gardiner Harris, "Will Cuts Hurt Diplomacy? Tillerson Tries to Ease Senate's Worries," *New York Times*, June 13, 2017, https://www.nytimes.com/2017/06/13/world /rex-tillerson-senate-state-department.html?searchResultPosition=37.

25. See 115th U.S. Congress, Senate Report 115-152, "Department of State, Foreign Operations, and Related Programs, Appropriations Bill, 2018," September 7, 2017, 1, https://www.congress.gov/congressional-report/115th-congress/senate-report/152. Senator Graham presented his views on the Service in "Message from the Hill: Time for a National Conversation," *FSJ*, March 2018, 18–19.

26. Graham, "Time for a National Conversation," 18.

27. Congressional Research Service, "Department of State, Foreign Operations, and Related Programs: FY2021 Budget and Appropriations," Report R46367, updated September 24, 2021, 1, https://crsreports.congress.gov/product/pdf/R/R46367.

28. Stephenson, interview, March 23, 2022.

29. Candidates listed at AFSA News, *FSJ*, April 2017, 54; and election results at *FSJ*, July–August 2017, 49.

30. The annuity exception allows officers and specialists below the rank of FS-1 who reach their time-in-class limit before they reach the age of 50 to remain in the Service without further promotion until they turn 50, at which point they retire with their

annuity and access to health insurance. Without this exception, such persons would be forced to retire before age 50 and would be ineligible for both the annuity and health insurance. The exception, which was introduced following the 1971 suicide of FSO Charles Thomas, came under attack during the Trump administration. See *FSJ*, June 2019, 44.

31. Stephenson, interview, March 23, 2022; and minutes of the Governing Board, October 5, 2016, and June 7, 2017.

32. For background on the professional policy issues directorate, see AFSA, "2016 AFSA Annual Report," 7, https://afsa.org/sites/default/files/flipping_book/ar2016/files/assets/basic-html/page-1.html. The Bureau of Human Resources changed its name to the Bureau of Global Talent Management, effective February 19, 2020. See "In Brief: Announcing the Bureau of Global Talent Management," *State Magazine*, https://statemag.state.gov/2020/02/0220ib07/.

33. *FSJ*, October 2017, 57; and Ken Kero-Mentz, interview, April 20, 2022. The relevant provision of the bylaws is Article VII, Section 1(a), https://afsa.org/afsa-bylaws#a07. The membership approved the revision of the bylaws in 2019.

34. Ian Houston, interview, April 14, 2022; and email to author, August 13, 2022. The reference to AFSA's past presidents is from Stephenson, interview, March 23, 2022.

35. Stephenson, interview, March 23, 2022.

36. Kero-Mentz, interview.

37. Rex Tillerson, "Address to State Department Employees on 'America First' Foreign Policy," Dean Acheson Auditorium, Washington, D.C., May 3, 2017, https://www.americanrhetoric.com/speeches/rextillersonbriefing05-03-17.htm.

38. See, for example, "AFSA Hosts Redesign Event," *FSJ*, October 2017, 49; "Heard on the Hill," *FSJ*, November 2017, 14; Alex Karagiannis, "Straight Talk on Diplomatic Capacity," *FSJ*, May 2018, 19–25; and Ken Kero-Mentz, "A Fresh Start," *FSJ*, June 2018, 49.

39. "Barbara Stephenson: What Tillerson's Actions Mean for Foreign Service Workers," interview by Tom Temin, Federal News Network, May 5, 2017, https://federalnewsnetwork.com/tom-temin-federal-drive/2017/05/barbara-stephenson-what-tillersons-actions-mean-for-foreign-service-workers/#.

40. During Secretary Powell's tenure, Foreign Service Day was relaunched as Foreign Affairs Day (see page 165). AFSA, however, prefers the original nomenclature.

41. Roger Cohen, "The Desperation of Our Diplomats," *New York Times*, July 28, 2017 (print edition July 30, 2017, under the title "The Diplomats Can't Save Us," SR1). Barbara Stephenson confirmed the shoving incident in a March 23, 2022, interview. Because she was pushed aside, Stephenson had no chance to brief the secretary on the details of the ceremony. As a result, Tillerson stood in the wrong place, and when the color guard entered, he was trapped behind the flags. See "2017 AFSA Memorial Dedication Ceremony," May 5, 2017, AFSAtube, youtube.com/watch?v=souX35GCnZs.

42. Stephenson, interview, March 23, 2022. She attributed the "tipping point" phrase to Liz Schreyer, chairman and chief executive officer of the U.S. Global Leadership Coalition.

43. Barbara Stephenson, "Time to Ask Why," *FSJ*, December 2017, 7. In absolute numbers, 60 percent of career ambassadors was three of five.

44. Barbara Stephenson, "Rapid Cuts at State Department Raise Concern, Says Former Ambassador," interview by Judy Woodruff, PBS *NewsHour*, November 8, 2017. https://www.pbs.org/newshour/show/rapid-cuts-to-top-leadership-at-state-department-raises-concern-says-former-ambassador.

45. "Two Trump Aides Indicted, Transcript 11/9/17," *Rachel Maddow Show*, MSNBC, November 9, 2017, https://www.msnbc.com/transcripts/rachel-maddow-show/2017-11-09-msna1038051.

46. Antony J. Blinken, "How Rex Tillerson Did So Much Damage in So Little Time," *New York Times*, November 30, 2017.

47. Bethany Allen-Ebrahimian, "Top U.S. Diplomat Blasts Trump Administration for 'Decapitation' of State Department Leadership," *Foreign Policy*, November 8, 2017, https://foreignpolicy.com/2017/11/08/top-u-s-diplomat-blasts-trump-administration-for-decapitation-of-state-department-leadership/; Joe Davidson, "Foreign Service Leadership Being 'Decapitated' and 'Depleted at a Dizzying Speed," *Washington Post*, November 17, 2017, https://www.washingtonpost.com/news/powerpost/wp/2017/11/17/foreign-service-leadership-being-decapitated-and-depleted-at-a-dizzying-speed/; Zack Beauchamp, "New Data Shows How the Trump Administration Is Destroying the State Department," *Vox*, November 9, 2017, https://www.vox.com/world/2017/11/8/16623278/trump-state-department-data-career; and Billy Perrigo, "Top Diplomat Says U.S. Has Lost 60% of Its Career Ambassadors under President Trump," *Time*, November 9, 2017, https://time.com/5016774/trump-ambassadors-state-department-lost-60-percent-afsa-barbara-stephenson/.

48. "The Dereliction of American Diplomacy," *The Economist*, international edition, August 13, 2020, https://www.economist.com/international/2020/08/13/the-dereliction-of-american-diplomacy; and "Diplomacy in Crisis: The Trump Administration's Decimation of the State Department: A Democratic Staff Report Prepared for the Use of Committee on Foreign Relations of the United States Senate," July 28, 2020, https://www.foreign.senate.gov/imo/media/doc/Diplomacy%20in%20Crisis%20--%20SFRC%20Democratic%20Staff%20Report.pdf.

49. Max Boot, "Time Is Up on Rex Tillerson," *Foreign Policy*, August 23, 2017, https://foreignpolicy.com/2017/08/23/time-is-up-on-rex-tillerson/.

50. "Moron" from Carol E. Lee, Kristen Welker, Stephanie Ruhle, and Dafna Linzer, "Tillerson's Fury at Trump Required Intervention from Pence," NBC News, October 4, 2017, https://www.nbcnews.com/politics/whitehouse/tillerson-s-fury-trump-required-intervention-pence-n806451; and "represent him credibly abroad" from Ilan Goldenberg, "A Requiem for Rex's Redesign," *Foreign Policy*, March 13, 2018, https://foreignpolicy.com/2018/03/13/a-requiem-for-rexs-redesign/. Goldenberg points out that "even President Trump does not always speak for himself."

51. Shawn Dorman, "Letter from the Editor: The State of State," *FSJ*, September 2018, 9.

52. See "Executive Office Appointments by Donald Trump," Wikipedia, last edited March 23, 2023, https://en.wikipedia.org/wiki/Executive_Office_appointments_by_Donald_Trump#Previous_officeholders_2.

53. Michael R. Pompeo and John J. Sullivan, "Welcome Remarks to Employees," May 1, 2018, https://2017-2021.state.gov/welcome-remarks-to-employees/index.html; and Scott Horsley, "Secretary Pompeo Promises New 'Swagger' at State Department Swearing-In," NPR, May 2, 2018, https://www.npr.org/2018/05/02/607728832/secretary-of-state-pompeo-promises-new-swagger-at-state-department-swearing-in.

54. Barbara Stephenson, "Getting Our Team on the Field," *FSJ*, July–August 2019, 7.

55. Barbara Stephenson, "Taking Stock," *FSJ*, October 2019, 7.

56. Michael Pompeo, "The State Department's Foreign Policy Strategy and FY20 Budget Request," Testimony before the House Committee on Foreign Affairs, March 27,

2019, https://www.youtube.com/watch?v=2gbN1WZzcbQ; and Barbara Stephenson, "The State of State: Putting the Back Channel up Front," *FSJ*, May 2019, 7.

57. Stephenson, interview, March 23, 2022. Stephenson said that when dealing with Sinn Fein during her tour in Belfast, she learned from George Mitchell and Richard Haass to highlight contradictions between their stated positions and their actions.

58. See, for example, Jon D. Michaels, "Trump and the 'Deep State,'" *Foreign Affairs*, September–October 2017, https://www.foreignaffairs.com/articles/2017-08-15/trump-and -deep-state; and Julie Hirschfield Davis, "Rumblings of a 'Deep State' Undermining Trump? It Was Once a Foreign Concept," *New York Times*, March 6, 2017.

59. Robbie Gramer and Colum Lynch, "Despite Pompeo's Call for 'Swagger,' Trump Slashes Diplomatic Budget," *Foreign Policy*, March 11, 2019, https://foreignpolicy.com/2019 /03/11/trump-federal-budget-steep-cuts-to-state-department-foreign-aid-development -diplomacy-pompeo/.

60. Nahal Toosi, "Emails Reveal Conservative Alarm over 'Obama Holdovers' in Trump Administration," *Politico*, March 15, 2018, https://www.politico.com/story/2018 /03/15/emails-trump-administration-alarm-over-obama-holdovers-465528; and Colum Lynch and Robbie Gramer, "Trump Appointee Compiles Loyalty List of U.S. Employees at U.N., State," *Foreign Policy*, June 13, 2018, https://foreignpolicy.com/2018/06/13/trumps -vino-vixen-compiles-loyalty-list-of-u-s-employees-at-u-n-state-mari-stull-political -appointee-state-department-international-organization-united-nations-political -retribution-chaos-dysfunction/.

61. U.S. Department of State, Office of Inspector General, "Review of Allegations of Politicized and Other Improper Personnel Practices in the Bureau of International Organization Affairs," ESP-19-05, August 2019, https://www.stateig.gov/report/esp-19-05; and U.S. Department of State, Office of Inspector General, "Review of Allegations of Politicized and Other Improper Personnel Practices Involving the Office of the Secretary," ESP-20-01, November 2019, https://www.stateig.gov/report/10587. When Mari Stull, the central figure in the scandal in the Bureau of International Organization Affairs, left the department in January 2019, *Politico* reported, "Many U.S. diplomats were sore that Secretary of State Mike Pompeo didn't fire Stull after the allegations against her became public last year. It was not clear Tuesday whether Pompeo played a role in Stull's departure." See Nahal Toosi, "'Vino Vixen,' Alleged Blacklist Creator, Leaves State," *Politico*, January 15, 2019, https://www.politico.com/story/2019/01/15/vino-vixen-out-state -department-1101555.

62. Stephenson, interview, March 23, 2022.

63. Barbara Stephenson, "Does America Spend Too Much on Diplomacy?," *FSJ*, March 2018, 8–9. "Core diplomatic functions" are defined in the column as the line item for ongoing operations (under administration of foreign affairs/State programs/ diplomatic programs) in the annual SFORP's Congressional Budget Justification. See also U.S. Department of State, "Ten-Year Appropriation History," *Congressional Budget Justification, 2018*, 22.

64. The actual funding for "Diplomatic Programs, Ongoing Operations" was $5.1 billion in FY2020. See U.S. Department of State, "Diplomatic Engagement and Foreign Assistance Request, FY 2020–FY 2022," *Congressional Budget Justification, 2022*, 1; and U.S. Department of State, "FY 2022 International Affairs Budget," https://www.state.gov /fy-2022-international-affairs-budget/. See also Secretary of State Mike Pompeo, Written Statement to the House Appropriations Committee, Subcommittee on State, Foreign Operations, and Related Programs on the FY 2020 Budget, March 27, 2019, http://docs

.house.gov/meetings/AP/AP04/20190327/109146/HHRG-116-AP04-Wstate-PompeoM
-20190327.pdf.

65. "2017–2019 AFSA Governing Board Term Report," AFSA News, *FSJ*, March 2020, 62.

66. Dan Sullivan, press release, "Sullivan, Van Hollen Launch Senate Foreign Service Caucus," May 19, 2017, https://www.sullivan.senate.gov/newsroom/press-releases/sullivan -van-hollen-launch-senate-foreign-service-caucus; and "Senate Foreign Service Caucus," https://www.legistorm.com/organization/summary/143914/Senate_Foreign_Service _Caucus.html.

67. "Membership Has Its Privileges (and It's a Bargain!)," *FSJ*, February 2018, 64. At that time, the State vice president supervised the labor-management directorate. In 2020 that role was reassigned to the AFSA president.

68. Sharon Wayne, USAID vice president's report, in AFSA, "2016 AFSA Annual Report," 10–11; and Colleen Fallon-Lenaghan, "AFSA and USAID Reach Agreement on FSL Hiring," *FSJ*, November 2017, 64.

69. The June 2016 issue included "Supporting FS Families with Special Needs Children" by Maureen M. Danzot and Mark R. Evans (pp. 17–19), and "Mental Health Support for Foreign Service Children: Parents Weigh In" (pp. 46–50). Danzot and Evans founded the Foreign Service Families with Disabilities Alliance, an affinity group that drove much of the progress on this issue. The December 2016 issue published a powerful letter, "Support for FS Kids with Special Needs," with the signatory's name withheld. The issue was personal for Barbara Stephenson, who has a special-needs child.

70. Jackie Spinner, "State Department Support for Diplomats with Children with Disabilities Is Contracting," *Washington Post*, October 29, 2017, https://www.washingtonpost .com/world/national-security/state-department-support-for-diplomats-with-children -with-disabilities-is-contracting/2017/10/29/86e2fff6-b4d4-11e7-be94-fabb0f1e9ffb _story.html.

71. Ken Kero-Mentz, "A Job Worth Having," *FSJ*, May 2019, 56.

72. "2017–2019 AFSA Governing Board Term Report," *FSJ*, March 2020, 68; and Papp, interview, May 20, 2022.

73. Eric Rubin, "Progress and New Priorities," *FSJ*, September 2019, 9.

74. Article VIII, Section 1, https://afsa.org/afsa-bylaws#a08.

75. Papp, interview.

76. Ibid.; and AFSA, "2016 AFSA Annual Report," 9.

77. Texts of Executive Office of the President, "Executive Orders 13836, 13837, and 13839," October 11, 2019, https://www.federalregister.gov/documents/2019/10/21/2019 -23021/executive-orders-13836-13837-and-13839.

78. See minutes of the Governing Board meeting, October 21, 2020, 27.

79. Executive Office of the President, "Creating Schedule F in the Excepted Service," E.O. 13957, October 21, 2020, https://www.federalregister.gov/documents/2020/10/26 /2020-23780/creating-schedule-f-in-the-excepted-service.

80. Jonathan Swan, "Trump's Revenge," *Axios*, July 23, 2022, https://www.axios.com /2022/07/23/donald-trump-news-schedule-f-executive-order.

81. Paige Hopkins, "D.C.'s Federal Workforce Fears Schedule F," *Axios*, August 17, 2022, https://www.axios.com/local/washington-dc/2022/08/17/dc-federal-workforce -schedule-f.

82. Loren DeJonge Schulman, "Schedule F: An Unwelcome Resurgence," *Lawfare* (blog), August 11, 2022, https://www.lawfareblog.com/schedule-f-unwelcome-resurgence.

83. Executive Office of the President, "Protecting the Federal Workforce," E.O. 14003, January 22, 2021, https://www.federalregister.gov/documents/2021/01/27/2021-01924 /protecting-the-federal-workforce.

84. The Senate had unanimously passed a funding bill that included no money for the wall. The president had initially said he would sign the bill but then changed his position. Republicans in the Senate lacked the time they would need to seek passage of a new bill under budget reconciliation procedures that would block the threatened Democratic filibuster. On January 3, the Congress elected in November was sworn in, and control of the House passed to the Democrats. The bill the president eventually signed contained no money for building the wall.

85. Ken Kero-Mentz, "Foreign Service Furlough Stories," *FSJ*, April 2019, 46.

86. Ken Kero-Mentz, "Even during (Another) Shutdown, AFSA Is Here for You," *FSJ*, March 2019, 57.

87. Matthew Lee, "Pompeo Says Diplomats' Morale 'Good' Despite Shutdown," AP News, January 12, 2019, https://apnews.com/article/north-america-international-news -politics-abu-dhabi-united-states-61aa9d45529c4788accoc932fe4cb22d; and Ben Phillips, "The Shutdown: Why Didn't AFSA Sue the Federal Government?," *FSJ*, May 2019, 61.

88. Barbara Stephenson, "Staying Constructive in Trying Times," *FSJ*, March 2019, 7.

89. Congressional Budget Office, "The Effects of the Partial Shutdown Ending in January 2019," January 28, 2019, 1, https://www.cbo.gov/publication/54937.

90. P.L. 116-1 of January 16, 2019.

91. "Talking Points," *FSJ*, June 2019, 11; and Susan B. Glasser, "Mike Pompeo, the Secretary of Trump," *New Yorker*, August 26, 2019, https://www.newyorker.com/magazine /2019/08/26/mike-pompeo-the-secretary-of-trump.

92. Eric Rubin, interview, June 7, 2022; and Glasser, "Mike Pompeo."

93. Rubin, interview.

94. "The Transformation of Diplomacy," *Foreign Affairs*, November–December 2020, https://www.foreignaffairs.com/articles/united-states/2020-09-23/diplomacy -transformation.

## 13. Which Side Are You On? 2019–2023

1. Thomas D. Boyatt, President's Report, *FSJ*, August 1974, 34. For Boyatt's role in the union elections, see chapter 4.

2. Rubin, interview, June 7, 2022.

3. Ibid. The Strong Diplomacy slate offered candidates for president (Eric Rubin), treasurer (Virginia Bennett), State and retiree vice president (Tom Yazdgerdi and John O'Keefe), and six State representative and two retiree representative positions. All Strong Diplomacy candidates were elected except John O'Keefe, who lost to independent candidate John Naland, and Don Jacobson, who was outpolled for the sixth State representative position by write-in candidate Matthew Dolbow. Write-in candidates Jason Singer and Michael Riedel were elected vice president for USAID and FAS, respectively. See AFSA, 2019–2021 AFSA Governing Board, https://afsa.org/2019-2021-afsa-governing -board; "2019–2021 AFSA Governing Board Election Results," *DilploPundit* (blog), https://diplopundit.net/2019/06/26/2019-2021-afsa-governing-board-election-results/; and "AFSA Governing Board Election for the 2019 to 2021 Term," AFSA News, Special Election Edition, April 2019, https://afsa.org/sites/default/files/candidate-statements -election2019.pdf.

4. Yovanovitch, *Lessons from the Edge*, 279.

5. Pompeo, *Never Give an Inch*, 275.

6. David Welna, "The Hold on Ukraine Aid: A Timeline Emerges from Impeachment Probe," NPR, November 27, 2019, https://www.npr.org/2019/11/27/783487901/the-hold -on-ukraine-aid-a-timeline-emerges-from-impeachment-probe.

7. Summary transcript of July 25 Trump-Zelensky phone call, released by the White House, September 24, 2019, available at *Politico* (https://www.politico.com/story/2019 /09/25/trump-ukraine-phone-call-transcript-text-pdf-1510770) and many other sites.

8. See House of Representatives, "Impeachment of Donald J. Trump, President of the United States: Report of the Committee on the Judiciary of the House of Representatives together with Dissenting Views, to Accompany H. Res. 755," 116th Cong., 1st sess., Report 116-346, December 15, 2019, https://www.congress.gov/congressional-report /116th-congress/house-report/346/1; and Yovanovitch, *Lessons from the Edge*, 292–308.

9. Rubin, interview: "All of our lawyers, all of our members' lawyers, everyone had the same answer, which is, if you're subpoenaed by Congress and you fail to appear, it's a crime."

10. Yovanovitch, *Lessons from the Edge*, 307.

11. Rubin, interview.

12. "We Defend the Foreign Service," *FSJ*, November 2019, 7; and "A Year of Challenge and Opportunity," *FSJ*, January–February 2020, 7.

13. Sharon Papp introduced the motion creating the Legal Defense Fund at a June 6, 2007, meeting of the Governing Board, which approved the motion by a vote of 10 to 3 (minutes of the meeting provided to the author). In November 2007, the fund was named in honor of the late Richard "Dick" Scissors, a member of the labor-management staff. See minutes of the Governing Board meetings, June 6, 2007, and November 7, 2007; and Susan Maitra, "Remembering Dick Scissors," *FSJ*, December 2007, 51–52.

14. Rubin, interview.

15. Papp, interview, May 20, 2022. Email to author from Sharon Papp, July 2, 2022; and email to Sharon Papp from David P. Huitema of the Office of the Legal Adviser, October 16, 2019, provided to the author by Sharon Papp.

16. Rubin, interview.

17. Robin Wright, "The Staggering (and Uncovered) Legal Bills Facing Impeachment Witnesses," *New Yorker*, January 21, 2020, https://www.newyorker.com/news/news-desk /the-staggering-and-uncovered-legal-bills-facing-impeachment-witnesses.

18. Rubin, interview.

19. Ibid. In December 2017, the Board of Governors resolved "that AFSA continue to restrict grievance counseling and legal assistance to AFSA members" and that "effective July 1, 2018, only members who have been in good standing for at least six months are able to receive LM grievance counseling and legal assistance." AFSA Governing Board Minutes, December 20, 2017, provided to the author.

20. Yovanovitch, *Lessons from the Edge*, 298, 306.

21. Shawn Dorman, "Going through Things," *FSJ*, March 2020, 9. Cited in Dmitry Filipoff, "Staying Diplomatic: The *Foreign Service Journal* during Controversial Times," *Signature*, November/December 2020, 36. (*Signature* magazine is a publication of the Specialized Information Industry Association.)

22. See CDC, David J. Sencer CDC Museum, "CDC Museum COVID-19 Timeline," https://www.cdc.gov/museum/timeline/covid19.html; "Trump Suggests Light and Heat Treatments," *Today*, NBC, April 24, 2020, https://www.youtube.com/watch?v

=K63t4fMTH6c; total COVID-19 deaths at Johns Hopkins University and Medicine, Coronavirus Resource Center, "COVID-19 Dashboard as of May 10, 2023," https://coronavirus.jhu.edu/map.html; and U.S. Bureau of Labor Statistics, "Unemployment Rate Rises to Record High 14.7 Percent in April 2020," TED: The Economics Daily, May 13, 2020, https://www.bls.gov/opub/ted/2020/unemployment-rate-rises-to-record-high-14-point-7-percent-in-april-2020.htm.

23. The *Foreign Service Journal* devoted much of its April 2021 issue to the practice of virtual diplomacy.

24. "The Foreign Service Responds to COVID-19," *FSJ*, July–August 2020, 50–71.

25. GAO, "COVID-19: State Carried Our Historic Repatriation Effort but Should Strengthen Its Preparedness for Future Crises," Report no. GAO-22-104354, November 2021, 1, https://www.gao.gov/products/gao-22-104354.

26. Rubin, interview. Credit for the department's changes in leave policy goes also, and perhaps mainly, to Balancing Act at State, an affinity group organized in 2012 by Foreign Service and Civil Service working mothers and others to address issues of work-life balance. See Lillian Wahl-Tuco, "Balancing Act's Formula for Driving Institutional Change," *FSJ*, May 2020, 45–47; and "AFSA and COVID," *FSJ*, May 2020, 57.

27. "AFSA Governing Board Election for the 2021 to 2023 Term: Governing Board Candidates," AFSA News, Special Election Edition, April 2021, 8, https://afsa.org/sites/default/files/afsa-governing-board-election-candidate-statements-2021-23-term.pdf. AFSA's election committee issued its call for nominations on January 15, 2021, in accordance with Article VIII(2)(a) of the bylaws.

28. AFSA, "2021 AFSA Election Results," https://afsa-nfe2015.informz.net/informzdataservice/onlineversion/ind/bWFpbGluZ2luc3RhbmNlaWQ9MTAwNjc5MTAmc3Vic2NyaWJlcmlkPTEwODM4MTI2NTA=; AFSA, "2021–2023 AFSA Governing Board," https://afsa.org/2021-2023-afsa-governing-board; and membership numbers at *FSJ*, July–August 2021, 65.

29. Rubin, interview.

30. Kim Greenplate, "Major Advocacy Milestones Achieved," *FSJ*, March 2022, 70. The key provisions of the National Defense Authorization Act for FY2022 (P.L. 117-81) are summarized at AFSA, "National Defense Authorization Act: AFSA Policy Priorities Become Law," https://afsa-nfe2015.informz.net/informzdataservice/onlineversion/ind/bWFpbGluZ2luc3RhbmNlaWQ9MTAzNjI2Mzkmc3Vic2NyaWJlcmlkPTEwOD M4MTI2NTA=#. For anomalous health incidents, see White House, "Memorandum on Implementation of the Anomalous Health Incidents Provisions in the National Defense Authorization Act for Fiscal Year 2022," February 1, 2022, https://www.whitehouse.gov/briefing-room/statements-releases/2022/02/01/memorandum-on-implementation-of-the-anomalous-health-incidents-provisions-in-the-national-defense-authorization-act-for-fiscal-year-2022/.

31. Greenplate, "Major Advocacy Milestones Achieved."

32. Kim Greenplate, email to author, August 1, 2022.

33. Darnella Frazier's video was amplified by video from other witnesses, security camera footage, and police body camera recordings. See Evan Hill, Ainara Tiefenthäler, Christiaan Triebert, Drew Jordan, Haley Willis, and Robin Stein, "How George Floyd Was Killed in Police Custody," *New York Times*, May 31, 2020, https://www.nytimes.com/video/us/100000007159353/george-floyd-arrest-death-video.html. Crowd size at Larry Buchanan, Quoctrung Bui, and Jugal K. Patel, "Black Lives Matter May Be the Largest Movement in U.S. History," *New York Times*, July 3, 2020, https://www.nytimes.com

/interactive/2020/07/03/us/george-floyd-protests-crowd-size.html. The article cited data from four polling organizations suggesting that "15 million to 26 million people have participated in demonstrations over the death of George Floyd."

34. American Academy of Diplomacy, "Rebuilding after the Violence: State Must Improve on Diversity," June 9, 2020, https://www.academyofdiplomacy.org/wp-content /uploads/2020/06/2020-06-09-AAD-Press-Release-State-Must-Improve-on-Diversity -final.pdf.

35. GAO, "USAID: Mixed Progress in Increasing Diversity, and Actions Needed to Consistently Meet EEO Requirements," Report no. GAO-20-477, June 23, 2020, https:// www.gao.gov/products/gao-20-477; and "State Department: Additional Steps Are Needed to Identify Potential Barriers to Diversity," Report no. GAO-20-237, January 27, 2020, https://www.gao.gov/products/gao-20-237.

36. "The Future of the Foreign Service: A Discussion with Nicholas Burns, Marc Grossman and Marcie Ries," *FSJ*, January–February 2021, 21.

37. Association of Black American Ambassadors, "Diversity and Inclusion in the U.S. Foreign Service: Recommendations for Action," November 2020, reprinted in *FSJ*, January–February 2021, 25–27.

38. AFSA, "AFSA Member Survey on Implicit and Explicit Racial Bias in the Foreign Service Workplace," August 12, 2020, https://afsa.org/sites/default/files/afsa-bias-survey -general-responses.pdf. See also "AFSA Works for Diversity and Inclusion: An Update," *FSJ*, December 2020, 69. About 25 percent of respondents reported that they had experienced some form of bias or discrimination in the Service. See also advocacy report, Governing Board packet for September 16, 2020; Jason Singer, "Words of Thanks," *FSJ*, June 2021, 49; and AFSA, "AFSA Retention, Diversity, Equity, and Inclusion Recommendations," https://afsa.org/sites/default/files/afsa-retention-dei-bullet-points.pdf.

39. The *Journal* covered its own history in its April 2018 issue, which included the following articles: Harry Kopp, "A Century of *Journals*," 22–33; Stephen R. Dujack, "The *Journal* in Transition: The 1980s," 34–41; Steven Alan Honley, "Now It Can Be Told," 42–49; and Dmitry Filipoff and Susan B. Maitra, "The Journal through Time," 50–67.

40. "Bylaws of the Editorial Board," adopted by the AFSA Governing Board, August 7, 2002.

41. Shawn Dorman, interview, June 22, 2022.

42. The archive includes the *Journal's* predecessor publication, the *American Consular Bulletin*, published from 1919 to 1924. For background on the launch of the archive, see Shawn Dorman's "Letter from the Editor: Where Diplomacy and Defense Meet," *FSJ*, May 2017, 10.

43. Dorman, interview.

44. Andrea Capellán, "On Our Own: Diplomats Deserve Equal Access to Reproductive Health Services," *FSJ*, May 2022, 19–21; and Robbie Gramer, "U.S. Diplomats 'Routinely Denied Access' to Reproductive Care," *Foreign Policy*, May 17, 2022, https:// foreignpolicy.com/2022/05/17/us-diplomats-abroad-denied-access-reproductive-care/.

45. Dorman, interview. The $20 annual subscription fee is for AFSA members only and has not changed since 2012. Fees are published each October. In 2022 the annual fee was $30 for students and $50 for others (*FSJ*, October 2022, 8).

46. "Significant space" in Letter from the Editor, *FSJ*, April 2020, 9; and "your magazine" in Letter from the Editor, *FSJ*, January–February 2017, 9.

47. "A Conversation with Harry W. Kopp and John K. Naland on *Career Diplomacy*, *4th ed.*," Georgetown University, https://www.youtube.com/watch?v=Q38fulqqqw4.

48. Rubin, interview, November 8, 2022.

49. "The End of an Era: What Lies Ahead?," *FSJ*, October 2021, 7. Jack Aubrey, the fictional eighteenth-century British naval master and commander in Patrick O'Brian's novel of the same name, pointed out, "When a man was obliged to say 'Yes, sir,' his agreement was of no worth even if it happened to be true."

50. As of June 30, 2022, the Senior Foreign Service was 84.5 percent white and 64.9 percent male. See "Department of State Fulltime Permanent Workforce Diversity," June 30, 2022, https://www.state.gov/wp-content/uploads/2022/08/Diversity-Report-6-30-2022.pdf.

51. Rubin, interview, November 8, 2022.

52. See, for example, Nicholas Burns, Marc Grossman, and Marcie Ries, "A U.S. Diplomatic Service for the 21st Century," Belfer Center, November 2020, https://www.belfercenter.org/publication/us-diplomatic-service-21st-century; William J. Burns and Linda Thomas-Greenfield, "The Transformation of Diplomacy: How to Save the State Department," *Foreign Affairs*, November–December 2020, https://www.foreignaffairs.com/articles/united-states/2020-09-23/diplomacy-transformation; Truman Center, "Transforming the State Department," March 5, 2021, https://www.trumancenter.org/issues-posts/transforming-the-state-department; and American Academy of Diplomacy, "Strengthening the Department of State," May 2019, https://www.academyofdiplomacy.org/publication/strengthening-the-department-of-state/.

53. Burns and Thomas-Greenfield, "Transformation of Diplomacy."

54. Marc Grossman and Marcie Ries, *The American Diplomacy Project II: Blueprints for a More Modern U.S. Diplomatic Service* (Washington, D.C.: Arizona State University Barrett & O'Connor Washington Center, September 2022), https://ldns.asu.edu/sites/default/files/events/2022-09/American%20Diplomacy%20Project%20-%20Final%20Report_0.pdf.

55. Rubin, interview, November 8, 2022. AFSA has a long history of opposition to mid-level hiring (see page 199).

56. U.S. Department of State, press release, "Secretary Antony J. Blinken on the Modernization of American Diplomacy," Foreign Service Institute, George P. Shultz National Foreign Affairs Training Center, Arlington, Va., October 27, 2021, https://www.state.gov/secretary-antony-j-blinken-on-the-modernization-of-american-diplomacy/.

57. U.S. Department of State, Fact Sheet, "Improvements in the Foreign Service Selection Process," April 26, 2022, https://www.state.gov/improvements-in-the-foreign-service-selection-process/.

58. AFSANET messages, "AFSA Statement on Concerns Regarding New Foreign Service Exam," April 26, 2022, https://afsa.org/afsa-statement-concerns-regarding-new-foreign-service-exam; and "Update: AFSA Concerns on New FSOT Process," April 28, 2022, https://afsa-nfe2015.informz.net/informzdataservice/onlineversion/ind/bWFpbGluZ2luc3RhbmNlaWQ9MTA1NjU4NTcmc3Vic2NyaWJlcmlkPTEwODM4MTQ1MDg=.

59. Rubin, interview, November 8, 2022.

60. Deidi Delahanty, "FSO Selection: Changing the Path to the Oral Assessment," *FSJ*, October 2022, 38–41. The *Journal* made the evergreen topic of reform the focus of its March 2023 issue.

61. Rubin, interview, November 8, 2022. AFSA regularly publishes its nuts-and-bolts (or bread-and-butter) objectives as an "advocacy update" on the policy page of its website. See, for example, https://afsa.org/afsa-advocacy-update-september-2022.

## Epilogue: AFSA Strong

1. Pollard, Ries, and Amiri, *Foreign Service,* 56.

2. Tim Weiner, in his review of Pompeo's 2023 book *Never Give an Inch*, wrote, "He describes them [America's career diplomats], by turns, as un-American, deceitful denizens of the 'deep state,' and 'overwhelmingly hard left.'" Tim Weiner, "Political Books Are Often Bland. Mike Pompeo's Is Savage," *Washington Post*, January 24, 2023, https://www.washingtonpost.com/books/2023/01/24/pompeo-trump-attack-memoir-review/.

3. Ásgeir Sigfússon, interview, July 11, 2022.

4. Data in this and preceding paragraph from Ásgeir Sigfússon, email to the author, January 30, 2023.

# BIBLIOGRAPHY

## ADST Foreign Affairs Oral History Collection

The Association of Diplomatic Studies and Training has produced more than 2,600 oral histories as part of its Foreign Affairs Oral History Project (OHP). These are available online at https://adst.org/oral-history/.

Adair, Marshall P. OHP interview by Charles Stuart Kennedy. September 1, 2011.
Bacchus, William I., and Thomas Stern. OHP interview by Charles Stuart Kennedy. February 19, 1990.
Bierce, Ambrose. Presentation at the Foreign Service Institute, OHP. September 30, 1992.
Black, Melville. OHP interview by Tom Dunnigan. August 25, 1999.
Boyatt, Thomas D. OHP interview by Charles S. Kennedy. March 8, 1990.
Constable, Elinor. OHP interview by Charles Stuart Kennedy. May 30, 1996.
Corell, Frank D. OHP interview by W. Haven North. September 29, 1998.
Crockett, William J. OHP interview by Thomas Stern. June 20, 1990.
Good, Barbara. OHP interview by Charles Stuart Kennedy. May 25, 1993.
Harrop, William C. OHP interview by Charles S. Kennedy. August 24, 1993.
Harter, John. OHP interview by Charles S. Kennedy. July 22, 1997.
Hays, Dennis. OHP interview by Raymond Ewing. November 28, 2008.
Hemenway, John. OHP interview by David T. Jones. August 10, 2010. Not available online.
Horan, Hume. OHP interview by Charles S. Kennedy. November 3, 2000.
Laise, Carol. OHP interview by Charles S. Kennedy. April 17, 1989.
La Porta, Alphonse F. OHP interview by Charles S. Kennedy. February 11, 2001.
Michel, James. OHP interview by Thomas Stern. September 10, 1991.
———. OHP interview by Charles S. Kennedy. October 21, 2005.
Quainton, Anthony. OHP interview with Charles S. Kennedy. November 6, 1997.
Rimestad, Idar. OHP interview by Thomas Stern. June 22, 1990.
Spiers, Ronald. OHP interview by Thomas Stern. November 11, 1995.
Stewart, John Todd. OHP interview by Charles S. Kennedy. October 25, 1999.
Veale, William. OHP interview by Thomas Dunnigan. June 27, 2000.
Viets, Richard N. OHP interview by Charles Stuart Kennedy. April 6, 1990.

Whitehouse, Charles. OHP interview by Roger Ernst. November 28, 1989.
Wilkinson, Theodore. OHP interview by Charles S. Kennedy. January 11, 1999.


## Published Sources

Acheson, Dean. *Present at the Creation: My Years in the State Department.* Rev. ed. New York: W. W. Norton, 1987.

Adams, Henry. *The Education of Henry Adams.* New York: Library of America, 1983.

———. *History of the United States of America during the Administration of Thomas Jefferson, 1801–1805.* New York: Library of America, 1984.

American Academy of Diplomacy and the Stimson Center. "A Foreign Affairs Budget for the Future: Fixing the Crisis in Diplomatic Readiness." Washington, D.C.: American Academy of Diplomacy and the Stimson Center, October 2008.

Bacchus, William I. *Inside the Legislative Process: The Passage of the Foreign Service Act of 1980,* replica ed. Boulder, Colo.: Westview Press, 2013.

———. *Staffing for Foreign Affairs: Personnel Systems for the 1980s and 1990s.* Princeton, N.J.: Princeton University Press, 1983.

Ball, George W. *Diplomacy in a Crowded World.* Boston, Mass.: Little, Brown, 1976.

Barnes, William, and John Heath Morgan. *The Foreign Service of the United States: Origins, Development, and Functions.* Washington, D.C.: U.S. Government Printing Office, 1961.

Bierce, Ambrose. *The Devil's Dictionary.* New York: Dover Press, 1993.

Bodine, Barbara. "Preemptive Post-Conflict Stabilization and Reconstruction." In *Commanding Heights,* ed. Michael Miklaucic, 31–38. Washington, D.C.: National Defense University, 2010.

Brookings Institution. *Administration of Foreign Affairs and Overseas Operations.* Washington, D.C.: Government Printing Office, 1951.

———. *Vital Statistics on Congress.* Washington, D.C.: Brookings Institution, November 2022.

Carlucci, Frank C., and Ian J. Brzezinski. "State Department Reform: Report of an Independent Task Force Cosponsored by the Council on Foreign Relations and the Center for Strategic and International Studies." Washington, D.C.: Council on Foreign Relations, 2001. https://www.cfr.org/sites/default/files/pdf/2005/10/state_department.pdf.

Caro, Robert. *The Years of Lyndon Johnson: The Passage of Power.* New York: Alfred A. Knopf, 2012.

Carter, Jimmy. *Why Not the Best?* Nashville, Tenn.: Broadman Press, 1975.

Committee on Career Principles, American Foreign Service Association. *Toward a Modern Diplomacy: A Report to the American Foreign Service Association.* Washington, D.C.: American Foreign Service Association, 1968.

Congressional Research Service. *Department of State Foreign Operations, and Related Programs: FY 2023 Budget and Appropriations.* Report R47070. Updated April 1, 2022. Washington, D.C.: Congressional Research Service, April 18, 2022. https://crsreports.congress.gov/product/pdf/R/R47070.

Daalder, Ivo H., and I. M. Destler. *In the Shadow of the Oval Office.* New York: Simon & Schuster, 2009.

Dobbins, James, Seth G. Jones, Benjamin Runkle, and Siddarth Mohandas. *Occupying Iraq: A History of the Coalition Provisional Authority.* Santa Monica, Calif.: RAND Corporation, 2009.

Fenzi, Jewell, with Carl L. Nelson. *Married to the Foreign Service: An Oral History of the American Diplomatic Spouse.* New York: Twayne Publishers, 1994.

Gill, Cory R., Marian L. Lawson, and Emily M. Morgenstern. "Department of State, Foreign Operations, and Related Programs: FY2022 Budget and Appropriations." R46935. Washington, D.C.: Congressional Research Service, June 27, 2022. https://crsreports.congress.gov/product/pdf/R/R46935.

Goodwin, Doris Kearns. *Team of Rivals: The Political Genius of Abraham Lincoln.* New York: Simon & Schuster, 2005.

Gregory, Bruce. "Union Representation in the Foreign Service." Paper presented at the 1977 Conference of the International Studies Association. St. Louis, Mo., March 16–20, 1977.

Grossman, Marc, and Marcie Reis. *The American Diplomacy Project II: Blueprints for a More Modern U.S. Diplomatic Service.* Washington, D.C.: Arizona State University, Leadership, Diplomacy and National Security Lab, September 2022.

Halchin, Elaine. "The Coalition Provisional Authority (CPA): Origin, Characteristics, and Institutional Authorities." CRS report no. RL32370. Washington, D.C.: Library of Congress, Congressional Research Service, updated June 6, 2005.

———. "Senior Executive Service (SES) Pay for Performance System." CRS report no. RL33128. Washington, D.C.: Congressional Research Service, 2007.

Harr, John E. *The Anatomy of the Foreign Service: A Statistical Profile.* Foreign Affairs Personnel Study no. 4. Washington, D.C.: Carnegie Endowment for International Peace, 1965.

Holmes, J. Anthony. "Where Are the Civilians? How to Rebuild the U.S. Foreign Service." *Foreign Affairs* 88, no. 1 (January–February 2009). https://www.foreignaffairs.com/united-states/where-are-civilians.

Hoover, Herbert. *U.S. Commission on Organization of the Executive Branch of the Government: The Hoover Commission Report.* New York: McGraw-Hill, 1949.

Hunt, Gaillard. *The Department of State of the United States: Its History and Functions.* New Haven, Conn.: Yale University Press, 1914.

Johnson, David K. *The Lavender Scare: The Cold War Persecution of Gays and Lesbians in the Federal Government.* Chicago: University of Chicago Press, 2004. Amazon Kindle edition.

Jones, Arthur G. *The Evolution of Personnel Systems for U.S. Foreign Affairs: A History of Reform Efforts.* Foreign Affairs Personnel Study no. 1. Washington, D.C.: Carnegie Endowment for International Peace, 1965.

Kahn, E. J., Jr. *The China Hands.* New York: Viking, 1975.

Kennan, George F. "Diplomacy without Diplomats." *Foreign Affairs* 76, no. 5 (September–October 1997): 198–212.

———. "The Future of Our Professional Diplomacy." *Foreign Affairs* 33, no. 4 (July 1955): 566–86.

———. *Memoirs.* Vol. 2, *1950–1963.* Boston, Mass.: Little, Brown, 1972.

Kissinger, Henry. *Years of Renewal.* New York: Simon & Schuster, 1999.

———. *Years of Upheaval.* Boston, Mass.: Little, Brown, 1982.

Kopp, Harry W. *Commercial Diplomacy and the National Interest.* Washington, D.C.: American Academy of Diplomacy/Business Council for International Understanding, 2004.

———. *The Voice of the Foreign Service: A History of the American Foreign Service Association.* Washington, D.C.: Foreign Service Books, 2015.

Kopp, Harry W., and Charles A. Gillespie. *Career Diplomacy: Life and Work in the Foreign Service*. 2nd ed. Washington, D.C.: Georgetown University Press, 2011.

Kralev, Nicholas. *America's Other Army: The U.S. Foreign Service and 21st Century Diplomacy*. Nicholas Kralev, 2012.

Macomber, William B. *The Angels' Game: A Handbook of Modern Diplomacy*. New York: Stein and Day, 1975.

Mattox, Gale A. "Report of the [Murphy] Commission on the Organization of the Government for the Conduct of Foreign Policy: Background and Principal Recommendations." Washington, D.C.: Library of Congress, Congressional Research Service, January 1975.

Mattox, Henry E. *The Twilight of Amateur Diplomacy: The American Foreign Service and Its Senior Officers in the 1890s*. Kent, Ohio: Kent State University Press, 1989.

McGlen, Nancy E., and Meredith R. Sarkees. "Gender and the Foreign Policy Institutions." In *Diversity and U.S. Foreign Policy: A Reader*, edited by Ernest J. Wilson III, 327–38. New York: Routledge, 2004.

Mee, Charles L., Jr. *The Marshall Plan: The Launching of the Pax Americana*. New York: Simon & Schuster, 1984.

Morgan, Ted [Sanche de Gramont]. *FDR: A Biography*. New York: Simon & Schuster, 1985.

Moskin, J. Robert. *American Statecraft: The Story of the U.S. Foreign Service*. New York: Thomas Dunne, 2013.

Nakamura, Kennon H. "Proposals for a New Foreign Service Compensation System in the 110th Congress." CRS report no. RL34668. Washington, D.C.: Library of Congress, Congressional Research Service, September 12, 2008.

Nasaw, David. *The Patriarch: The Remarkable Life and Turbulent Times of Joseph P. Kennedy*. New York: Penguin Press, 2021.

Nathan, James, and James Oliver. *Foreign Policy Making and the American Political System*. 3rd ed. Baltimore, Md.: Johns Hopkins University Press, 1994.

Nevin, Jack, and Lorna Nevin. *Federal Union: The Story of the American Federation of Government Employees*. Washington, D.C.: American Federation of Government Employees, 1976.

Parker, Richard B. *Uncle Sam in Barbary*. Gainesville: University Press of Florida, 2003.

Plischke, Elmer. *U.S. Department of State: A Reference History*. Westport, Conn.: Greenwood Press, 1999.

Pollard, Michael S., Charles P. Ries, and Sohaela Amiri. *The Foreign Service and American Public Opinion: Dynamics and Prospects*. Santa Monica, Calif.: RAND Corporation, 2022.

Pompeo, Mike. *Never Give an Inch: Fighting for the America I Love*. New York: HarperCollins, 2023.

Poole, DeWitt C. *The Conduct of Foreign Relations under Modern Democratic Conditions*. New Haven, Conn.: Yale University Press, 1924.

Porter, William Sydney (O. Henry). *Cabbages and Kings*. New York: McClure, Phillips, 1904. Chapel Hill: University of North Carolina. http://docsouth.unc.edu/southlit/henry/henry.html.

Rice, Condoleezza. *No Higher Honor: A Memoir of My Years in Washington*. New York: Crown Publishers, 2011.

Rowe, James H., Jr., Robert Ramspeck, and William E. DeCourcy. *An Improved Personnel System for the Conduct of Foreign Affairs*. Washington, D.C.: Government Printing Office, 1950.

Rusk, Dean, as told to Richard Rusk. *As I Saw It*. New York: W. W. Norton, 1990.

Safire, William. "On Language: The Way We Live Now." *New York Times Magazine*, July 22, 2001.

Schaffer, Howard B. *Ellsworth Bunker: Global Troubleshooter, Vietnam Hawk*. Chapel Hill: University of North Carolina Press, 2003.

Schlesinger, Arthur M., Jr. *A Thousand Days: John F. Kennedy in the White House: A Pulitzer Prize Winner*. New York: Mariner Books, 2002.

Shapiro, Bruce. "A House Divided: Racism in the State Department." *The Nation*, February 12, 1996. Reprinted in *Diversity and U.S. Foreign Policy: A Reader*, ed. Ernest J. Wilson III, 91–98. New York: Routledge, 2004.

Shimabukuro, John. "Collective Bargaining and Homeland Security." CRS report no. RL31520. Washington, D.C.: Government Printing Office, Congressional Research Service, November 18, 2002.

Shultz, George P. *Turmoil and Triumph: My Years as Secretary of State*. New York: Charles Scribner, 1993.

Smith, Jean Edward. *FDR*. New York: Random House, 2008.

Stuart, Graham H. *American Diplomatic and Consular Practice*. New York: Appleton-Century-Crofts, 1952.

———. *The Department of State: A History of Its Organization, Procedures and Personnel*. New York: Macmillan, 1949.

Thompson, Richard. *Duty and Danger: The American Foreign Service in Action*. Washington, D.C.: American Foreign Service Association, 1988.

Trask, David F. *A Short History of the U.S. Department of State, 1781–1981*. Washington, D.C.: U.S. Department of State, 1981.

U.S. Commission on Organization of the Executive Branch of the Government. *The Hoover Commission Report*. New York: McGraw-Hill, 1949.

U.S. Congress, House of Representatives, Committee on Foreign Affairs. *Hearings on H.R. 17 and H.R. 6357, 68th Congress, 1st Session*. Washington, D.C.: Government Printing Office, 1924.

———. *Hearings on H.R. 4674 [The Foreign Service Act], before the Subcommittee on International Operations of the Committee on Foreign Affairs and the Subcommittee on Civil Service of the Committee on Post Office and Civil Service, 96th Congress, 1st Session, June 21, 28; July 9, 11, 17, 18, 24; September 6, 11, 19, 20, 27; and October 16, 1979*. Washington, D.C.: Government Printing Office, 1980. https://www.flra.gov /system/files/webfm/Authority/Archival%20Decisions%20&%20Leg%20Hist/LEG %20HIST%20OF%20THE%20FOREIGN%20SERVICE%20ACT.pdf.

U.S. Department of State. *America's Overseas Presence in the Twenty-First Century: The Report of the Overseas Presence Advisory Panel*. Washington, D.C.: Government Printing Office, 1999.

———. *Biographic Register*. Washington, D.C.: Government Printing Office, 1969.

———. *Congressional Budget Justification: Department of State, Foreign Operations, and Related Programs, Fiscal Year 2018*. Washington, D.C.: Department of State, 2018. https://2017-2021.state.gov/wp-content/uploads/2020/11/FY-2018-Congressional -Budget-Justification-FINAL.pdf.

———. *Congressional Budget Justification, Foreign Operations, and Related Programs, Fiscal Year 2022*. Washington, D.C.: Department of State, 2002. https://www.state .gov/wp-content/uploads/2021/05/FY-2022-State_USAID-Congressional-Budget -Justification.pdf.

———. "Directive to Improve the Personnel Program of the Department of State and the Unified Foreign Service of the United States." Washington, D.C.: Government Printing Office, March 1951.

———. *Executive Budget Summary, Function 150 and Other International Programs, Fiscal Year 2013*. Washington, D.C.: Department of State. https://2009-2017.state.gov /documents/organization/183755.pdf.

———. *Foreign Relations of the United States, 1969–1976*. Vol. 2, *Organization and Management of U.S. Foreign Policy, 1969–1972*, edited by David C. Humphrey and Edward C. Keefer. Washington, D.C.: Office of the Historian, Bureau of Public Affairs, 2006.

———. "Report of the Secretary of State's Advisory Panel on Overseas Security." 1985. https://irp.fas.org/threat/inman/index.html.

———. Report to the Speaker of the House of Representatives and the Committee on Foreign Relations of the Senate concerning Implementation of the Foreign Service Act of 1980. February 1, 1983. [AFSA Archives]

———. *State 2000: A New Model for Managing Foreign Affairs: Report of the U.S. Department of State Management Task Force*. Washington, D.C.: Government Printing Office, 1992.

———. *Toward a Stronger Foreign Service: Report of the Secretary of State's Public Committee on Personnel*. Washington, D.C.: Government Printing Office, 1954.

U.S. Department of State, Bureau of Diplomatic Security. *History of the Bureau of Diplomatic Security of the United States Department of State*. Washington, D.C.: Global Publishing Solutions, October 2011. www.state.gov/documents/organization/176589.pdf.

U.S. Department of State and U.S. Agency for International Development. *Enduring Leadership in a Dynamic World: Quadrennial Diplomacy and Development Review, 2015*. Washington, D.C.: Department of State and USAID, 2015. https://2012-2017 .usaid.gov/sites/default/files/documents/1870/QDDR2015.pdf.

———. *The 2010 Quadrennial Diplomacy and Development Review (QDDR): Leading through Civilian Power*. Washington, D.C.: Department of State, 2010. https://2009 -2017.state.gov/s/dmr/qddr/2010/index.htm.

U.S. General Accounting Office [GAO]. "Equal Employment Opportunity: Women and Minority Representation at Interior, Agriculture, Navy, and State." Report no. GAO/ GGD-95-211. Washington, D.C.: Government Printing Office, September 1995.

———. "State Department: Minorities and Women Are Underrepresented in the Foreign Service." Report no. GAO/NSIAD-89-146. Washington, D.C.: Government Printing Office, June 1989.

———. "State Department: Professional Development of Foreign Service Employees." Report no. GAO/NSIAD-89-149. Washington, D.C.: Government Printing Office, July 1989. http://www.gao.gov/assets/220/211579.pdf.

U.S. Government Accountability Office [GAO]. "Department of State Overseas Comparability Pay." Report no. GAO-11-772R. Washington, D.C.: Government Printing Office, June 30, 2011.

———. "Foreign Service Mid-level Staffing Gaps Persist Despite Significant Increases in Hiring." Report no. GAO-12-721. Washington, D.C.: Government Printing Office, June 2012. http://www.gao.gov/assets/600/591595.pdf.

———. "State Department: Staffing Shortfalls and Ineffective Assignment System Compromise Diplomatic Readiness at Hardship Posts." Report no. GAO-02-626. Washington, D.C.: Government Printing Office, June 2002.

U.S. Office of Management and Budget. "Historical Table 4.2: Percentage Distribution of Outlays by Agency, 1962–2017." Washington, D.C.: The White House. https://www .whitehouse.gov/omb/budget/historical-tables/.

U.S. Senate. "Washington's Farewell Address to the People of the United States." Senate Document no. 106–21, 106th Congress, 2nd session. Washington, D.C.: Government Printing Office, 2000. www.gpo.gov/fdsys/pkg/GPO-CDOC-106sdoc21/pdf/GPO -CDOC-106sdoc21.pdf.

Walker, Lannon. "Our Foreign Affairs Machinery: Time for an Overhaul." *Foreign Affairs* 47, no. 2 (January 1969): 309–20.

Warwick, Donald P. *A Theory of Public Bureaucracy: Politics, Personality, and Organization in the State Department*. Cambridge, Mass.: Harvard University Press, 1975.

Werking, Richard Hume. *The Master Architects: Building the United States Foreign Service, 1890–1913*. Lexington: University Press of Kentucky, 1977.

Wilkinson, Stephan, Richard Wolf, and Dick Young. *Profiles in Democracy: The U.S. Foreign Service*. Video. Alexandria, Va.: WETA.

Wilson, Ernest J., III. *Diversity and U.S. Foreign Policy: A Reader*. New York: Routledge, 2004.

Yovanovitch, Marie. *Lessons from the Edge: A Memoir*. New York: Mariner Books, 2022.

# INDEX

# ABOUT THE AUTHOR

Harry W. Kopp was a member of the Foreign Service from 1967 to 1985. He was deputy assistant secretary of State for international trade policy in the Carter and Reagan administrations. He served abroad in Warsaw, where he directed the United States–Poland Trade Development Center, and Brasília, Brazil, where he was deputy chief of mission. He received superior and meritorious honor awards from the Department of State and a presidential award for public service from President Ronald Reagan. In 2024 DACOR (originally Diplomatic and Consular Officers Retired) awarded him the Foreign Service Cup, in recognition of his distinguished Foreign Service career and significant post-retirement contributions.

Kopp is the author of *Commercial Diplomacy and the National Interest* (American Academy of Diplomacy, 2004) and, first with the late Tony Gillespie and then with John K. Naland, of four editions of *Career Diplomacy: Life and Work in the U.S. Foreign Service* (Georgetown University Press, 2008, 2011, 2017, and 2021). His short story "Trotsky in the Bronx" won the 2012 Goldenberg Fiction Award.

Kopp was a founding partner of L. A. Motley and Company, a consulting firm. He is a graduate of Hamilton College and holds a master's degree in Russian and East European studies from Yale University. He lives with his wife, Jane, in Baltimore, Maryland.

www.ingramcontent.com/pod-product-compliance
Lightning Source LLC
Chambersburg PA
CBHW030354130626
46549CB00004B/1486